WELL BEING

WELL BEING

A Personal Plan
for Exploring and Enriching
the Seven Dimensions of Life:

■

Mind, Body, Spirit, Love,
Work, Play, the Earth

Howard Clinebell, Ph. D.

HarperSanFrancisco
A Division of HarperCollins*Publishers*

1992

Credits appear on p. 347

Harper San Francisco and the author, in association with Treepeople and the Rainforest Action Network, will facilitate the planting of two trees for every one tree used in the manufacture of this book.

FIRST EDITION

Library of Congress Cataloging-in-Publication Data

Clinebell, Howard John.
    Well being: a personal plan for exploring and enriching the seven
dimensions of life . . . / Howard Clinebell.—1st ed.
        p.   cm.
    Includes bibliographical references.
    ISBN 0-06-061503-6
    1. Self-realization. 2. Self-care, Health. 3. Love. 4. Spiritual
life. I. Title.
BF637.S4 1991   90–55293
158—dc20   CIP

---

92 93 94 95 96 MAL 10 9 8 7 6 5 4 3 2 1

This edition is printed on acid-free paper that meets the American National Standards Institute Z39.48 Standard.

To Your Health!

The Health of Those You Love!

and The Health of Your World!

Contents

How to Get the Most from This User-Friendly Guide

Barbara spotted this new book in the health and self-care section of her neighborhood bookstore. "I wonder if this one will get me moving to take better care of myself? I've started dieting and exercising more times than I like to think. Look at me now! I hope this one works for me."

The key to unlocking Barbara's dilemma is learning to love herself more. This book is about love—loving self-care. The book offers a wide variety of practical insights and tools for devising your personal well-being program. If you develop and use such a program, I expect that you'll help yourself in some of these ways:

- Acquire strategies for outwitting your self-sabotaging, the big *R*'s of *rationalizations* and *resistances* to healthy self-care;

- Discover methods to feel more alive and fit for living and loving by investing some more of your valuable time in self-care each day;

- Find ways to turn some of your crises and losses into opportunities for whole-person growth;

- Learn some ways to enjoy avoiding burnout on your job;

- Develop methods to get and keep yourself healthier at this stage on your life journey;

- Learn techniques for generating mutual love and wellness in your intimate relationships;

- Discover fresh approaches to enjoying sensual-sexual aliveness in loving relationships;

- Find ways to liven up your spirituality by grounding it in love—of yourself, other people, nature, and the divine Spirit;

- Discover how to help your loved ones increase their well being;

- Learn to heal yourself by helping to heal a wounded planet;

- Find ways to let the little girl or boy inside you laugh and play more, for the health of it.

The book gives you regular how-to pointers for building your personal well-being plan. Near the end of each chapter I invite you to create a small piece of your plan. When you complete the book, I encourage you to put it all together and implement it as a workable plan of self-care.

Here are five suggestions to increase the healing and help you receive as you use this book.

1. Use the well-being checkups and other exercises. Self-healing and self-care involve both your left- and right-brain abilities. The left hemisphere of your brain specializes in the analytic, rational, verbal, conceptual, problem-solving functions of your mind. The various checkups and inventories are left-brain well-being tools. Your right hemisphere specializes in intuitive, nonverbal, imaging, metaphoric, holistic problem-solving functions. The guided imaging and action exercises throughout the book are designed to activate these right-brain functions. They are planned to balance the left-brain exercises and to bring alive the book's working concepts in your own experience.

2. Keep a *Well Being Self-Care Journal* by using a notebook, or underline and make notes in the book's margins. Journaling is a valuable self-care method in itself. Using it here will be an asset in generating and refining a workable plan for your well being.

3. Enrich the experience by inviting a friend or family member or a small group to try the book's well-being program with you. If you do this in a spirit of mutual support and playful challenge, it may help you overcome resistances to improving your health care. You may decide to use the book in your organization, school, work setting, or congregation as an easily planned series of programs or lessons on self-care for better health. You'll find some guidelines for doing this near the end of the book.

4. Make the book work for you by using it playfully, in your own way. Ignore the things that don't fit your unique way of living and learning. At least sample the things that attract you as you scan the chapters. Or, after you've gone through the book on the fast track, come back to read the relevant sections carefully and do the checkups and exercises that you find most attractive.

5. If you have access to a VCR, use the companion video programs. These show members of a wholeness group I led using some of the key exercises. In some scenes I comment on what's happening and offer additional suggestions for self-care. The videos and the book, fortunately, can be used independently, but they also complement each other. You may want to explore the advantages of using the two together. For information about tapes, write me at the address below.

A few words about the Windows of Wholeness. The people I selected to highlight were chosen because their lives dramatically illuminated some aspects of love-centered wholeness. They're all finite and fallible humans. Like the rest of us, they have weaknesses in some areas of their lives. Fortunately for us all, limitations can be intertwined with whatever degree of well being we have, without canceling it out.

How to Use Guided Imaging Exercises

Numerous guided meditations and active imaging exercises are available throughout this book. Let me offer some guidance for using these helpfully. Forming pictures in your mind is a spontaneous, right-brain activity of the human psyche, for example, in daydreaming and in dreams during sleep. Apparently these images have a powerful impact on your mind-body organism. The unconscious mind seems to be unable to distinguish between your mental images and the reality you face. Therefore your organism responds as if the images were reality. It is important to become aware and change the negative images of self-deprecation, powerlessness, failure, hopelessness, and catastrophes you may tend to form. These images diminish the effectiveness of your behavior and the defensive power of your immune system. They also produce unnecessary stress and lower your self-esteem. Intentionally substituting positive images of healing, success, self-worth, and wellness is one of the simplest ways of accessing the power of the subconscious-unconscious mind for self-healing and well being.

I recommend that you use such exercises in a spirit of playful seriousness. To pursue wellness with heaviness is a catch-22 approach, something like the uptight health fanatic who reported, "I'm relaxing as hard as I can!" If active imaging is new to you, it usually takes practice to use it effectively. If a particular exercise seems promising but isn't effective when you first try it, it may be worthwhile to repeat it for several days to discover how useful it may be for you.

You can do guided imaging exercises alone, with a friend, or in a group. If you're doing them with others, select someone to read the instructions aloud, stopping at each slash (/) for a brief time while everyone (including the reader) does what has been suggested. If you're alone, read the instructions until you come to a /, then stop and do what has been suggested, including closing your eyes when appropriate.

Before starting an exercise loosen or remove tight garments, including your belt or necktie, take off your shoes, and unplug the phone so you won't be disturbed. Imaging exercises are most effective when your body-mind organism is in a state of relaxed alertness. The flow of energy in your body is best when you are sitting comfortably but with your spine erect and with both feet flat on the floor. The problem with lying down is that it's easy to be very relaxed but not to stay alert. If you doze off during an exercise, your nonconscious mind may be resisting something threatening, or you may simply be tired. Remember any dreams you have so that you can discover their messages to you from your deeper mind.

Well Being By Experience

In this book I share the most helpful insights, tools, and resources that I have discovered and developed in my work as a teacher, pastoral counselor, psychotherapist, workshop leader, and struggler for my own well being. The book draws on the experiences of real people struggling with real-life issues of healing and health. I have been careful to maintain the confidentiality of my professional relationships with students and clients by altering all identifying information or creating composite cases to illustrate important points.

I hope to convince you that many of the challenges explored here are important for you. Mark Twain is alleged to have declared: "To be good is noble. To tell other people how to be good is even nobler— and much less trouble." The same is true of telling people how to be healthy. Like you, I suspect, I'm a frequent fitness backslider. My resistances to doing what's "good for me" often overwhelm my passion for a long, healthy, productive life. But I'm also very grateful for the ways in which my own health has been enhanced by practicing the things recommended here.

In writing, I kept in mind the people I've met who are searching for practical ways to take better care of themselves, often in the midst of hectic schedules, to be healthier and happier. They are people who are hungry for more fulfilling, more adventuresome lives. They are from diverse backgrounds and cultures and are in various life stages.

This book can be useful to parents and grandparents looking for ways to enhance their family's health style, thus helping their children and grandchildren learn lifelong well being *by experience.* I think teachers, therapists, clergy, and medical professionals will also find it helpful for their students, clients, parishioners, patients, colleagues, and work associates.

It gladdens my heart to say a rousing "Thanks!" to many people—friends, family members, graduate students, clients, and colleagues at the School of Theology at Claremont, the Institute for Religion and Wholeness, and the American Association of Pastoral Counselors. Many of them helped, directly or indirectly, in the writing of this book. In particular I express my gratitude to four persons: Erma Pixley and Rugeon Peters—who have graduated to the life of larger well being—and LeRoy and Gladys Allen. I have been inspired and informed by their visions of healing and well being centered in healthy spirituality.

I also have heartfelt appreciation for the late Norman Cousins. His lifelong commitment to enhancing the well being of both persons *and* the planet has been an empowering model for me during the struggles of wholeness and peace work. I'm particularly thankful for his encouragement and support during the difficult birthing years of the Institute for Religion and Wholeness.

To family members (including my long-time best friend and partner), friends, and colleagues who gave me valuable feedback and critiques or helped with the research that undergirds the book, my heartfelt thanks. They include Jim Farris, Mary Lautzenhiser, Tim Locke, Emily Chandler, Art Madorsky, Harville Hendrix, Ruth Krall, Kaofang Yeh, Bill Bray, David Richardson, David Augsburger (who suggested the Windows of Wholeness idea), and Steve Jackson, my partner in developing the videotapes. My daughter Susan was of great help with her skills as a writer, her keen awareness of contemporary idioms, and her sensitivity to ecological and feminist issues. I'm also grateful to the hundreds of people with whom I've enjoyed working and learning—in workshops, retreats, classes, as well as in psychotherapy and couple and family therapy sessions. In this book you learn the tools these folks have identified as most helpful.

As you and I touch minds in these pages, my fondest hope is that you will experience some fresh healing and hope, some liberating spirituality, and—very important—more love and laughter!

Howard Clinebell
2990 Kenmore Place
Santa Barbara, CA 93105, USA

Practical Methods for Enhancing Well Being in the Seven Dimensions of Your Life

Walking the Sevenfold Path of Love-centered Well Being

 Several years ago I enjoyed an incredibly beautiful day of snorkeling in a lovely undersea garden in Hawaii with a dear friend. We luxuriated in the sensuous azure water filled with gorgeous schools of multi-colored tropical fish in beautiful canyons of coral. As we relaxed on the beach between snorkeling excursions, a man walked slowly toward us holding an electronic device over the sand. Occasionally he stopped to dig in the sand. I greeted him and asked what he was up to. He laughed and replied, "This is an electronic treasure finder, a metal detector. I'm hunting for coins, wrist watches, rings, and other precious metal that unlucky folks like you have lost in the sand!" We laughed with him and wished him happy treasure hunting, adding that we hoped it wouldn't be at our expense.

I hope you'll keep a treasure finder in your imagination as you read this book. There *is* a precious treasure within you waiting to be discovered and used. It is the treasure of your potentialities—your possibilities for a healthier, more alive, more fulfilled, productive, and love-energized life. *Nothing* is more important to your overall happiness than your health. The purpose of this book is to put a treasure finder in your hands. It will give you a variety of practical tools for discovering how to develop high-level well being in all of the seven major areas of your life.

Before going further let me clarify some terms. *Well being* and *wholeness* are used interchangeably in these pages. *You are whole or have well being to the degree that the center of your life is integrated and energized by love and healthy spirituality.* This wholeness at the center of your life influences and is influenced by the well being of all the dimensions of your life and relationships. Your well being intertwines in widening circles with the well being of the important people in your life and the well being of your community, culture, and world.

Wholeness or well being is not the absence of brokenness. Instead it is what you choose, at the center of your life, to do with your brokenness. René Dubos's non-grandiose definition of health is close to the meaning of well being or wholeness in this book: "A method of living which enables imperfect persons to achieve rewarding and not too painful existences while they cope with a very imperfect world."[1]

The book's central message is one of reality-based hope: It *is* possible to develop and enjoy more love-empowered wholeness in yourself, your family, your work, your world, in spite of the losses and crises, failures and limitations in your life. This book provides a smorgasbord of practical guidelines, do-it-yourself methods, and down-to-earth coaching on how to accomplish this. It will offer you a strategy for developing your personal self-care-for-wholeness program using resources you select.

Love—The Heart of Well Being

Philosopher-theologian Paul Tillich, a mentor of mine, declared that love is "the moving power of life."[2] It's true. Love is the moving power of both your life and your health. The Trappist mystic Thomas Merton coined the apt phrase *the wholeness of love.*[3] Without love there can be no well being. Love is the heart of well being! It's the power, the means, the meaning, and the goal of wholeness. The great French scientist-philosopher Pierre Teilhard de Chardin puts this truth well: "Love alone is capable of uniting living beings in such a way as to complete and fulfill them, for it alone takes them and joins them by what is deepest in themselves. This is a fact of daily experience. . . . And if that is what it can achieve daily on a small scale, why should it not repeat this one day on world-wide dimensions?"[4]

Whole person well being includes

• **Loving yourself** by developing your unique gifts of body, mind, and spirit, as fully as you can, at each life stage.

• **Loving other people** by encouraging them to develop their unique gifts.

• **Loving your work and your play,** your vocation and avocation.

• **Loving the planet,** our Mother and her wonderful network of living things, by caring for her and helping to heal her wounds.

• **Loving the divine Spirit,** the source of all healing and wholeness.

ROSA BEYER

This fascinating item appeared in the *Los Angeles Times:* "Rosa Beyer wanted one thing in particular for her 106th birthday, 'All I care is that we go out and dance. I want to celebrate,' Beyer said at a party in her honor at the Colerain Township Senior Citizens Center. . . . Beyer is a celebrity on Cincinnati's west side, where her family operated a home-grown vegetable stand for years. Last year she was grand marshal of a local parade. Although she has cut back on her activities, Beyer said she is not ready to join what she calls the 'can't' club. 'I figure it this way: I have lived this long because God has something he wants me to do, and I haven't done it yet,' she said. 'But you know what? Even if I knew what he wanted, I think I'd wait a couple of years yet to do it.' "

Rosa Beyer's sense of humor and zesty love of life sparkles in this brief vignette. Intrigued by this account, I tried to get in touch with her. By the time I made contact with her family, she had graduated to heaven. From her daughter and great-granddaughter, I learned that she *did* dance on her 106th birthday, as she had hoped. They said that Rosa had immigrated from Switzerland with her parents when she was a little girl. Soon after they arrived in Cincinnati, her mother died from the flu. Eventually Rosa married. She and her husband raised five children on the small farm they purchased. While her husband worked for a railroad, Rosa plowed their farm (with a horse-drawn plow), raised and sold vegetables, flowers, and fruit, as well as milk and eggs. One foggy morning her husband was struck by a car and killed while walking to his job. She continued to work outdoors on the truck farm until her eyesight failed at about age 103.

Her daughter remembers her as "loving children, nature and growing things, the Bible, baseball, and life. She always saw the good in people" (letter of February 27, 1990. I am indebted to Ruth B. Allen, her daughter, and Tonya Gabard, her great-granddaughter, for their generous response to my request for information). Rosa reached out to help troubled families and took battered wives and their children into her home. She made stuffed animals as gifts for the children at a nearby home for the mentally retarded.

Rosa was devoted to her church, attending almost every Sunday until her final hospitalization a few months before her death. Her pastor interviewed her during the Mother's Day service when she was 105. The tape recording is sprinkled with her delightful sense of humor. The congregation laughed with gusto when she admitted that she and her family went to church each Sunday when she was a girl "because there wasn't anything else to do." Rosa mentioned what must have been a key to her continuing aliveness and love of life—in spite of having her share of crises and griefs: "The one gift that I share with my family and friends is love—plenty of it because it's free" (interviewed at the Monfort Heights Methodist Church in Cincinnati, May 12, 1985).

Rather than settling down and being resigned to die, Rosa was still kicking up her heels—literally—at 106! She obviously had a sense of a larger purpose in her life. She had little doubt that God had something in mind for her. Like most of us, she wasn't quite sure what it was. So let's have a toast to Rosa Beyer and the many other Rosas of all ages and both sexes who enjoy well being by staying playful, loving, and alive all their lives!

In case all this emphasis on loving seems a little much for you, let me say that wholeness or well being as understood here includes the pain and frustration, the anger and brokenness that are a part of everyone's life, sooner or later. Agony as well as ecstasy are present in most people's experience of giving and receiving our very human and imperfect but oh-so-needed love. Like a rose, most love seems to have thorns. But rather than complaining that roses have thorns, it's better to rejoice that some thorns have roses![5]

Love is a verb. It is something you *do* as well as feel and enjoy. Loving of course often involves such intense, delicious feelings as passion and sensuality, compassion and caring. These feelings are very important to us. But love is much more. It is doing those things that help enable whoever or whatever you love to develop the treasure of their possibilities and thus move toward "life in all its fullness"—an ancient phrase for the experience of well being.[6]

Wholeness-nurturing love begins with yourself but must not stop there. Whether your ability to love others is limited or liberated depends on how fully you love yourself. You really love yourself only to the degree that you do those self-caring things that help improve your own health, creativity, aliveness, and joy. In a parallel way your love for the earth is effective only to the degree that you live in ways that respect and protect the environment. Since your health and that of all God's creatures ultimately depend on the health of the environment,

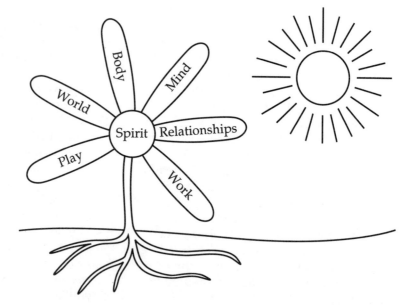

loving the planet is really another way of loving yourself, other people, and all living things.

Relationships of mutual love are the garden where well being grows. Health-generating love is love with muscles, a love expressed in active responsiveness to one another's needs. Giving this love is as important to your health as getting it. Reaching out with warmth and caring is as essential to your well being as taking in this indispensable food of the human spirit.

Wholeness or well being is not some kind of perfect halo of health at which you aim and hope some day to reach. Rather well being is a trip of emerging possibilities. This book is a user-friendly guide to this, your most important journey—the journey of well being through all the years of your life.

The Flower of Spiritually Centered Well Being

Wholeness, like a flower, is a living, growing, ever-changing unity among all its parts and with its environment. The center of the flower stands for healthy spirituality. Such spirituality holds the petals of wholeness together and gives them organic unity. The center is also where the petals are nourished and the seeds of new life grow. The roots of the wholeness flower go deep to draw nutrients from the soil of our common humanity and from the biosphere, the wonderful web of living things from which all our food comes. The air with which the flower interacts for its life, surrounds it. Above the flower is the sun of Love—the divine source of healing and wholeness. This sun supplies the energy that enables the flower to continue to grow, stay beautiful, and, in due time, produce seed. Like the flower, wholeness has its seasons and its birth-life-death-rebirth cycles. There are times of seed-planting and germination, blossoming and seed-making, withering and dying, returning to the earth—in preparation for the new generation in the cycle of continuing creation.

The Rewards of the Sevenfold Path of Well Being

The chapters of Part 1 will explore seven dimensions of wholeness depicted by the flower above. It will give you practical self-care methods to raise your wellness level in each area. To whet your appetite, here is a sneak preview of these seven paths of healthy living, focusing on what you might gain from better self-care.

1. **Your spiritual well being.** Wholeness-nurturing spirituality involves enjoying a growing intimacy with the divine Spirit of love and liberation. Human love at best is fractured, time limited, and partial. Therefore, as precious as human relationships are to you, it is vital for your well being to have a source of unconditional Love from beyond those relationships. The quality of your relationship with this divine Spirit influences how alive and loving you are

in the other dimensions of your life. Ours is a world of severe spiritual drought in which ethical confusion and spiritual emptiness cause sickening guilt, cosmic loneliness, and despair. In such a parched world a lively relationship with the divine Spirit can be a bubbling spring of healing, renewing power to help you become a more healing person—in your inner life, in your relationships, and in the world. (See chapter 2.)

2. **Your mind-personality well being.** Current research makes it clear that our minds and bodies are profoundly interdependent, in both health and sickness. Taking good care of your body helps enhance your mental and emotional health. Conversely, how you use your mind can help keep you healthy or make you sick. Chronic feelings of helplessness and hopelessness can make your body more vulnerable to all sorts of illnesses. Hopefulness can facilitate more rapid healing and help keep your body well. Furthermore, the untapped intellectual and creative resources of your mind are immense. The challenge is to love, empower, and enjoy your mind by using it in an adventure of lifelong, self-directed learning. In a world with a knowledge explosion and lightning-fast social change, such continuing learning is the secret of ongoing mental sharpness and well being. (See chapter 3.)

3. **Your body's well being.** Self-care to nurture physical well being provides a solid foundation on which to build. To the degree that you keep your body fit, it will be more pain free, energized, sensually alive, functionally effective, and supportive of your mental and spiritual well being. This is true no matter what your disabilities or how little your body happens to match our culture's superficial stereotypes of "body beautiful." Learning to love your body is the secret of caring for it like a good mother or father. (See chapter 4.)

4. **The well being of your relationships.** Chronic loneliness and lack of love can be hazardous to your health. Are loving relationships in short supply in your life? If so, enriching and deepening love in your relationships may be a very important way of moving to higher wellness levels. But to enhance wholeness and bring healing, love needs to embody mutual respect, integrity, open communication, and mutual commitment to each other's full becoming. Increasing loving well being in intimate relationships usually requires learning more effective communication and conflict-resolution skills. (See chapter 5.)

5. **Well being in your work.** Is your work a major source of self-worth and satisfaction? Or is it mainly a source of stress, boredom, and frustration? Because most of us invest a large part of our total

lives in work, it's important to discover how to make work less stressful and more health nurturing. Once you find that what you're doing has some meaning beyond its pragmatic role of providing money for life's necessities, you'll probably develop more love in, for, and from it. (See chapter 6.)

6. **Well being in your play.** Play is linked with work wholeness because they are complementary. Both have to do with how healthfully we use our time. If you know how to balance your work with revitalizing re-creation, you will nurture well being in both areas. Furthermore, laughter and playfulness can enrich all the other dimensions of your wholeness. (See chapter 7.)

7. **The well being of your world.** Your personal and family health is inseparable from the health of the important institutions in your life and the health of the natural environment. There's slim chance that the environmental crisis will be interrupted until you and I, and millions of our species, learn to care more lovingly for this incredibly beautiful and vulnerable planet. We need to develop the environmental conscience and caring that will motivate us to live in more ecologically healthy life-styles. (See chapter 8.)

Helping heal our planet includes working with others to enhance the health of all your community's people-serving institutions. The goal is to help change them so that they'll stimulate rather than stifle the mind-body-spirit wellness of everyone whose lives they touch, including yours. Thinking of the social context of your life as an essential dimension of your well being may be a startling idea at first. But your individual well being can be maximized only if it is supported by the institutions in which you are vitally involved. Your children's intellectual wholeness, for example, will flourish fully only if their schools are like fertile gardens of the mind. In such schools well-respected and well-paid teachers who love the adventures of the mind will nurture this love in your children.

Love-centered wholeness flows from the awareness that we human beings are all profoundly interconnected with each other and with the biosphere. Well being is inherently interpersonal and social. Your illness and health are inseparably intertwined with the illness and health of your family and your community, your nation, and your world. In our interdependent world, investing some of your time and passion to reach out in healings ways beyond yourself is enlightened self-interest. For in a profound sense no one can be totally whole until all are whole. Methods for healing your world are described throughout the book, particularly in chapters 8 and 11.

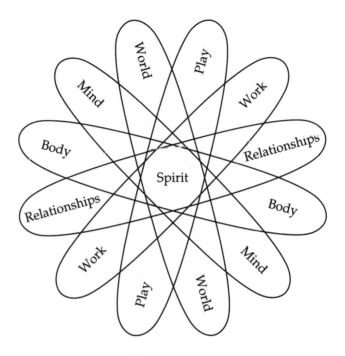

The Energy of Well Being

I'm grateful to Nelle Morton, pioneer feminist and friend, for suggesting this dynamic alternative image of wholeness. She sketched it for me one day and sent it with this comment: "Wholeness is never static, always in ferment and growth. Since we live in a global community and are rapidly emerging into a cosmic mind, could we not think of spirit as that flow of energy that brings us and the other six aspects of wholeness into dynamic relationship with one another and with the whole—ever in movement, in tension, interactive, interconnected, and interdependent, yet powerfully present?"[7]

Each aspect of our lives touches all the other aspects. The spiritual dimension is formed by the convergence of all the other dimensions, rather than being only one among the others. Your spiritual life, to the degree that it's health-giving, isn't a separate "sacred" area. Rather it's a vital part of all the mundane, earthy, ridiculous, sexy, playful, and painful aspects of your life.

This image resembles the representational drawing of an atom in old physics books. Collectively atoms constitute what appears to be solid, fixed matter. As we now know, each atom actually is an energy field in continuous dynamic interaction with countless energy fields all around it. This atomic image seems to fit us humans in all our interacting complexity and our potential power, for better or for worse. Like the genie the atomic scientists let out of the bottle nearly half a century ago, human power is both awesome and potentially awful in its possible impact on the health of the planet in the years ahead.

Light is not just the absence of darkness. It is energy moving at a certain frequency. Similarly well being is much more than the absence of sickness. It is the presence of the dynamic energies of love and healthy spirituality producing a positive aliveness, an inner power and creativity. In playful moments I've imaged how handy it would be if someone devised an AQ test to measure a person's Aliveness Quotient. Such an instrument would give us a well-being reading on individuals, families, and institutions. To the degree that people are well, they're inwardly alive. This inner vitality is one reason others are attracted to them and influenced by them. And, as we'll see in chapter 5, both aliveness and inner deadness are contagious.

Well being produces a joy that's very different from happiness. It's deeper, an inner joy that can exist when more surface-level happiness and pleasure are missing from our lives. The joy of wholeness is the joy of celebrating the precious gift of just being alive. The expressive French term *joie de vivre* (''joy of life'') says it well. This joy is rooted in wonder; life can be wonder-full for children and the child in each of us if we are aware of the miracle of ordinary things.

Wholeness in a Broken But Birthing World

The situation in which you and I search for well being is a mixed bag, at best. Problems and losses are persistent frustrations in most people's lives—in their health, families, job situations, or spiritual lives. No approach to well being can fly if it ignores the fact that most of us get dumped on at times. This on top of the abuse we heap on

I FIND IT INCREASINGLY DIFFICULT TO REMAIN MAN'S BEST FRIEND

ourselves by our mistakes and irresponsibilities. Violence and brokenness also flourish in our frantic, fragmenting society. Societal crises such as these complicate personal brokenness and make healing more difficult:

- the violence against mother nature by the pollution of our rivers, lakes, oceans, air, soil, and by toxins in the food we eat and in our homes;

- the widespread breakdown of families in industrialized, hi-tech, urban societies;

- the explosive, often violent, alienation among ethnic, racial, and national groups;

- the runaway crises of drug and other chemical dependencies in our addiction-spawning society, striking young people, seniors, women, and minorities with particular fury;

- the pandemic, planet-wide AIDS plague;

- the ravaging violence (sexual and otherwise) against those defined by society as lesser—women, children, ethnic minorities, the disabled, gays, to name a few;

- the violence of poverty—in the pockets of poverty within affluent nations and in the dehumanizing poverty in poor nations being exploited by rich nations;

- the epidemic of teen suicides rooted in the "radical futurelessness" of youth in our age of unprecedented global threats;

- the violence against future generations inherent in staggering national debts caused by our greedy, wasteful life-styles and the arms race;

- the profound spiritual and ethical crisis of our world.

But in the midst of this dark picture, there are some promising rays of light and hope, suggesting that our broken world is also a birthing world! Consider these harbingers of hope that may signal the birth struggles of an age of growing compassion and community, of justice and freedom:

- the ways our economic and ecological survival needs are pushing us, as never before in human history, to discover and strengthen our basic unity as one human family on a fragile, precious planet;

- the birth of new freedom in Eastern Europe, the superpowers' dramatic moves—ending the cold war and slowing the insane arms race;

- the growing recognition that the smallest unit of security and survival for any group on the planet is the whole human species together with other species;

- the coming together of the planet-wide environmental and peace-making movements (governmental and non-governmental), with their growing commitment to save the planet for all its human children and for its marvelously diverse flora and fauna;

- the flowering of *whole-person* health movements in many countries;

- the empowering ways women are redefining themselves and moving into leadership in politics, education, religion, and all the professions;

- better health resources contributing to extended lifespan, opening up unprecedented opportunities for longer, more whole lives;

- the proliferation of lay self-other help groups (on the model of Alcoholics Anonymous), enabling millions to find well being through recovery from a variety of life problems;

- the incredible new potentials of computers, video-taping, and other hi-tech communication tools to reduce human drudgery and enhance effective global communication and education;

- the spiritual awakening of countless persons who have risked letting go of old authority-prescribed certainties to discover new ways of deepening their spiritual lives.

Of course, the darkness is still deep in many places. The dawning of a new stage of civilization is now only a very promising potential. The full birthing depends on our willingness—yours and mine—to help midwife the process in ourselves, our families, our communities, and our world. The good news is that to respond to this challenge with informed passion, zest, and commitment, can in itself do wonders for our wholeness.

I recall a cartoon showing two white-coated, proper-looking doctors talking in a hospital corridor as a bearded doctor (without a stethoscope) passes them. One of the two says to the other, ''I can't stand his more-holistic-than-thou attitude!'' This kind of humor points to a significant new reality in our society—a growing concern for healthy living, healing, and whole-person well being. Fortunately, this concern is shared by an increasing number of health professionals as well as by the general public.

The interest in whole-person health is only the tip of the iceberg of a wider search for new ways of understanding ourselves and our world. Profound changes are taking place in many of the sciences including modern biology and physics, the human, psycho-social sciences, as well as the healing arts. These changes all move away from compartmentalized, hyper-individualistic understandings of persons and their world. They're toward relational, ecological, social systems—understandings that all things are interrelated, and that humans can best be helped to heal and grow when seen in their total interpersonal, cultural, and natural environments. The many encouraging trends in this direction today suggest that wholeness is a valuable guiding image whose time has come, a guiding image for the nineties and into the next century.[8]

A Guided Meditation For Enhancing the Seven Dimensions of Your Health

This exercise has two purposes: (1) to enable you to check out your wellness in each of the seven dimensions experientially and (2) to discover ways to increase your wellness in areas in which you decide you need help. To get the most from this exercise, you'll need fifteen to twenty minutes in a quiet place where you won't be interrupted. If you can't make time to do all seven steps at one sitting, try dividing the exercise between two sessions. You may want to review "How to Use Guided Imaging Exercises" on pp. xi–xii.

1. Sit in a comfortable position with your spine in vertical alignment and your feet flat on the floor. / Close your eyes and become aware of how you feel—about this exercise and in general. / Focus for a minute or two on how your body feels. / Hunch and wiggle your shoulders and neck, taking several deep breaths. As you inhale be aware of the flow of energy revitalizing your mind and the parts of your body that feel discomfort or tension. / As you continue to breathe deeply, tense and hold your muscles tight all over your body as you count to five (silently). Then exhale deeply as you count to five. Hold for another count of five and then repeat the cycle. Do this several times, especially in the areas in which you're carrying tension. Do this until your whole body is very relaxed *and* very alert. / Do whatever else you need to in order to feel more energy and aliveness throughout your body. / Be aware of how you have intentionally nurtured and enlivened your body.

2. Staying in touch with your body, picture your consciousness as a room within yourself. Be alone in that room now. / Look around the room. Be aware of its size, color, furnishings, its smells, sounds, temperature—and how you feel right now in the room of your consciousness. / Do whatever you need to do now, in your imagination, to make your room a better place in which to be at home with yourself. For example, if it feels cramped, push back the walls and raise the ceiling to give yourself more inner space. Do whatever you wish to make it a good, warm, love-filled place to

be with yourself—clear the clutter, change the decor, add some comfortable furniture, a fireplace, some music, flowers, a picture window. / Now just enjoy your inner space in a quiet, renewing way for a little while. / Reflect on this part of the exercise. What did you learn about making your conscious mind a better place to be with yourself?

3. Staying aware of your body and your inner room, picture clearly the person or persons you'd most enjoy being close to right now. / Experience relating in warm, loving ways to that person(s). / Be aware of how your feelings have changed since you were alone in your inner room. / If you're doing this exercise with others, join hands now, keeping your eyes closed to focus on what you're experiencing. / Be aware of the person(s) with whom you're connected by touch or in your imagination. They are persons with feelings, hopes, loves, fears, joys, and pain—many of these like yours. Be aware that each of these persons is, like you, a loved child of God, of irreducible worth. Open yourself to experience your basic oneness as sisters or brothers in one family—the human family. Experience your deep connectedness in spite of differences between or among you. / Reflect for a few moments on what you learned about deepening your relationships.

4. Staying in touch with your body, the room of your consciousness, and your important relationships, become aware of the world of nature. Allow your body to experience being *grounded*—supported securely by the chair, the floor, the building's foundation, and all this by Mother Earth. / Now, in your imagination go to your favorite place of beauty in nature. / Enjoy being in this place for a little while, letting yourself be nurtured and energized by the wonderful aliveness there. / Reflect on what you have just learned about making your relationship with nature more intimate, energizing, and renewing.

5. Staying aware of your body, your inner room, your relationships with people and nature, form a vivid picture now of the place where you work. / Be in that place for a little while, being aware of how you feel when you're there. How nurturing is the climate of relationships there? How satisfying and worthwhile does your work seem? / For a little while be in that part of your job situation in which you feel most alive, esteemed, and empowered. / Now move to that part of your job situation in which you feel unappreciated, depressed, and deenergized. / Move back and forth between the two places several times, seeing if you can take some of the energy from the healthy place to help heal the other place in your work situation. / Reflect on what you might do to make your organization more wellness nurturing for yourself and others. / Be

aware of what you've learned as you have been in touch experientially with whatever health is in your work setting.

6. Now, in your imagination, have some fun. Enjoy being playful with a friend or lover for a little while. Have a good laugh. Play a game you both like, or enjoy goofing off or making love. Just let yourself go. Really enjoy! / Be aware of how you feel when you're playful. / How can you bring more of this lightness and joy into your work, your family life, or your spirituality?

7. Keeping in touch with what you have experienced in the first six dimensions, become aware of the divine Spirit of love who is present here right now, in this very moment. Fling open the windows of your mind and your body. Let the energy of God's healing Love flow in a warm healing light. / Now, beginning with your body, surround and fill it with the light of this Love. / Do the same with your inner room. / With your most intimate relationships. / With your relation to Mother Nature. / Do the same with the setting where you work and the people there. / Now let your experience of playfulness be infused with God's love. / Notice how opening your awareness to this spiritual energy changes your experiences in the other dimensions. / Think of someone you care about who is sick or troubled or oppressed. / Hold a picture of them in your mind surrounded by the healing light of God's love and yours. / Reflect on what you learned as you focused on enjoying your relationship with the divine Spirit. /

Finish the exercise in whatever way you choose to give it a sense of completion. Then, before opening your eyes, reflect for a while on what you've learned that may be useful for enhancing your well being. / Now, gently open your eyes and, if you wish, jot down notes about your important learnings in your *Well Being Self-Care Journal*. / When it's possible, share the highlights of this exercise with someone you like and trust.

I hope this guided meditation helped bring the seven dimensions of well being alive in your experience, and that in the process you discovered some simple things you can do to enrich your life in one or more of these crucial areas. If you found the exercise useful, I recommend repeating it each day for several days. With practice it will become even more helpful. Over time you may discover that this meditation is an excellent way to check out as well as strengthen your development in each of the seven dimensions of well being.

Enriching and Enjoying Your Spiritual Life—Wellspring of Love, Well Being, and Joy

 At age 43 Pete was an outstanding "success" in his business as well as a leader in his church and community. He came for pastoral psychotherapy, pushed by an agonizing crisis, the suicide attempt of his only child, a teenage son, Ted, who was in trouble at school for cutting classes, drinking beer, and smoking marijuana with two other students. The hidden pain of the whole family came out during the second session, to which the therapist had recommended that they all come. It became clear that Pete and his wife, Carla, were living alone together in painful alienation. During several months of combined couple and family therapy, along with some individual therapy for Ted, they gradually learned ways to heal their family pain, which was a major cause of Ted's self-destructive action.

A deeper problem behind their marital problem emerged during a couple session with just Pete and Carla. Each was struggling with an acute crisis of life's meaning and priorities. Both were feeling what Carla described as "a vacuum," a painful inner emptiness. Their spiritual crisis was an issue all three family members were suffering from and expressing in different ways. Their pastoral therapist was able to help Carla and Pete learn how to deal more constructively with their midyears spiritual values crisis.

We humans are "spiritual" creatures, whether or not we have any interest in organized religions. We are creatures who live in our meanings and in our hopes and beliefs about what is ultimately important in ourselves and our world. By these hopes and beliefs and the religious practices that may express them, you and I create some

GOD LOVES YOU AND I'M

TRYING!

—bumper sticker

The glory of God is the glory of people fully alive.

—Irenaeus of Lyon

(A.D. 130–200)

Existence will remain meaningless to you if you yourself do not penetrate into it with active love and if you do not in this way discover its meaning for yourself. Meet the world with the fullness of your being and you will meet God. . . . If you wish to believe, love.

—Martin Buber

sense of order and meaning in our turbulent lives. Without at least a minimal sense of meaning, we cannot be sane or whole.

This is why humans are "incurably religious" and why religious beliefs and practices of some type have been found in all the diverse societies studied by historians and anthropologists around the planet and back through time. Whether we recognize it or not, we are inherently, inescapably transpersonal and transcending beings. *Our most powerful well-being need—often hidden from us in our secularized world—is to develop our spiritual powers and potentialities.* An often-hidden cause of other painful alienations is our alienation from our spiritual Selves, the integrating center of our beings. This core Self includes all the things that are creative, transcending, and unique about us human beings. In traditional religious language, this core Self is called our soul. But it doesn't matter what you call it, as long as you know it's there and know how to keep it alive and well.

Though sometimes ignored in biomedical discussions of health, this spiritual-ethical dimension often is the key to increasing whole-person wellness. The quality of your spiritual beliefs and ethical practices has a profound influence on all dimensions of your health. It influences your subconscious picture of yourself (your identity). It strengthens or weakens your self-esteem, your ability to give and receive love, and your inner strength for coping with life's losses and crises. The health of your relationship with the divine Spirit influences the aliveness of your relationships with yourself, with other people, and with the earth's wonderful network of living things. If your religious-spiritual-ethical life is a wasteland, it will lessen your well being in other areas. If it is a verdant garden, it will help your whole self flower by opening to the sunlight of God's loving Spirit.

For these reasons, awakening and revitalizing your spiritual life may be *the* key to getting more love-centered wholeness in your life. How does your personal spirituality affect your well being? What methods can help you empower and enjoy this side of your life?

Perhaps "religion" isn't your thing, and you feel no need for any of the many forms of organized religions in our society. Whether or not you're "religious" in the traditional sense, as a human being you have spiritual longings and hungers. And it is crucial to your well being to learn how to satisfy your inescapable human needs for meaning, purpose, and transcendence, in the most health-giving ways possible.

A Spiritual Well-Being Checkup

This checkup nurtures your well being in two interrelated ways. First, it gives you a quick evaluation of your spiritual-ethical health. It helps you identify areas in which you may decide to do some spiritual growth work and play. Second, it lists practical suggestions for increasing your spiritual-ethical wellness.

WINDOW OF WHOLENESS

HILDEGARD OF BINGEN

Living in lush, beautiful Bavaria nearly nine hundred years ago, Hildegard was a remarkable renaissance woman, intellectual and spiritual. Her many-faceted genius was expressed in her life as abbess, doctor, dramatist, musician, physicist, liberation theologian, prophet, poet, mystic, and painter. She was also the foremother of a refreshing movement of sensuous spirituality, focused on wholeness as "the complex interweaving of the human, the cosmic, and the divine in a many-splendored and deep oneness" (from Matthew Fox's introduction to *Meditations with Hildegard of Bingen* by Gabriel Uhlein).

Hildegard was one of the great pioneers in understanding the spiritual basis of human well being. She was also a pioneer in the struggle to heal the planet and bring ecological wholeness. Injuring the earth, the air, the water was for her a sin against God's creation. Only by liberating all of creation can humankind be truly free and whole (Uhlein, *Meditations*, 7–12).

Savor these beautiful words from her inspired life and pen:

> The soul is kissed by God, in its
>   innermost regions.
> With interior yearnings, grace and
>   blessing are bestowed.
>
> And so, humankind full of all creative
>   possibilities, is God's work.
> Humankind alone, is called to assist
>   God.
> Humankind is called to co-create.
>   (Uhlein, *Meditations*, 92, 106)

Truly Hildegard had a lifelong love affair with the earth, with humankind, and with all of life because she had a love affair with God.

CHECKLIST

Instructions: In front of each item put one of three initials: E = I'm doing excellently in this area of my spiritual life; OK = I'm doing passably in this, but things could be a lot better; NS = I need strengthening in this area.

_____ My spiritual life increases my capacity to love myself, other people (including my enemies), and nature, and enables me to express love in my world.

_____ It strengthens my sense of being forgiven and accepted (rather than causing guilt trips); it helps me affirm rather than reject my sexuality; it increases my inner lightness and my zest for living.

_____ My spiritual beliefs and experiences help me cope constructively with my losses.

_____ I have learned to use tragedies, crises, and losses as opportunities to let my faith grow tougher and more able to cope with painful realities.

_____ I have evaluated the beliefs and values I learned in my childhood, reaffirming and retaining only those that still ring true in my adult life.

_____ I have learned to respect my honest doubts, viewing them as healthy growing edges of my faith, even when they disturb my nostalgic security.

_____ My guiding values are in harmony with my understanding of love, justice, and wholeness.

_____ My conscience is responsive to social evils that are among the root causes of the pain and brokenness of individuals.

_____ My priorities (as reflected in my use of time) are in line with the values, people, and causes that are most important to me.

_____ My beliefs and values build bridges not barriers between myself and those with different understandings of life.

_____ I practice spiritual self-care each day, spending some time generating the serenity, joy, forgiveness, and love I need by spiritual disciplines such as meditation, prayer, and study.

_____ My experiences of God's love and forgiveness help me to reach out as a channel of that love to others, especially those wounded by personal tragedies and those put down by society.

_____ I've made friends with my spiritual Self, the divine light within me; and I have committed myself to making this spiritual core the unifying center of my whole being.

_____ I feel and celebrate a sense of wonder, joy, and gratitude for the good gift of life.

_____ It's easier to accept the unlovely aspects of myself and others because I know that I am accepted unconditionally by the loving Spirit of the universe.

_____ I have a sense of the purposes of the divine Spirit for my life, which adds meaning to my everyday relationships and work.

_____ I experience spiritual highs regularly through a variety of nonchemical activities—such as prayer, being in nature, music, loving relationships, worship, exciting ideas.

_____ I'm sometimes aware of the everyday miracles in mundane things and ordinary people in whom I sense extraordinary spiritual gifts.

_____ I participate in a caring community of shared faith (e.g., a support group, a congregation) that provides meaningful festivals, rituals, celebrations, and support to nurture my spiritual-ethical growing.

_____ I enjoy both the caring, passionate, nurturing, mystical side of my spiritual life and the rational, ethical, assertive, responsible side.

_____ I enjoy a sense of the wisdom and wonder of the natural world as God's handiwork, loving it by a life-style that's respectful of its wonderful diversity and aliveness.

_____ I affirm that all of us humans, with our many differences, are daughters and sons of the loving Spirit, each one of irreducible value.

_____ I rejoice that I am called by God to help create a world of greater caring and compassion, of justice and community, to make greater well being possible for everyone, including the poor and oppressed.

_____ I face my feelings about death in the context of a vital faith, so that they become sources of energy to live with more zest and creativity.

_____ I have a growing awareness that I am at home in the universe, that I really do belong.

_____ My beliefs and spiritual experiences foster love, hope, trust, self-esteem, joy, responsibility, empowerment, inner freedom, and the acceptance of my body and its pleasures; they also help me overcome destructive feelings such as fear, guilt, childish dependency, prejudice, hate, body rejection, and inner trappedness.

_____ I have discovered spiritual approaches that help me move from the alienation (from myself, others, and God) caused by guilt to the wonderful healing reconciliation of forgiveness.

_____ My spiritual life helps keep me in touch with the creative resources of my unconscious mind, through living symbols, meaningful rituals and myths, and vital festivals celebrating life transitions such as birth, aging, and death.

_____ I'm aware of and enjoy the mystery and wonder of life.

Using Your Findings: Take time now to scan the initials you placed in front of these spiritual beliefs, attitudes, and practices. What is your overall feel for the wellness of your spiritual life? In your *Self-Care Journal* jot down the NS and OK items that seem most important to you. Next to those items write any tentative ideas you have about how you can improve your spiritual self-care and health in those areas.

Further suggestions for using your findings are given near the end of this chapter.

Your Spirituality— Power to Hurt or Heal

A dear friend named Erma Pixley, shortly before she died, shared this powerful image with me: "Religion can be either a set of wings with which our souls can fly or a lead weight around our necks!"[1] I remember a book by a psychiatrist entitled *Religion May Be Hazardous to Your Health.*[2] When I first read it, I scoffed. But my years as a teacher-therapist have convinced me that the author was on target. I picture in my mind now some of the many people I have known whose religious beliefs and practices were a source of guilt, fear, and self-rejection, a health-crippling weight rather than liberating wings with which they could soar. On a personal level I have some first-hand acquaintance with wholeness-diminishing religion and moralism (about sex, anger, and aggressiveness) from my own early life. The various religious groups that breed hate and paranoid suspicion and that exploit believers are examples of pathogenic spirituality.

The distinction between health-giving (salugenic) and sickness-causing (pathogenic) religion was recognized early in the discipline of psychology of religion. The field's foremost pioneer, psychologist-philosopher William James, distinguished between the religion of healthy mindedness and that of the sick soul.[3] Many psychologists and therapists have added important light to our understanding of religio-ethical beliefs and attitudes that hurt or facilitate wholeness. They include Sigmund Freud, Erich Fromm, Roberto Assagioli, Karen Horney, Carl Jung, Ruth Benedict, Gordon Allport, Rollo May, Abraham Maslow, and Carol Gilligan.[4] There is a circular interrelationship among the spiritual-ethical side of our lives and all the other aspects of our personalities. Pathogenic spirituality both reflects and reinforces personality problems and sick relationships. Conversely, salugenic spirituality both reflects and enhances well being in other areas of our lives.

What Is Spiritual Health?

High-level wellness in your spiritual life comes from satisfying seven basic spiritual needs in healthy, growthful ways. These spiritual hungers are present in all human beings in some form, including those of us most secularized in our thought. These needs are existential needs, meaning they're inherent in our very existence as self-aware, meaning-seeking creatures who know we will someday die. They produce deep though often-repressed existential longings, hungers that can be satisfied only by spiritual, religious, or philosophy-of-life food. Psychoanalyst Erich Fromm observes: "Because the need for a system of orientation and devotion is an intrinsic part of human existence, we can understand the intensity of this need." He goes on to point out that there is no more powerful source of energy in human beings.[5] It is by the constructive satisfaction of our existential hungers that spiritual health flowers and in turn nurtures physical, mental, and interpersonal health.

In our society and world there is an epidemic of life-constricting approaches to religion. The power of spiritual needs is so great that people who do not develop health-enhancing spirituality in their lives tend to develop health-depleting beliefs and commitments. Many of us seek (unsuccessfully) to satisfy our spiritual hungers in ways that diminish our spiritual, mental, and physical health. We worship a variety of little gods—success, money, power, health, our family, group, religion, or nation. Eventually we suffer more as we discover the profound inadequacies of our idols. The religious life of most of us is a paradoxical blend of pathogenic and salugenic aspects, of limiting and liberating spirituality.

Improving your spiritual self-care means discovering healthier ways to meet your spiritual needs. Your personal religion tends to create wholeness when you satisfy your spiritual hungers in open, loving, growing, life-celebrating, esteem-strengthening, and reality-respecting ways. Conversely, your religion tends to diminish wholeness when you satisfy these needs in rigid, moralistic, authoritarian, idolatrous, reality-denying, or fear- and guilt-generating ways. The attitudes and practices in the spiritual health checkup above listed some of the important ingredients in good spiritual self-care.

Let's have a closer look at the seven basic spiritual needs now, one by one, and try some spiritual self-care methods. To maximize what you get from this section, I suggest that you ask yourself two questions about each of the seven needs: (1) How well am I doing in satisfying this need? (2) What can I do to satisfy this need so as to give myself more peace, joy, love, and courage?

Spiritual Need Number 1. *All of us need to experience regularly the healing, empowering love of God.* This need is for a growing relationship with the divine Spirit, whose acceptance of you has no strings attached and whose love is always available to heal your brokenness and liberate you to live and love more fully. The very heart of spiritual growth work is learning how to open our lives to become more receptive to the healing, cleansing energy of God's Love. The transforming light of this Love can bring inner warmth that helps melt the cold places of fear, guilt, and self-rejection in you. In the midst of the repeated small and heavy blows to our trust and self-esteem in everyday life, we need the comfort and care of a trust-full relationship with the divine Spirit of love. My friend theologian John Cobb says it well: "Above all, the spiritual life can be healthy only as it is grounded in the assurance of an acceptance that no human being can give, the ultimate acceptance that is God's."[6] The *quality* of your relationship with God is the foundation of your spiritual health. It can become a wellspring of wholeness in all aspects of your life.

Scott Peck points to one of the exciting rewards of a growing, empowering relationship with the divine Spirit: "The experience of spiritual power is basically a joyful one. . . . It is the joy of communion with God. . . . Those who have attained this stage of spiritual growth . . . are invariably possessed by a joyful humility. Their efforts at learning are only efforts to open the connection."[7]

A time-tested path to opening up your awareness of God's presence involves practicing one or more of the variety of spiritual disciplines. Through the centuries a dynamic prayer life has helped millions of people develop deeper relationships with God's enlivening Spirit. When experienced as an intimate conversation with a deeply trusted friend, prayer can be an energizing and healing spiritual practice. There are various types of prayer, verbal and nonverbal. Many find contemplative prayer spiritually enlivening and healing. Its goal is simply to develop a heightened awareness of the ways God is present in all experiences, including the most earthy and mundane. A great spiritual leader, Julian of Norwich, who wrote about the motherhood and goodness of God around the troubled times of the black death in Europe, declared, "The fullness of joy is to behold God in everything."[8]

I find Matthew Fox's understanding of contemplative prayer both wholeness oriented and playful. He sees prayer as a growing, transforming awareness of life and its mysteries: "To be aware in a prayerful way is to be sensitive to the pathos of the present. An aware person grows in realizing that every day bears its mystery, every person one meets, every event in the news, every feeling felt deeply by oneself." He adds, "Prayer is a psychological reality to the extent that it is the process of the individual growing, becoming, and being changed. . . . The essence of prayer is the way we are altered to see everything from a life-filled dimension, to feel the mysteries of life as they are present (and are presented) within us and around us."[9]

Health-giving prayer changes the glasses through which you see yourself, other people, and life. Carolyn Bohler's *Prayer on Wings: A Search for Authentic Prayer*[10] offers a liberating variety of fresh approaches to prayer, as do the books by Matthew Fox. Bohler's book invites readers to revitalize their prayer life by enlisting their imagination and choosing fresh metaphors for God that increase openness to experiencing the divine.

If praying has lost its vitality for you, or if it simply isn't your thing, you may find it helpful to try meditation and self-guided imaging. Many have found that these methods open new doorways to experience the healing love of God. By "meditation" I simply mean any of a variety of methods for focusing your awareness, quieting your consciousness (by temporarily not attending to the busy flow of thoughts, feelings, images, and sensations), and thus getting into what has been called your serenity zone. When you're in such a quiet, uncluttered consciousness, the use of spiritual images that are really alive to you may let you experience the divine Love in fresh, energizing ways. Morton Kelsey's book *The Other Side of Silence: A Guide to Christian Meditation* presents an approach to the inward journey via meditative prayer and imaging, to experience God's presence. (For help in learning meditative methods, see chap. 3, pp. 66–68.)

Spiritual Need Number 2: *All of us need to experience renewing times of transcendence regularly.* This could be called getting high without drugs. Psychologist Abraham Maslow coined the phrase *peak experiences* to describe wonderful fleeting moments of wonder and uplift, precious moments of transcending the flatness of the two-dimensional, space-time, objective world. He observed that people who have a high degree of wholeness (he called them "self-actualizing" people) tend either to have more of these experiences or be more aware of them when they occur. Maslow believed that peak experiences are life validating. They can give life meaning and help to heal the splits, both within us and between us, other people, and the natural world. Nondrug ways of getting high can be surprisingly stress reducing. They can enable you to forget your "pocket dictator" (your datebook) and your wristwatch temporarily and lay down your backpack of stress for a welcome rest. Peak experiences can be spiritual door openers to the healing inflow of God's love.

In my experience, times of transcending often are not really peaks. Rather they are quiet moments when you know you are on holy ground, in touch with the eternal within yourself, and aware—as the lyrics of a song I heard put it—that you "are related to everything and therefore every place is home." In his latter years Maslow became aware of a type of spiritual experience that he called high plateaus. He observed: "I have noticed that it's possible to sit and look at something miraculous for an hour and enjoy every second of it." He added, somewhat whimsically, I suspect, "You can't have an hour-long orgasm."[11] High plateaus are sustained levels of awareness of that sacredness which infuses the ordinary. When they occur, it's a gift, as though an inner light has been turned on by someone else.

If you had trouble recalling any peak experiences, you may feel sad or mad now. But you may have an important clue about some

Cf. Maslow, Religion, Values, and Peak Experiences!

spiritual awareness work you probably need to do. It may help to remember that increasing your experiences of wonder can be a matter of increasing your awareness of the little miracles that happen in everyday life. These are so easy to miss in the hectic pace and harassed space of most people's inner lives.

In our society many people try to find their highs in limited ways. Some of these ways can become addictive and disastrous to health. For example, if you seek peak experiences only via alcohol and drugs, you're inviting addiction. Even sex, one of the most pleasurable and popular ways of getting high, can become tragically addictive, losing its spontaneity and joy. For your health it's important to learn a broad range of nonaddictive ways to get the peak experiences you need. A young woman who was involved in the high school drug scene became part of a whole-person wellness group in her congregation. After several months she wrote a letter to her minister expressing thanks for the group, in which she had "learned how to get high on people, music, books, laughter, religion, and helping people in need"!

Wholeness Exercise

> **Reliving a Peak Experience.** Recall the most meaningful peak experience you've had in the last year. (If it has been a flat year spiritually, go back further in memory until you find a mountaintop experience.) / Relive that experience, letting it happen again right now. Let yourself enjoy its energy and uplift—in your body, your mind, and at the spiritual center of your being. / Become aware of how you just energized your inner life by drawing on your memory-treasury of peak experiences. I recommend that you make a plan (perhaps jotting it down in your *Self-Care Journal*) to give yourself such a gift whenever you feel a need for a spiritual refill. /

Spiritual Need Number 3: *All of us need vital beliefs that give some sense of meaning and hope to our lives in the midst of our losses, tragedies, and failures.* What you really believe—in your heart as well as your head—and what you value most can either help keep you healthy or increase your vulnerability to illnesses. The deep conviction that your life has some meaning and worth and that you are really loved can help you live a more whole life right in the midst of life's difficulties. Devastating experiences during the Nazi holocaust, like those of Anne Frank, Viktor Frankl, and Elie Wiesel, make something very clear. We humans have the capacity to bear incredible hardships, deprivation, and even humiliation without being destroyed. But this seems to happen only if people have two things: a sense of meaning, however tenuous, and one or more mutually

"It's been such a struggle, but we've managed to keep alive his belief."

caring relationships. A sense that life has a larger spiritual meaning can help keep hope and courage alive in otherwise hopeless situations.

Among the most troublesome inner blocks to a lively, functional faith and a healthy conscience are the frozen religious beliefs and the obsolete shoulds and oughts from our childhood. These are "hangover beliefs." We no longer accept them with our adult intellects, but they cling leechlike in our feelings. They function like paint we throw on the window through which we otherwise could experience the light of God's healing love now. Immature, trivial guilts tend to waste our moral energies, preventing us from investing them in important matters like justice and integrity. This old spiritual-ethical baggage was formed by childhood experiences of religion and by the way we absorbed uncritically the beliefs and values of our parents, other authority figures, and our religious group.

Wholeness Exercise

Updating Obsolete Beliefs and Values. This exercise is designed to help you discover and replace obsolete beliefs and values with those which are current and health sustaining. Complete the unfinished sentences below in your *Self-Care Journal*, being aware of what you are feeling as you do so.

The beliefs from the religion of my childhood that no longer make much (any) sense to me are . . .

The ethical values (do's and don'ts) from my childhood training that I now question or actively reject are . . .

The beliefs that I now experience as true and really important are . . .

The values that are exciting and worth living for today are . . .

My life has the most meaning, hope, and purpose when . . .

The parts of religious life that help me handle crises and losses are . . .

To make my spiritual-ethical life more whole through better spiritual self-care, what I need to do is . . .

The feelings (fears, guilts, etc.) that make me resist taking these new steps are . . .

The actions I'll take to overcome these resistances and thus take better care of my spiritual-ethical health are . . .

Now, take time to discuss fully, with a trusted friend, the key issues, feelings, and plans that emerged in your mind. Pick a friend who'll listen with warm understanding and without judging or advising. This will let your conversation be both candid and clarifying. If possible, choose a friend who has some insight and aliveness from her or his own spiritual journey. Continue the conversation until you get some real light on your obsolete beliefs, your ethical hangovers, and what may be hindering your spiritual growth. You'll know how much you've let go of obsolete, wholeness-diminishing beliefs and values by the degree of inner lightness you feel. You can now use this energy to replace your worn-out spiritual baggage with healthier, more functional beliefs and values.

What if you're having trouble letting go of obsolete beliefs and values that you know are a burden on your soul? I recommend that you find a competent, caring pastor, priest, or rabbi who is trained in counseling and spiritual guidance on theological-ethical problems. (To locate such a pastoral counselor, contact the American Association of Pastoral Counselors, 9504A Lee Highway, Fairfax, VA 22031, phone: 703-385-6967.)

It takes spiritual courage to respect your honest doubts and to let go of childish guilt feelings over moralistic trivia. It isn't easy to remove the paint from the window of your soul. But the reward for doing so is freedom to replace these outdated beliefs and values with what you really believe and prize in your adult experience. Such a process of spiritual maturing, though painful, can liberate you to live with more spiritual, ethical, and psychological power, joy, and aliveness today.

Spiritual Need Number 4: *All of us need to have values, priorities, and life commitments centered in integrity, justice, and love, to guide us into personally and socially responsible living.* (This spiritual need is inter-twined with number 3. You've already begun to work on this by using the spiritual-ethical updating exercise above.) Your values are guideposts on the road of your life that are essential to making countless decisions each day. These include the decisions that deter-mine the health of your life-style. Chronic problems in living often result from distorted or impoverished values. Psychologist Abraham Maslow held to a deep conviction that all human beings need to experience certain wholeness-enhancing values—truth, goodness, beauty, justice, playfulness, meaningfulness. He called these B (for being) values and regarded them as necessary for psychological well being as basic food elements and vitamins are for physical health. To the degree that you're living by these life-affirming values you'll be less vulnerable to the epidemic of spiritual illnesses in our world. These illnesses include hopelessness and despair, meaning-lessness, existential depression, boredom, addictions, and loss of zest for living a life with inner joy and purpose.[12]

Psychiatrist Jean Baker Miller and psychologist Carol Gilligan add an invaluable new insight to Maslow's understanding of healthy values. They show how women have been programmed in male-dominated cultures to overdevelop, while men are programmed to underdevelop, certain essential capacities and values. These include sensitivity and responsiveness to feelings, cooperation with and car-ing for others, compassion, and responsibility for intimate relation-ships. These humanizing values are desperately needed by many men and by our male-dominated institutions. Only by learning to prize and practice these values more can men humanize the capaci-ties and values that they have been programmed to overdevelop in patriarchal cultures—competition, conquest, power over others, ra-tionality, control, analysis, technical mastery. More about this in chapter 11, which is about women's and men's well being.

The inventory that follows is a companion to the exercise you just did. It should help you develop ways to use your precious time to do more of what's really important to you. Both exercises are based on the awareness that the way we choose to use our limited time in any day or any lifetime determines both the values we live out and the quality of our life-style, for better or for worse.

Wholeness Exercise

Self-critiquing and Revising Your Values. In your *Well Being Self-Care Journal* list the ten most important things (people, activities, causes, possessions, goals) in your present life. / Now, beside each of your top ten values, note approximately how much time you actually devoted to them in the last two weeks. / In light of your time-identified priorities, reflect on the following queries, perhaps writing your responses in your *Journal:*

Do my real values and the life-style they produce enable me to

- Give adequate attention to the most important things in my life? (Pause while you reflect on each question.)
- Take good care of my body? My mind? Avoid burnout in my work?
- Enjoy my favorite people? Nature? My creativity? My sexuality? My playfulness and sense of humor? The things I love to do most?
- Enjoy working hard with others for a more livable planet, for myself, my loved ones, my children and grandchildren, and for all the members of the human family?
- Do the exciting and worthwhile things I really want to do during whatever long or short time I may have left on planet earth?
- Do the spiritual self-care that could enhance my total well being?

Now, in light of your self-evaluation, ask yourself two more questions: **Does my present life-style allow the urgent things to push aside the important things (and people) in my life?**[13] / **What exactly will I do to bring my life-style more in line with what is most important to me?** Note your answers in your *Journal.*

**Time, Values,
Life-Style
Inventory**

Instructions:

1. Look down the column of time-consuming activities on the left, adding others that consume significant amounts of your time. /
2. After each activity check one of the three columns to the right. TIME OK = "The time I'm spending at present seems appropriate to me"; MORE TIME = "This activity has more value to me and therefore deserves more of my time"; LESS TIME = This activity is less valuable to me and deserves less time than I'm giving it."/
3. Evaluate the priorities and values inherent in your present allocation of time in light of your own important values, including those you still accept from your religious tradition. /

4. Develop workable plans to change your schedule to give more of your time to higher-priority values and less to those that have lower priority. Jot down the gist of your self-change plan, including a time line for implementing your plan, in the right column./

5. Implement your plans, rewarding yourself in some way each time you use your time more intentionally and well. Remember, your time is your life! To use it well is to live life well!

TIME-CONSUMING ACTIVITIES	TIME OK	MORE TIME	LESS TIME	CHANGE PLANS
Work				
Rest and Sleep				
Play				
Body Self-Care				
Mind Self-Care				
Spiritual Self-Care				
Time with My Family or Friends				
Serving Others				
Creative Activities				
Free, Unstructured Time				
Time Wasted				
Other Uses of Time				

Changing long-established values, priorities, and commitments is far from easy, even if your present life-style is killing you (literally). It often takes a painful medical or family crisis to motivate us to make the changes that will make our lives more whole and fulfilling. It is obviously wise to make these changes before such a costly confrontation occurs.

Spiritual Need Number 5: *All of us need to discover and develop the inner wisdom, creativity, and love of our transpersonal or spiritual Self.* In traditional religious language the spiritual dimension of your life is called the soul. Roberto Assagioli, the Italian psychiatrist who founded the school of therapy called psychosynthesis, coined the term *higher Self* to describe this dimension. Swiss psychiatrist Carl G. Jung used "Self" to distinguish this spiritual aspect from the "ego." Both therapists understood the Self as having the wisdom and empowering love to become the integrating center of optimal human wholeness. I agree. The more you make your spiritual Self the integrating center of your life, the more your whole being is energized by openness to God's Love.

Donald and Nancy Tubesing put this well: "The process of touching and being touched by your core is an experience that creates wholeness and gives you energy. Enthusiasm, that bubbling of life energy, comes from tapping into the spirit of God within—deep within. The Greek word for enthusiasm originally means 'in God,' filled with and able to express God's energy as it flows through. When you're touched by that energy, you know you're alive."[14]

Some years ago I had a psychotherapeutic "retread" during a period of painful struggles with personal and relationship issues. The therapist, trained in psychosynthesis, sensed my deep frustration in attempting to use only ego-level understandings to solve my problems and resolve the hard lumps of grief and anger within me. The turning point in the session came when he invited me to "go to the place within you where you're together and whole and at peace. Look at your issues from that perspective." As I did this, I was

Wholeness Exercise

> Stop reading, close your eyes, and see if you can get in touch with your core Self—the loving place deep within you where you're "together" and at peace, even when there are storms on the surface of your life. / If you find that place, let yourself simply enjoy being there for a little while. / Now, look at whatever problems you're facing from that perspective and see what happens. / If you found this simple technique helpful, you may want to jot down your discoveries in your *Journal.*

The first seed of the longing

for Justice

blows through the soul like

the wind.

The taste for good will plays

in it like a breeze.

The consummation of this

seed is a greening in

the soul

that is like that of the

ripening world.

Now the soul honors God by

the doing of just deeds.

The soul is only as strong as

its works.

—*Hildegard of Bingen*

All the messages I have

suspected were from God

have come anonymously,

with no return address, and,

occasionally, with postage

due.

—*Ruth Bebermeyer*

surprised that the lumps of painful, frozen feelings began to melt. My complex problems weren't magically solved, of course. But I experienced a sense of release and a gentle flow of healing energy. It gradually became clear that I could use this energy either to continue working on the issues (less obsessively) or release them as beyond my power to resolve.

In our busy, surface-living world, it's easy to lose contact with your deeper transpersonal Self. But discovering and caring for this spiritual center is a way of meeting another deep spiritual hunger—the need for a sense of purpose in your life and work. When people get in touch with their spiritual Self and begin to search for ways to express the love they experience by reaching out to others, they often discover their vocation. By "vocation" I mean an awareness of where you need to invest your talents and energy in ways that can make a small but constructive difference in the lives of others. For both youth and adults few things contribute more to "getting it together" than a clear sense of vocation—a purpose that excites them to commit themselves to some work or cause whose value transcends their own self-interest. This experience can be pivotal in restoring zest to your life and work. (More about this in chapter 6.)

George Fox, the seventeenth-century founder of the Society of Friends (also called the Quakers), had a passionate respect for the divine image and spark in every person. He called this the "inner light," believing that one must express this in the world, helping make society a little more just and compassionate.

Perhaps you are skeptical, as I often am when I encounter folks who think they have some sort of special God-appointed mission. I remember how many destructive things have been done throughout history using this as a justification.

Spiritual Need Number 6: *All of us need a deepening awareness of our oneness with other people and with the natural world, the wonderful web of living things.* The essence of human brokenness is feeling cut off from aspects of ourselves, other people, nature, and God. An alcoholic with whom I was counseling described his sense of deep aloneness in these poignant words, "Howard, I feel like an orphan in the universe." Lover of the High Sierras John Muir said it well: "When we try to pick out anything by itself, we find it hitched to everything else in the Universe. . . . No particle is ever wasted or worn out, but eternally flowing from use to use."[15] An ecological consciousness rooted in a spirituality of relationships seems to bring an awareness that you are really at home in the universe. You really belong! Such a sense of organic interrelatedness with the biosphere can help to heal our body-mind-spirit brokenness and keep us grounded.

An ecological consciousness flows from what Matthew Fox calls a creation-centered spirituality. It produces a "sensual spirituality" which is fed by a deep awareness of interconnectedness with the universe. Teilhard de Chardin describes the spiritual depth of our relatedness to the universe: "The human soul . . . is inseparable, in birth and growth, from the universe in which it is born. In each soul, God loves and partly saves the whole world which that soul sums up in an incommunicable and particular way."[16] He believed that the dawning of human personality, in the eon-spanning continuing creation of the evolutionary process, marked the emergence of an exciting new dimension of reality—the network of minds and spirits that he calls the noosphere. As integral parts of this network, we are mutually nurtured by other minds and by the creative, loving Spirit of the universe. But to be whole our connection with this psychospiritual network must be kept grounded in an awareness of our bodies and nature and the wider web of living things.

Spiritually centered wholeness grows best in the loving relationships of a small group or community committed to mutual spiritual growth around shared values. Our human longing for spiritual intimacy was expressed by a young student in a spiritual growth group who said wistfully: "Once before I die I would like to get close enough to another human being to really touch souls." Finding what has been called a soul friend can occur in a deep friendship or in a creative marriage or in a small spiritual growth group committed to mutual caring and spiritual-ethical discovery. It often occurs in a faith community, a creative church or synagogue, or in a Twelve-Step recovery group. In such an environment, mutual caring, refreshing honesty, and open communication combine to generate healing and health.

The beautiful Hebrew word *shalom*, like the parallel Arabic word *salam*, though usually translated "peace" also means to be healthy or whole in community. To greet another with "shalom" is to wish that person health and well being. A student from the Near East said that to him the salutation means "May that which is good within you richly abound and flow out to those around you."[17] Shalom appears over 350 times in the Hebrew Bible. It is understood as a gift from God. This gift is received in a spiritual community united by a covenant of mutual caring that helps empower persons within it to develop their God-given possibilities. If you don't have a shalom community, it's worth whatever you must do to discover or develop such a spiritually nurturing network.

Spiritual Need Number 7: *All of us need spiritual resources to help heal the painful wounds of grief, guilt, resentment, unforgiveness, and self-rejection. We also have a need for spiritual resources to deepen our feelings of trust, self-esteem, hope, joy, and love of life.* Methods of meeting these essential needs will be described in the next chapter in the discussion of salugenic and pathogenic feelings.

Creative Coping with Our Planet's Spiritual Crisis

Satisfying your deep spiritual hunger in healthy ways is more difficult today because of the planetwide spiritual crisis of humankind. Spiritual transcendence as a vital experience has largely disappeared from the lives of millions of us in Western societies. The mind-boggling speed of social and technological changes has produced a massive breakdown of traditional belief and value systems. Millions of us are flatly rejecting old authority-centered ways of defining what is really good or ultimately true. There seem to be more questions than believable answers today, more options and more opinions, too. Old ways of believing and valuing are no longer accepted or satisfying. But many have not yet developed new ways. Painful meaning and value vacuums proliferate, rooted in our profoundly materialistic, thing-worshiping life-styles.

Grasping the enormous power of spiritual needs and the urgency of satisfying them in constructive ways requires understanding *existential anxiety.* This is the normal, non-neurotic anxiety flowing from our human awareness that we will someday die. In our death-denying culture we have countless ways of deadening the awareness of our vulnerability and mortality. Psychoanalytic pioneer Karen Horney suggests, for example, that neurosis is a way of avoiding one's fear of death by avoiding being fully alive. If I keep myself feeling half-dead by compulsive work, guilt, depression, and unawareness, death becomes less threatening because I have so little to lose.

Some vital thinking by existentialist psychologists in recent decades has shed light on this non-neurotic anxiety. Therapists and other thinkers as diverse as Carl Jung, Otto Rank, Karen Horney, Erich Fromm, Ernest Becker, Rollo May, Abraham Maslow, Norman O. Brown, and Laura Perls, Paul Tillich, Tennessee Williams, and Woody Allen have wrestled with this fundamental human dilemma. In a moving scene in Tennessee Williams's play, "Cat On a Hot Tin Roof," Big Daddy is confronted by his son Brick, who demands to know why his father had not told his family about his cancer. Big Daddy's response is simply that it was because he "lacks the pig's advantage"—i.e., ignorance of his mortality.

Philosopher Martin Heidegger spoke of *Urangst* (the German word for existential anxiety) as the background music that plays continually so that ordinarily we don't even hear it. But in the pressure-cooker developmental transitions of life, and in unexpected crises along the way, the volume gets turned up. It becomes nearly impossible not to listen. When personal crises happen in the context of massive social traumas, like the environmental-nuclear crisis today, existential anxiety becomes even more powerful, pervasive, and inescapable.

We humans flee from existential anxiety into all manner of addiction. We make idols out of success, power, prestige, things, drugs, alcohol, religion, work, sex, our country, our families. By obsessively centering our lives around these addictions, we avoid facing our own mortality and finitude. But like Janus (the Roman god after whom the first month of our calendar was named), our idols all have two faces. One face eventually turns out to be that of a demon who betrays its worshipers, leaving them in greater despair. When the false gods of our addictions betray us, we hit bottom, as they say in AA.

How can existential anxiety be handled constructively? Since it's a normal, inescapable part of the human awareness, there are (in contrast to neurotic anxiety) no psychological or psychotherapeutic ways of healing it. The grandfather of existentialism, Danish philosopher Søren Kierkegaard, pointed to the answer. He observed that it's possible to transform this anxiety into what he called a school—a stimulus to creativity, an opportunity for learning. The bottom line is that this transformation can happen only in the context of a meaningful faith undergirded by a trustful experience of the divine Spirit.

In other words, the only way to cope creatively with existential anxiety is to experience a love-empowered spirituality that lets you risk really coming alive in the present moment. The authentic answer to the terror of death is to experience really being alive in this moment. As philosopher Mary Daly observes, some people in religion "seek to overcome the threat of nonbeing by denying the self. The outcome of this is ironic: that which is dreaded triumphs, for we are caught in the self-contradictory bind of shrinking our being to avoid nonbeing. The only alternative is self-actualization in spite of the ever-present nothingness."[18]

Out of the ancient wisdom of the East, Lao-tzu declares: "A man of **outward courage** dares to die; a man of **inward courage** dares to live."[19] A client in long-term art therapy (who painted her unconscious conflicts, impulses, fears, and fantasies), taught me this truth. As she completed her rebirth into greater well being via her therapy, she declared with passion, "I came for help because I was afraid of dying, but I discovered I was really afraid of living!" Generating the inward *courage to be and to become* requires power from a vital love-saturated spirituality. It's like the radical climate change that brought the end of the last ice age. The warm, healing Love of God can melt the ice of the soul (existential anxiety), transforming it into living water that nurtures life in all its fullness. The fear of death thus becomes a primary motivation and power for the flowering of creativity. Existential anxiety is transformed into a "school" (Kierkegaard), an experience of growing in the aliveness of love.

The spiritual crisis of our culture (and ourselves) leaves us terribly vulnerable to the ego-chill of existential anxiety. But this crisis also is an unprecedented challenge and opportunity for us humans to grow up spiritually and ethically. It is spiritually healthy that millions of us are no longer giving away our spiritual power to authoritarian religious institutions and authority figures. As never before in human history, we're challenged to use our new spiritual freedom to relinquish childish things in our religious lives. We're confronted by the necessity to develop healthy, self-validating beliefs and values, beliefs that we can affirm wholeheartedly and values that we can live by with zest and love and joy. This is the direction of our exciting spiritual journey into the future.

Spiritual Sources of Well Being

The passion for love-centered well being is deeply rooted in many of the world's religious traditions. Consider a few examples.

Among the great spiritual heritages of the East, Taoism is the tradition that most clearly has as its goal what is called well being today. In 600 B.C. the founder Lao-tzu, in his book *The Way of Life*, described the tao (life principle, force, or way) as an inclusive interrelatedness. Today this might be described as an ecological view of the healthy life. He wrote: "Perhaps I should have called it 'fullness of life,' since it implies widening into space . . . until the circle is whole. . . . The surest test if a man is sane is if he accepts life whole, as it is."[20]

The Buddhist tradition offers insights that help correct certain views of wholeness in Western religions. For example, the path to finding fulfillment in Buddhism is by lightening one's load of desires rather than by satisfying more and more of them. In our world of gross consumerism and shrinking resources, this understanding is a healthy corrective to our view that happiness comes mainly by achieving and getting.[21]

The Sufi mystical tradition within Islam also has insights that are potential wholeness resources. Regarding spiritual enlightenment, a great Sufi teacher once said, "Make God a reality and he will make you the truth." Reflecting on the mystery of love, Mevlana Jelalu'ddin Rumi stated: "Reason is powerless in the expression of Love. Love alone is capable of revealing the truth of Love and being a Lover. . . . If you want to live, die in Love; die in Love if you want to remain alive." Muhyi-d-din Ibn Arabi, another Sufi sage declared, "God is never seen immaterially; and the vision of Him in woman is the most perfect of all."[22]

In the Jewish Bible, the wonderful potentialities of human beings are communicated by the story of being created in God's image. In the second testament, Jesus' purpose in coming is described in wholeness terms—to enable persons to find "life in all its fullness" (John 10:10). All seven dimensions of well being are affirmed in the sacred writings of Judaism and Christianity:

Spirit: Spiritual wholeness is a main theme of both testaments. A poetic paraphrase of the letter to the Romans by J. B. Phillips communicates the conviction that the gravitational energy of the spiritual universe is on the side of our becoming more whole: "The whole creation is on tiptoe to see the wonderful sight of the children of God coming into their own" (Rom. 8:19).

Mind: Quoting the two great commandments of his Jewish Bible, Jesus enjoined his hearers to love God with their whole mind, heart, soul, and strength (Mark 12:30).

Body: The human body is understood as a temple of the Spirit in St. Paul's writings. He asked the recipients of one of his letters to "glorify God in your body" (1 Cor. 6:19–20).

Relationships: In the second great commandment, Jesus emphasized love, the heart of wholeness, by instructing people to love their neighbor as they loved themselves (Mark 12:30).

Work: The wisdom literature of the Hebrew Bible invites believers to "commit your work to the Lord" (Prov. 16:3).

Play: The recognition that playfulness is healthy is reflected in this proverb from the First Testament, "A cheerful heart is good medicine" (Prov. 17:22).

The World: In the first of the two creation stories in the Torah, after each epoch of creation, God looked at what had been made and affirmed it as good (Gen. 1), thus highlighting what is called ecological wholeness today. Increasing societal wholeness by enhancing justice is the strong message of the Hebrew prophets of the eighth century B.C.

Both testaments understand wholeness as a process of growing. A good person is like "a tree planted by streams of water, that yields its fruit in its season" (Ps. 1:3). The earthy stories told by Jesus of mustard seeds, leaven in bread dough, a farmer who sowed seeds in a field describe the growth process by which the new era of caring and community, justice and wholeness is coming.

The Bible emphasizes the profound brokenness and resistances to wholeness in us humans as much as it does our remarkable capacities. The biblical writers were aware that the potential for wholeness is a gift of God. But they also knew that it takes discipline and struggle to claim and develop this gift. Images of rebirth and the new age of shalom are affirmations of the power for transformation in spiritually-energized human beings. It is very clear that well being involves investing oneself in helping others find well being: "For whoever would save his life will lose it, and whoever loses his life for my sake will find it" (Matt. 16:25). In both the Hebrew and the Christian heritages one persistent theme is that we're all members of one family—the human family—with a common spiritual Parent (Acts 17:25).

A Spiritual Empowerment Exercise

Hildegard of Bingen uses wonderful water images in speaking of the divine Spirit: "The soul that is full of wisdom is saturated with the spray of a bubbling fountain—God himself." "Like billowing clouds, like the incessant gurgle of the brook, the longing of the soul can never be stilled."[23]

In the spirit of her flowing images here is a guided meditation[24] I hope you find spiritually empowering. (Remember, the slashes mean pause a while, close your eyes, and do what has been suggested.)

In your imagination, picture a small, rough irrigation stream (perhaps a foot or so wide and just a few inches deep). / Notice that in spite of its small size the stream is carrying a steady flow of clear, refreshing water into some dusty, barren places. As the water spreads out on the parched earth, be aware of the tiny seeds that have been waiting, like wildflower seeds in the desert longing for the spring rains. Rejoice as they begin to sprout in a glad awakening. / Keep watching while the little plants begin to flower, seeing them blossom (as in a time-lapse movie) into a dazzling, multicolored carpet of flowers, nodding gently in the breeze. Experience the wonder of the flowering that occurs with the continuing flow of life-awakening water, from even this small irrigation channel. /

Now, follow the irrigation channel to its visible source—a wonderful little bubbling spring that seems to laugh and dance as it reaches the surface from a deep, hidden source. Watch the water in the little stream as it continues to dance and play, catching the sparkles of sunlight on its ripples. Enjoy the miniature sailboats bobbing playfully along with the flow of the stream where a child has placed them. / In your imagination follow the spring below the ground until you come to its hidden source—a wonderful, ever-flowing river of clear, refreshing water. Experience the joy of the discovery that the source of the water that flows into the little surface stream has no limit. It won't run out, no matter how dry and hot it gets on the surface! /

Come back up now to the little irrigation stream, observing that it has a sluice gate that releases or blocks the flow. Be aware that you can decide whether the gate is closed or how wide it is open. / Let your eyes and your spirit feast on the beautiful flowers blossoming in all directions from the little stream. / Now, finish this guided meditation in whatever way you choose, to give it a sense of completion for you. / Reflect for a few minutes on whatever you learned that promises to be useful in enhancing your spiritual life. / Now, take a little while to jot down in your *Self-Care Journal* insights and images for further reflection. /

In your use of this meditation I hope you discovered some ways your spiritual Self can become a channel through which divine Love can flow out to others, making parched places flower with new life.

Create Your Spiritual Self-Care Fitness Plan

Having finished this chapter, develop a tentative spiritual Self-Care Plan for yourself in your *Self-Care Journal*. Write down at least six things you can do to increase your spiritual health. Use the important checkup items you marked OK or NS, plus insights and methods you found relevant in this chapter. Your plan will be more likely to work if you include (1) concrete, realizable objectives that you really want to achieve; (2) practical plans for moving toward these; (3) a time line, especially when you'll begin; (4) rewards you'll give yourself as you take each step toward objectives or withhold if you backslide; (5) a record of your progress in your *Journal*.

Be sure to keep your plan love centered and spiritually energized. Also, activate your inner child to give your plan's implementation a touch of playfulness to balance your serious intentions.

Pick one or two attractive and achievable objectives and begin moving toward them immediately, if only for ten or twelve minutes a day. In overcoming resistances to self-change, momentum from small early successes often helps. I wish you empowering self-care of your spiritual life as you implement your plan.

Empowering Your Mind for Healing and Creativity

I cannot tolerate bigots.

They are all so obstinate, so

opinionated.

—*Senator Joseph McCarthy*

If ignorance is bliss, why

aren't there more happy

people?

—*Milton Berle*

 Your mind—with its ideas, attitudes, perceptions, feelings, and images—has incredible power to help heal and keep you well or to make and keep you sick. Duke University Medical School studied 255 male doctors who graduated between 1954 and 1959, dividing them into a "cynical and hostile" group and a "trusting and positive outlook" group. A follow-up study in 1980 revealed that the hostile and cynical group was almost five times more likely to have developed heart disease and died than the group that had a positive mental outlook. The researchers concluded that negative, cynical attitudes can harm the heart as much as high blood pressure, smoking, and cholesterol.[1]

This study is but one dramatic illustration from contemporary scientific evidence of the impact your mental and emotional health, or lack of it, has on your overall well being. *The dual keys to maximizing love-centered well being in your whole life are the health and aliveness of your mind and the health and aliveness of your spirit.*

Zen scholar D. T. Suzuki and psychoanalyst Erich Fromm collaborated to produce an illuminating book on the relationship of Zen Buddhism and psychotherapy. They declare: "The aim of life is to be fully born, though its tragedy is that most of us die before we are thus born. . . . The answer is . . . to develop one's awareness, one's reason, one's capacity to love, to such a point that one transcends one's own egocentric involvement and arises at a new harmony and a new wonder with the world."[2] The journey of whole-person fitness is a lifelong process of becoming more *fully born*—to the wonder and challenges, the potentialities and love of life! Being

"I think of you as being enormously alive."

We are entering a new level in the scientific understanding of mechanisms by which faith, belief, and imagination can unlock the mysteries of healing.

—Joan Borysenko, Director of Mind/Body Clinic, Harvard Medical School

Get wisdom, get insight . . . love her and she will guard you. (Proverbs 4:5–6)

fully born is one way of understanding the words attributed to Jesus about being born again (John 3:3).

Loving, empowering, and renewing your mind is a path to continuing transformation. Contemporary psychological approaches to this process parallel the wisdom articulated by Paul of Tarsus when he urged first-century Christians to "be transformed by the renewal of your mind" (Rom. 12:2). Furthermore, as we saw in the last chapter, the quality of your values and spirituality profoundly influences how you use your mind.

Psychologists like Abraham Maslow have estimated that most of us use only a small part (perhaps 15 to 25 percent) of our potential intelligence, creativity, and problem-solving ability. Most people die without ever discovering more than a fraction of their minds' powers and possibilities. You're probably much more creative and mentally resourceful than you think! Learning to use more facets of your mind, including your creativity, is a vital secret for enhancing your overall fitness. This chapter will focus on both left-brain and right-brain tools to increase the power of your mind as an instrument of love-centered learning, healing, problem-solving, and creativity.

Mental Well-Being Checkup

This checkup can help you increase the fitness of your mind in two ways. (1) It can help you quickly identify areas of your mind and personality where you are strong and those where you may need to grow. (2) The items in the checkup offer a variety of practical things you can do to empower your mind, increase its creativity, and use it to help heal yourself.

CHECKLIST

Instructions: In front of each statement put one of three initials: E = I'm doing excellently in this; OK = I'm doing acceptably, but there's room for improvement; NS = This is an area where I definitely need strengthening.

_____ I enjoy a sense of wonder, a childlike curiosity that makes learning new ideas and skills energizing.

_____ I'm aware of some of my unused intellectual and personality assets, and I'm taking steps to develop these gifts.

_____ I regularly exercise my intellectual and creative muscles by reading, by wrestling with tough issues, and/or by taking a refresher class.

_____ I enjoy using my mind to "spark off" new ideas with others by spirited dialogue and debate with stimulating people.

_____ I regularly balance my rational, analytical, verbal, quantitative left-brain functioning with intuitive, playful, nonanalytical right-brain activities, such as music, drawing, gardening, joking, storytelling, imaging.

_____ I practice the principle of healthy alternation, intermingling intellectual, physical, and people activities.

_____ I have a sense of inherent worth as a precious child of the divine Spirit, self-worth not derived from collecting achievements or the approval of others.

_____ I have learned to resolve my so-called negative feelings, such as guilt, shame, jealousy, unforgiveness, anger, resentment, loneliness, despair, fear, so that they don't diminish my well being.

_____ I nurture positive feelings, such as hope, trust, serenity, love, caring, connectedness, playfulness, joy, and zest for living, so that they will enhance my wholeness.

_____ I practice the fine art of forgiving myself, thus becoming better able to forgive others and life.

_____ I affirm my sensual-sexual feelings, without guilt, and enjoy their ability to bring sparkle and passion to my life and relationships.

_____ When crises occur I mobilize my coping abilities effectively. I learn from the pain, losses, and tragedies without losing touch with the beauty, love, and just plain fun in my everyday life.

_____ I avoid wasting energy on useless remorse about things past as well as unrealistic fearful fantasies about the future. I enjoy the good gift of being alive and aware in this present moment.

_____ I have sufficient self-esteem and awareness so that I usually avoid responding to threatening situations in self-defeating or paranoid ways.

_____ I check out my perceptions of events and people with those I trust, to increase the likelihood that my understanding is based on the real situation I face.

_____ I enjoy stretching my mental horizons by reading and thinking about issues outside my everyday experience.

_____ I avoid depressing myself by turning anger in on myself or striking out in unconstructive ways.

_____ I give my mind-body-spirit the daily gift of a quiet time, such as deep relaxation, meditation, inspirational reading, or prayer, to reduce stress and recharge my batteries.

_____ I know and use effective self-help techniques for healing painful memories and using my mind to keep my body-mind fit.

_____ If inner conflicts and unresolved problems continue to plague me, I have the courage to seek help from a competent counselor or therapist.

_____ I prefer to live with the anxiety of unanswered questions rather than settle for easy answers to life's complexities, paradoxes, and dilemmas.

_____ I have reasonable and achievable (not perfectionistic or grandiose) goals for my life, as a basis for planning and prioritizing my use of time and to avoid the fragmentation of going off in all directions.

_____ I'm friendly with my hidden, less attractive "shadow" side, thus avoiding fighting or fearing in others what is really in me.

_____ I befriend my dreams and spontaneous fantasies, using them to stay in touch with the energies and wisdom of my deeper mind.

_____ I keep the responsible adult side of my personality in the driver's seat, but also regularly let my playful inner child and nurturing inner parent enjoy playing and caring to enrich my life experience.

_____ I enjoy awareness of the profound interconnectedness of my head, heart, body, and sexuality, with themselves and with other people, nature, the divine Spirit, and the whole network of living things.

_____ I find satisfaction in using my mind, heart, and hands to help other people and my community with troubling problems.

Using Your Findings: How can you get the most benefits from what may feel like a heavy-duty checklist? First, scan the three types of initials to get an overall feel for your mental self-care and fitness. Give yourself a mental pat on the back for the E items. Go through the OK and NS items quickly, picking out those which seem important to you, jotting these down in your *Self-Care Journal.* For future use, beside these note your tentative ideas concerning what you might do to strengthen your health care in those areas.

Your Mind's Remarkable Power to Hurt or Heal

The mind's power to hurt or heal the body has been demonstrated repeatedly. Scientific experiments have documented negative body changes resulting from job loss, divorce, and bereavement as well as positive body changes from getting a pet, meditation, psychotherapy, spiritual healing, and leaving a miserable marriage. Studies of heart, cancer, and rheumatoid arthritis patients have revealed that hopelessness often appears to be a crucial factor in the onset, and hopefulness an important resource in persons who recover.

Positive feelings like joy and hope have a correlation with healing and longevity. Louis A. Gottschalk, psychiatry professor at the University of California at Irvine, has developed a "Hope Scale" to measure patients' degree of hope.[3] Sandra Levy, a psychologist at the Pittsburg Cancer Institute, discovered that a factor she called joy (including mental resilience and vigor) was the second strongest predictor of the longevity of patients with recurring breast cancer.[4]

Biofeedback researchers also have demonstrated that the mind has unsuspected power to influence the body. They have concluded that the mind can exercise some degree of voluntary control over any internal biological function of which individuals can become aware. This includes functions previously believed to be completely beyond conscious control, for example, blood pressure, heart rate, skin temperature, and brain waves.[5]

The body's responsiveness to even erroneous beliefs is dramatically illustrated by the use of placebos in medical research. After receiving totally inert pills (lookalikes of the medication), subjects who believe they have been given genuine medicine experience real relief from chronic pain, high blood pressure, arthritis, hay fever, asthma, headaches, diabetes, seasickness, and warts. Placebos often produce even the expected side effects of the drugs they mimic.

An exciting new medical field called PNI (psychoneuroimmunology) is shedding light on how the mind-body connection works. The conclusion of scores of independent scientific studies is that there is a circular interaction between the immune system, which protects and heals the body, and the mind-brain. The higher brain or cortex—usually equated with the "mind"—seems to influence the immune system through its language capacities and its ability to think and store massive quantities of information, thoughts, feelings, images, beliefs, and experiences. The immune system is controlled by the brain, but it apparently "talks back" to the brain, sending messages via hormones from the endocrine system that affect emotions and other mental states. This body-mind interaction produces increased vulnerability to illnesses or enhances the likelihood of recovery or of staying well.

Jeanne Achterberg, director of research at the University of Texas Health Science Center, describes the mind as "the link between disease and the environment, the controlling force of the body's protection system, the storehouse of the secrets of health and disease."[6] *Most if not all illnesses are really psychophysiological (psychosomatic) illnesses*, to some degree, in that psychological, interpersonal, and spiritual factors are among the multiple causes of them. Therefore these factors should not be ignored if either prevention or treatment is to be fully effective.[7] Mental and behavioral therapies are being used as an essential part of the treatment for migraines, high blood pressure, colitis, ulcers, sexual dysfunction, pain problems, cancer, heart disease, and other illnesses.

There is a real danger in all this. It is blaming victims who don't get better, for not using their minds more effectively. Often the blame is self-blame. Jane's breast cancer was discovered during a routine medical checkup, soon after her youngest child started school. Jane was excited about launching a new chapter in her musical career. She was devastated by the diagnosis. On top of all this, having read articles on the mind-body movement, she felt acute guilt and failure for having contracted cancer.

It was essential for her therapist to help Jane let go of this self-blaming. The therapist did this by reminding her of the evidence that many causes probably converge when people acquire major illnesses. These include factors over which one has little or no control, such as genetic vulnerability and environmental toxicity. Mental factors, she pointed out, may play a tiny or a large role among the causes, and letting go of self-blaming may help activate the body's malignancy-fighting inner resources. In Jane's case it also freed up previously wasted energy for use in her whole-person treatment—through exercise, diet, imaging, and a support group, as well as conventional medical approaches.

I recall a cartoon showing some slaves with ropes around their middles, struggling mightily to move some huge blocks of stone

"Look out! Here comes Denis Farnell and his 'wellness unto death.'"

toward an unfinished pyramid. One of the slaves is saying heatedly to another: "Do me a big favor! Quit saying 'Happiness is within one's self!'" This points to the catch in any approach that emphasizes the power of your mind while ignoring your external situation. Your mind *does* have incredible power—to influence how happy you are, whatever your circumstances, and to influence your body's capacity to heal itself. But, as you're probably painfully aware, there are also limiting or oppressive things in your external life situation that cannot be changed merely by altering the way you use your mind.

Empowering Your Mind for Well Being

What is "empowerment"? Three fundamental human needs—for self-esteem, competence, and inner strength—constitute personal empowerment. You (along with other human beings) need profound awareness of your inherent, irreducible worth. You also need the knowledge and skills to accomplish things that are important to you and to your society. And you need inner strength to guide your own life and to influence others in constructive directions. In our mega-society, with its depersonalizing technology and giant bureaucracies, millions of us can resonate to the feeling expressed by Tom, a depressed, cocaine-dependent young adult: "I often feel like a damn computer punch card with the corner torn off."

An epidemic of personal powerlessness is at the root of many of our society's problems. Only when you and I feel at least a minimal degree of self-esteem, competence, and inner strength will we be able to respect others, cope constructively with life's demands, and know that our lives can make a small but significant difference in the world. Without this cope-ability, it is very difficult to handle ordinary (not to mention extraordinary) challenges and crises without developing dis-ease in one or more areas of our lives.

There are four types of human power: power *over* (dominance, control of others, often rooted in hidden feelings of impotence); power *against* (attacking, subduing, even destroying others, often rooted in fear); power *for* (nurturing and caring for others); and power *with* (mutual empowering through cooperation and collaboration).[8] Health-giving empowerment excludes power *over*. It uses power *against* mainly to gain just and necessary objectives for the well being of oneself or others. Healthy empowerment employs power *for* only when it may strengthen the person being "helped." Power *with* is the primary mode of love-centered wholeness. Such power generates mutual empowerment that increases the esteem, competence, and inner strength of all the persons involved. The remainder of this chapter describes tools you can use for this kind of empowerment.

Empowering Your Life by Self-Responsibility

One of the important things you can do for self-empowerment and higher-level wellness in your life is to take (back) responsibility for your own health. It is you, not your physician (as competent as she or he may be), who has the ultimate responsibility and opportunity to do the many things you *can* do today to enhance your fitness. Self-responsibility means using whatever options you have in each life situation to choose to step in a constructive direction. Self-responsibility is the opposite of a passive victim response, which puts you at the mercy of circumstances and thus makes you more of a victim.[9]

Many of us (including myself) wouldn't be alive without the marvels of modern medicine. Unfortunately, our worship of medical miracles has fostered health-sabotaging responses in many people. These include passivity in relating to physicians; exaggerated expectations of medical miracles on demand; overdependency on medications; reliance on medical treatments as a cure for self-neglect; and a tendency to ignore the responsibility and opportunity to develop a healthful life-style.

What can you do to enhance your fitness by self-responsibility?

You can accept the fact that many if not the majority of the life-style decisions that influence the length, quality, and health of your life are within your control. Of course, factors over which you have little or no control also influence your degree of wellness. But whatever your health limitations, if you put yourself in the driver's seat of your life, you can devise ways to reshuffle these givens so that you raise your general wellness level. You also can increase your knowledge about preventing health problems and wellness self-care through reading or workshops. As recommended in these pages, you can develop and use a personal fitness program that fits your preferences and life situation. And finally, you can use competent therapists and health professionals as needed, but use them as enablers, resource persons, and guides to your own wellness care. Insist on being an active collaborator and partner rather than a passive recipient of their services. Only you can walk the road of your own personal fitness journey. But having their expertise as wise guides at critical points on the journey can be important, even lifesaving.[10]

Empowering Your Mind Through Exercise

Consider two disturbing facts. The average American watches between four and five hours of television each day. The average college or university graduate reads slightly less than one book each year. These are but two symptoms of the intellectual flabbiness that produces low levels of mental fitness in our society. This is particularly tragic in light of the undiscovered intellectual potentialities of most people, mentioned earlier. The development of some of these capacities can help folks suffering from intellectual malnutrition and suffocating from boring TV addictions to get back into mental trim.

Perhaps you're wondering why so many educated people do not enjoy having their minds challenged and enriched by the adventure of reading? A major cause is the crippling of creativity resulting from traditional, authority-centered educational methods which tend to stifle rather than reward creative thinking. They force students to memorize endless boring content which often has little or no relation to their real interests and actual needs-for-living. As you probably remember, most of what is crammed in to pass exams is forgotten just as fast when the threat of failure is past. Years of such externally motivated education extinguish the spark of spontaneous curiosity which motivates young children to explore their world and learn new things eagerly.

Paulo Freire, the courageous Brazilian philosopher of education, makes something frighteningly clear in his confronting classic, *Pedagogy of the Oppressed* (see Recommended Reading). He shows how authority-centered education prepares people mentally to be submissive conformists to authoritarian leaders. As he told me when I visited him in Sao Paulo in 1990, it's an encouraging sign of the persistent passion for freedom of the mind that his book sold a million copies in seventeen languages during the first two decades after it was published.

Most adults are motivated to engage in lifelong learning only in areas they regard as useful or interesting. To contribute most to your mental fitness, your reading and study must serve your self-defined needs and interests. Such need-fulfilling learning is inherently satisfying to us curious human animals because it increases our options for living more fully.[11]

Whole-person learning (also called "confluent" education[12]) occurs best in relationships that are both affirming and challenging. Students learn much more if their teachers believe they have the capacity to flower intellectually. Thirty years of teaching taught me that a teacher's most important contributions to students' mental empowerment are believing in their intellectual potentialities more than they do and communicating what is taught with passionate aliveness and with caring for students as unique, valuable persons.

Actually, life taught me this long before I ever thought of becoming a teacher. As a child I suffered from miserably low self-esteem and paralyzing shyness, which produced painful failure experiences in my earliest school years. I became convinced that I was at best a slow learner and at worst stupid. Like all negative self-images, mine functioned as a self-fulfilling belief system, causing me to appear to myself and my teachers less able than I actually was.

It was not until my second year in high school that I began to pull out of this intellectual tailspin. A social studies teacher who was excited about teaching modern history took an interest in this shy, awkward, pimply-faced teenager. He affirmed my mind by challenging me to read, think, discuss, and write down my thoughts. I sensed that he believed I could do this and do it well. To my surprise I began to discover that I enjoyed and could in fact excel in intellectual pursuits. I shall always be profoundly grateful for that teacher. He enabled me gradually to revise my negative self-image, enjoy using my mind, and gain a sense of my real inner strength. He embodied a transforming truth for me—that, as someone has put it, "People don't really care how much we know until they know how much we care."

There are many satisfying ways to enjoy strengthening your mental muscles through exercise. One of the best is reading. Books let you touch minds and hearts with mental and spiritual giants and giantesses of our day and of centuries past. Via books you can travel to distant places and faraway times, without leaving your living room. Reading can stimulate your own creative thought, widening your horizons of understanding of yourself, as well as today's exciting world with its mind-boggling information explosion. You're too busy to read? A friend named Jerry was frustrated because he hadn't

GEORGE WASHINGTON CARVER

George Washington Carver was born a slave baby in 1864 to Mary and Moses Carver on a plantation near Diamond Grove, Missouri. When he was only a few weeks old, he and his mother were stolen by night raiders. His master ransomed them back with a race horse worth three hundred dollars. Young George nearly died from whooping cough and remained frail and sickly throughout his childhood. His parents wanted him to get an education, but they couldn't afford to help him. No school nearby would admit black children. His mother gave him a speller and later a Bible. With her help he got his first education from these. At ten he left home to attend a grammar school, supporting himself by odd jobs. Two years later he moved to Minneapolis, Kansas, where he completed high school, doing laundry, knitting, embroidery, and odd jobs to support himself. He then worked his way through Simpson College, graduating in three years. After that he enrolled in Iowa State College of Agriculture and Mechanical Arts, where he earned bachelor of science and master of science degrees. He remained there on the staff for two years, directing the research work on systemic botany and bacteriology. In 1898 Booker T. Washington learned about him and invited him to join the faculty of the Tuskegee Institute in Alabama. He remained there for more than forty years.

One of Carver's first interests in the South was the pressing need for crop rotation. Based on his research he recommended peanuts, sweet potatoes, and pecans as money crops to replace cotton, which was depleting the soil. Peanuts at that time were considered an unimportant crop, so he set about to find new ways of using them as well as sweet potatoes and pecans. Years later, when asked to testify before a congressional committee, Carver described 145 products he had made from peanuts, 100 from sweet potatoes, and 60 from pecans. These included condiments, axle grease, flour, insulating board, starch, plastics, coffee, and library paste. When he prepared to stop after the ten minutes alloted for his testimony, the congressmen clamored for him to continue. He did for an hour and forty-five minutes, while they listened in fascination. From Alabama red clay Carver extracted blue, purple, and red pigments; from cornstalks, fiber and rope; from cotton stalks he made gums, starch, and dextrins. From palmetto roots he made veneers. He made paving blocks from cotton, dyes of nineteen colors from peanuts, and others from tomato vines and dandelions. Through the years his incredible contributions to the field of agricultural chemistry tremendously enriched and diversified the entire southern agricultural economy.

As word of Carver's brilliant achievements spread, he was consulted and honored by distinguished leaders and by societies of scientists in this country and abroad. He came to be called Wizard of Tuskegee, Columbus of the Soil, and Goober Wizard. As his reputation spread, he received high-paying offers to do his research elsewhere. But Carver chose instead to give his services freely. A group of farmers sent him a check for eradicating a peanut plant disease. He returned it with thanks. In 1940 he gave his life savings (thirty thousand dollars) to establish the George Washington Carver Foundation at Tuskegee dedicated to continuing his research on soil fertility problems, new uses of native plants, and development of useful products from otherwise wasted materials.

George Washington Carver had a deep, spiritually grounded loveing respect for nature, nurtured by his intimate relationship with her. His mental, ecological, and spiritual well being is reflected, simply and beautifully, in this response to a questioner who asked the secret of the incredible quantity of his creative and productive work: "I have made it a rule to get up every morning at four. I go into the woods and there I gather specimens and study the great lessons that Nature is eager to teach us. Alone in the woods each morning I best hear and understand God's plan for me" (*Current Biography*, 1940, 148–49). In spite of the severe limitations of his humble beginnings, Carver's contributions to society through his brilliant achievements as an agricultural chemist are without equal in the long human story of seeking new ways to cooperate with Mother Earth. His life and work are an inspiring example of loving God, nature, and human beings *with one's mind!*

the time to read several books he was interested in. So he bought some books on tape and now listens to current best-sellers or classics while he drives to and from work each day. He reports that this makes even the L.A. freeways in "crush hour" at least bearable.

Alan Paton, the courageous author who first made the agony of apartheid in South Africa visible to the world, toward the end of his life wrote a letter to Norman Cousins. He told of his love of great books and mentioned some that, in his youth, had helped shape his life. He declared: "In heaven I shall ask to be excused the harp so that I can read all of these again."[13] It's clear that reading as well as writing was for Paton an adventure of the mind.

Wholeness Exercise

Stop and think for a few minutes about three or four things you'd like to do that would open up your understanding of areas of life you're interested in. This could be, for example, reading a book whose title intrigues you, taking an adult ed class to learn Spanish, or getting coached by a friend on using a home computer. / Jot these down in your *Self-Care Journal* and then decide which one of these you will do first and take whatever steps are necessary to start this adventure of your mind.

Empowering Your Mind by Enhancing Your Creativity

Brain research has discovered that we humans have one brain but two interconnected minds centering in the two hemispheres of the brain. In most schools one side of the brain (the left in most right-handed people) receives most of the attention and rewards and therefore the development. This side specializes in rational, analytical, cognitive, verbal, mathematical, and scientific functions. Because it dominates our technological, scientific culture, its functioning gets the psychic energy of most of us during 75 percent or more of our waking hours. The full development of the intuitive, imaging, nonverbal, artistic, relational, and holistic functions of the right hemisphere are downgraded by the values of our culture. This tends to produce a lopsided development of our mental potentialities. Yet creativity is a kind of playful but serious dance between the left- and right-brain functions.

The ancient wisdom of the founder of Taoism provides an image for whole-brain creativity and wisdom:

Can you, mating with heaven,
Serve as the female part?
Can your learned head take leaven
From the wisdom of your heart?[14]

The history of science makes clear that the vast majority of scientific discoveries came as hunches when the scientists were relaxing after a time of intensive research or theory building.[15] Albert Einstein, for example, mentions playing with visual images long before he undertook the tough left-brain work that connected these intuitive images with words, concepts, and mathematical explanations, resulting in one of the most exciting breakthroughs in our modern understanding of the world.

For many of us, whole-brain healing and creativity involves developing more of our latent right-brain capabilities so as to balance our overdeveloped left-brain functions. Sustaining personality wholeness in our left-brain society requires investing some time each day in right-brain activities such as music, drawing, moving to music, whittling, storytelling, imaging, sculpting, meditating, doing yoga, gardening, playing, and clowning around.

> Can you,
>
> mating with heaven,
>
> Serve as the female part?
>
> Can your learned head
>
> take leaven
>
> From the wisdom
>
> of your heart?
>
> —Lao-tzu

Wholeness Through Creativity Exercise

Studies of how creative minds generate new ideas and inventions show that there often are four steps by which this occurs.[16] Here's a left-right brain exercise in which you will use these steps. Try it now.

Stage 1: Preparation. Select a difficult project you need to accomplish, an actual problem you're trying to solve, or a complex decision you need to make. In this stage work intensively, using your logical, analytical left-brain abilities as follows. Keep careful notes, defining the problem clearly; identify its various parts; get as much relevant information about it as possible, and then brainstorm (by yourself and with others who are interested) to generate a variety of possible solutions. List all the options you can come up with, including those which seem "way out." Keep working until the intertwined parts of the issue and the obstacles to any easy solution become visible. Keeping notes on all this left-brain work will help you analyze and organize your information and options. /

Stage 2: Incubation. After you've done this disciplined preparation as fully as possible, put the whole thing on the shelf for a while. If you can, just table the pressure to solve the issue right away. Relax and let the problem stew on the back burner of your mind, remembering that a different, perhaps wiser, part of your mind is now working on the problem. Your right, intuitive brain will work on the issues if you release it from left-brain preoccupation. If it fits your personal beliefs, it may be helpful to turn the problem over to God, as you understand her or him. /

Stage 3: Illumination. Light often comes spontaneously, with the sudden or gradual dawning of a hunch, an image or an insight that you recognize as the solution or perhaps the direction out of the tangled thicket of your problem. It may help the light to come on to do some diagramming, doodling, or other free (unplanned) drawing of whatever images or thoughts come to you. Just jot down your free associations—words, stories, daydreams, ideas, images, pictures— that bubble up into your conscious awareness. In my experience as a left-brain-dominant person, illumination often happens during a second or third time of intensive thought or writing, after a period of relaxed right-brain activity, either awake or more often while I'm asleep. /

Stage 4: Verification and Implementation. Now, take whatever has come to you intuitively and test its validity by some tough-minded, critical thought. Organize the parts that are confirmed as valid into a workable plan, complete with a strategy concerning how and when you'll implement it. / Implement your plan. /

Certain things tend to cripple innovation and creativity in many people. Emotional blocks such as being hypercritical of your own ideas; being afraid to make mistakes, look foolish, or stick your neck out are prime creativity diminishers. So are two widely held, fallacious beliefs: that creativity necessarily diminishes with age and that only the superintelligent can be creative. Countless late bloomers have demonstrated that creativity often flowers after retirement, when people have the time to play with ideas. Some (not all) people with IQs in the genius range are creatively productive, but only average intelligence seems to be necessary to enjoy and even excel in creative activities.[17] Don't let the word *creativity* scare you. I'm not talking only or mainly about doing something "artistic"—like writing a poem or becoming a Grandma or Grandpa Moses, whatever your age. Your creativity may take such a form, but creativity also means using your mind to play with a new idea, cope constructively with a problem, whittle a whistle for a child, or whatever your creative "thing" happens to be. Whatever your form of creativity, it can be an opportunity to enrich your life and, in the process, become a co-creator, in some small but significant way, with the divine Source of all creativity.

Using Your Mind to Cope Constructively with Stress

[handwritten marginalia: Of naturopathy and homeopathy !]

According to psychologist Joan Borysenko, "Recent major studies indicate that approximately 75 percent of visits to the doctor are either for illnesses that will ultimately get better by themselves or for disorders related to anxiety and stress. For these conditions, symptoms can be reduced or cured as the body's own natural healing balance is reinstated."[18]

Chronic self-stressing is a significant contributor to many illnesses and to low levels of wellness. A study of college students found that even the stresses and anxieties around exams decreased the functioning of the valuable "killer cells," the crucial immune system lymphocytes responsible for patrolling the body and destroying viruses and cancer cells.[19]

Overloading your circuits with stress results from interaction among internal and external stressors and between mental and physical pressures. It is very important to your self-care, therefore, to learn how to de-stress your total mind-body self regularly. A variety of stress-reducing techniques will be presented in discussing burnout in chapter 6. But what is the role of the mind in handling stress constructively?

The chronic stress that cripples the health of many people today results from their fight-flight response being activated almost nonstop. This response evolved over eons of time as an essential human survival mechanism. When a wave of fear from an objective danger like a saber-toothed tiger hit cavepersons, having their blood pressure, muscle tension, and energy level skyrocket, as their bodies were flooded with hormones, enabled them to survive by running very fast or defending themselves. But most of the anxieties in today's society cannot be handled by fight or flight, for example, losing your job, the environmental crisis, or chronic fear about economic survival. But these threats still trigger the same biochemical response, keeping the body chronically tense and blocking deep rest and relaxation. Furthermore, two of the hormones that are

Wholeness Exercise

Moving from Depression to Self-Esteem. This is a method that, in my experience, helps many people turn off their depressed, put-down feeling and awaken feelings of hope and self-worth. It is a self-help version of what is called cognitive therapy, which is based on the assumption that negative feelings often are generated by faulty perceptions, thoughts, attitudes, images, and beliefs. The following four-step approach is adapted from rational emotive therapy, a form of cognitive therapy pioneered by psychologist Albert Ellis. I suggest that you try it now on an episode about which you still feel some depression or injured self-worth.

1. Recall the activating event, for example, you failed at something or someone criticized you unfairly and harshly. / Relive that painful experience to become aware of the negative feelings that are still attached to that memory.

2. Become aware of the distorted, irrational beliefs triggered by the event that color your perception and memories of what happened in gloomy or catastrophic hues. Typical irrational beliefs: we say to ourselves: "My worth is dependent on being approved by everyone and never making serious blunders." "My failure on this occasion shows that I am a born loser!" (In transactional analysis terms, the irrational beliefs usually were programmed in us by parenting persons in our childhood. They continue as the punitive parent voice in our heads.)

3. Let yourself experience your inappropriate emotions again, for example, anger, rage, shame, guilt, depression, worthlessness, failure, or fear, being aware that these negative feelings probably flow mainly from the irrational beliefs, repeated in your head.

4. To interrupt these feelings you must identify, challenge, and gradually correct the obsolete and/or irrational beliefs expressed by what you are saying to yourself in your mind and then substitute more rational and affirming beliefs. Begin doing this now. To illustrate, instead of saying to yourself the self-depressing, "I can never do anything right" or "It's a catastrophe for me to not behave perfectly," you can learn to substitute a more objective and rational, "So I made a serious goof. No reason to put myself down because I make occasional mistakes like everyone else." Some people find it useful to write down their "favorite" crazy beliefs about themselves and then write beside each of them the more

positive beliefs they know to be truer. It may help to put the latter up on cards as affirmations where you can gradually reprogram old messages in your head by seeing them several times a day. / In this process the irrational beliefs behind the depression and self-rejection may be gradually transformed to more reality-based and positive beliefs about yourself. To the extent that you do this, hope and self-esteem will tend to grow, and you won't be as vulnerable in the future when similar criticisms or failures occur. Thus you deactivate the activating events.

released, cortisol and adrenalin, are powerful inhibitors of the immune system.

I use the term *self-stressing* intentionally. Research by physiological psychologist Barbara Brown, an expert on biofeedback and stress disorders, has discovered that "stress is 90 percent how the mind looks at difficulties in life and relieving stress is 100 percent the way the mind uses its resources to . . . deal with stress without distress." She continues, "If we review the dis-ease process, the fundamental causes of stress are easily recognizable as a distressing perception of one's circumstances and its implication for future well being. The stress itself is actually the effect of uncertainty, frustrated problem solving (unsuccessful coping), and negative images that evoke mind and body tensions. The entire process occurs within the thought and idea generating systems of the mind."[20]

This is good news. Whatever the external pressures (stressors) in your life, it is your response to these that determines how stressful they actually are to you. You have considerable freedom to choose your attitudes toward unfortunate circumstances and irritating people so that they won't get to you as much in self-damaging, stressful ways. This is often easier said than done, but with practice you can learn to protect your mind-body self from external stressors to a greater degree than you probably think.

A helpful guide to using your mind in stress-reducing and healing ways is *Minding the Body, Mending the Mind* by Joan Borysenko. It describes the treatment process developed at the Harvard Medical School's Mind/Body Clinic, of which she was the director. Here are some guidelines for handling stress constructively—guidelines drawn in part from Borysenko's approach and from my own professional and personal experience with stress.

Reframe your stresses as challenges and opportunities (which they are, at least potentially). Thus you take steps to get on top of them by overcoming feelings of helplessness and regaining control of your life. This is in the category of making lemonade out of the lemons life gives you.

Learn to interrupt the vicious cycle of negative feelings (especially worry, guilt, and anxiety) and the buildup of stress and tensions in your body. The feelings cause the tensions to grow and vice versa, on and on, unless you interrupt the circular process. (See Borysenko's chapter 3 on "Breaking the Anxiety Cycle.")

Learn to apply Twelve-Step recovery programs' Serenity Prayer to stress-producing circumstances in your life. This simple, profound prayer is worth its weight in psychoactive drugs (and more) in enabling you to ask for and get the serenity to accept what you can't change, the courage to change what you can, and the wisdom to know the difference.

Practice some form of quieting your mind-body organism deeply at least once each day. This can be much more renewing than an equal amount of time spent sleeping. If you're in a pressure-cooker situation, it can do worlds for your wellness. (See the discussion of meditation below.)

Practice the complete breath (see chap. 4) when you're getting uptight, and also do some quick stretching and relaxation exercises. These are ways of breathing through and releasing the tensions in your body-mind.

Remember that "this too shall pass." This thought may give you a larger, somewhat liberating perspective on time-limited frustrations, irritating people, and even your own failures.

Do whatever is necessary to heal those wounded and wounding emotions that cause chronic self-stressing. (Borysenko's chapter 7 is very helpful.)

Do whatever is necessary to increase your experience of positive, wholeness-generating feelings, including hope, self-esteem, forgiveness, joy, and, most of all, love. (More about the last two below.)

Keep your playfulness operating, especially in situations where you are likely to tense up. Laughing at yourself is especially helpful. I keep a cartoon (courtesy of my best friend) above my word processor when I'm writing. It shows a superserious-looking man facing a computer screen on which these words have mysteriously appeared: "What makes you think that your words are worth processing?"

If all your self-help efforts are not sufficient, invest in your wholeness and longevity by enrolling in a mind-body stress reduction program and/or consulting a holistic counselor.

The Serenity Prayer

God

Grant me

Serenity

To accept the things I

cannot change

Courage

To change the things I can

and Wisdom

to know the Difference.

Liberating the Light Trapped in Emotional Black Holes

Astronomers have identified what they think are "black holes" in various parts of the universe—strange areas that are invisible, apparently because they suck in all the light and energy that come near them. The black holes in our psyches are chronic, unresolved negative feelings, including low self-esteem and depression, resentment and anger, unforgiveness and guilt, fear and anxiety, and long-unhealed grief. When these feelings build up in our subconscious or unconscious minds, they rob our creative life of energy and our body-minds of wellness. Healing emotional black holes and liberating the light of positive feelings can be a tough process. It may require professional therapy, but if the negative emotions aren't rooted in deeply buried conflicts, self-help methods often suffice. Let's look at a few self-help tools.

A valuable self-help manual using a cognitive therapy approach similar to the one on pp. 60–61 is David D. Burns's *Feeling Good*. It provides a wide variety of exercises for systematically transforming your black holes by releasing the energy of the positive feelings they gobble up. Depression, the "common cold of the mental health field," has a variety of causes, including anger turned on the self, grief, and probably biochemical and genetic vulnerability factors in some cases. If depression is severe, the use of psychic energizing drugs prescribed by a physician may help the person continue to function and become accessible to other therapies.

There are a variety of other things you can do to help your feelings work *for* rather than *against* your mind-body wholeness.

1. **Deal healthfully with anger, resentment, and fear, so as to move to greater peace within yourself and with others by**

- Openly discussing small irritations and frustrations in close relationships and seeking to resolve the issues before they accumulate and produce painful alienation;

- Vigorous, aggressive, big-muscle exercise such as jogging or kicking a cardboard box in your garage are good ways to drain off anger nondestructively and helpful in reducing mild depression;

- Learning to distinguish between appropriate assertiveness and being destructively aggressive; and then using assertiveness to correct injustices that should produce anger;

- Becoming aware of how much inappropriate anger flows from being deflated by someone or something after being puffed up.

Lao-tzu, the wise founder of Taoism, provides this apt image to describe the fragile nature of defensive pride based on inflated self-image:

He who feels punctured
Must once have been a bubble.[21]

He who feels punctured

must once have been a

bubble.

—Lao-tzu

On the subject of anger, it's noteworthy that a recent study discovered that chronic anger and conflict with work associates is a much more important cause of burnout than the level of pressure on the job.[22]

Some years ago when I was in a storm at sea in a twenty-eight-foot sailboat, a surprising thing happened. An old saying that I must have heard somewhere popped into my mind: "Cowards die a thousand deaths; brave people only one!" I was astonished that my fear level immediately declined. Since then in several fear-triggering situations, recalling that statement helped reduce my fear to manageable levels as I decided that dying once was plenty for me. I hope that the statement will help you mobilize your coping energies (rather than spending them on fearing) when you're facing rational fears in a scary crisis.

2. Resolve guilt and unforgiveness and move to reconciliation with yourself and others by

• Learning to distinguish between your neurotic guilt feelings and appropriate guilt. The latter is appropriate for any of us to feel when we have misused our freedom in ways that hurt other people or ourselves or alienate us from ourselves, others, nature, or God. In contrast, neurotic guilt is usually associated with ethical trivia and sexual or aggressive impulses. The two varieties of guilt require different treatment. Unfortunately, they are usually tangled together when they occur.

• Using the time-tested wisdom of the Western spiritual heritage to move from appropriate guilt to the healing reconciliation of genuine forgiveness. There are five steps in this process: self-confrontation, confession, forgiveness, restitution, and reconciliation. (The twelve steps of AA and the sacrament of reconciliation in the Roman Catholic tradition include these steps.)

• Recognizing that the source of neurotic guilt feelings (which are not healed by the five-step path above) is in transgressing childhood prohibitions. Learning to take these feelings less seriously and even to laugh at them often helps. The cognitive therapy approach outlined above also may help. If neurotic guilt feelings persist and interfere with your living, it's wise to get some counseling to change the obsolete self-punishing messages from your inner parent to your inner child. As Erma Bombeck is alleged to have said, "Guilt is the gift that keeps on giving!" This certainly is true of neurotic guilt.

• Becoming aware that forgiving yourself and forgiving others are two sides of the same coin psychologically. The person you help most when you forgive someone else is yourself. Harry Emerson Fosdick once observed, "Hating people is like burning your own house down to get rid of a rat."[23]

3. **Increase feelings of genuine self-worth.** Our self-esteem or lack of it is formed in childhood as we internalize the appraisals of parents and other important adults in our lives. Loving acceptance by them, with no strings attached, is the prerequisite for robust self-esteem. To the degree you and I experienced that in our formative years our feelings of self-worth are strong. As children grow in their autonomy, power, and competence in such an environment of loving acceptance, their sense of inner worth is self-reinforced. They become less dependent on others for their core feelings of esteem. Helping children learn this solid self-love is the most important gift parents can give.

Many of us grew up with parents who had painful self-esteem problems that prevented them from giving us a sturdy sense of our inner power and worth. We try to get feelings of worth by achievements and by the praise of others. Or perhaps we use alcohol and drugs to give us a temporary sense of relief from nagging self-doubts and self-put-downs. None of these strategies is effective in the long run.

There seem to be only three dependable sources of self-esteem. One is the inner empowerment of growing competence so that we *know* that what we can do is good and worthwhile, regardless of what others think. The second source is learning to treat ourselves with more grace—to love and care for ourselves in spite of all our limitations and failures. Some folks reach a point in their maturing where they seem to mellow grace-fully. They stop struggling to be OK in the eyes of others and just accept themselves as they are, which allows them to choose to change if they wish.

The third dependable source of self-esteem is the *experience* deep in our spiritual Selves that, though we are anything but perfect, we are precious and of infinite worth to our loving God. This spiritual source of self-esteem depends, of course, on how alive and love centered our relationship is with the divine Spirit. Physician Bernie Siegel puts it well: "Self-love is an acknowledgment of the spark of the Divine that's in each of us, no matter what our imperfections."[24]

4. **Generate reality-based hope.** According to some studies, as long as cancer patients feel hopeless, their bodies do not fully mobilize their immune systems to fight the malignancy. In a real sense, while there's hope, there's life. Hope consists of having a positive expectation about your future. A sense of having a viable future toward which you have some real power, however small, to move,

is a wellspring of hope. Adrienne Rich asks, "What would it mean to live in a city whose people were changing each other's despair into hope? You yourself must change it. . . . What would it mean to stand on the first page of the end of despair?"[25]

Using Meditation for Healing and Stress Reduction

A graduate student came into my office one day wearing this lapel button; LEARN TO MEDITATE. MAKE GOOFING OFF RESPECTABLE! Actually, focusing and quieting your mind through meditation once (or better twice) each day for fifteen to twenty minutes can be a valuable investment in your mind-body-spirit wellness. Meditation is any method that enables you to focus your attention and thus quiet your consciousness and your body systems and increase your awareness. Studies of various Eastern and Western meditative and relaxation techniques show that they can produce salutary psychological and spiritual as well as physiological benefits.[26] Scientific journals have reported more than twenty-six types of healthful bodily changes resulting from the regular practice of meditation and other contemplative, mind-quieting disciplines. These changes include lowering of blood pressure and slowing of heart rate, breathing, and brain waves—the opposite of high stress fight-or-flight responses triggered by threatening circumstances. A Harvard study of older adults who learned and practiced meditation discovered that their lifespans were significantly longer than their nonmeditating peers. Several aspects of the meditators' mental functioning improved. The psychologist who co-led the study observed that meditation induces "a distinctively deep state of rest" while the mind is alert but "in a very settled, quiet state."[27]

When you're feeling stress overload or "beside yourself," quieting the racing motor of your stream of consciousness and rediscovering your spiritual center via meditation can be refreshing and stress reducing. There is evidence that regular meditation activates your immune system and "releases the inner physician by quieting your mind so that the body's own wisdom can be heard."[28] It also gives you a welcome mini-vacation in the quiet place that's always there at deeper levels of your mind, even when there's a storm on the surface. In addition it may give you a fresh perspective on the things that trigger your stress. Furthermore, those who meditate regularly often report that their inner lives have more serenity on a *continuing basis*.

Eileen Caddy, one of the co-founders of the remarkable Findhorn Community in Northern Scotland, uses this apt image: "When a musical instrument is out of tune, time has to be taken to get it into tune again. When you are out of tune, you have to take time to get into tune once again."[29] Meditation is an excellent way to help yourself get back in tune with yourself, other people, nature, and the universe!

The meditation technique that's probably used most widely in many faith traditions and cultures around the planet involves simply focusing your attention entirely on your breathing. Stop now and try the following exercise. It uses focused breathing plus a spiritual opening step.

Learning to meditate is difficult at first for many of us, particularly if we're extroverts whose primary focus is on the outer world. The

Wholeness Exercise

> **Meditation Exercise.** Locate a quiet place where you can be alone and uninterrupted for the next fifteen to twenty minutes. (Once you've learned to meditate, you'll probably discover you can use it effectively in unquiet settings, such as on buses or planes.) / While standing, stretch and yawn and tighten, hold, then release all your muscles several times. Wiggle parts of your body that feel stressed, letting the tension flow out as you wiggle. / Sit in a comfortable straight-back chair with your spine vertical and both feet on the floor. / With your eyes closed, focus your full attention only on your breathing for the next few minutes, concentrating on the inflowing and outflowing of air, in and out of your nostrils. / Don't try to make something happen. Whatever happens will be OK. Just keep concentrating fully on your breathing—in-out, in-out, in-out. If stray thoughts, sounds, images, feelings, worries, or itches interrupt your one-point focusing, don't try to get rid of them. Instead just be a passive observer of them as they pass through your awareness and disappear, while you continue to focus on your breathing. If a bright insight comes, you won't need to interrupt your focused attention to jot it down. In all likelihood you'll remember it after meditating. / Gradually your breathing will slow and you'll begin to feel increasingly clear and at peace with yourself and life. As this happens let yourself enjoy being in this peaceful place for about ten minutes, continuing to focus exclusively on your breathing. / After you've savored this inner quieting for ten minutes or so, you may want to try this: Choose a religious symbol or other image that is very much alive for you— light, burning bush, Jesus Christ, the star of David, Mother Earth, for instance. Focus your attention on this image for a while. Experience a warm, healing light flowing from it into your body-mind-spirit, energizing and awakening your whole being. / When you're ready, conclude the meditation in your own way to give it a sense of completion. / Sit quietly for a few minutes and let yourself enjoy the inner serenity and aliveness. / If it feels helpful, jot down in your *Well Being Journal* the things you found important to your wholeness in this experience.

rewards tend to be subtle and non-dramatic at first. But regular meditative practice often brings increased inner calm, clarity, insight, and empathy. Those who discipline themselves to practice intense and ongoing meditation often report transformative experiences of joy, deep serenity, and love—frequently with profound spiritual dimensions.

Keeping your attention focused isn't easy at first for most people. Fortunately, it becomes easier and more satisfying with practice. You may find it helpful to try focusing on a single object—a lighted candle or a single flower, for instance. Or try repeating a single word such as *one* or a short phrase from your religious tradition each time you exhale. It is wise to try meditating each day for at least two or three weeks. It usually takes that long to discover its potential benefits. For further help in learning to meditate, see the books by Herbert Benson, Daniel Goleman, and Lawrence Le Shan, in the Recommended Reading for this chapter and Morton Kelsey's book in the Recommended Reading for chapter 2.

Using Dreams for Healing and Stress Reduction

Like daydreams and guided imaging, your dreams while sleeping are valuable pathways to your deeper mind and self-healing. By working with your dreams you may identify and resolve hidden stress-producing conflicts while gaining access to the rich healing wisdom of your unconscious mind.

Wholeness Exercise

Dreamwork Exercise. To use this method, pick any dream you remember well and write it down in your *Self-Care Journal* in the present tense (as if it were happening right now). List in detail all the persons, objects, feelings, and events in the dream. Don't try to analyze these. / Or, as an alternative to journaling, with your eyes closed tell the dream out loud in the present tense to someone who's a good listener. Thus you let yourself relive the dream fully. / When you have relived the dream to the point where it stopped during sleep, continue living it out in your imagination until it's finished, describing what's happening to your listener (or in your *Journal*). / Then, *become* each part of your dream, one at a time. Carry on a lively dialogue among the parts of yourself represented by the parts of your dream. Continue this until you have made friends with these alienated parts of you and conflicts among these have been resolved. As you do this, the wasted energy tied up in those rejected parts gradually becomes available for use in coping and creativity.

I find the gestalt therapy approach to dreams (used in the above exercise) to be most healing. All parts of a dream are understood as disowned aspects of the dreamer and therefore unfinished wholeness work. If you meet, befriend, and integrate these parts of yourself into the jigsaw puzzle of your identity, you'll be stronger and more whole.

Discovering Your Hidden Treasure

A wellness life-style starts with the awareness that you're capable of developing more life and health than you are enjoying at this moment. The pioneer psychologist-philosopher William James once declared: "Most people live, whether physically, intellectually or morally, in a very restricted circle of their potential being. They make use of a very small portion of their possible consciousness, and of their soul's resources in general, much like a man who, out of his whole bodily organism, should get into a habit of using and moving only his little finger. Great emergencies and crises show us how much greater our vital resources are than we had supposed."[30] (See the Wholeness Exercise on p. 70.)

A New Mind for a New World

There's more than a little truth in the familiar line from the comic strip Pogo: "We have met the enemy and he is us." Two Stanford University professors, Robert Ornstein, a research psychologist, and Paul Ehrlich, an expert in population problems and ecology, have shown why there is an urgent need for us to change radically our traditional ways of thinking about and understanding our collective problems. Our minds have been conditioned through eons of time to think tribally, that is, in we-versus-them terms; to focus on immediate information rather than long-term consequences; and to judge everything from automobiles to presidents by superficial appearances. All this "old think" had survival value for our species in the old world. However, that world was radically transformed by the multiple revolutions that produced lightning-fast social change, the global electronic communications village, the exploding human population, planetwide environmental deterioration, and the technology for a thermonuclear Armageddon.

In *New World, New Mind: Moving Toward Conscious Evolution*,[31] Ornstein and Ehrlich call for a "new-mindedness" that fits the radically different world we now live in. They show how education, reoriented in both content and methods, can and must now produce rapid, "conscious evolution." Such education will enable our human species to

• learn how to handle and guide rapid and continuing social change;

Wholeness Exercise

Guided Imaging Exercise. The purpose of this exercise is to help you discover more of your treasures.

Stretch all your muscles tightly and then relax them like limp rubber bands. Repeat this several times until your body is energized and your mind alert but relaxed and receptive to new experiences. / Create a moving picture of a beautiful meadow in your imagination. / Be in the meadow now. Let yourself enjoy being nurtured by this lovely, inviting, peaceful place. /

Become aware that this meadow is a special place with many valuable and beautiful things to be found. Wander playfully around the meadow now—like a child on a fun treasure hunt. See what treasures you can find. / Remember, this is *your* meadow. You created it. Its treasures are yours, a part of your inner life. They're talents and gifts, possibilities and potentialities waiting to be discovered and used. Continue to explore the meadow, asking yourself what each treasure you find represents and how you might use it in your everyday world. /

Be aware that there's a special treasure in one part of the meadow to which you feel powerfully drawn. You sense that it's a special unused gift, a precious resource you need to develop to make life more fulfilling and whole for you. / Move toward where that treasure is and uncover it. / Walk around it, examining it from all sides. / Decide what you'll do to claim and use this special gift. If you're ready, make concrete plans for how you'll move ahead to develop and enjoy this special treasure you've discovered within yourself. / Create a movie screen in your mind as you are in the meadow. On the screen watch yourself using this treasure and perhaps others you've discovered, to make your life more fulfilled and joyful and whole. / Become aware of the source of this wonderful gift—the divine Spirit of love and light and liberation, whose energy is available, at this very moment, to empower you in using the treasures you've decided to develop. Open the windows of your soul to let this empowering, healing energy flow in now. / Complete this meditation in whatever way you choose to give it a sense of closure. / Jot down in your *Self-Care Journal* whatever you learned in this awareness exercise, including the plans you are formulating to use one or more of your gifts more fully. / Share the significant discoveries you've made with someone you trust, and invite their feedback on your plans. / If this exercise has been meaningful to you, as I hope it has, I suggest that you commit yourself to explore other treasures in your meadow and implement plans for their use during the months ahead.

- understand the long-range consequences of today's social practices and change those that will be destructive to humanity and the world;

- recognize that violence, including war, is an obsolete, ineffective method for resolving individual and group conflicts, and develop constructive alternatives to replace it;

- integrate modern scientific understandings of human well being with the best wisdom of the world's great religions;

- think globally and be concerned about the well being of all humanity and the global environment with all its interdependent life forms.

An ancient Chinese saying uses a powerful metaphor to describe the constricted vision of provincialism: "To see the world from the bottom of a well."[32] In the same vein, a saying from Southeast Asia observes that people who know and appreciate only their own culture are like frogs under coconut shells. It is clear that in the future our planet increasingly will be one world or none. In such a world, living under a coconut shell or seeing the world from the bottom of a well will be increasingly hazardous to the health of our whole species as well as that of the planet's biosphere.

All human beings, with our many diversities, are really one family. Genetically, we're all members of the human family, whether or not we recognize or like it. Norman Cousins observed that biologically no person can be more distantly related to any other person on earth than fiftieth cousins. (When anthropologists and mathematicians construct and connect genealogical lines by going back generation after generation they come to this conclusion.)[33] To develop global mindedness, as described above, is a biologically based affirmation of our membership in the human family. It is also the most sane and healthy way to use our minds today for the well being of tomorrow's children.

Create Your Mind-Personality Self-Care Fitness Plan

Review key insights that you gained as you read this chapter, perhaps noted by underlining or in your *Self-Care Journal*. Review those items you checked OK or NS on the checkup that now seem like areas in which you'd like to implement some changes. Using insights and methods you found in this chapter, create and write out a realistic Self-Care Plan for self-healing and developing more of the unused treasures of your mind and personality.

It is important that your plan include five things: (1) concrete, realizable objectives that you really want to achieve; (2) practical strategies for moving toward these; (3) a time line, especially when you'll begin; (4) rewards you'll give yourself as you take each step toward objectives or withhold if you backslide; (5) a record of your progress in your *Journal*. Be sure to keep your plan love centered and energized by your spiritual resources.

Pick one or two especially attractive objectives and begin moving toward them immediately. Remember, in overcoming resistances to self-change, the hope and momentum from small early successes often helps.

I wish you empowered self-care of your mind.

Loving and Empowering Your Body for Fitness

 A study of the sex life of middle-aged male joggers by a California physician revealed that they made love 3.2 times each week on the average. This is significantly more frequent than their nonjogging counterparts.[1] The study reached a striking conclusion. After examining and rejecting a variety of physiological possibilities (including the increase of the male sex hormone testosterone), the researcher concluded that the joggers do more loving because they have increased self-esteem! Toning up their bodies, losing weight, and feeling stronger and more alive enhanced their positive feelings about their bodies *and* increased their sense of self-worth. Whatever helps us say "yes!" to our full, embodied selves tends to improve our health as well as our love life.

One of the most important things you can do for self-healing and higher-level wellness is to care for your body more lovingly. It is also one of the most potentially pleasurable. In *High Level Wellness*, Donald B. Ardell declares: "If you want to pursue a lifestyle of high level wellness, you really ought to think of fitness as both an integral and pleasurable part of your routine; valued not only for the good things it does for your body, but equally for the satisfactions it provides and the added zest it gives to nearly everything you do."[2] Speaking from the perspective of women's body alienation, the authors of *The New Our Bodies, Ourselves* put the importance of body care powerfully: "Learning to understand, accept, and be responsible for our physical selves, we . . . can start to use our untapped energies. Our image of ourselves is on a firmer base, we can be better friends and better lovers, better *people*, more self-confident, more autonomous, stronger and more whole."[3] This also applies to men, whose body alienation is different but often also very deep.

Whatever your present physical condition (even if you're a couch potato), or whatever limitations and disabilities your body has, there's good news. You probably can enjoy more fitness in your body through regular self-care than you now suspect is possible. Bodily self-care means loving it like a good mother-father, befriending it, and respecting it with all its assets as well as imperfections. Befriending your body means giving it four things—enlivening exercise, healthy nutrition (including eliminating toxins), renewing rest, and sensual satisfactions (preferably low calorie).

It's obvious that we can ignore the fact that we are embodied selves only at a high cost to our physical wholeness. What's not so self-evident is that neglect of bodily self-care usually has a deleterious impact on our mental and spiritual wholeness as well. (This was the point of the midyears joggers story, of course.) Speaking personally, when I neglect vigorous exercising for several days or have a junk food relapse, my mind slows down and my soul feels like it has a layer of dust over it.

A body that's as alive and fit as possible provides a strong foundation for your overall wholeness, including your spiritual wholeness. Thinking of their body from a wholistic, spiritual perspective helps some folks get motivated and moving to better self-care. These ancient words, from Saint Paul, express such a spiritual perspective: "Your body is a temple of the Holy Spirit within you, which you have from God. . . . Therefore glorify God in your body."[4] From this viewpoint, methods of body self-care are really spiritual disciplines. If you've been treating your body carelessly or shabbily, establishing a loving reconnection with it via better self-care can be a kind of bio-spiritual rebirth. As body therapist Alexander Lowen puts it, you may reclaim your "forsaken body with all the fervor of the lost child finding its loving mother."[5] Matthew Fox calls such a warm, wonderful body-awakening "sensual spirituality."

The key to enhancing your body's wellness via better self-care is learning to love your whole self more, including your body. Yale University physician Bernie Siegel has had lots of experience with what he calls "exceptional" cancer patients. They defy gloomy prognoses, learn to love themselves, become active participants in seeking to heal their malignancy, and often live much longer than anyone expected. Siegel declares: "The fundamental problem most patients face is *an inability to love themselves,* having been unloved by others during some crucial part of their lives. This period is almost always childhood. . . . As adults we repeat these reactions and make ourselves vulnerable to illness. . . . The ability to love oneself, combined with the ability to love life, fully accepting that it won't last forever, enables one to improve the quality of life. My role as a surgeon is to buy people time, during which they can heal themselves."[6]

This chapter is a how-to guide to loving your body in active ways that can help heal, awaken, and empower it. How can we love our bodies? By listening to them and understanding them better and thereby learning how to give them the vital care they need to get or stay whole. The full enjoyment of your mind and the blossoming of your spirituality both can be helped by keeping your body as fit as possible.

For those who are getting older, hear this: There's increasing evidence that the physical aging process can be accelerated or slowed by how well we care for our bodies. Even if loving physical self-care doesn't add years to your life, it probably will add aliveness and joy to your years!

There's a danger in all this: The obsessive focus on the body and on fitness, called "healthism,"[7] is a popular addiction in affluent societies like America. Robert J. Crawford (who coined the term) believes that overfocusing on healthiness or on a "healthy life-style" enables us to deflect our attention from the larger, more difficult and important goals of social justice and saving the planet. Psychologist Anne Wilson Schaef observes that a woman's obsession with weight and dieting often reveals that she is alienated from a natural source of female power—her body. It also reveals that she has not been allowed (by her programming in a sexist culture) to develop a reverential feeling for her body. Her "sexist inner critic" keeps telling her that her body is not OK.[8] Whether one is a woman or a man, gaining some liberation from body addictions is essential for full body wholeness. This happens as you learn to accept and even love your body with all its imperfections, even though you still wish it were different. Such loving acceptance is an essential first step toward better self-care, which can both strengthen your body esteem and enhance its wholeness.

Body Well-Being Checkup

This checkup can help you increase your physical wholeness in two important ways. (1) It gives you a quick reading on your self-care practices that are strong and those that are weak. (2) The checkup items are practical things you can do to increase the fitness, strength, and aliveness of your body. You will find it helpful to choose from these in developing your body Self-Care Plan.

CHECKLIST

Instructions: In front of each statement, place one of three initials: E = I'm doing excellently in this; OK = I'm doing acceptably, but there's room for improvement; NS = My self-care definitely needs strengthening here.

_____ I'm a self-disciplined but noncompulsive fitness fan.

_____ I listen to my body and learn from what it's trying to tell me (like, "Slow down and play a little!").

_____ I enjoy spending some time each day giving my body loving self-care to increase its aliveness, its attractiveness (especially to myself), and its power to function with high energy, strength, and effectiveness.

_____ I'm cultivating my body's awareness and sensuality, letting myself enjoy discovering its pleasuring potentials.

_____ I have one or more forms of big-muscle exercise (appropriate to my age and health level) which I enjoy doing three or four times a week, for twenty to thirty minutes—for example, brisk walking, biking, jogging, swimming, aerobics, vigorous sports.

_____ I know and practice the basic principles of healthful nutrition in my eating, drinking, and reducing or eliminating toxic substances.

_____ By eating lower on the food chain, I give myself healthier food and also do not contribute as much to the problem of world hunger.

_____ I balance my calories and my exercise so as to maintain my weight within ten pounds of the optimum for my height and gender.

_____ I eat a healthful breakfast to get each day off to a good start nutritionally.

_____ By not smoking, using street drugs, or misusing prescribed drugs, I respect my body and also avoid a variety of dangerous health hazards.

_____ If I drink alcohol, I limit myself to one or two drinks a day, and then only when I'm not driving or otherwise needing to be mentally sharp and responsible.

_____ I practice one or more forms of deep body-mind relaxation at least once a day, to reduce my stress load and increase my energy level.

_____ I sleep seven or eight hours (or less, if my body and mind require less for full renewal) at least four nights a week.

_____ I satisfy my skin hunger and my sexual needs regularly in enjoyable ways that contribute to my wellness and also my partner's, if one is involved.

_____ I wear a seat belt when I'm in an automobile and drive responsibly when I'm at the wheel.

_____ I read current wellness literature to keep myself updated on body self-care.

_____ I don't waste creative energy feeling guilty if I take an occasional holiday from simon-pure health practices.

_____ I avoid damaging my skin by long exposure to the sun without a sunscreen.

_____ My care for my body is strengthened and enhanced by my spirituality.

Using Your Findings: Scan and tally the initials in front of these fitness-nurturing practices to give yourself a rough evaluation of your overall physical self-care. /

Congratulate yourself on the items you could honestly score E. / For future reference jot down (in your *Self-Care Journal*) those OK and NS items about which you'd like to take some action to make your body feel, look, and function better. Also note what you might do. /

Loving Your Body by Exercising for Fitness

Donald Ardell shares this delightful story: A certain middle-aged executive had suffered a series of nearly fatal heart attacks. He was severely restricted in his physical activity because he was in terrible physical shape. Very depressed by his situation, he decided to end it all. Out of concern for his family, he chose a method that would hide his suicidal intent and thus not embarrass them or keep them from collecting his life insurance. He borrowed a jogging suit and set off running fast. He soon collapsed but neither died nor had a heart attack. He tried it again the next day and the next, collapsing each time. On the fourth day he did not collapse. By the second week of running he felt much better about himself and life, so much so that he decided he wanted to live after all![9] I hasten to add that this is definitely not a safe way to get back in shape if your main exercise for years has been lifting your fork and spoon to your mouth and pushing yourself back (reluctantly) from the table.

To enjoy higher levels of fitness, vigorous, big-muscle exercise must be a regular part of your life-style. Giving your body such exercise is the first leg of the three-legged stool of body wellness. The good news is that increasing numbers of men and women in high-tech, mechanized societies are engaging in regular fitness routines. The bad news is that a life-style of inactivity is still a major health robber for millions of people in Western cultures. Forty percent of adult Americans, for example, say they never exercise. Fewer than 10 percent exercise vigorously and regularly. Americans average five hours each day immobilized in front of TV screens, ingesting the "plug-in drug." They also consume thousands of tons of junk food and drinks with empty calories while watching TV. It is now clear that a wide variety of medical problems—including heart disease, premature aging, hypertension, chronic fatigue—have a common

W I N D O W   O F   W H O L E N E S S

WILMA "SKEETER" RUDOLPH AND BLANCHE RUDOLPH

The first woman in the history of the Olympic games to win three gold medals for running was Wilma Glodean Rudolph (see *Current Biography*, 1961, 399–401). People who knew her in her early childhood could never have imagined that she would be a candidate for such a spectacular sports achievement. Wilma was unable to walk from age four until she was eight. Born in 1940 in a tiny town in Tennessee, she was a frail baby of only four and a half pounds. Her parents, Ed Rudolph, a retired porter, and Blanche Rudolph, a domestic, were afraid she would not survive. At age four scarlet fever, followed by polio, left Wilma's left leg paralyzed and useless. Her mother took her to Nashville, where she was told by medical specialists that daily therapeutic massage offered the only hope that Wilma's leg might recover. Blanche devoted many hundreds of hours, after finishing her work as a domestic servant, massaging her daughter's leg. Often she continued until long after Wilma had fallen asleep. She also taught three older siblings how to help with these therapeutic massages.

Eventually the family's devotion enabled Wilma to begin to walk again, using a specially constructed orthopedic shoe. By age eleven she had discarded this shoe and was shooting baskets in their backyard. Only three years later she had become a star high school athlete,

scoring 803 points, a new record for girl basketball players in Tennessee. After graduating she enrolled in a small predominantly black university, Tennessee Agricultural and Industrial State University. There she excelled in track as well as basketball.

In the 1960 Rome games she tied an Olympic record in winning the women's 100-meter dash. She also won the 200-meter dash, setting a new Olympic record, and anchored the winning women's 400-meter relay team, all classmates at her university. Her still-segregated hometown decided to have a parade honoring her. She told them she would not attend if it were segregated. Thus she broke the racial barrier there. Following her stellar Olympic performance, she won races in various international track meets in Europe. Spectators marveled and French journalists called her "La Gazelle" for her remarkable speed and flowing stride. She endeared herself to fans in the U.S. and abroad. She was honored in 1960 as "America's Female Athlete of the Year." Wilma Rudolph, and her mother, together had demonstrated remarkable capacities to turn a miserable minus into an inspiring plus! She is now track director and Special Consultant on Minority Affairs at my alma mater, De Pauw University in Greencastle, Indiana.

underlying cause: a vicious cycle of overeating and underexercising. Furthermore, being sedentary is costly, to yourself and to society. A Rand Corporation study concluded that inactivity costs industry an average of $1,900 during an employee's lifetime—from medical costs, sick-leave pay, disability insurance, and loss of job productivity. The total subsidy would be considerably higher except that sedentary people tend to die considerably younger.[10] The average forty-year-old male who doesn't exercise, smokes two packs a day, is 30 percent overweight, and doesn't wear his seat belt costs his employer $1,292 a year in medical bills, two times that spent on someone the same age who has healthier habits.

In case you have doubts about the longevity benefits of regular exercise, consider this summary of studies (from three different countries) of communities with unusually high numbers of people over age one hundred: "Physical activity is . . . unequivocally the most important factor in the longevity and optimum health exhibited in these centenarian communities. . . . After extensive physical examination of the people in the Caucasian village of Duripshi, [Dr.] Alexander Leaf concluded that physical activity was a potent preventive measure against cardiovascular diseases . . . and other disorders such as osteoporosis [weakening of bones]. . . . Among the centenarian communities, the evidence of the value of regular exercise . . . confirms the research concerning the psychophysiological imperative of aerobic activity."[11]

A widely publicized study reported in the *Journal of the American Medical Association*[12] followed 10,224 men and 3,120 women for just over eight years. The subjects, ranging in age from twenty to sixty, were mainly white professionals in the middle to upper socioeconomic strata. They were divided into five levels of cardiovascular fitness at the beginning of the study, by the use of a treadmill stress test. Here is a reporter's colorful summary of the findings—"Get off your duff and live longer." Among the men, death rates among the least fit were 3.4 times higher than among the most fit, and 4.6 times higher for the women. Moderate amounts of exercise were found to reduce the risk of death from all causes, including heart disease and cancer. A striking finding was that the biggest health gains came, for both sexes, from just getting out of the most sedentary, least fit category. Dr. Carl Caspersen of the Federal Center of Disease Control in Atlanta commented: "This is a hopeful message. . . . You don't have to be a marathoner. In fact, you get much more benefit out of being just a bit more active. For example, going from being sedentary to walking briskly for a half hour several times a week can drop your risk [of death] dramatically."[13] In other words, you need to sweat a little but not gallons. If you substitute "human power" for electricity or gasoline more of the time, you'll probably live longer.

Do you have a problem generating the discipline to exercise regularly? If so, welcome to the club. It may help you be seduced less often by the two big R's—resistances and rationalizations—to remind yourself that we human beings are made for vigorous, big-muscle exercise. We're designed for it by our ancient biological heritage and the particular attributes that enabled our ancestors to survive and pass on their genes. An anthropologist declares, "When we run, we are . . . reviving the work of yesteryear, hunting-gathering work. The muscles, bones, cartilage, lungs, heart and mind of the primate best adapted to running *want to be used*."[14]

Loving your body by engaging in some form of vigorous, big-muscle exercise that you enjoy, at least three or four times a week, can give you a payoff from your investment of generally improved well being. A Gallup Poll discovered that people who work out regularly are two and a half times more likely than sedentary folks to say they're happy. It also revealed that the regular exercisers feel that they are more in control of their health, are more able to relax, and better equipped to talk to their doctors about health issues. Sixty-four percent of the exercisers report they're eating a healthier diet (compared with 47 percent of the sedentary people) and 43 percent have lost weight (compared with 31 percent of nonexercisers). The most intriguing finding was that those who work out regularly are more open to spiritual experiences than nonexercisers.[15]

Your exercise-for-wellness program needs to include three basic types of exercises:

Type 1—Aerobic Exercise.

This helps your cardiovascular and cardiorespiratory system fitness by enabling your heart, lungs, and blood-delivering network to stay tuned up and efficient. For both your fitness and longevity, this is the most important of the three types. Fast walking, jogging, cycling, swimming laps, roller and ice skating, cross-country skiing, aerobic dancing, and rope jumping are among the popular forms of aerobic exercising. The objective is to increase your aerobic capacity—the amount of oxygen your body can process in any given period of time—and thus increase the quantities of cleansing, energizing oxygen and blood delivered to every cell in your body, including your heart and brain.

Regular aerobic exercise improves wellness in these ways:

- It strengthens the muscles of breathing and the heart, enabling an increase in the oxygen of each breath and the blood pumped with each heartbeat.

- It tones up all the body's muscles, thus decreasing the heart's work and possibly lowering blood pressure.

- It increases the amount of blood, the number of red blood cells and hemoglobin, enabling the blood to carry more oxygen to and wastes away from all parts of the body.[16]

Aerobic exercising also increases stamina, improves utilization of the food you eat, and decreases the fat stored in body tissues, consuming it as energy and replacing the fat by muscle. In addition, if you exercise regularly and vigorously, you probably won't consume as much caffeine, alcohol, refined sugars, fat, salt, drugs (prescribed or recreational), and junk food. This is because increased respect for your healthier, more attractive body (and for your whole self) tends to diminish the craving for these polluting chemical frustration comforters.

To have aerobic benefits, exercise must elevate your pulse rate to an optimal level (as indicated below) and keep it there for a sustained period, four or five times a week. The standard fitness recommendation is twenty to thirty minutes of sustained aerobic exercise four or five days a week. If you have difficulty finding time to work out on such a schedule, a recent study brings welcome news. An exercise physiologist at Stanford Medical School had twenty men walk briskly or jog at a moderate pace nonstop for thirty minutes, five times a week. A matching group did three mini-workouts of moderate intensity, three times a day for ten minutes. After eight weeks, both groups had achieved practically identical levels of improved fitness.[17]

If you're over thirty, and out of condition, or have any history of heart disease (personally or in your family), it's crucial to have a physical checkup (with an electrocardiogram) and get a physician's guidance before beginning any vigorous exercise program. If you have no history of heart problems, the following heart rates are recommended as safe and high enough to increase aerobic capacity: Age 20—160; 30—152; 40—146; 50—140; 55—137; 60—128; 65+— 120.[18] (It's a good idea to check with your health professional to make sure these heart-rate levels are OK for your level of fitness and that they are the most recent recommendations by heart specialists.)

The safest, least expensive lifelong exercise is walking. Studies have shown that walking briskly (not strolling), three and a half to four and a half miles per hour, benefits nearly everyone, regardless of their starting levels of fitness. Slower walking (two MPH) can enhance the health of most elderly people as well as those recovering from illnesses. Aerobic benefits from walking can be increased by swinging your arms vigorously to give your upper body some workout.[19]

I enjoy walking fast up and down the hilly streets near our home. Riding a stationary bike is also a part of my exercise plan. It has movable handlebars, which allows a workout of arms and torso as well as legs. An exercycle has the advantages of providing all-weather aerobic exercise that one can do while watching the TV news (an asset if you're a type A person like me). My sister (who's not a type A) has clocked over eleven thousand miles in the last five years. She has kept herself remarkably fit this way. The stationary bike's disadvantage is that one misses the renewal that comes from biking, walking, or jogging outdoors with changing scenery and the nurture of nature.

Three-Minute Fitness Check

Heart rates immediately after exercise are a rough measure of cardio-vascular efficiency. An easy way to check your physical fitness is the Three-Minute Step Test devised by Dr. Fred W. Kasch, director of the Exercise Physiology Center at San Diego State University. Don't use it if you have any heart problem.

Instructions: 1. Select a step that is twelve inches high. 2. The stepping is done in a brisk four-part sequence—step up right foot, up left, down right, down left. Practice doing twenty-four of these four-step sequences per minute. / Rest for a few minutes. 3. Do the actual test now, performing the stepping sequence at the set speed for three minutes. / 4. Then sit down, wait five seconds, and count your pulse for exactly ten seconds (beyond this, the pulse rate drops rapidly). Compare your count with the following table:

Classification	Women	Men
Excellent	16 or less	17 or less
Good	17–18	18–20
Average	19–22	21–23
Fair	23–25	24–26
Poor	26 or more	27 or more

If your heart rate is fair or poor, you need an aerobic conditioning program very much. Start soon but be sure to begin gradually, walking at a moderate pace for at least twenty minutes three times a week.[20]

Type 2—Flexibility Exercises.

These stretch muscles, keep joints more mobile, make body movement more graceful and posture more comfortable and attractive. This type is very important for lifelong body-mind-spirit wellness. Any type of gentle, full-body stretching that you enjoy and do regularly (for as little as five minutes a day) can give you the benefits of this type of exercise. (See the book by Bob Anderson in Recommended Reading.) Popular forms of flexibility exercises include isometrics, vigorous dancing, hatha yoga, tai chi (a kind of gentle flowing dance that evolved from Taoism), and some forms of calisthenics. I like hatha yoga because of these advantages:

- It is gentle, quieting, and energy renewing.

- You can begin it at any age and continue it with beneficial results throughout most of your life.

- Accompanied by healthy nutrition, yoga helps keep the body flexible and trim, retarding the physical aging process.

- Some of its tension-reducing, energy-raising stretching can be done while seated in an office, on a plane, and in other such settings.

- Even five minutes of gentle yoga movement can make you more wide awake and energized.

Incidentally, you can benefit from the yoga movements without necessarily accepting all its philosophical and theological assumptions. To teach yourself the basic yoga exercises in a systematic and gradually more advanced way, I recommend Richard Hittleman's *Yoga Twenty-eight Day Exercise Plan.*[21]

Type 3—Strength-increasing Exercises.

These increase the bulk, tone, and power of your muscles. Weight lifting, weight machines, and many types of calisthenics (like pull-ups and push-ups) are popular forms of Type 3. Although strength-increasing exercises don't take the place of the other two types, they do have many benefits. These include improved strength, greater freedom of movement, and greater muscle reserve for times of stress, injury, or surgery. Having a stronger, firmer body often helps boost morale. It tends to give both men and women a sense of

Wholeness Exercise

Body Enlivening Experience. Stop reading now and enjoy a brief period of body awakening. Put your favorite relaxing music on the tape player. Then enjoy moving freely around the room for a few minutes, letting your body flow with the music as you stretch gently in all the directions that you find comfortable. Be aware of what happens to your energy level. If you want to really boost your energy, try moving to your favorite rock music, or, if you're fifty-something or older, perhaps your favorite jitterbug music.

psychological empowerment, a more positive body image, and the self-confidence of having a stronger, more attractive body. Muscle-building exercise also helps those preparing for competitive sports that require greater strength. It can help prevent physical difficulties such as back strain, which is often caused by weak abdominal muscles.

Doing muscle-strengthening exercises combined with yoga-type stretching several times a week can help keep your "growing edge" from gravitating to your body's sagging places, where they tend to go as you get older. In case you're thinking that weight lifting is only for the young, consider this. A study of ten residents ages eighty-six to ninety-six in nursing homes found that training with a weight machine, *carefully monitored by medical professionals*, enabled them to triple and quadruple their muscle strength in as little as eight weeks. This undoubtedly also helped their morale. The ten subjects weren't exactly in robust health. Six had coronary heart disease, seven had arthritis, six had suffered bone fractures from osteoporosis, four had high blood pressure, and all of them had been inactive physically for years.[22] The study's findings are significant, since the muscle strength of adults decreases an average of 30 to 40 percent during their lifetimes. Also, recurrent falls by the elderly, a leading cause of immobility and death, have been linked to muscle weakness.

In case you suffer from the exercise blahs, here are some further suggestions for enlivening your body-mind-spirit lovingly with regular exercise:[23]

1. Variety is the spice of our exercise life for most of us. Try blending the three basic types of exercises, alternating among more than one form of each type. Cross-training, as it's called in sports, is also valuable for fitness. If you use this, it will also reduce the risk of injuries by distributing stress on different joints and muscle groups.

2. Choose forms of exercise that you enjoy. This is the best cure for the exercise blahs. It also increases the likelihood that you'll continue long enough to begin getting the rewards of feeling better. Satisfying exercise lets you raise your overall pleasure quotient while staying fit. If you exercise only out of a sense of duty, you'll miss the rewarding pleasure of "fittening up" your body. Be disciplined about exercising but take it with a smile. Exercise is hard work, but the way you do it can also add some fun. "Jocks" (compulsive competitors) tend to cheat themselves of the fun of playful exercise and also depress themselves by self-rejection when they lose.

3. Many popular sports (e.g., golf, softball) are good for your psychological well being, but they're not substitutes for exercise

that increases your aerobic capacity. Playful sports can reduce chronic stress (provided your need to win doesn't raise your stress level) and drain off built-up aggression from frustration and anger. Enjoyable sports provide mini-vacations from the responsibilities and frustrations of everyday living. Exercise and sports with friends or family adds the joy of sharing with people you like.

4. To avoid overdoing, listen to your body; and increase the amount of exercise you do from day to day only gradually. Sudden, very intense stress on the heart and vascular system may be harmful unless you have gotten in condition by training over time. The high costs of ignoring this guideline are the too-familiar heart attacks of middle-aged males who try to be week-end athletes after a week of almost nonstop sitting at their desk and in front of the TV.

5. Prevent injury and increase benefits by

   • having regular medical checkups, particularly if you have pain or discomfort during or after exercising;

   • warming up and stretching before you work out and cooling down gradually, doing more stretching after you finish;

   • choosing a low-impact aerobic exercise like swimming or cycling to reduce wear and tear on your joints, muscles, and bones;

   • getting adequate footwear;

   • getting some coaching on proper sports training and techniques;

   • paying attention to aches and pains.

6. Develop an uncomplicated fitness routine that's realistic for your life-style. In spite of their popularity, health clubs have a large percentage of dropouts. The same is true of diet programs and shape-up-fast schemes.

7. In addition to regular workouts, find ways to make increased activity an ongoing part of your life-style. For example, stop riding elevators and use the stairs instead (unless you work in a place like the Empire State Building). Stair climbing uses five to ten calories a minute. Cleaning the house uses three to six a minute. Gardening and hoeing uses five to nine calories. So go back to a hand mower to cut the grass; or park several blocks from work and get there by a brisk walk. Having a healthy exercise-oriented life-style lets you use the spare moments of waiting to do a little tension-releasing stretching, isometrics, or deep breathing.

8. Remember that exercise is a must in any effective approach to weight loss or control. To keep your body weight at a healthy level, you must keep your intake of the food and drink energy units (calories) in balance with the burning of this energy through exercise. Effective weight loss usually requires both reducing calories and increasing exercise. (To lose a pound of fat without reducing your food and drink intake requires walking thirty-five miles.) Regular vigorous exercise can help redistribute weight, reduce the total fat and increase the muscle of your body, and possibly even raise your metabolic rate. (After strenuous exercising, some people burn more calories for a given amount of body movement.)

9. Use mental goals and images to challenge, encourage, and guide your body. Pick realistic, graduated goals for your workouts, goals you can reach by pushing yourself a little more each time, without overdoing. The self-rewarding satisfactions of progressively achieving your goals may be enough to let you overcome resistances to continuing. In addition it may help to hold in your imagination a mental picture of yourself doing the sport or exercise skillfully, with pleasure, and with maximum benefits to your whole being. (The "inner game of fitness," anyone?)

10. Get your spouse or other family member or a friend involved in a shared exercise program. Invite your children to join you. Remember, active parents tend to have active kids. Sedentary parents tend to have sedentary kids. Exercising together can enrich your relationships in a variety of ways.

Perhaps you're thinking to yourself, "I've taken my body for granted and neglected it for years. What've I got to gain from all the effort it'll take to shape it up now?" A study of more than twelve thousand middle-aged men discovered that those who were given help to stop smoking, reduce their weight, lower their blood pressure, and go on cholesterol-lowering diets cut their risk of heart attacks substantially.[24]

Or perhaps you're wondering, Am I too ancient to start? People who get and stay in shape can continue exercising vigorously throughout their lives. More than ten thousand (42 percent) of the runners in the New York Marathon in 1989 were over forty. Of these, fifty-six were over seventy. The oldest person to finish the twenty-six-mile-plus race was ninety-one. He did it in six hours and forty-three minutes![25] If you're forty or older, and your body is feeling it as well as showing it, you still can get with an exercise program that will make you more fit for the years ahead.

Loving Your Body by Eating for Wellness

Many of us in affluent countries suffer from spoon-in-mouth disease. A healthful, nutritious diet is the second essential leg of the three-legged stool of physical wellness. It should be seen as a partner, with adequate exercise and rest-relaxation, in your fitness program. A study of seven thousand adults over a five-and-a-half-year period sought to identify factors related to increased life expectancy and general health. They found seven factors. It's worth noting that four of these have to do with diet:

- Three meals at regular times each day and no snacks
- A healthy breakfast each day
- Moderate exercise two or three times a week
- Adequate sleep
- No smoking
- No alcohol or only in moderation
- Moderate weight [26]

Obesity is a major problem in most affluent countries (Japan being an exception). At least thirty-four million Americans, according to a government study, including one out of four children, are seriously overweight. Only 20 percent of the overweight men and 30 percent of the overweight women are trying to do anything about it, like increasing physical activity and reducing calories. Obesity has long been known to contribute to heart disease in men, along with cancer, high blood pressure, and diabetes in both sexes. A recent study of 115,889 women showed that those even slightly overweight are 80 percent more likely to have heart attacks than slim women are. Those 30 percent or more overweight (one-quarter of U.S. women ages 35 to 64) were found to be more than three times as prone to heart attacks.

W I N D O W   O F   W H O L E N E S S

FRANK JONES

His name was Frank Jones. His body had been grotesquely deformed by rheumatoid arthritis during his boyhood. In his midyears, when I knew him, he had to be lifted into the wheelchair where he spent most of his waking hours. Because of the arthritis, he could open his mouth only enough to get a graham cracker between his teeth. Yet, in spite of his terrible physical disability, Frank was one of the most whole individuals I have ever known! His life-affirming attitudes, spiritual aliveness, and loving relationships with others were incredibly healing.

When we first met, my response to Frank's terribly deformed body was repugnance. But as I grew to know him as a person, this initial response was replaced by respect and affection for a person of great caring and spiritual depth. When I felt discouraged about myself and my work, as a struggling young adult, I often went to see Frank. His clear perspectives and very gentle confrontations brought healing to me. When I was about to leave that community, I went to tell him my sad good-bye. I arrived at his home to find him holding a much-used book in his misshapen hands, ready to give it to me. It was a modern translation of the New Testament. I told him that, though I deeply appreciated his wanting me to have it, I couldn't accept what obviously was one of his favorite books. He insisted that I take it as a small token of his thanks for our friendship and all that I had given him. I responded that he had given me far more than I possibly could have given him. Seldom in my life have I been so deeply moved as when Frank handed me his precious gift. That battered book from a remarkable friend is one of the most cherished gifts I have ever received.

As I think of Frank I'm aware that he had used his miserable physical brokenness as an opportunity for developing spiritual depth and interpersonal, loving wholeness. His body was terribly crippled but his mind and spirit were incredibly whole. Frank was a "wounded healer," a wonderful channel for the healing love of the divine Spirit, for me and countless others. By who he was, Frank helped me learn that wholeness is not the absence of brokenness in your body but what you choose to do with it.

Overweight women who smoke are five times as likely to have heart attacks as nonsmoking overweight women.[27]

Here are some down-to-earth things you can do to enable your eating and drinking to maximize your wellness, raise your energy level, and increase the odds that you will live a long, healthy life.

1. Eat a balanced and varied diet, including appropriate amounts of the six types of nutrients needed for your body's health—

proteins, carbohydrates, fats, water, vitamins, and minerals. Put the emphasis in your diet on unrefined complex carbohydrates, fruit, and vegetables.

2. Reduce drastically your intake of all kinds of fat, especially those from animal sources. Too much fat is the number one enemy in many people's diets.[28] Our bodies need only about one teaspoon of fat each day for healthy functioning. The average American eats six to eight teaspoons. High fat consumption is now associated with a host of medical problems—heart attacks, diabetes, kidney disease, gallbladder attacks, premature aging caused by athero-sclerosis (clogging of the arteries by fatty deposits), and some forms of cancer. Yet more than one-third of the calories consumed in industrialized, developed countries consists of fat (in the U.S. it's 37 percent). Saturated fats from animal sources seem to be the main villain in heart attacks, but overconsumption of vegetable fats (polyunsaturated) can cause health problems, too. Fat has more than twice the calories found in equivalent weights of protein or carbohydrate foods. Cutting your fat consumption in half can be a big help in staying near your optimal weight.

3. Improve the quality of the protein you eat by eating more vegeta-ble proteins (such as those found in grains and beans), fish, and the white meat of turkey and chicken, thus reducing drastically your consumption of red meat. Eating even a serving or two of fish a week apparently reduces the risk of fatal heart attacks, according to a study in Wales. Red meat is more difficult to digest, is not the "perfect protein," contrary to what lots of people believe, and is environmentally problematic, since it takes much more out of the land to produce. Reducing your consumption of animal proteins, including eggs, whole milk, and meats, lessens your intake of serum cholesterol, which has been linked to heart problems. Sub-stituting nonfat milk for whole milk gives you the considerable food values of milk without the fat and cholesterol and with about half the calories.

4. Increase the unrefined, complex carbohydrates in your diet—such as potatoes, whole grains, beans, fruits, vegetables—to get up to 60 percent of your total calories. A healthful diet should be built around complex carbohydrates (not proteins). Boycott or reduce drastically processed carbohydrates like refined sugar, bleached flour, and white rice. Junk foods and processed foods such as candy, ice cream, alcohol, sodas, most packaged cereals, and many frozen meals, contribute heavily to excessive sugar and, in some cases, fat and salt intake. These foods are hyped to children by TV advertising. They provide largely empty calories, lacking any significant amounts of vitamins, minerals, and fiber. (Chil-

dren and teens are the best customers of junk foods including candy.) Always read the labels before deciding to buy packaged foods!

5. Eat fresh, organically grown fruit and uncooked vegetables each day. These are rich sources of vitamins, minerals, and fiber. Cooking—particularly frying and boiling at high temperatures—destroys much of the nutritional value in foods. Steaming vegetables or eating them raw tends to leave subtle food values intact. Cooking in fat significantly increases the calories and the fat you consume.

6. Increase the fiber in your diet by eating more whole grains and cereals, beans, and raw fruits and vegetables. High-fiber diets help to facilitate digestion and elimination, reduce cholesterol and blood sugar levels, and lessen chances of colon cancer.

7. Make sure you are getting at least the RDA (Recommended Daily Allowance) of vitamins and minerals. A well-balanced diet with lots of unprocessed foods supplies most if not all of these. But consumption of highly refined foods, as well as fast and junk foods, increases the likelihood that you won't get the vitamins that help to regulate metabolism and the minerals that serve as rebuilding materials for your body (including bones and teeth). It makes sense to learn the best food sources of the essential minerals and vitamins.[29] But, if you live in the fast lane, it's wise to supplement your food with a multi-vitamin and mineral tablet, to be on the safe side.

8. Recognize and interrupt vicious cycles of using food to temporarily deaden emotional pain, loneliness, and spiritual emptiness. Such vicious cycles often go like this: One overeats (or overdrinks) in an attempt to anesthetize painful feelings about one's body and perhaps one's life. But this self-medication with food or alcohol increases one's pain because overconsumption makes one look and feel worse. Using food to try to meet nonfood needs sets one up for a food addiction. Interrupting such destructive cycles is imperative if one is to recover nutritional sanity and the satisfactions of an alive body, enhanced self-esteem, and positive self-image. Even if your emotional life and relationships are in reasonably good shape, it isn't difficult to become a junk food junkie in our pressure-cooker society plagued with its epidemic of "hurry-itis." Eating for wellness in such a context takes commitment and discipline.

The Stress Diet

BREAKFAST

½ Grapefruit
1 Piece Whole Wheat Toast
8 oz. Skim Milk

LUNCH

4 oz. Lean Broiled Chicken Breast
1 Cup Steamed Zucchini
1 Oreo Cookie
Herb Tea

MID-AFTERNOON SNACK

Rest of the Package of Oreo Cookies
1 Quart of Rocky Road Ice Cream
1 Jar Hot Fudge

DINNER

2 Loaves Garlic Bread
Large Mushroom and Pepperoni Pizza
Large Pitcher Beer
3 Milky Way Bars
Entire Frozen Cheesecake, Eaten Directly
   From the Freezer

9. You may find that it helps to take a positive approach and also use humor to cope constructively with frustrating eating problems. A positive approach means concentrating on eating healthful foods you really like and doing it with style, rather than focusing on foods you shouldn't like, but do. A cartoon shows two midyears women at a restaurant. The thinner one is enjoying a mountainous hot fudge sundae. The plumper one is having a salad, saying: "Why didn't I order a sundae? Because my doctor gave me two choices—either hate myself and eat what I like, or like myself and eat what I hate." Fortunately, it's possible to eat a healthy fare that is also tasty, though probably not as orally gratifying as a hot fudge sundae. Food binges lack both style and joy. They involve gulping food compulsively without really savoring it. On the subject of eating with style, chef Julia Child once declared, "Life itself is the proper binge."[30] People who are living and loving life fully don't need to binge on food. Many problematic food preferences are acquired tastes, such as for heavily salted food. It takes some motivated discipline but it is possible to unlearn such preferences by just not practicing them for a while.

Bill Cosby's delightful essay "Lead Us Not to McDonald's" illustrates the use of humor in handling eating problems constructively. He talks about "the culinary minefields of America" and says the first thing he's going to do when he turns seventy is go to a restaurant like the one across the street from the Mayo Clinic—"a feeder system for the Clinic." There all the food is covered with chocolate, sugar, or grease. He makes an aside, "They might as well have served you a plate of corks for your arteries."[31]

Eating and Drinking Rituals: Responses to Life's Mystery

There are deep-seated social and existential rituals related to eating and drinking. People in many cultures bring and eat food gifts when there is a death. Years ago, as a young workaholic pastor of a congregation composed mainly of German descendants on Long Island, I was struck by the lavish feasts that followed funerals there. All the family and friends gathered for several hours of eating and drinking, weeping and laughing, grieving and reminiscing about their departed loved one. Gradually it dawned on me that these meals were profoundly earthy healing rituals—ways of saying a collective "yes!" to the ongoingness of life in spite of the awful tear in the fabric of their families.

Since then I've experienced eating and drinking rituals in a variety of cultures, rites of passage around stressful transitions, sad endings and scary though exciting new beginnings. Such boundary events confront us humans with the mystery of time and our yearning to transcend the painful limits of our mortality. Formal and informal food rituals associated with these feelings are intimately linked with the many sacramental meals in the great religions of humankind.

Even in the daily-ness of our everyday lives, eating and drinking often are much more than simply ways of meeting biological and pleasure needs. There's an existential-spiritual dimension that sheds light on why so many people are moved to express ritual thanks before they eat together. Perhaps there's a dim, subconscious awareness in us of the biological miracle by which what we eat and drink is transformed into music, love, sexuality, thoughts, words, passion, poetry, and prayers.

Awareness of the bio-social-spiritual meanings of consuming food with others may be of help in transforming self-destructive eating and drinking attitudes and behavior. It certainly can increase our understanding of why it's difficult to change destructive eating patterns learned early in life. In the midwestern ex-farm family in which I was reared, growing, canning, preparing, talking about, and eating food (much of it very high in fat, sugar, and salt) were a continuing preoccupation and major motifs of family communication and festivals. It has taken great effort to change my eating habits in healthier directions. But the wellness rewards, such as fewer colds and increased energy and aliveness, make the struggles worthwhile, though I still backslide occasionally.

You may be thinking to yourself, Since I've been eating in highly gratifying but unhealthful ways for years, is it really worth the sacrifice to learn to eat more wisely? If you feel like a nutritional lost cause, consider a study of fifty patients by a professor of medicine at the University of California. It revealed that changes in diet and life-style can reverse a leading cause of heart disease—arteriosclerosis. A very low-fat vegetarian diet, combined with meditation and moderate exercise, widened partially blocked arteries, reduced stress, and lowered cholesterol. The oldest people, interestingly enough, with the most severe arteriosclerosis showed the most improvement.[32] It's never too late to turn over a new (table) leaf.

Eating Wholistically in a Hungry World

It can be important to our wholeness to see our eating, problematic or basically healthy, in its global as well as a spiritual context. At least one-third of the planet's children went to bed hungry or malnourished last night. This happens every day in a world with the capacity to feed everyone adequately. In such a world, hunger is totally unnecessary, an avoidable tragedy. Yet sixty thousand people, including some forty thousand children, die each day from starvation and the diseases associated with malnutrition.[33] From this perspective think about the overuse and waste of food in affluent countries like America.

A humane and genuinely wholistic approach to eating must include a commitment to doing everything we can—through personal eating choices, hunger programs, political action, and the United Nations—to create a world in which all our sisters and brothers on planet earth have enough nutritious food to sustain their wholeness. This certainly includes the tragic millions of homeless and hungry individuals and families in the "pockets of poverty" in wealthy countries. Supporting one or more of the organizations working to end hunger is an appropriate and effective way to put your money where your mouth is on this issue.[34] Fortunately, speaking of mouths, eating lower on the food chain is both a small contribution to solving the hunger problem and better for your health. Books to help you do this include *Diet for a Small Planet* by Frances Moore Lappé; *Diet for a New America* by John Robbins; and *The New Laurel's Kitchen* by Laurel Robertson, et al. *The New Our Bodies, Ourselves* by the Boston Women's Health Book Collective has excellent guidelines on nutrition, as well as on alcohol, drugs, and smoking. It's also helpful on exercise and sexuality.

Loving Your Body by Reducing or Eliminating Toxins

Another important way to increase your body's wellness is to reduce radically or eliminate your intake of nicotine, caffeine, alcohol, so-called recreational drugs, pesticide residues, and potentially toxic food additives. Alcohol, nicotine, and caffeine, like junk food and sugar, are popular self-medications for stress, depression, boredom, anxiety, emotional conflict, low self-esteem, sexual frustration, loneliness, and painful emotional hungers caused by unhappy relationships. Unfortunately these temporarily comforting tranquilizers tend to increase the very pain and emotional problems they temporarily relieve.

We live in a psychochemical age. Our culture conditions us to use mood-changing chemicals to cope with stress and painful feelings, especially loneliness. Alcohol is humankind's favorite, domesticated mood-altering drug. It has been used in almost all known cultures since long before recorded history. The vast majority of drinkers think of it as a solution rather than a problem. What are the facts about its relationship to high-level wellness? Very moderate drinking (not more than two glasses of wine or the equivalent alcohol in beer or hard liquor a day) probably doesn't pose major health problems for most people. But keeping your drinking at a low-risk level is difficult in a high-stress society that pushes alcohol at us from all sides. This is especially difficult for adolescents struggling to find their identity in troubled times. It is hard for anyone with considerable psychic and spiritual pain, the very ones who most need to limit or avoid drinking because they're most at risk of losing control.

Beverage alcohol, though taken for granted by the majority of adults in our society, is a powerful drug with biochemical properties which make it problematic for many people. Alcohol addiction is a sneaky illness. It creeps up on people gradually without their being aware of what is happening. They are hooked long before they are clobbered by evidence that is painful enough to shatter the rationalizations we humans use to avoid facing our loss of control over anything. In America it is estimated that some ten million persons are addicted to alcohol, to a damaging degree. Furthermore, most addicted people are surrounded by circles of tragedy composed of at least three or four others who are hurt by their addictive behavior.

Many adults and youth suffer from multiple addictions, to alcohol and also to one or more of the following—nicotine, tranquilizers, sedatives, antidepressants, barbiturates, amphetamines (pep pills), diet pills, and street drugs such as cocaine. Unfortunately psychoactive drugs such as tranquilizers frequently are prescribed for ordinary life stresses and losses, occasional insomnia, and mild depression. Two-thirds of psychoactive drugs used in America are prescribed to women, mainly by male physicians. All these drugs have some addictive properties, meaning that one's body chemistry can adapt to them so that the body requires more and more to get the same effects. Addiction to prescribed drugs is very prevalent among women.

Chronic, heavy drinking increases the risk of a number of physical diseases including heart attacks, strokes, liver damage, pancreatitis, phlebitis, lowered resistance to infections, malnutrition (alcohol is a super–junk food that provides only empty calories), gastrointestinal problems, certain types of cancer (liver, colon, stomach, breast, mouth, and thyroid), and, in cases of prolonged excessive drinking, damage to the brain and nervous system. Among pregnant women even very moderate drinking may cause "fetal alcohol syndrome," irreversible abnormalities, including growth deficiencies and mental retardation. Pregnant women, therefore, should avoid all use of alcohol. The greatest health danger for youth who drink and/or pop pills is mixing these with driving. More than half of their fatal accidents (the leading cause of teenage death) involve alcohol, drugs, or a combination of both.

Nicotine is a highly addictive, legal, and relatively cheap drug from which you can get many "hits" for a few cents. Most people don't think of it as a drug, but it has produced an epidemic of lethal addictions in our society. Tobacco is the leading cause of premature deaths in the U.S. Smoking-related, debilitating illnesses account for over 1,000 unnecessary deaths each day, mainly from heart attacks and strokes. The 600 billion cigarettes smoked by Americans each year account for 15 percent of all deaths (over 350,000 a year). As many people die from smoking in three years as from all the wars in U.S. history. The diseases associated with smoking cost somewhere between fifty and sixty billion dollars each year to treat. These include hypertension, heart disease, emphysema, bronchitis, and cancer of the lungs, kidneys, and uterus.

So, if you smoke, do whatever you must to stop! This may include taking advantage of the low-cost or free programs sponsored by some hospitals, churches, and community groups such as the American Lung Association and the American Heart Association. In spite of the terrible tenacity of this addiction, millions of persons have stopped and stayed stopped. You can, too. You couldn't give your health and longevity a more valuable gift. Even "passive smokers" who breathe others' smoke regularly experience serious health hazards.[35] If you're living with someone who smokes, take a firm stand and insist that they do it outside.

Pre-addiction Checklist

Ask yourself these questions, jotting down candid answers in your *Self-Care Journal:*

1. Is my use of my favorite mood-altering chemical causing or contributing to problems in any important area of my life, including my health?

2. When I feel mad, sad, or glad, do I automatically reach for a drink or cigarette or pop a pill?

3. Do I have to take more of my chemical to get the effects I desire?

4. Have I caught myself feeling guilty or sneaking my favorite chemical when no one was looking?

5. Do I feel I *have* to have a drink or a pill at particular times of day, for instance, to get going in the morning, to relax after 5:00 P.M., or to go to sleep?

6. Do I ever have trouble meeting responsibilities because of my use of alcohol or pills?

7. Has my spiritual life been hurt by this use?

8. Do I feel defensive about this checklist, tempted to skip it, or annoyed at the person who suggested I question my drinking or use of pills?[36]

If, in all honesty, you had to answer even a qualified "yes" to any of these questions, you may be on thin ice. Your favorite chemical probably is beginning to control you rather than vice versa. Even if you answered yes only to question 1, you probably are already hooked, to some degree. It's vitally important to your health to mobilize the courage and strength it takes to seek help. If you think you even *might* need such help, give it a try. There are many resources—AA, Al-anon (for family members), Women for Sobriety, NA and CA (Narcotics Anonymous and Cocaine Anonymous), along with numerous professionally staffed addiction-treatment programs. Help that could save your health and even your life is available. Use it!

Loving Your Body by Renewing Rest and Relaxation

Giving your body-mind organism the regular renewal of adequate rest and relaxation is the third leg of the stool of healthy self-care. Sleep researchers understand its main function as restorative—to renew both the body and mind by restoring what was depleted during waking hours. Deep sleep in the first few hours probably alleviates physical fatigue, whereas dream sleep (also called REM, rapid eye-movement sleep) during the latter part of the night alleviates mental fatigue.

How much sleep do you need to stay in robust health? The amount needed to function at one's optimum level varies from person to person, and at different ages for the same individual. The average is about seven and a half hours in twenty-four. But sleep needs of individuals vary as much as three hours in either direction from this average. Many people are sleep deprived without being aware of it. A study was done of generally healthy college and graduate students between the ages of eighteen and thirty who got an average of seven to eight hours a night. Although they seemed to be alert and functioning well, when the students got to bed an hour to ninety minutes earlier than usual for one week, their performance on cognitive and psychological tests improved markedly.[37] How do you know whether or not you're getting enough sleep? A sleep researcher at the University of Florida gives this guideline: "The rule of thumb is very simple. If you wake up spontaneously, feeling well rested, and if you don't struggle through periods of intense sleepiness during the day, then you're getting enough sleep."[38]

Insomnia is a common problem. Among its several types, having trouble staying asleep in the hours after midnight is a common form, especially among older people. Unless a shorter night is interfering with effective functioning during the day, there's probably nothing to worry about. But awaking frequently with agonizing forebodings before dawn is often a symptom of depression that needs treatment. Insomnia involving trouble dropping off to sleep usually happens because something the person is thinking (e.g., heavy worries) or doing is interfering with the natural onset of sleep. Sleeping pills don't cause you to sleep. They just dull whatever was causing you to stay awake. Chemical depressants like alcohol and barbiturates (sleeping pills) suppress REM sleep with its restorative function and may cause broken sleep as they wear off.

Here are a few suggestions for increasing the probability of falling asleep.

- Avoid drinking any caffeine (including coffee, tea, and cola) after breakfast.

- Do something quieting during the hour before bedtime, for example, full-body relaxation exercises, listening to soothing music, or reading something comforting or boring.

- Take a long, warm bath and drink a glass of non-fat milk or one glass of wine.

- Avoid heated argument just before sleeptime.

- Release the cares of your day by letting the divine Spirit "take the night shift."

- Before you go to bed, hold a peaceful mental picture in your mind, seeing yourself being warmly and safely nurtured as you sleep. Such intentional preparation can enhance the quality of sleep as well as facilitate its onset.[39]

"I've tried relaxing, but—I don't know—I feel more comfortable tense."

There is scientific evidence that we human beings may have an inherent tendency to sleep in the early afternoon as well as at night. Researchers who compared the 50 percent of Greek men who nap with those who don't found that the nappers are 30 percent less likely to develop heart problems.[40] Whenever possible I take a brief siesta after lunch as an efficient way of freshening up for the rest of the day. Winston Churchill was a well-practiced napper, feeling that a nap broke his day into two productive halves.

Many people live pressure-cooker lives in which they seldom if ever relax deeply. Yet chronic stress is a major cause of a plethora of physical, emotional, psychosomatic, and interpersonal problems. Learning and practicing a method of deep relaxation several times a day can raise your wellness level and prevent illnesses. One enjoyable way to do this is to give yourself the gift of at least two mini-vacations each day. These are five- to fifteen-minute breaks when you do something that's a renewing change of pace and very relaxing. In addition to the "Mini-Ways to Wellness" you'll find in chapter 7, here are some samples of renewing mini-vacations you might enjoy:

• Stop and go outside to sit in the sun or walk around the block with the wind on your face.

Wholeness Exercise

> **Deep Relaxation Exercise.** (Takes only a few minutes.) Breathe deeply from your belly for one minute. As you breathe out, say the word *release* in your mind, forming a picture of the tension in your body flowing out with each exhalation. / Tighten the muscles of your scalp as tight as you can and hold this as you silently count to three; then release the tension, letting your scalp relax like a limp rubber band. / Stay deeply relaxed as you count to three, continuing to breathe from your belly. / Repeat this sequence three times. / Now go down your body, repeating the full sequence in each area: your face (making a funny face and releasing tension in your jaw) / neck / shoulders (rotate your neck and shoulders several times) / arms / hands / chest / stomach / back / pelvis / buttocks / thighs / calves / ankles / feet. / Now tense your whole body and repeat the sequence until your entire body is deliciously relaxed. /
>
> If you're too busy to do the full relaxation exercise, try doing just the tense-hold-release-hold sequence two or three times with all the muscles of your body.

- Look briefly at something beautiful—really look so that you take it in.

- Let the kid inside you chuckle playfully at a memory of something funny or at the heavy adult seriousness around you.

- Stretch vigorously and yawn for a minute or two, breathing deeply.

- Ask yourself, Where in my body am I holding tension? Then release it intentionally.

- Enjoy a brief fantasy that happens to float through your consciousness or draw on your memory bank, and relive being in a beautiful place you love.

- Play your favorite music for a few minutes, out loud or in your head.

Loving Your Body by Nurturing-Cleansing Breathing

The words for spirit and breath are the same in several languages, including Hebrew, Greek, Latin, and Sanskrit. It's also noteworthy that various approaches to deep relaxation and self-nurture—bioenergetics, meditation techniques, gestalt therapy, and yoga—emphasize learning to breathe more deeply and fully to energize your whole body, awaken sensuousness, help you relax deeply, and

Wholeness Exercise

> **Complete Breath Exercise.** Here, from the ancient wisdom of India, is a way of doing enlivening, full-lung breathing. Sit or stand in a comfortable position, emptying your lungs as fully as possible by exhaling through the nose as you pull your abdomen in as far as you can. Hold this for five seconds. / Inhale slowly through your nose, pushing your abdomen way out to let air enter the lower part of your lungs which are usually underused. Continue the slow inhalation by also expanding your chest as far as possible and then raising your shoulders as high as possible, thus allowing air to enter the higher area of your lungs. Hold the breath in your lungs for a count of five, allowing the oxygen in the air to be fully absorbed. / Now, slowly exhale as deeply as you can, relaxing your shoulders and chest and contracting your abdomen to expel as much waste-laden air as you can. Hold this for five seconds. / Repeat the whole breath cycle ten times or so, pausing between cycles if necessary. Be aware of how full of energy your body feels when you finish. / Practice this deep, natural, unblocked breathing for several days in succession until it becomes automatic.[41]

release painful, hidden memories. Most of us breathe in shallow, constricted ways, using less than half of our potential lung capacity.

Another form of body self-care is to take advantage of the skills of a licensed chiropractor. This modern health science has deep roots going back many centuries. In my experience, problems caused by non-alignment of vertebrae and the pelvis can be relieved in a few sessions with a competent chiropractor. Many chiropractors also are trained to give guidance in nutritional problems.[42] Chiropractic approaches are appropriately used to complement, not substitute for the expertise of orthopedic and other physicians. Physicians trained in osteopathic medicine combine expertise comparable to that of M.D.'s with hands-on methods of body adjustments which can be both healing and wellness-sustaining.

Create Your Body Self-Care Fitness Plan

Review insights and methods that impressed you as you read this chapter, including at least six items you marked OK or NS when you took the checkup. Using your creativity and playfulness, write down a realistic Self-Care Plan to make your body more fit. Remember, your plan will work better if it includes five things: (1) concrete, realizable objectives that you really want to achieve; (2) practical strategies for moving toward these; (3) a time line, especially when you'll begin and when you expect to achieve your various objectives; (4) rewards you'll give yourself as you take each step toward objec-

Wholeness Exercise

> **Energizing-Healing Breathing Exercise.** As you practice the complete breath exercise, close your eyes and see a moving picture in your imagination of the fresh oxygen flowing throughout your body, energizing each cell as you inhale. / Pick a part of your body that is tense, tired, or in some discomfort or pain. / Imagine that you are breathing in and out through that part in a very focused way. Let each inhalation bring healing energy and each exhalation carry away tensions, impurities, and pain, gradually leaving that part of your body refreshed, cleansed, and healed. / When you have a headache or your mind feels fuzzy, try this method of energizing breathing. If you feel anxiety, keep breathing through it deeply and intentionally and see what happens. You may discover why Fritz Perls, the father of gestalt therapy, once said that the difference between fear and excitement is breathing.

tives or withhold if you backslide; (5) a record of your progress in your *Self-Care Journal.* Be sure to make what you do love centered. Genuinely loving your body is the key to fitness. Also, activate your inner child to give whatever you do a touch of playfulness to balance your serious intentions and self-discipline with pleasure and satisfactions.

Pick one or two especially attractive objectives and begin moving toward them immediately. In self-change it helps overcome resistances to savor the sweet taste of success in the early phases.

I wish you satisfying, strengthening self-care of your one and only body.

Nurturing Well Being Through Love: Strategies for Use in Your Family and Other Intimate Relationships

Aloha Airlines Flight 243 was almost five miles above the Pacific near Hawaii when a huge part of the 737 jet's fuselage ripped off, sweeping a flight attendant out to her death. Bob Nichols was one of the ninety terrified passengers. Believing that the crippled plane was about to crash, he frantically scrawled these notes to his family on a scrap of paper: "Overhead blown out. Can see sky & clouds. A/C [aircraft] turbulent. Going down fast. . . . No word from pilot. Terrible (sometimes) noise." Fearing he was running out of time, he scribbled, "I love you Jan my love [his wife]. I love Jenny, Shayne [their daughters] & Robert [their son] and all others. No time left. Love Dad." Miraculously the plane was able to land.[1]

One of the most important things you can do for your total wellness and longevity is to nurture healthy love in your intimate relationships. To help you get well or stay that way, you need the mutual love of at least one other caring person. It's much better, of course, to have a small network of friends and/or family with whom you have honest, caring communication and with whom you both give and receive the essential soul foods of mutual caring, respect, and loving.[2] Wholeness, like brokenness, is contagious. This chapter is about how to catch it and help others catch it from you in your close relationships.

Your well being is inherently and inescapably relational. The recognition that people must have people to be whole is deeply embedded in the folk wisdom of many cultures. In ancient China, for example, this awareness was expressed in this image: *It is impossible to clap with only one hand.* For your healing and health, nothing is more important than satisfying your deep *will-to-relate.*[3] The need to re-

Wholeness Exercise

Imagine that you are in a situation like Bob Nichols's. / In the brief time you have available, who are the folks to whom you would most want to say "I love you" or "thank you" or perhaps "I'm sorry"? / Make a list of these dear ones—your inner circle of mutual love. / Now, before you do anything else, take time to express your feelings to each of these precious persons, face-to-face, by phone, or by writing them a note. Tell them what you would long to say if you thought your life was about to end.

ceive and give love is the most powerful of our basic heart hungers. A study of emotional factors in illness was done by scientists at the University of Michigan. By reviewing a variety of studies of stress and sickness, as related to longevity, they discovered that the mortality rate was three times higher among persons with the fewest close relationships. They concluded that social isolation (loneliness) is a "major risk factor" for mortality, perhaps as important as smoking cigarettes.[4] In a Missouri School of Medicine study of factors in longevity, seventeen hundred persons were interviewed in 1966. The survivors were contacted again after twenty years. Participation in formal social networks, such as churches and community groups, was found to be the most important factor for predicting longevity. A researcher concluded: "Regardless of health problems, people who had formal social networks in 1966 were more likely to remain independent and survive."[5]

To grasp the biological and genetic depth of our need for love, it is helpful to look far back to the dawn of our human species. Anthropological evidence suggests that we are the descendants of ancestors who learned to survive by forming mutually protective, supportive relationships. Through small family clans our remote ancestors enabled their highly vulnerable children to survive and pass on their genes. Cooperation for mutual survival probably evolved into loving relationships. Thus, in spite of our sorry record of mutual destructiveness, we humans are inherently a bonding, loving species, in our genes as well as deep in our unconscious minds. Those who didn't bond didn't survive. From an eon-spanning perspective, we humans have been appropriately called "passionate survivors."[6]

For your health and longevity there is an incredibly profound truth in the New Testament's beautiful hymn to love—"The greatest of these is love"(1 Corinthians 13:13). In this ancient wisdom, love is identified, as it is in contemporary psychotherapy, as the most im-

A faithful friend is the

medicine of life.

(Ecclesiasticus 6:17)

If my wife really loved me

she would have

married someone else!

—Milton Berle

portant ingredient in life. When love is missing from the equation of relationships, it never balances. Without love other human values fade in importance.

Unfortunately much that passes for love in our culture is actually hazardous to your health. Here's a down-to-earth definition of the kind of love that does enhance wholeness: *Love is caring about and commitment to one's own and the other's continuing growth, empowerment, and self-esteem.* This kind of love is radically different from the love that's identified only with romantic feelings. The latter is an obsessional state of mind into which (and out of which) people "fall." Your love is health-giving to the degree that it involves ongoing commitment to and joy in helping each other develop your fullest self-esteem, dreams, and gifts at each stage on your journeys together, in spite of the conflicts and limitations in any close relationship. Such love often includes very passionate feelings, of course. But its key is behavior that encourages mutual growth. You can measure this kind of love by what you do to encourage, challenge, support, and empower the continuing fulfillment of both your own and each other's possibilities.

Health-nurturing love grows in relationships where there are what I like to call covenants of mutual wholeness. (A covenant is simply an agreement with a spiritual dimension.) Such covenants

"And do you promise to love, honor, cherish, obey, respect, uplift, understand, encourage, involve, revitalize, inspire, admire, entertain, relate to, communicate with . . ."

can be either implicit or explicit. They're grounded in appreciation of the image of the divine in oneself and the other. They're rooted in some awareness of each other's unique, God-given potentialities, dreams, and purposes in life.

Relationship Well-Being Checkup

This checkup helps you enhance your intimate relationships in two ways. (1) It can provide you with a quick self-evaluation of the health of your relationships. (2) The checkup items are attitudes and behaviors that help nurture love and wholeness in relationships. If you have a close, committed relationship now, I recommend that each of you take the inventory separately. Then use what you learn to enrich your relationship. If you are in a lonely place on your life journey, this checkup may be painful. But it can also be useful as you search for ways to enrich your caring community of relationships.

CHECKLIST

Instructions: In front of each statement put one of three initials: E = I am (we are) doing very well (excellently) in this; OK = I am (we are) doing all right, but there is room for improvement; NS = I (we) definitely need to strengthen this area.

_____ I have a strong, loving network of friends and/or family in which we all feel mutually respected, cared for, and empowered to grow.

_____ I love and respect myself, which enables me to do the same for those I care about most.

_____ The give and take in my close relationships are generally balanced and fair to both sides.

_____ I (we) communicate regularly about the things that really matter to us, including clearing the air of irritants in our daily living.

_____ I'm often playful in my close relationships, laughing at myself and with them about our shared foibles.

_____ I have close, meaningful relationships with persons of both genders.

_____ I respect my partner's differences and have accepted the futility of trying to re-form him or her to be like myself. (A difficult lesson to learn.)

_____ I (we) deal with interpersonal conflicts openly and regularly rather than letting them grow huge or grind on without resolution.

_____ I'm often able to learn from the inevitable conflict, pain, and mistakes in my close relationship(s).

_____ I give and receive forgiveness, appreciation, warm support, and *constructive* criticism in these relationships.

_____ I ask for what I need and say what I believe in an honest but not attacking manner.

_____ I can express my real feelings and discuss my problems honestly with the person(s) with whom I'm closest.

_____ I'm not a people-pleaser nor do I play phony, manipulative games to be liked or keep peace at whatever price in my relationships.

_____ Meeting my partner's needs is satisfying to me because I really care about that person's well being.

_____ I enjoy and affirm the successes, accomplishments, and strengths of my partner, and vice versa.

_____ I (we) enjoy participating in meaningful groups and organizations in which I (we) have a sense of belonging.

_____ I get and give as much touching and hugging as I need.

_____ I enjoy making new friends as well as savoring old friends.

_____ My closest relationship(s) is (are) strengthened by shared spirituality and values.

_____ My partner and I work together in one or more causes aimed at enhancing the quality of life in our community and/or world.

Using Your Findings: Scan your responses and get an overall feel for your relationship's strengths and weaknesses, congratulating yourself on the E items. In your *Self-Care Journal*(s) jot down a list of the important items you evaluated as OK and NS—areas where constructive changes would increase your relationship's loving wholeness.

If you're doing this chapter with your partner, share and compare your responses with your partner's, discussing differences and similarities and possible changes each of you desires. Jot down in your *Journal*(s) your preliminary ideas regarding what you might do to enhance love, esteem, and communication in your relationship.

The Care and Feeding of Intimate Relationships

Sustaining love over the years is far from easy, as you probably know from experience. Most of us fumble and stumble now and again in our efforts to be more adequate friends, spouses, lovers, children, or parents. Erich Fromm is right when he declares: "That nothing is easier than love—has continued to be the prevalent idea about love in spite of the overwhelming evidence to the contrary.

WINDOW OF WHOLENESS

WILL AND ARIEL DURANT

For more than three decades, Will and Ariel Durant collaborated in researching and writing a "biography of the human family," the series of volumes entitled *Story of Civilization*. They pioneered together in making the knowledge of the ages available to ordinary people, highlighting the human and cultural heart of history. When asked to sum up civilization briefly, Will responded: "Civilization is a stream with banks. The stream is sometimes filled with blood from people killing, stealing, shouting and doing the things historians usually record, while on the banks, unnoticed, people build homes, make love, raise children, sing songs, write poetry and even whittle statues. The story of civilization is the story of what happens on the banks. Historians are pessimists because they ignore the banks of the river" (*Current Biography*, 1964, 116).

In October 1963 Will and Ariel celebrated their golden wedding anniversary at their home in Los Angeles. Ariel was a continuing, behind-the-scenes collaborator with Will for most of their monumental writing project. Their earlier relationship, in which she mainly supported his career, reflects the late nineteenth and early twentieth centuries in which they grew up. It was not until the seventh volume in their series that her name appeared as coauthor. The emergence into the open of this professional partnership would seem to point to their movement toward a more egalitarian understanding of women-men relationships (*Current Biography*, 1964, 114–16).

The Durants have a daughter and a son. The eighth volume of their *Story of Civilization* is dedicated to their granddaughter, Monica. Will was once asked to give his definition of happiness. He responded that he had searched for it in vain—in pleasure, in work, in travel, in knowledge, in writing, in achievement and wealth. Then he shared this touching story about a day with their daughter:

Today I have neglected my writing. The voice of a little girl calling to me, "Come out and play," drew me from my papers and books. Was it not the final purpose of my toil that I should be free to frolic with her, and spend unharassed hours with the one who had given her to me? And so we walked and ran and laughed together, and fell in the tall grass, and hid among the trees; and I was young again. Now it is evening; while I write, I hear the child's breathing as she sleeps in her cozy bed. And I know I have found what I sought. . . . Gladly I surrender myself to nature's imperative of love and parentage, trusting in her ancient wisdom. . . . There can be no real or lasting happiness without love" (from Lillian E. Watson, ed., *Light from Many Lamps* [New York: Simon & Schuster, 1951], 246).

There is hardly any activity . . . which is started with such tremendous hopes and expectations, and yet, which fails so regularly, as love."[7]

Yet the tender joys and soul-satisfying caring in intimate relationships that are working can make all the struggles worthwhile. As someone has said, at the close of your day or the close of life's day, there is only one fully convincing answer to the question, What really matters to me now? Clearly, for most of us, the answer is *people*—the people with whom we have the deepest ties of love, however mixed our feelings may be.

Have a look at a rose bush. To continue to flourish and flower it must be cultivated, fertilized, weeded, pruned, and watered. Love is like that. If we learn how to care for love, it will flower. If we neglect love, it will wither and eventually die.

Most people are aware at some level that love is important in their lives. But they lack the knowledge and skills needed to keep love going and growing. Two kinds of interpersonal skills are essential in nurturing the flower of loving wholeness—honest, caring *communication* and effective *conflict resolution*.

The twelve strategies that follow are ways of nurturing love by using and strengthening these skills in your intimate relationships. I have derived these strategies from more than three decades of doing counseling and enrichment work with couples. They also come from four-plus decades of on-the-job training in my own most important, challenging, and enriching relationship. These strategies are designed to be practical tools for you to explore and enrich what Thomas Merton called "the wholeness of love" in your important relationships. To get the most help from the strategies, pause after reading each one and ask yourself two questions about your close relationship(s): (1) How well am I (are we) doing in using this strategy? (Put a number from 1 to 10 in front of each strategy, 10 meaning "I am doing great in this area; 1 meaning "This is a disaster area that I urgently need to strengthen!") (2) What do I (we) need to do to enrich our mutual love and wholeness in this way? Jot down in your *Self-Care Journal* any tentative ideas that come to you as you reflect on these strategies, building on insights gained from the relationship wholeness checkup. If possible, I recommend that you invite your spouse, close friend, or lover to share the experience. Just read the strategies aloud, pausing to talk after each one, applying it to your relationship. Whether you're using these strategies solo or as a couple, be sure to consider concrete steps you'll take to help your relationship(s) become more mutually loving and nurturing.

Love-Nurturing Strategy Number 1: *Set aside some time each day (at least ten to fifteen minutes) to communicate about what really matters to* *each of you.* Communication is to your relationships what oxygen is to your body. Your basic personality needs (including your need for love) can be met and conflicts resolved only by effective communication. An old cartoon shows a couple leaving a marriage counseling session. The wife is saying, "Now that we've learned to communicate, shut up!" Obviously the quality and spirit of communication makes all the difference in its impact on the health of your relationships. Another cartoon I enjoy shows a man saying heatedly to his wife, "If you wanted a communicator, you should have married Walter Cronkite!"

Can you imagine any deeper or more painful loneliness than where two persons live for years in the same house, sleep together, struggle to raise their children, and yet seldom if ever communicate about their despairs and dreams, their hopes and fears, the things that really matter to each of them? The good news is that most people have the potential ability to strengthen their communication skills. Doing this involves learning to do three things more effectively:

1. Express your own ideas, feelings, and needs clearly and honestly.
2. Listen more carefully to help yourself understand what the other is really communicating, both verbally and nonverbally.
3. Check out what you heard to make sure you got the message accurately.

Love-Nurturing Strategy Number 2: *Feed each other's heart hungers regularly and intentionally, particularly the deep needs for mutual appreciation, respect, touching, warmth, caring, laughter, and joy.* Loving wholeness is nurtured by responsiveness to each other's basic personality needs. Love withers when reciprocal need satisfaction is neglected or replaced by toxic communication, producing mutual need hunger. Later in this chapter you'll learn two practical tools for increasing your skill in feeding each other's heart hungers.

Love-Nurturing Strategy Number 3: *Continue to grow as individuals, developing your own special gifts and talents. And make healthy spaces in your togetherness.* As persons in a close relationship develop their own unique gifts and enhance their own wholeness, they have much more to give to each other. The wisdom of Lao-tzu, time-tested through twenty-six centuries, describes the way inner aliveness and warmth in persons enriches their intimate relationships:

> If the sign of life is in your face
> He who responds to it
> Will feel secure and fit
> As when, in a friendly place,
> Sure of hearty care,
> A traveler gladly waits.[8]

If the sign of life

is in your face

He who responds to it

Will feel secure and fit

As when, in a friendly place,

Sure of hearty care,

A traveler gladly waits.

—Lao-tzu

Learning to balance times together, times alone, and time with others can be difficult. But it can also be essential to the health of relationships. Carlos, a long-distance truck driver, and Martha, a court stenographer, have been married for some seventeen years. Their relationship works reasonably well as long as Carlos's job keeps him on the road at least a third of the time. But when his union was on a three-month strike and he was home most of the time, they experienced unprecedented and painful conflict. Struggling to find a workable togetherness-apartness balance is a challenge to many couples, especially if one wants more and the other less together-ness. This is a sticky issue that recently retired couples often find they must negotiate. Many women, because of being overpro-grammed as care givers of others, have a pressing need for what Virginia Woolf aptly called "A Room of One's Own."

This strategy runs parallel to the Buddhist belief that love can flower in a relationship only if there is "non-attachment" between the persons. Translated into Western terms, this means giving up the possessiveness that causes some couples to believe (erroneously) that each owns the other. To the degree that they believe this, real respect for each other's autonomy and differentness, and therefore real intimacy, are diminished. They have a symbiotic, meaning a mutually parasitic, relationship.

Love-Nurturing Strategy Number 4: *Affirm each other's gifts, both actualized and potential, by providing maximum and equal opportunities for developing these.* As suggested above, loving wholeness is alive in a close friendship (including a marriage) to the degree that the partners support the fulfillment of each other's dreams and possibilities. For this to happen, your working agreement (your relationship cove-nant) must be as fair and just as you can make it. Without a firm foundation of fair play, the house of love is like the house in Jesus' parable—built on unstable sand so that it cannot survive any storm or flood. The crux of wholeness for countless intimate male-female relationships, in this time of changing identities, is providing equal opportunities for both persons to develop their unused or partially used gifts.

Love-Nurturing Strategy Number 5: *Learn more effective ways to prevent the cold wall of unhealed conflict, hurt, anger, and resentment from blocking the flow of caring, passion, joy, and love between you.* Milton Berle tells about a man who said, "My wife and I never go to bed mad. We stay up until the problem is resolved. Last year we didn't get to sleep until March."[9] Actually, anger and resentment from accumulated hurts is a major cause of devitalized relationships, robbing them of joy and playful passion. Even if you "married an angel," you've probably discovered that the shadow side of human angels is usually at least a little demonic.[10] As Elizabeth Taylor is alleged to have said, "People who have no faults have some pretty annoying virtues."

Long-accumulated hurt and anger can produce tragic explosions of rage, as is evident in the epidemic of domestic violence. One-fourth of all the murders in the U.S. are by spouses and other live-in partners.[11] In addition, there's the enormous trauma of emotional and spiritual violence in families—violence that deadens joy and cripples love, even when there is no physical violence.

The tender, promising plant of new love can be strangled by a thicket of unresolved resentment and anger, unforgiven hurts, and frustrated heart hungers. Learning how to heal the hurt and resolve the conflicts is essential if loving wholeness is to grow.

As Ben and Peggy agreed, after a couples' enrichment weekend highlighting creative handling of conflict, "It's great to discover that our most painful conflicts occur right at the places where we have the best opportunity to grow and get more satisfaction in our marriage!"

> Remember,
>
> if you have a fight
>
> and don't learn from it,
>
> you've wasted a good fight!
>
> —Howard Clinebell

Love-Nurturing Strategy Number 6: *Keep your friendship strong and growing. Include having fun together regularly.* A *Psychology Today* survey of 351 couples married fifteen years or longer (300 of whom said they were happily married) revealed these surprising findings. When asked what had kept their marriages going, the first and second most frequently mentioned reasons, for both women and men, were these: "My spouse is my best friend," and "I like my spouse as a person." Among the top ten reasons given by both sexes were "My spouse has grown more interesting," and "We laugh together." "We agree about our sex life" was twelfth for men and fourteenth for women among the list of reasons for their relationships continuing. Sex is a powerful factor that draws couples together initially. But the best long-term cement for sustaining an intimate relationship (and also for keeping the fires of romance glowing) is *liking each other as friends!*[12]

Laughing and playing together are vitally important as well as enjoyable ways to cultivate your love. Being able to laugh at yourself and with each other is a like a breath of cool, fresh air on a hot, smoggy day. Stop reading now and plan a shared mini-vacation—a brief fun time of playful relaxation you will both enjoy sometime today. While you're at it, why not take time to plan a fun "date" this week with your spouse, lover, or friend? Such dates once or twice a week can be refreshing oases of intimate reconnecting. These are particularly important if you're in the desert of a distancing time, a pressure-cooker life-style, or a two-career relationship. In his insightful book, *Getting the Love You Want*, Harvel Hendrix observes: "When couples have exuberant fun together they identify each other as a source of pleasure and safety, which intensifies their emotional bond. . . . Partners begin to connect with each other on a deeper, unconscious level."[13]

Love-Nurturing Strategy Number 7: *Open yourselves regularly to "peak experiences"—times of enjoying your spiritual lives together.* In the *Psychology Today* study of couples, spiritual and value issues were high on the list of the couples' reasons for their long-lived marriages. In fact, "Marriage is sacred," and "We agree on aims and goals" were the fourth and fifth most frequently cited reasons. Just over two decades ago, in a very different world, my partner Charlotte and I wrote about the power of spiritual intimacy: "In the fullest expression of intimacy there's usually a vertical dimension. . . . This both strengthens the relationship and is strengthened by it. . . . The spiritual dimension of marriage is a practical source of food for marital growth and health. No single factor does more to give a marriage joy and keep it both a venture and an adventure in mutual fulfillment than shared commitment to spiritual discovery. The life of the spirit is deeply personal, so the moments of sharing on the spiritual level are tender, precious moments in a relationship."[14] In today's anxious, alienated world, with its epidemic of spiritual loneliness and value confusions, what we said then is even more relevant to the struggle to find creative closeness.

Our Western religious tradition understands human love as rooted in and empowered by God's love. Here is a first-century way of putting this: "God is love, and he who abides in love abides in God, and God abides in him. . . . There is no fear in love, but perfect love casts out fear" (1 John 4:16–17). It can be an exciting moment when you discover unexpectedly that your finite, fractured human love has become an imperfect but real doorway through which you can experience the Love of the universe.

Perhaps you recall the story of the little boy who was afraid to go to sleep in a dark bedroom. His father tried to comfort him, saying, "You shouldn't be afraid. God is here." The boy responded, "I want God with skin on his face!" Something miraculous occurs when our ambivalent human love becomes—in special moments of agony or ecstasy—a very partial but very real embodiment of God's Love. When this occurs, the healing presence of divine Love becomes alive in our very human relationships. In our rootless world, being rooted in this Love can be a wonder-full source of a sense of groundedness. The imagery in this biblical line is an invitation to open ourselves to receive this healing, transcending love: "May your roots go down deep into the soil of God's marvelous love" (Ephesians 3:17, NEB).

Good news! You and your partner can use the spiritual enrichment methods described in chapter 2 to help deepen both spiritual and values intimacy between you. Remember the image of the bubbling spring and the irrigation channel? If you are with your partner, take time now and see if you can open the sluice gate to Love together. Some couples do this by sharing spiritual enrichment practices such as meditation, prayer, inspirational reading, worship, communion with nature, and helping those in need. Increasing spiritual intimacy can enhance creative closeness in other areas of your lives.

Love-Nurturing Strategy Number 8: *Take good care of your caring community—the close friends and extended family members who love you and support your relationship in all the ups and downs of the passing years.* Studies of healthy families show that they are "open systems." This means that they do lots of interacting with their biological extended family, their "friend family,"[15] which is their mutual support system, and other meaningful individuals and groups. Isolated nuclear families miss the enrichment that comes from interacting with a wider circle of caring people from a variety of life stages, backgrounds, and life-styles. Isolated nuclear families also are extremely vulnerable when crises strike. In our mobile, cut-flower society one family in five moves each year. Sustaining a health-nurturing caring community requires continuing cultivation of friendships for most of us. As many have discovered, a warm, familylike congregation is one of the best places to put down roots quickly when you're uprooted and move to a new community.

Love-Nurturing Strategy Number 9: *Discover and enjoy together the special romance, challenges, opportunities, wisdom, and gifts of your present life stage.* Each family stage (like each individual life stage) has a new set of losses and problems. It also has a whole new set of assets and possibilities. Learning to savor the changing seasons of your life together, with all their shadows and sunlight, is an essential art in these times of extended life spans. It's an art that can add life and zest to your growing relationship. One of the joys of leading midyears "retread" enrichment retreats is helping couples make a wonderful discovery: that there's a special depth romance that is possible for them because of all they've shared on their journey together. If you're a younger person, I hope you know at least one older couple who demonstrate that the belief that "romantic love is only for the young" is an ageist fallacy that's true only if you believe it.

Love-Nurturing Strategy Number 10: *Find an exciting cause for which you can enjoy working together.* Your love for each other will deepen if you express it, among other ways, through working to help make your community and world a little healthier for the human family. The great pastor-preacher Harry Emerson Fosdick once ob-

served that persons wrapped up in themselves make very small
packages. The same is true of intimate relationships such as families.

Broadening your circle of caring beyond your immediate self-
interests stretches your intimate relationships, making them more
whole. Thus your life together can avoid the trap of family narcis-
sism, which is something like an ingrown toenail. The various
healing-yourself-by-healing-the-planet methods described in chapter 8 can be used in your biological family or friend family to broaden
your horizons of caring together. In doing this you may enjoy the
shared satisfactions of helping, in small but significant ways, to heal
the brokenness in your community and your world. (For ways to
involve your children in peace, justice, and environmental awareness and action, see the books by James and Kathleen McGinnis, and
by Joseph Cornell in the Recommended Reading for chapter 8.)

Love-Nurturing Strategy Number 11: *Develop and implement an
intentional plan of mutual care for your relationships, incorporating these
strategies as well as others you devise.* Long-term studies of marital
happiness have produced a challenging discovery; namely, levels of
satisfaction tend to decline as the years pass unless couples learn to
work together to keep their relationships growing. Those who continue to be friends and lovers after even a few years together are
couples who, in most cases, have done just this.

There are complex factors that influence how happy or unhappy
folks are in intimate relationships. Many people are attracted to their
lovers and mates by the (vain) hope of finding the parent(s) they
longed for but did not have as children. Parentifying one's partner is
one of the most widespread forms of neurotic interaction in intimate
relationships. Using a relational growth plan does not, for these and
other reasons, guarantee a blissful relationship. What it does is increase the odds that mutual satisfaction and loving wholeness will
flourish rather than founder in your relationship.

If, in spite of your best efforts at intentional enrichment, your
mutual sabotage continues unabated, I recommend that you do two
things. First, read and digest a book that describes an effective approach to transforming old, unconscious programming so that you
can become "passionate friends." It's *Getting the Love You Want: A
Guide for Couples* by Harville Hendrix. Second, if that doesn't help as
much as you'd like, get some individual psychotherapy and/or
couple therapy. Do this with a relationship counselor who is trained
in helping people gain liberation from living today's relationships in
terms of yesterday's programming.

Love-Nurturing Strategy Number 12: *If you don't have time to care
for your intimate relationships, you've got a problem. You probably need to
revise your priorities and the schedule overload these priorities generate in*

your life. Love takes time. In our hectic lives it's easy to let the pressure of less important things squeeze love nurturing out of our prime time. Perhaps you have felt what couples in counseling sessions often say, wistfully or angrily, "We only communicate on the run, like ships passing in the night." How often do you take or, more accurately, make time to communicate heart to heart? Are you investing only leftover time in your important relationship(s)?

If, in your judgment, your most important relationships are being shortchanged, it may help to remind yourself that each of us has 1,440 minutes each day and 10,080 minutes each week. The moment-by-moment decisions regarding how we'll invest our precious time each day are guided by our working values and priorities. So if you want more time for communicating and loving, the way to start may be by revising your guiding priorities. If you'd really like some time each day to enjoy and care for your important relationships, you may find the Time-Values Inventory in chapter 2 helpful.

The two self-change exercises that follow—The Intentional Relationship Method and the Relationship Satisfaction and Justice Inventory—can be used to reduce conflicts, increase mutual fulfillment, and thus enhance love by revising the working agreement in your relationship. If you're in the fast lane and are tempted to skip these, I recommend that you make a date with yourself, and your partner, to come back and experience these. I think you'll discover that they're two of the most useful tools in this book.[16] These tools will work only if both partners have some openness to changing the relationship to make it more mutually satisfying. The less-motivated one may be willing to cooperate, of course, because of the other's desire for improvement.

The Intentional Relationship Method (IRM)

This communication method can be used to enhance any personal relationship—friend-friend, wife-husband, parent-child, colleague-colleague, lover-lover, and others. Of all the communication tools I've experimented with through the years, more couples have evaluated this one as "most helpful" than any other. Mary Ann and Larry, a couple in their early thirties, use this exercise regularly around their anniversaries to remind themselves of strengths and resolve conflicts in their marriage. A counselor in Arizona builds his preparation-for-marriage sessions around coaching couples in using this method. Several organizations have used it as a part of leadership planning retreats to strengthen relationships and resolve covert conflicts. I encourage you to try the IRM now.

Instructions: This exercise is most productive when done with a relationship partner. However, if you're using the book alone or aren't in a committed relationship currently, the steps may help you gain insights about how to build and enrich close relationships.

Using it solo can be good preparation for doing it with a partner, later, if you choose. Set aside at least forty-five minutes to do the first three steps. You'll need your *Self-Care Journals* (or some other paper) and a pen. The instructions are given as one might present them in a couples' workshop, so you'll need to adapt them for solo use. Remember that the / sign means stop reading now while you do what has been described.

Step 1:   **Enjoying the Strengths in Your Relationship.** Find a comfortable place to sit facing each other, on the floor if you like. / Begin by becoming more aware of some of the strengths and assets you already have going for you. First, each person write a list of all the things you can think of that you enjoy and appreciate in the other person and the relationship. / Now, using your written lists to jog your memory, one of you complete this sentence to the other, "I appreciate in you (or us)—" as many times as you can. When expressing what you appreciate, it's important to table for the time being the things you don't appreciate. When you're the recipient, just listen and enjoy the warm glow of affirmation from your partner. / After the first person has completed Step 1, reverse roles. / Share with each other now what you experienced as you were giving and receiving these affirmations. / If it feels appropriate, give each other a hug. / It may be helpful to jot down what you and your partner each appreciates in the other. /

Sincere appreciation is the language of love. Lovers know this intuitively and practice it spontaneously. But some of us longer-coupled folks tend to forget this vital truth. Step 1 can provide a launching pad of warmth, hope, and motivation for taking the other steps. If your relationship has a sexual side, you may discover that this step is a good warmup for sexual intimacy. If you enjoyed this step, decide on a time to repeat it just for fun.

Step 2:   **Identifying the Growing Edges of Your Relationship, the Unmet Needs, Wants.** There is, of course, room to grow in all relationships, including those that are working well. This second step enables you to zero in on areas in which you can grow together, if you choose. Begin this step by each person jotting down a needs/wants list. Include all the concrete needs or desires you wish your partner could or would satisfy. (Don't concern yourselves at this point about whether your partner can or will respond to them.) / Using your lists to prompt you, one of you complete this sentence aloud to the other, as many times as you wish: "I need (or want) from you—." When you are the recipient, listen as carefully as possible, trying to remain nondefensive. Remember that meeting all of each other's needs is neither desirable or possible in any human relationship. The purpose of this step is simply to get your druthers out on the table, to become aware of them, and thus to have them available to work with in the third step. /

After each person has completed the list, jot down in your *Self-Care Journal* what you heard your partner express. / Then, as a communication check, compare your list with your partner's list of needs and wants. Discover how clearly each of you stated your needs and how carefully each listened and remembered. /

Now, discuss how you feel about this step. / You probably found it more difficult than the first. It's easy to feel defensive when you hear needs and wants that your partner feels are not being met. Remember that unmet or partially met needs in any close relationship are the places where conflicts occur most often but also the places where growth has the greatest benefit. That's one reason why it's valuable to state and hear each other's needs and wants.

It is useful to know that there are three types of needs in close relationships. (1) Shared needs are those that are felt by both parties. For example, many couples share a pressing need for more time alone together to talk and play. (You may find it helpful to put an *S* beside all the shared needs on your lists.) (2) Conflicted needs are those around issues on which one partner wants more (sex or time together, for example) and the other wants less. (Put a *C* beside these needs on your lists.) (3) Parallel needs are those that don't contradict each other but are simply different. For example, when you eat out, one may prefer Chinese food and the other Mexican, but you both also enjoy the other type of food. (Put a *P* beside all the parallel needs on your lists.)

Step 3:   **Planning to Nurture Your Love by Intentionally Increasing Your Mutual Need Satisfaction.** You've now completed preparation for making your relationship more mutually nourishing. You're ready to make some satisfying changes intentionally. In making desired changes in intimate relationships, nothing succeeds like success. Each step forward gives a little additional momentum for taking the next step. It's easiest to make changes in the area of shared needs, since both of you will find these changes rewarding. So, to move into action, discuss the shared needs on your two lists now, and decide on one or two that seem important to both of you.

Now, through dialogue, work out a Mutual Change Plan that you agree will meet the shared need(s) you have selected. / Outline what each person will do and when as you implement your plan. Writing down your joint plan lets you check back later and be aware of the progress you've each made in fulfilling your plan.

Step 4:   **Implementing Your Self-Change Plan.** This is the payoff step. Some couples find it helpful to launch their joint plan in a symbolic or ritual way, confirming their agreement by some kind of brief ceremony that they devise. If it feels meaningful to both of you, do this now. / As you put your plan into action, it's a good idea to discuss your progress and to keep daily notes in your *Self-Care Journal.* Be sure to reward yourselves for each small step you take. One way to do this is to congratulate each other as you strengthen your relationship together. Through intentional affirmation and planning you have added or improved one or more small but significant clauses in your relationship covenant. Through your actions, you have intentionally made your relationship more mutually fulfilling and thus helped your love to grow.

If a particular plan doesn't work, for whatever reason, use your creativity to modify it or scrap it, go back to the drawing board, and devise a more workable one to satisfy these or other needs.

Step 5: **Choose Another Shared Need (or Two Parallel Needs) and Develop and Implement Plans to Meet this Need.** By continuing this process from one pair of unmet or partially met needs to another, you continue on the path of intentional renewal of your relationship. Be sure to repeat the "I appreciate in you (or us)—" step regularly. / When you move from shared to parallel needs, you'll be working out a Mutual Change Plan for a more fair *quid pro quo,* the Latin legal term meaning "something for something." Translated into this context, it means "I'll be glad to scratch your back if you'll scratch mine."

The greatest challenge is to develop workable plans to satisfy conflicted or contradictory needs. The not-so-easy communication skill required is *effective negotiation that produces win-win compromise agreements.* These are agreements by which each person gets some but not all of what she or he needs, wants, or hopes for. If you want sex four or five times a week, for example, and your partner wants it only once or twice, a win-win compromise would be to agree to make love three times a week. In other words, you meet in the middle. Win-lose "solutions" of conflicted needs in intimate relationships are really not solutions at all. Both of you really lose if you follow a regular win-lose pattern favoring one partner, because your relationship will be hurt by this unfairness. In contrast, win-win solutions tend to nurture love by satisfying some of each of your needs in a fairer way.

A win-win resolution of conflicted needs often involves finding a third option. Mary Ann and Larry identified several conflicted needs as they used the IRM. For example, Larry abhors and Mary Ann adores camping. Larry loves vacations involving lots of "culture"— art galleries and concerts—which Mary Ann can take or leave. Fortunately, they discovered several vacation options about which both were enthusiastic—for example, a cruise or a week in a hideaway

"I am not leaving you, I'm just going somewhere to do a little work on my autonomy."

cottage on a secluded beach. They actually decided on a win-win compromise—to go to Yosemite but to stay in a comfortable lodge rather than a tent.

The Relationship Satisfaction and Justice Inventory (RSJI)

As mentioned above, love, respect, and passion in any intimate relationship flower best in a climate of fairness and equality. Perhaps your relationship isn't working as well as you'd like. If so, it's probably because your basic covenant or agreement needs revising. Knowing how to do this is one of the most important tools for keeping long-term relationships going by growing. The IRM and RSJI are two do-it-yourselves inventories devised to help couples revise their working agreement. The RSJI complements and goes beyond the IRM by providing specific information about where in the couple's covenant satisfactions and fairness are in short supply.[17] Both instruments can be used in any close relationship.

Instructions: This exercise can be used solo or with your partner. In either case, set aside twenty minutes to take the inventory individually. If you're using it with a partner, set aside at least another thirty minutes to begin sharing your findings and developing practical plans for eliminating injustices and dissatisfactions. Use this inventory when you're both feeling relatively good about your relationship and communicating well. If you're in time of distancing and pain, it may open up areas of conflict that are difficult to resolve by your-selves. If this happens, it's important to get the assistance of a com-petent relationship therapist. You'll need to make two copies of the inventory and decide who will be Partner A and who will be Partner B.

Step 1:   Each of you complete your copy of the inventory by yourself. Begin by looking down the lists of "Areas of Our Relationship" on the left. (These represent clauses of your relationship covenant.) / Add other significant areas in your relationship in the blanks near the bottom of the inventory on the left. / Go back to the first item on the list. If you feel your present division of responsibility for house, yard, and other "dirty work" is fair and satisfying to both partners, put an *F* and an *S* in the blank to the right of this item. If you feel that your present arrangement is unfair or unsatisfying to Partner A, put *US* or *UF* in the middle blank. Do the same for Partner B in the space on the right. Now do the same for each area on the list.

AREAS OF OUR RELATIONSHIP	FAIR AND SATISFYING TO BOTH PARTNERS	*UF* OR *US* TO PARTNER A	*UF* OR *US* TO PARTNER B
Responsibility for dirty work			
Educational-growth opportunities			
Opportunities for fulfilling work			
Child-rearing responsibilities			
Money decisions			
Opportunities for self-care			
Opportunities for hobbies and fun			
Sexual satisfaction			
Leadership in the relationship			

Self-esteem enhancement opportunities			
Decisions about moving			
Relations with relatives			
Spiritual life responsibility			
Community service responsibility			
Other areas:			
_____			
_____			
_____			
_____			
_____			

Step 2: Compare your two sets of responses, paying special attention to the *UF*s and *US*s—areas where either of you feels that fairness or satisfaction is lacking. I think you'll find that these are the places where conflicts occur most often. They're also the places where growth is most necessary and most potentially rewarding. Affirm yourselves for having the courage to face these conflicted areas. You have taken an important step toward making intentional changes to correct the problem. If your perceptions of these areas are similar, consider this a strength in your relationship on which you can build.

Now, list in your *Self-Care Journals* the areas either of you marked *US* or *UF*. Leave some room beside each item for notes.

Step 3: Go down the list item by item, discussing and jotting down your tentative ideas about what you can do to make your relationship more just and satisfying by negotiating plans for constructive changes in your relationship covenant. Bear in mind that as you do this you'll be nurturing your love.

Step 4: Pick one area in which you agree that things are either unsatisfying or unfair for one of you and a second area where things are unsatisfying or unfair to the other. / Discuss your ideas about what you can do to increase satisfaction and fairness in these two areas. Then work out a Mutual Change Plan together. Be sure to include a clear statement of who is agreeing to do what by what time. If one of you has been getting the short end of the stick in your relationship, concentrate on correcting those injustices. But also make sure that both of you will get some increased satisfactions from your overall plan. / Write down your agreed-upon plan, so you'll both have a written record for future reference.

Step 5: Commit yourself to implementing your plan, and go for it! After each step you take toward a more fair and satisfying relationship, give yourselves a congratulatory hug and reward yourselves by doing something you both enjoy. Use your imaginations to create rewards to offset any frustrations from having to give up satisfying but unfair aspects of your relationship. (Of course, many of the changes should prove to be rewarding in and of themselves.) Agree in advance what rewards will be withheld if one or both of you blows it by not doing what you each agreed you'd do.

After you have made changes in the initial areas, go back and select two other areas in which both of you agree changes are in

"It was like any other day . . . a few carefree moments tidying up the place, a joyous and fulfilling hour playing with the kids, a couple of hours of spontaneous creativity in the kitchen . . ."

order, and repeat steps 4 and 5. If one or both of you foul up your efforts to take a step in your change plan, don't waste energy with mutual accusations and futile postmortems. The withheld rewards should be enough motivation to do better next time. Just devise a more workable plan to enhance fairness and satisfaction in that area or put that one in the refrigerator (cool it) and focus on making changes in a less difficult area for a while.

Beyond Enlightened Self-Interest

Are you troubled by this chapter's theme, that increasing justice and need satisfaction in your relationship is the path to enriching your love? Perhaps this seems selfish and/or legalistic. Let me emphasize that negotiating a more fair and satisfying relationship covenant (contract) is a good place to start but not to stop in enlivening your love.

When couples are suffering from severe need hunger and therefore are feeling hurt, hostile, low self-esteem, and emotional alienation, *enlightened* self-interest is the most effective place for them to begin healing their woundedness. This may help them gradually replace their unenlightened self-serving with increased mutual satisfaction. This in turn may enable them to move from negative cycles of escalating need deprivation and mutual attacking to more mutually satisfying cycles.

As Thomas Merton observes, "to consider love *merely* as a matter of need and fulfillment, as something that works itself out in a cool deal, is to miss the whole point of love, and of life itself."[18] As love matures, two exciting relational dynamics begin to operate. First, couples discover the "new math" of loving—that *giving love away by satisfying the other does not diminish it. Instead this is the only way to increase the love that comes back to you.* An image from the Talmud expresses the reality of mature loving well: "Many candles can be lighted from one candle without diminishing it."[19] As lovers know intuitively, lighting the other's candle of passion can make one's own candle glow with heat as well as light. If you're in a nontoxic relationship, you probably can increase self-rewarding, mutual-caring cycles intentionally, so that both of you receive and give more caring love. As mentioned above, if your relationship is toxic and afflicted with poor communication, you'll probably need the help of a trained counselor-therapist who will help you learn how to accomplish this.

Someone has observed that children need a lot of love, especially when they don't deserve it. This certainly applies to the little girl or boy within all of us adults. The kid who gets activated when we're sick, discouraged, or exhausted from having to parent others too long needs feeding with some unearned loving. In healthy intimate relationships each person's inner child can get loving care on occasions without the other expecting reciprocity right at that time. Going

Many candles can be lighted

from one candle without

diminishing it."

—Talmud

the second mile in relationships can work and be healthy when there is sufficient mutual esteeming and caring so that each is willing to give occasionally when the other isn't in the mood to reciprocate at that time. But the give and take of any relationship must be fairly balanced if it is to generate well being in both partners.

The second, closely related dynamic in relationships where love is maturing is the gradual *overlapping and merging of some needs.* Wholeness-oriented psychologist Abraham Maslow puts this well: "One important aspect of a good love relationship is what may be called need identification, or the pooling of the hierarchies of basic needs in two people into a single hierarchy. The effect of this is that one person feels another's needs as if they were his own."[20] Of course, self-serving needs continue in all of us, to some degree. Being willing to ask for what one needs is healthy for relationships, provided it is a two-way street. But as loving relationships mature, reciprocity often is transcended, as each partner gets more pleasure from giving the other pleasure.

It's when we go beyond enlightened self-interest that love becomes most enjoyable and transforming. Thomas Merton's insights illuminate this transition: "In reality, love is . . . a transcendent spiritual power. It is, in fact, the deepest creative power in human nature. . . . It is a living appreciation of life as value and gift. . . . Love has its own wisdom . . . its own way of exploring the inner depths of life in the mystery of the loved person. . . . When people are truly in love, they experience far more than just a mutual need for each other's company. In their relation with each other, they become different people; they are more than their everyday selves, more alive, more understanding. . . . They are transformed by the power of their love."[21]

What I think Merton is saying is that in the midst of all the grubby earthiness and conflict in any live human relationship, it really is possible at times to experience some transforming power.

Relationship Well Being for Singles

From the perspective of wholeness the single life has both problems and possibilities. Single and unsingle people share many if not most of the rough places and detours on the life journey. But single, divorced, separated, or widowed persons also confront a variety of special challenges. As emphasized earlier, everyone needs a caring community of friends and/or family to support their well being with a sense of belonging and some no-(or few)-strings-attached love. Singles often have to work harder and more intentionally to sustain their health-nurturing support system. This is especially true for those who are living alone, without a familylike harbor of acceptance, where they can really relax and refuel for facing the storms at sea.

A societal challenge to singles' self-esteem is the widespread biases and discrimination (often illegal) against unmarried people, single parents, and anyone else who doesn't fit the old pattern of the traditional two-parent family. This prejudice ignores the fact that the majority of Americans no longer live in such families. But being married is still considered the norm. This means that adults who are divorced, widowed, or who have never married (by choice or by circumstance) often feel less valued by society and like fifth wheels in social situations. Older unmarried women may suffer their culture's cruel stereotyping and put-downs. Many people-serving institutions, including congregations, conform to rather than challenge the culture's bias against being uncoupled. Family-centered programs, as important as they may be for those who fit the old definition of family, frequently make singles feel like outsiders. (A healthy development in contemporary society is the broadening of definitions of "family" to include the whole spectrum of intimate supportive relationships.)

Other factors that may pose health hazards for singles include the high-stress life-style of the singles scene, where some seek to satisfy their needs for emotional and sexual intimacy. Singles bars and condo complexes illustrate this pressure. Unhealed, infected wounds from close relationships that have died but have not been fully buried take their toll on the health of some singles. Loneliness may push them into unhealthy relationships, where their pain and grief from earlier relationships, still unhealed, is increased by new suffering.

Some singles avoid long-term commitments because they fear a repetition of the deep hurts experienced in childhood or in previous adult relationships. They suffer from the dilemma described in the old fable, retold by the philosopher Schopenhauer, about the two freezing porcupines. They're caught between huddling together to avoid freezing and being pushed away by the pain from each other's sharp quills. Singles growth groups and therapy are good investments for such persons to enable them to strengthen relationship-building skills and to unlearn emotional blocks to mutual, growthful intimacy.

Many people who live alone tend to eat less healthily because they are less motivated to prepare nutritious meals. They may overdo fast foods and TV dinners loaded with fat, salt, and refined sugar. Live-alone singles often have less interpersonal support and help to deal constructively with crises. If singlehood carries a load of loneliness, grief, or diminished self-esteem, singles are vulnerable to the addictive dangers of self-medicating these painful feelings with excessive drinking or drug use (prescribed or street drugs), or by overeating and underexercising.

But singlehood also has some unique positive potentialities for well being. For one thing, being self-liberated from a toxic relationship can be a valuable contribution to one's wholeness. The negative health impact of an unwholesome marriage is considerable. Sally, at age thirty-one, finally mustered the courage to leave such a stifling marriage. She laughed from deep inside her as she told how much better she felt in her whole being, quoting one of her heroes (Martin Luther King, Jr.), "Free at last! Thank God Almighty, I'm free at last!" Because singles cannot hide behind safe but neurotic and deadening marriages, they have the freedom and often the motivation to develop healthier relationships and life-styles. They make time to care for their bodies and invest the energy required to keep their "friend family" in robust condition.

Sex is complicated enough for married people. It is often even more problematic for singles. Our society's current attitudes about sexuality are chaotic and in transition. Sex is glamorized in the media and exploited by Madison Avenue, and yet traditional social attitudes still seek to deny sex to millions of single adults. Along with many married people, singles often need encouragement to discover what constitutes wholeness-generating sexuality for them. More about this in chapter 10.

It's a healthy development in contemporary society that marriage is becoming somewhat less glamorized and singlehood is becoming more of a genuine option, a fully legitimate life-style. As young people are freer to choose to remain single longer or permanently, they're less likely to run into bad marriages in vain attempts to escape from childhood families or from their own loneliness and low self-esteem. Both marriage and singlehood can be hellish hazards to health. But, fortunately, both can also be wholeness nurturing, depending on the quality of the lives and relationships of the persons involved.

A valuable guide to creative singlehood is John R. Landgraf's *Singling: A New Way to Live the Single Life.* He redefines singlehood as a positive state of being "well married to yourself." His key idea is that being fully single in this sense is a prerequisite for being creatively coupled or creatively noncoupled. Convincing evidence is offered that:

- Singlehood can be a state of high-level wellness;

- One can be single and sexually whole (he recommends becoming your own best lover);

- Once wholly single, a person is free and equipped to have a lifemate—or not to have one.[22]

Alternative Relationship Styles

The basic methods of couple enrichment and enhancement (described above) can be valuable tools for any close relationship. Certainly this includes unmarried heterosexual couples living together in committed relationships. Many such couples are reacting against the emotional hypocrisy and deadness of some conventional marriages among their parents' generation. They are searching for more humanizing ways to satisfy the basic human needs for companionship, emotional support, and sex. Some older couples living together "without benefit of clergy" are seeking to satisfy these emotional and sexual needs without the complications and loss of income that a formal marriage sometimes brings.

Couples living in alternative life-styles and also gay and lesbian couples often experience interpersonal conflict and pain like those in traditional marriages. But additional burdens frequently make relational wholeness even more of a challenge. These burdens include being given cold shoulders by families or congregations who are embarrassed by and reject their life-style or sexual preference. Other burdens include society's judgmental, discriminatory attitudes and practices. Such couples face the same types of challenges encountered by minority groups suffering from a one-down position in their community and society. Such punishing pressures make it even more important that these couples work together to enhance their love and wholeness. Those of us in people-serving institutions should do everything within our power to erase the judgmentalism and homophobia that cripples the effectiveness of these institutions as resources for enriching the lives of such individuals and couples.[23]

Nurturing Parent-Child and Family Wholeness

Healthy families are the world's greatest wholeness resource. Why? Because wholeness is "home grown," families are the main garden, and parents (along with teachers) the primary gardeners. There is no doubt that we parents, individually as well as collectively, have the future wholeness of the planet at our fingertips—literally. What an awesome responsibility—and opportunity!

An enlightening survey of 550 professionals who work with families identified the traits of healthy families.[24] They discovered that such families

AVENGE YOURSELF!

LIVE LONG ENOUGH TO

BECOME A PROBLEM

TO YOUR CHILDREN!

—*lapel button*

• communicate and listen

• affirm and support one another

• teach respect for others

• develop a sense of trust

• have a sense of play and humor

- exhibit a sense of shared responsibility

- teach a sense of right and wrong

- have a strong sense of family in which rituals and traditions abound

- have a religious core

- respect the privacy of one another

- value service to others

- foster family table time and conversation

- share leisure time

- admit to and seek help for problems

The good news is that most of the methods for enhancing individual and relationship wholeness described in this chapter can be applied to your family. Use these to help increase characteristics such as those identified in this survey. For example, many families discover that the IRM and the RSJI are valuable tools for increasing love-nurturing communication and resolving conflicts.

What If Self-Help Tools Don't Do It?

What can you do if you've tried the do-it-yourselves strategies, communication exercises, and conflict-resolving tools and found that they don't give you the wholeness you want? I recommend that you get the coaching of your pastor, priest, or rabbi (if he or she is trained in counseling), or the help of a competent relationship counselor-therapist.[25] A series of sessions with such a wise guide may help you renegotiate a more fair, mutually satisfying, love-generating relationship agreement. After getting some expert professional help, you may find that the strategies and communication tools in this book are useful to you. Getting such help is a good investment in yourself, your family, your future, and your children's future well being.

We're in the early stages of a new era of human history with respect to marriages and families. The identities, roles, and relationships of persons within them is being redefined in profound ways. Many people are struggling mightily to discover and retain whatever is healthy from their old understandings, yet become more open to necessary changes in the new world of the 90s and the next century. John Shelby Spong is on target in this description of the huge challenges we face: "Marriage is ceasing to be a power relationship between two unequal persons. Increasingly it is seen as a relationship between two persons who want to create a new life together, share sexual pleasure, work in concert for the economic well-being of the family unit, and be partners in planning their older years together. In such a relationship the possibility of open conflict will necessarily be greater. . . . In a partnership marriage, the oath of fidelity and care for the well-being of the other will bind both partners, or it will bind neither."[26]

If you're sweating and struggling to redefine an intimate relationship with a person of the other sex, let me recommend three books. One is psychologist Herb Goldberg's *The New Male-Female Relationship*, a guide written in popular style. (See Recommended Reading for all three.) *The Dance of Intimacy* by Menninger psychologist Harriet Goldhor Lerner is the second book. Although the subtitle is "A Woman's Guide to Courageous Acts of Change in Key Relationships," it also can be valuable for men. For genuine intimacy and solid connectedness to happen in "stuck relationships," she holds, at least one person must stop focusing mainly on the other (in a negative or worried way) and invest that energy in developing a clearer and stronger sense of personhood.

The third book is *The Chalice and the Blade* by Riane Eisler. She looks at partnership relationships between the genders as part of the new "partnership society" now struggling to be born around the globe. In this society women and men will be full partners, and social institutions like families, schools, and governments will be based more on linking than ranking in hierarchical pyramids. She predicts, "Along with the celebration of life will come the celebration of love, including sexual love between women and men. Sexual bonding through some form of what we now call marriage will most certainly continue. But the primary purpose of this bonding will be mutual companionship, sexual pleasure, and love. . . . And other caring relationships, not just heterosexual couples, will be fully recognized."[27] *The Partnership Way*, a more recent book by Riane Eisler and her spouse, David Loye, is a practical companion to *The Chalice and the Blade*.

Several years ago I met Sandra, a remarkable young woman. She'd lost her husband, Mark, in their midtwenties, after his long struggle with cancer. It was obvious that she had grown tremendously through her agonizing grief. A year after his death she wrote these moving words to her friends and relatives: "To all of you I would say (as I'm sure Mark would wish me to): Live out your love for one another now. Don't assume the future; don't assume all kinds of healing time for the bruised places in your relationships with others. Don't be afraid to touch and share deeply and openly all the tragic and joyful dimensions of life."[28] Wise words, don't you think? They're words flowing from facing the fragile splendor of a truly loving relationship.

Create Your Relationships Self-Care Fitness Plan

Go back and review the insights and methods that you liked as you read this chapter. Include at least six ideas you came up with around your OK or NS issues on the checkup. You'll find more grist for the mill by looking at the other chapters, which also have resources for enriching intimate relationships—sex and wholeness (chapter 10), women's and men's wholeness (chapter 11), and the discussion of parenting for peace, justice, and the environment (chapter 8).

Using your creativity, write out a realistic Self-Care Plan to enjoy and increase the wholeness of your intimate relationships. If you're working with a partner, create a joint plan, using what you learned from the IRM and the RSJI.

Remember, your plan probably will be more effective if it includes five things: (1) concrete, realizable objectives that you really want to achieve; (2) practical strategies for moving toward these; (3) a time line, especially when you'll begin; (4) rewards you'll give yourself as you take each step toward objectives or withhold if you stay stuck; (5) a record of your progress in your *Journal.* Keep what you plan playful (as well as serious) and spiritually energized.

Pick one or more especially attractive and achievable objectives and begin moving toward them immediately. I wish you love-nurturing, mutual self-care in your most important relationships.

Enhancing Well Being and Avoiding Burnout in Your Work

The trouble with being in

the rat race is that even if

you win, you're still a rat!

—*Lily Tomlin*

EMPLOYEES WHO DON'T

HAVE HERNIAS AREN'T

CARRYING THEIR SHARE OF

THE LOAD!

—*sign in a business office*

Ask yourself this important question: Do I enjoy my work enough that I'd choose to do at least parts of it for the satisfactions it gives, even if I were not paid to do it? I've asked several hundred workshop participants this question. I point out that those of us who can say yes are part of a fortunate minority in our society who love their work enough that it contributes significantly to their psychological and physical wellness.

A crucial way to enhance your overall well being is to make your work as fulfilling and self-esteem building as you can. This may not be easy, but it *is* possible. If you're like most of us, your work consumes forty hours of each week for forty-eight to fifty weeks a year, for about forty years, a huge portion of your total life. Doing work that you hate all this time can be destructive to your health in many ways. In contrast, doing work that you like can nurture your wellness in several ways. It can give the warm satisfaction of providing financially for yourself and the people and causes you care about. Competence in your work and the accomplishments that flow from it can undergird awareness of your self-worth. Constructive work can increase your zest for living by the knowledge that you are doing something worthwhile in a needy society.

The world of work in industrialized countries is convulsing in a major earthquake today, an earthquake caused by rapid social change and triggered by the hi-tech revolution. Millions of people feel caught in its epidemic of work-related problems. Their work is a burden.[1] Rather than enhancing their health, it diminishes their total well being. Many hate what they feel they must do to survive. They

IF YOU CAN'T GET YOUR

WORK DONE IN 24 HOURS,

WORK NIGHTS!

—lapel button

feel trapped in no-exit jobs. Their only work-related rewards are the things the paycheck buys, the TGIF release, and short-term liberation during vacations. In addition, countless people suffer from some degree of painful burnout. Having lost any love of and meaning in their jobs, they drag themselves through their work days. They put in their time, often inefficiently and ineffectively.

In addition to boring, meaningless jobs, a plethora of other work-related problems diminish the wholeness of millions. These include menial, repetitious, underpaid work; work addictions; chronic unemployment; underemployment (working far below one's potential); misemployment (round pegs in square holes); cutthroat, dog-eat-dog jobs; career trauma from technology-caused obsolescences; and uncreative retirement. Other common work-related problems are the cruel pressure of having to hold two low-paying jobs to make ends meet; the underpaying of women and their ghettoization in poorly esteemed, underpaid occupations; job discrimination against ethnic minorities and the disabled; and a variety of health hazards from toxic chemicals, pollution, and radiation in the workplace.[2]

In a recent issue of the *Los Angeles Times* four large ads appeared

"My day? One amazing slam-dunk after another."

Work can be used, as can anything and everything we do, to communicate our love for self-and-others.

—Marsha Sinetar

(next to the ads seeking game show contestants). The bold-faced headlines seemed to shout: "JOB PRESSURES TOO MUCH? OVERWORK? HEADACHES? STRESS? HARASSMENT? EMOTIONAL OR PHYSICAL PAIN? DEPRESSED? BURNED OUT? UNFAIRLY FIRED? MISTREATED? POOR SLEEP? CALL WORK TRAUMA HOTLINE ANYTIME!" Those who develop such hotline services are cashing in on our society's epidemic of work-related frustration, anger, and health problems.

All these challenges make it increasingly urgent that we all discover ways to enhance wholeness in the workplace—for ourselves and our society. How can you change your work or your workplace and your attitudes toward your work so they stimulate your wellness? What follows will focus on job issues, but the ideas, with some adaptations, apply to everyone's work. This includes the learning work of students; homemaking work of housewives and househusbands; the valuable work of countless volunteers who empower community services and religious organizations; and the continuing productive activities of the retired.

Work Well-Being Checkup

CHECKLIST

Taking this checkup can be useful to you in two ways. (1) It's a way to give you a quick diagnostic feel for your work's impact on your health. (2) It provides a variety of suggestions for avoiding burnout and increasing your wholeness in and through your work.

Instructions: In front of each statement put one of three initials: E = I'm doing excellently in this; OK = I'm doing all right, but there is room for improvement; NS = Things definitely need strengthening in this area.

_____ I love my work and find it generally challenging and fulfilling.

_____ I'm paid adequately for my work so that I have basic economic security.

_____ My work enables me to enjoy using many of my talents and skills.

_____ If I could live my life over several times, I'd choose the same work in at least one of them.

_____ After retirement, when I look back over my job history, I'll feel generally satisfied with what I did. (If you're retired, put this in the present tense.)

_____ I don't overload my work day with too many demands or with unrealistic expectations. When I have many things to do, I prioritize and focus on one thing at a time.

_____ I'm not compulsive about my work and keep a healthy balance between work and play in my life.

_____ I approach at least some aspects of my work playfully and laugh frequently with others there.

_____ I feel that I'm fulfilling my purpose in life by my work, at least in part. I know it helps rather than hurts people.

_____ I have constructive relationships with most of the people at work and I don't let the difficult people get to me for long. When conflicts arise, I face them and work out fair compromises.

_____ I receive the appreciation I deserve from my boss and give appropriate appreciation to anyone I supervise.

_____ I eat a healthful breakfast before work and enjoy a nutritious lunch without frequent high-pressure lunchtime business.

_____ The stresses and frustrations in my work don't hurt my mental or physical health.

_____ I don't use alcohol or other recreational drugs during the work day to prop up my self-confidence or deaden my frustrations.

_____ When I'm under pressure, I give myself several change-of-pace breathers during my work day.

_____ I can laugh at myself when I put absurdly high expectations on myself.

_____ When something unfair, unhealthy, or demeaning (to myself or others) happens on the job, I cooperate with others to protest and work for constructive changes.

_____ If my work situation should become chronically frustrating or conflict painfully with my basic values, I'll change jobs.

_____ My work and my leisure activities complement and balance each other.

_____ I let myself really savor my work successes, large or small.

_____ I learn from mistakes in my work and don't waste energy brooding over them.

_____ I usually don't take my work home with me either literally or emotionally.

_____ I don't lose sleep over job problems.

_____ I get out of bed on work days with some feelings of zest.

_____ I don't frustrate myself or cripple my job effectiveness by chronic procrastination.

_____ Fears of failure don't push me unmercifully or prevent me from doing some creative risking in my work.

_____ I function effectively in the system within which I work, without feeling I'm selling my soul to it.

_____ I don't give or tolerate sexual, racial, or ageist harassment in the workplace.

_____ I plan my ongoing work life as a part of intentional life planning and goal setting.

Using Your Findings: To derive the most benefit from this checkup, scan the items you marked E, OK, and NS. This will give you a general impression of your job well being. Give yourself a deserved pat on the back for the E items.

Now, for future use, jot down (in your *Self-Care Journal*) the items you scored either NS or OK that are important to you, along with tentative thoughts about what you might do to increase your work wholeness in those areas.

Understanding Work Burnout

Before focusing on practical things you can do to prevent or treat burnout, let's look at the nature and causes of this widespread problem. The term *burnout* refers to what happens to rockets after they consume all their fuel and rush ahead on sheer momentum, until air friction or gravitation slows them and eventually drags them back to earth. Do you ever feel like that in your life and work?

What are some warning symptoms of burnout? It's a sneaky malady, so recognizing the early signs can help you nip it in the bud. The most prominent symptom is a creeping loss of purpose, passion, and zest in your life and work, a feeling of being stressed out. Other closely related symptoms include

- feelings of having to run to stand still;

- chronic fatigue, in spite of having spent enough time resting and sleeping;

- lack of adequate energy to handle the demands of your work and relationships;

- increased feelings of self-doubt, inadequacy, irritability, ethical confusion, depression, hopelessness, helplessness, cynicism, and failure, and inability to laugh at oneself or one's situation;

- multiple psychosomatic illnesses such as frequent colds, headaches, stomach problems, and back pains.

Who is work burnout most likely to hit? It is epidemic among those in people-helping and healing occupations, like teachers, doctors, nurses, and clergy. It is also prevalent among those in high-pressure business and industry positions, especially those with Type A drivenness, fierce competitiveness, and chronic conflict with co-workers. It occurs, too, among persons in menial, undervalued, and underpaid jobs. It is common but often unrecognized among over-loaded homemakers, especially single parents and mothers with young children whose mates shirk their fair share of the dirty work around the house.

Perfectionistic, idealistic, self-driving, go-it-alone workaholics are especially vulnerable to burnout. Their problems often stem from a lack of mature, self-worth-strengthening answers to the basic identity questions, Who am I? What am I worth? What can I do that really matters? Because of their low self-esteem, such persons fear displeasing others. They are reluctant to say no even to unrealistic demands by others. Unfortunately, there is an abundant supply of dependent people waiting to attach themselves to "helpers" who can't protect themselves from others' neediness. For this reason, folks who are overcommitted to helping dependent people—at the price of neglecting their own self-care—are cases of burnout waiting to happen.

For preventing as well as treating burnout, it's important to distinguish internal and external causes. External causes usually produce burnout only if persons are rendered vulnerable by inner factors. This is good news, since most of us have more potential control over internal than external causes. Internal causes include one's attitudes and feelings, with low self-esteem and lack of a sturdy sense of purpose being central. Other inner causes include

- fear of anger and conflict, producing avoidance rather than resolution of conflict and injustices;

- painful inner fights between your idealized self-image and your human needs and impulses;

- time crunches among three conflicting demands: the demands of your job, your family (or other loved ones), and your self-care needs. In people flirting with burnout, family needs and especially self-care usually get terribly shortchanged.

External contributors to burnout come from unhealthful work environments. These usually have

- high levels of conflict and criticism and low morale;

- poor communication among different parts of the organization;

- authoritarian or weak, vacillating leadership;

- exaggerated expectations, producing chronic overwork;

- economic exploitation through inadequate pay and overwork;

- unfair evaluation and advancement on the job, and lack of affirmation for work well done;

- sexist, racist, ageist, and classist harassment and discrimination;

- little or no sense of mutual support or teamwork;

- lack of caring about persons who are hurting;

- lack of humor except hostile, put-down humor.

Whether they're businesses, industries, schools, service agencies, government institutions, or voluntary agencies, including congregations, such organizations are "craziness making." The pathology of these organizations produces dangerous health hazards for everyone they touch. (Suggestions for helping reduce institutional pathology are found later in this chapter.)

The Importance of Life-Work Planning

A key to avoiding burnout and enhancing your work wellness is building intentional life-career planning into your life-style. Richard Bolles, innovative author of vocational self-help books, makes it clear that career planning can be done effectively only in the context of developing more workable plans for your life as a whole. He declares: "The key to finding a job or career in which one can be most effective and productive is to discover what skills one has and most enjoys using, and to find what one's enthusiasms are. . . . For, in finding the work you truly enjoy, you will also find the work you will do best, and—thus—your mission in life."[3]

Life-Work Planning Tool

Here is a life-work planning tool, developed by John Landgraf, which you can use now to gain insights about your basic skills, enthusiasms, values, and style.[4] Take fifteen minutes to complete this now.

Instructions: In the upper left quadrant jot down what you regard as your best skills and abilities. / Now do the same with your keenest interests, in the upper right; your highest values in the lower left; and your personal style, in the lower right quadrant. /

Additional Instructions: Evaluate your present paid or volunteer work—or the work for which you're preparing—by putting plus marks in front of the skills, interests, values, and style characteristics that are used or expressed well in your work. / Put minus marks in front of those skills, gifts, and so on that are not used or expressed well. /

Put two or more plus or minus marks in front of items that are wonderfully used or grossly neglected. /

Note the rough ratio of plus and minus marks to see how well your present or anticipated job utilizes your unique resources.

MAJOR CONSIDERATIONS IN CAREER-LIFE PLANNING

My best abilities and skills are, or I'm very good at (e.g., public speaking; carpentry; selling; teaching):	My keenest interests are, or I get most excited about (e.g., studying other cultures; helping others; music; science):
1.	1.
2.	2.
3.	3.
4.	4.
5.	5.
Etc.	Etc.
My highest values are, or it is most important to me (e.g., that I make lots of money; stay healthy; make a difference):	My personal style is, or I'm the type of person who (e.g., likes variety; being my own boss; working out of doors):
1.	1.
2.	2.
3.	3.
4.	4.
5.	5.
Etc.	Etc.

Now, as the payoff step, let your imagination play as you create a picture in your mind of yourself doing work that respects your skills, values, interests, and style very fully. For the time being, don't worry about how realistic your picture is. Just experience how it is to be doing the ideal work for one unique person—you.

Reflect on your ideal job in light of the realities of your training and the current job market.

Using Your Time to Move Toward Your Life-Career Goals

Do you ever feel that your date book is a pocket dictator, that your schedule is running you rather than vice versa? If so, to grow in well being on and off the job you probably need to increase your control over your time so that you can use it more intentionally. One simple technique to bring some order to an overloaded schedule is to write out a "To-Do" list, updating it as you plan each day (usually the night before). It's helpful to put a star beside the items on the list that are the most urgent and those most important to complete.

Planning your time so that you will move toward both your short- and longer-term goals is a central ingredient of life-career planning. A classic guide to doing this is Alan Lakein's *How to Control Your Time and Your Life*.[5] His philosophy is that time is life. Therefore by using planning to gain control of your time, you increase control of your life and also make the most of whatever time you have available. He sees planning as a way of bringing the future into the present, and thus doing something constructive about it. Even brief planning periods at the beginning and end of your day can repay your time investment in ways that may surprise you. A crucial first part of planning your days, your career, your leisure, or your life is setting self-chosen, realistic goals.

Wholeness Exercise

Goal-Setting Exercise. Here's my version of Lakein's basic goal-setting tool.[6] Use it now—it requires only about fifteen minutes—to identify concrete long- and short-range goals. At the top of a page in your *Well Being Self-Care Journal* write: *What are my lifetime goals?* / Now, in not more than five minutes, list all the things you want to accomplish during the rest of your life. Include all your goals—personal, family, career, social, financial, creative, ecological, spiritual, community service, recreational, etc. List everything that seems truly important for you to accomplish. / Are some of your goals rather amorphous, like more love, happiness, health, peace of mind, success, enjoying my loved ones, having fun, improving my community? To make these goals more focused and concrete, write this question at the top of another page: *What would I like to accomplish in the next five years?* / List your answers in not more than five minutes. / Now, shorten your perspective by writing at the top of another page: *If I knew that I would be struck dead by lightning six months from today, what would I want to do before then?* (Assume that you've already taken care of the things related directly to death, such as making a will.) In not more than five

I think you will find that if
you arrange things so that
you find time to relax and
'do nothing,' you will get
more done and have more
fun doing it.

—Alan Lakein

minutes list the things that are important to accomplish in your radically reduced future. /

Now, pick the three most important goals from each of your three lists. Entitle another page *My Most Important Life-Work Goals,* and list these nine on that page. / Number them in order of importance to you. This is your Lifetime Goal Statement (LGS). / Decide on concrete, do-able activities, things you can start doing immediately, to move toward the top four goals on your LGS. / Put these on your to-do list each day, and schedule at least fifteen minutes to move toward one or more of these very high priority goals. As you do this, you may discover that you can gradually add more time and eventually also add more goals from your LGS.

The problem that stops me in my tracks when I use this exercise is that I usually want to accomplish two or three times what is possible for me in any given period. Because of this, I often find Lakein's suggestion to "repeal Parkinson's Law" useful. This means not allowing the food (time) to fill (or overfill) all the available space in the refrigerator (your schedule). To accomplish this, prioritize your goals and then use what Lakein calls the 80/20 Rule. You'll probably find that 80 percent of your satisfactions will come from 20 percent of the items on your daily (or your lifetime) To-Do list. If so, work out ways to spend larger chunks of your time on your most valued items. In case you're wondering if Alan Lakein's methods are suited only to charter members of Work-Addicts Anonymous, consider his statement: "I think you will find that if you arrange things so that you find time to relax and 'do nothing,' you will get more done and have more fun doing it." [7]

The Competence-Satisfaction Cycle

Ramon, age twenty-six, was in a frustrating job situation that provided him with an easy excuse for resting on the oars and doing sloppy work. In so doing he expressed his resentment toward a "stupid, slave-driving boss" and a company that didn't appreciate his abilities. But he began to realize that as long as he did this, he was putting himself in a self-sabotaging double bind. His anger was turned inward, producing depression, slipping morale, and burnout, all of which increased his sloppy work. The more his work deteriorated, the more criticism he deserved and got, and the more reasons he had to feel disgruntled about his job and crummy boss.

Are you in a toxic job in which you feel caught in a double bind like Ramon's? If so, there are two parallel paths you can take to help interrupt self-defeating cycles and, in the process, perhaps find a little more work satisfaction. (The same general options exist in most other difficult situations, including toxic relationships.) The two

I'M NOT TRYING TO WORK

HARDER, JUST SMARTER

—bumper sticker

main possibilities you have are (1) to change your *attitudes* (discussed below) and (2) to change your *behavior*, for example, by increasing your skills and improving your quality of work, or by choosing to relate more cordially and cooperatively to the people with whom you work. It might help your sagging morale and self-esteem to do both (1) and (2) simultaneously. If you decide you will do higher-quality work, the results could surprise you pleasantly. Who knows, you might get some appreciative feedback from your shocked boss. In any case, your self-esteem probably will rise as you feel better about yourself and become more employable. This will be a valuable asset if you decide to exercise your third option, finding a healthier job and telling your present employer to stuff it.

Creative Coping with Job Pressures

I hope you've already picked up some practical ideas that you can use to avoid burnout and enjoy more work wellness. As you'll recall, the checkup earlier in this chapter was full of suggestions. To highlight some of the crucial steps you can take, here is a baker's dozen of guidelines for making your work life healthier.

1. As suggested above, use intentional life and career planning regularly, especially during times of loss and transition. In this way you can get into the driver's seat of your life. You can use prioritizing and planning to avoid letting an overstuffed schedule run your life, and run you into the ground.

2. Plan your schedule to have regular times for self-care and fun. Include three or four mini-vacations each day. Take one or two real "days off" each week and a real vacation each year.

3. Plan your schedule to have some quality time with your family and friends each day.

4. Take good care of your body with healthful nutrition, regular big-muscle exercise, adequate rest, and satisfaction of your sensual needs. Be extra good to yourself when you're physically run down and therefore especially vulnerable to stress-caused illnesses and burnout.

5. Balance work and play, spicing your work with playfulness. Laugh with others, at yourself, and at the craziness in your workplace. (More on this below.)

6. Don't store up anger, resentment, guilt, or anxiety on the job or elsewhere. Burnout blossoms around the buildups of these heavy feelings.

7. Learn to replenish your inner springs and reduce stress each day at home by using methods such as meditation, full body relaxation, imaging, music, prayer, poetry, creative movement, art,

inspirational reading, making love, meaningful communication, recreation, and playfulness.

8. Practice the principle of alternation, mixing left-brain and right-brain activities. If your work uses mainly left-brain analytical, verbal, and mathematical skills, mingle in a right-brain break occasionally (like those in number 7).

9. Be open to letting others appreciate and nurture you, as you do the same for them. (More on this below.)

10. If your priorities, self-demands, and life-style are causing you to flirt with burnout, revise these to reduce pressure and give yourself more self-care.

11. Practice the fine art of saying no whenever your circuits are getting overloaded, people are making excessive demands, or you're shortchanging your self-care.

12. Keep growing and excited about something that's important in your life, your work, and your world. Thus increase the overlap of your work life and your life work.

13. Treat yourself with more love, caring, and self-forgiveness as a precious daughter or son of the divine Spirit, both on and off the job.

Liberating Yourself in Your Workplace

There are frustrations, person-to-person conflicts, and at least a little craziness even in relatively healthy workplaces. These burnout producers result from the flawed interaction of us imperfect human beings, as well as the chaotic work scene. Perfect jobs, like perfect marriages, seem to exist only in fairy tales and fantasies. If you decide to stay in a frustrating job, after you've done whatever you can to eliminate injustices and other stressors, there are things you can do to help yourself stay relatively sane. Deciding to change your attitudes from negative, self-hurting ones to positive, relationship-building ones is the heart of these self-caring strategies. Let's look at some self-protective attitudinal and relationship changes.

If you have a vocational lemon and you choose to stay with it, see if you can discover some way to make lemonade. I'm not suggesting that you stay in a deadend, toxic work situation. Having the courage to get out of a debilitating job, like taking the risk of leaving a toxic relationship, is often an essential and courageous step toward wholeness. But if you elect to stay with a frustrating job, for whatever reasons, exercise your ultimate freedom, the freedom to choose your attitude toward external situations. Remain open to the positive possibilities that often are well-hidden in negative situations. For example, if you're stuck with doing boring, repetitive work, on your job or at home, you'll probably discover that your mind can function on two levels, doing routine tasks and wrestling with something more creative, playful, and interesting simultaneously.

Another thing you can do is *find ways to get more satisfactions and self-esteem nurturance outside your job.* Don't put all your eggs in your job basket. Do more smelling of the roses and enjoying members of your family, your friends-and-fun circle, and your community or congregation. Many folks stay relatively healthy in frustrating jobs they choose not to leave by cultivating mutual support and appreciation with people outside work.

You can also make a frustrating job healthier for you by *cultivating mutually supportive relationships with one or more compatible friends there.* Such friendships can be fun as well as strengthening for each person's self-esteem. Some job conflicts can be avoided by such a strategy. Denis Waitley and Reni L. Witt, in *The Joy of Working*, highlight the crucial importance of self-worth in both job effectiveness and enjoyment: "Self-esteem is the first key to finding happiness on the job. Self-esteem is the cornerstone of success. It's that deep-down feeling in your soul of your own self-worth. Individuals who enjoy their work develop strong beliefs of self-worth and self-confidence. They weren't necessarily born with these good feelings. They might have even been made to feel clumsy and stupid in their youth. But as working adults, they learned to like themselves through practice."[8]

Unfortunately, the way people are treated in many workplaces lessens their self-esteem. Particularly in hi-tech workplaces, the hi-touch of supportive relationships and good positive communication is essential to wholeness.[9] A younger colleague of mine shared these moving memories of his father's long career with a large corporation: "Watching him work, the conviction has grown in me that to work can be a great joy. But it's the people, the relationships that transform it into something of great value in the course of a lifetime. As I have listened to my father talk about his work, it is not so much what he did as who he worked with and came to know that is of importance to him now [that he is retired]."[10]

Here are some suggestions for increasing mutual support and people satisfactions in your workplace.

1. Do the communicating (including listening) it takes to build a friendship with work associates with whom you feel some rapport and who share your interests. Speaking personally, it helped me survive three decades of graduate teaching with some semblance of sanity to have a colleague who became a close personal friend, confidant, and trusted source of mutual support. In spite of his busy schedule, he was there for me in both the ups and downs of my personal and professional life. I think that he would say the

same of me. Our regular lunch talks were like refreshing oases in the parched terrain that the academic world can sometimes be for faculty as well as for students.

2. Find something to appreciate (honestly) in your colleagues, telling them what you like. I suspect you've noticed that mutual affirmation is in short supply in many workplaces, particularly those where the emotional climate is chilled by conflict and fierce competition among peers. A gift of honest appreciation from another bolsters your self-esteem. It also nurtures mutual respect and caring. Stay open to opportunities to give positive strokes as an expression of your regard for your work associates. It may shock them a bit at first and they may suspect manipulation, but never mind, they'll love it. If you're a supervisor, it's very important to give sincere affirmation whenever possible, particularly when you must also give correction or criticism. The IRM described in chapter 5 can be used to prevent as well as resolve conflicts and to enhance staff relationships.

3. Open yourself to receiving whatever affirmation and caring feedback is available in your workplace. For several years I noted a strange fact about my fluctuating energy levels on my job. After certain days of doing my usual thing (teaching, counseling, committee work, and relating with colleagues), I felt wiped out. I was exhausted both emotionally and physically. On other days with comparable work, I came home physically tired but emotionally energized. It finally dawned on me (why did it take so long?) that there was one simple difference. On the wipeout days I had approached my work from a kind of professional Charles Atlas posture. Without being aware, I was carrying an enormous burden. I was shouldering the heavy, hard-driving (and also lonely) feeling of responsibility for "making it happen," whatever "it" happened to be on a particular day. Though I often worked as long and as hard on the other days, I was somehow more open, receptive, and vulnerable. In terms of my responsibilities, I felt less like a one-person band and more like a player (or, at times, a conductor) of an orchestra. I enjoyed students and staff, clients and colleagues more and did more laughing with them.

4. Keep in touch with your playful inner child while working. It's healthy to heed poet Ruth Bebermeyer's advice to "cherish the child playing hide and seek in your soul with your grown up self."[11] For the sake of your well being on the job, laugh within yourself as well as with others at the funny, stupid, and absurd things that happen in your workplace. By adding a playful touch whenever it's appropriate, you may lighten your own work load as well as bring a welcome gift to others there.

Hans Selye, the Canadian physician who did pioneering research in understanding stress, observed that ideally work should be joyful play.[12] In most people's work world of deadly drudgery, a goal such as this may seem to be middle-class vocational elitism. But consider the ways oppressed human beings in many cultures have learned to cope with their drudgery and to create a saving sense of community within it by singing and enjoying camaraderie while working.

In my memory bank I cherish a picture from early boyhood of my mother, standing at the kitchen sink, softly humming hymn tunes she loved while doing monotonous chores. My daughter Susan, in reflecting on a frustrating job she had, observed: "I've found that in my job, characterized mainly by endless repetition, learning how to laugh and relate to the people I work with is the only thing that gives it any meaning."[13] More about intermingling playfulness and work in the next chapter.

5. Release the inner pressure to be a people-pleaser and to always say yes. High vulnerability to the inflated expectations of controlling or dependent people is rooted in shaky self-esteem. This produces an exaggerated need to be liked and excessive fear of rejection if one says no. This syndrome is a major cause of stress overload and burnout. Protecting yourself involves gaining a tad more self-esteem so that you can respect your own needs more and practice the fine art of saying no, thus making time for the self-care you need.

If all these do-it-yourself techniques don't do it for you, I urge you to make a valuable investment in yourself and your work wellness by having at least a few sessions with a competent career counselor, preferably one with psychotherapeutic skills needed to deal with personality issues that frequently sabotage sound career decisions.

Recovering from Work Addiction

Work addiction is a widespread socially rewarded illness. It is characterized, like all addictions, by progressive loss of the freedom to live a sane, balanced life. This obsessive-compulsive process diminishes the health of millions of people. Such persons often are praised at their funerals for being so "dedicated to providing for their families," even though their families probably were often ignored in their consuming work addiction. Workaholics often have these characteristics. They

• work punishingly long hours with little real time off;

• get adrenalin highs from being "on a roll" of nonstop working;

- feel jittery and guilty when not working;

- make work even out of their play;

- always seem to be caught in hurry-itis, allowing too little time for most tasks and trying to do several things all at once;

- carry work home with them nights and weekends, and they may sneak work along on vacations, as a kind of anxiety-allaying security blanket;

- get chronic complaints from their loved ones about their missing important family events because they "have to work";

- suffer from a wide variety of stress-caused psychological and physical ailments;

- can stop working without overwhelming anxiety and guilt only when they get sick;

- have rationalizations that justify (to them) their need to work incessantly;

- spin their wheels while working compulsively but inefficiently;

- don't "waste time" on self-care and play.

Perfectionistic self-demands, the driving force in many work addictions, can kill whatever joy is potentially available in your work. Although perfectionism drives its sufferers to exhausting efforts, it's compulsivity tends to block the real creativity which flows from playfulness. It also ensures that nothing is ever quite good enough to permit them to enjoy their small successes. If you struggle with perfectionism, learn to practice what psychiatrist Karen Horney called "the courage of your imperfections." To do so can be good for your creativity as well as your well being. If your perfectionism is intertwined with the need to comply automatically with the expectations, unreasonable as well as reasonable, of others, it's crucial for your wholeness that you diminish or release this need also. To the degree that you can do this, you'll probably find a welcome lightening of your inner load.

Hard-core work addictions are difficult to interrupt because they're socially rewarded and because hitting bottom, so as to become open to help, happens very gradually—in slowly developing health problems in most cases. Twelve-Step group recovery programs like Workaholics Anonymous can be an effective treatment for the severely addicted who are motivated to change.[14] Individual and group psychotherapy to exorcise the psychological demons driving the compulsion may also be useful adjuncts to a Twelve-Step program, at some point in the recovery process.

*"It's for workaholics. It's a combination computer
terminal and microwave oven."*

All this isn't easy, of course. Art Buchwald once wrote an entertaining column entitled "If There's a Cure for Work Addiction, It Doesn't Work." He tells of trying (unsuccessfully) to spend a weekend away, playing with his wife, without writing. By Saturday morning he began to get the shakes as he experienced withdrawal and craved a fix of working. Although he clothed his insights in delightful humor, he illuminated vividly the drivenness of the underlying addictive process.

Workaholics often find it helpful to become aware that their exaggerated, perfectionistic self-expectations are the demanding inner parent voice (in transactional analysis terms) saying, "You'll never get my love and acceptance until you're perfect [which *is* never]. Because being perfect is the price of my love, you must keep driving yourself, hoping that you will achieve the impossible." Like other old tapes playing in our heads since childhood, it may not be possible to turn them off totally. What is possible and helpful is to turn the volume down on these tapes and learn to laugh at them when they turn on. (The re-parenting exercise described in chapter 12 may also be helpful.)

It is important to distinguish between compulsive workaholics and highly productive hard workers. The latter seem to thrive on hard work, often for long hours. Usually they love what they are doing, so there is overlap between work and play for them. Unlike the workaholic, they can relax and enjoy real re-creation in their times of playfulness.

Improving Your Workplace

It can be a contribution to your own wholeness to do whatever is possible to enhance the healthfulness of your work environment, thus reducing the organizational causes of burnout. To increase your understanding of the wholeness impact of your organization(s)—work or otherwise—I recommend that you now examine and perhaps use the survey instrument entitled "Helping Your Organization, Congregation, or Workplace Support Whole-Person Well Being," the final section of this book.

In their illuminating book *In Search of Excellence,* Thomas J. Peters and Robert H. Waterman, Jr., report on their study of thirty of America's best-run, most productive companies. Among the basic principles operative in these diverse companies was what they call "productivity through people," meaning treating employees with dignity and respect, as adults and partners whose best efforts are valued and essential. The authors declare: "There was hardly a more pervasive theme in the excellent companies than respect for the individual. . . . What makes it live in these companies is a plethora of structural devices, systems, styles and values . . . so that the companies are truly unusual in their ability to achieve extraordinary results through ordinary people. These companies give people control over their own destinies. . . . They turn the average Joe and the average Jane into winners. . . . We are not talking about mollycoddling. We are talking about tough-minded respect for the individual and the willingness to train him, to set reasonable and clear expectations for him, and to grant him practical autonomy to step out and contribute to his job."[15] Incidentally, this basic principle is one key to increasing wholeness in all types of organizations, not just businesses.

Providing family counseling or personal therapy for employees suffering from family disruption, addictions, and burnout is a growing expression of enlightened self-interest on the part of some employers. Rehabilitation of experienced workers is usually far less expensive than training replacements. It also contributes to the humane values and therefore the wholeness of the organization.

Many organizations also are adding fitness programs to their health-care benefits. (More than fifty thousand U.S. companies now have such in-house programs.) Exercise equipment, jogging tracks, weight reduction and stop-smoking programs, and lectures on fitness are among the free services provided. Some companies also open their fitness programs to families and retirees. Studies have found that programs like these reduce absenteeism, raise employee morale, and (not to ignore business's bottom line), are cost effective, increasing production and profits.[16]

It's important to cooperate with others in your workplace to eliminate unnecessary stressors, frustrations, and unfairness. Much of the wear and tear on workers can be eliminated by person-respecting personnel practices. These create a healthier work climate for everyone. Injustices of any kind militate against not only the wholeness of individuals but also of the organization. Using employee grievance procedures and, if those fail, legal recourse can be crucial to the health of both the individuals involved and the organization.

It's healthy to experience anger and take appropriate action when someone (including yourself) is being exploited or discriminated against in ways such as inadequate pay, unfair advancement and hiring and firing practices, or sexist or racist harassment—a misuse of authority. For the sake of your mind-body wholeness, not to mention your financial well being, don't smolder quietly, unless you feel you must do so temporarily to protect a job you can't afford to lose right now.

What you can do depends on your position in the power structure. If you're in a decision-making position, you have an obvious opportunity to initiate changes that may make your organization healthier for everyone. Of course, making waves in any social system upsets the people who have benefited from the unfair status quo. If you're in a subordinate position in your workplace's power structures, networking with peers is safer for you and more likely to be effective than attempting to be a one-person crusader for justice. There's a third, more desirable option to simply taking injustices passively or being a Don Quixote in the workplace. It's to come up with strategies collaboratively with your peers, rallying as many as possible around the issue. If you're part of a union, that's often an effective way to exercise this option.

Changing Jobs and Coping with Unemployment

A refreshing development in the contemporary job scene is the freedom many midyears adults exercise in having more than one career in their life spans. Perhaps you've outgrown your earlier vocational choice. If so, an exciting new chapter may be opened in your life by taking the scary leap of faith and moving into a new career. The same challenging opportunity confronts you if your present work is toxic to your health.

If your present job involves work that conflicts with important values in your life, a career change can contribute to your integrity and ethical wholeness. Joe, an electronics engineer in his early forties, now works as an administrator of a human services program. He gets less than half the pay he received for his work in a so-called defense industry. But he reports that the "people compensations" from his new job are great, "even though they don't pay the bills." He sleeps better than he has for years.

Before Joe resigned his job, he struggled through months of soul searching and late-night discussions with his wife, Jennifer. They knew that if Joe moved into a much lower paying job, she probably would have to get a full-time job and postpone the additional education that her part-time work was making possible. But the two of them had pangs of conscience from their awareness that Joe's engineering skills were helping to develop weapon systems capable of obliterating millions of innocent children and adults and doing irreparable damage to the biosphere in a few minutes.

Many of their friends have expressed admiration of the couple's considerable ethical courage in the joint decision to change Joe's job. Several of his former colleagues have affirmed his courage and have spoken of their own uneasy consciences, even though they haven't made the same decision. The most difficult adjustment has been for Joe's and Jennifer's teenage son, David. He is upset about the economic pressure the whole family is experiencing, even though his parents included him in some of their discussions before they made their decision.

Before making a career change, for whatever reasons, it's important to look and plan carefully before you leap. Do an analysis of your gifts, interests, and aptitudes in relation to the fluctuating job market. Which work options will contribute most to your fulfillment and sense of purpose in life? The assistance of a competent vocational guidance professional can be especially valuable in making a wise decision when you're at a vocational crossroads.

IF YOU THINK THE SYSTEM

IS WORKING, TALK TO

SOMEONE WHO ISN'T

—*bumper sticker*

The crisis of unemployment forces many people to turn in a new direction vocationally. Unemployment is a triple threat for nearly everyone—hitting them in the pocketbook (often disastrously), shaking their self-esteem, and often disturbing family stability. Few life crises threaten most people's overall well being more than prolonged unemployment. Here are some suggestions for coping constructively with the impact of this crisis.

1. Recognize that you are in grief from multiple losses and do your grief work (see chapter 9).

2. Turn toward people, accepting their help, rather than turning away out of embarrassment. Join a job transitions support group if one exists near you or take the initiative in starting one.[17]

3. Use your work crisis as an opportunity to do a careful evaluation of your career direction, perhaps with the help of a vocational counselor. Consider redirecting your vocational life.

4. Read Richard Bolles's *What Color Is Your Parachute?* and use the "Quick Job Hunting Map" in that book.

5. If the crisis disturbs your family relationships seriously, seek the help of a well-trained specialist in marriage and family counseling.

W I N D O W   O F   W H O L E N E S S

DOROTHY DAY

Journalist, social worker, and crusader for society's rejects, Dorothy Day was wonderfully responsive to the suffering of the victims of work trauma, the unemployed, the poor, and the homeless. While a reporter for a New York newspaper, she was horrified by what she observed in the slums. Like Mother Teresa, whose philosophy she shared, she decided that she must share the misery of the poor by living and working with them in voluntary poverty. A convert to Roman Catholicism, she felt deeply alienated from any religion that ignores the misery of the world.

In 1917 she picketed the White House for women's suffrage and was arrested and put in jail. At the height of social devastation of the Great Depression, she started a one-cent monthly newspaper, the *Catholic Worker.* It wedded the spirituality of her religious tradition and a passionate challenge to awaken the consciences of her church and her country on social issues. She became painfully aware of the profound interrelatedness of widespread poverty, the inequities of our society's economic system, and other peace and justice issues. Living out its credo—"Immediate response to the need of the other person"—the Catholic Worker Movement that she inspired and led established a network of "houses of hospitality" in almost every major American city. The hungry were fed and the homeless given shelter, and countless young people, living in hopelessness because they could not find jobs, were helped. With the dawn of the nuclear age, Day and her movement steadfastly opposed the "warfare state's" preparation for a nuclear war. She was imprisoned several times for protesting compulsory civil defense drills and demonstrating in support of the United Farm Workers' boycott.

Dorothy Day chose to live among the poorest of the poor. She developed a deep bond of love for them. Amid the exhausting struggles for justice, she often renewed her inner strength by spending time by the sea and engaging in prayer retreats. She was like Gandhi in many ways, including finding relaxation in spinning wool. She died in her eighties at the Catholic Worker's hospice on New York City's lower east side in 1980. Her tough love, rooted in justice, had impelled her to continue her work until the time of her death. Her inspiring life and passion for economic wholeness were a key force in mobilizing the witness and caring of her whole church for those crippled by social, economic, and job oppression.

Work Spirit and a Sense of Vocation

From counseling with people who were struggling with painful work problems, I have concluded that *nothing is more important to work wellness than discovering some sense of meaning in one's work.* Have you noticed that people who are on fire with love for their work and see it as somehow expressing their basic purpose in life thrive on challenges, stresses, and hard work? Most such persons are not only highly productive, they usually don't suffer from either work addiction or burnout. Why?

The answer was identified by USC professor Sharon L. Connelly, who did a study of twenty people whom she described as possessing "work spirit." This meant that they enjoyed their work tremendously and had outstanding levels of achievement and excellence in it. The qualities she identified as essential to work spirit included "a sense of vision and purpose with a commitment to a larger meaning in their work," "a sense of oneness with a higher order giving a sense of calling," and "tremendous energy often described as channeled *through* them."[18] It's noteworthy that work spirit seems to be precisely what empowered Dorothy Day.

The Buddhist way of describing this vocational alignment in one's life is "right livelihood."[19] In the Christian tradition such a love affair with your work is called having a "vocation" (literally a calling) or a "mission from God." A wholistic perspective on work sees *all* constructive work as being of genuine worth in the wider context of the universe. Therefore, everyone who is so engaged can understand their work as a calling, not just those whose work is so designated by their religious groups. This way of talking about work may seem a bit too lofty if you're not spiritually inclined. But finding a wider purpose in your work is essential for you to feel genuinely fulfilled there.

From a wholeness perspective, each of us has a calling—a calling to use our brains, imaginations, gifts, skills, and love in ways that may help make the world a little more loving and whole for all the children of the human family. When you're doing that, your work is expressing, to some significant degree, the loving purposes of the universe for you. Here's the key question to ask yourself: Where do my unique gifts and the world's crying needs intersect? That is the point where you'll find that your work life and your life work coincide. When these two come together in you, they will enliven and empower your life and work in ways that enhance your wholeness and bring wholeness to others through you!

Create Your Work Self-Care Fitness Plan

Go back and review the ideas that attracted you as you read this chapter. Include the items you marked OK or NS on the checkup and those derived from the picture you generated of the ideal work that would fully use your abilities, values, interests, and personal style. Pick at least six things from these items, and decide on actions you want to take to increase the wholeness of your work life. Using your creativity, write out a realistic Self-Care Change Plan to make your work life more whole, fulfilling, and zestful.

Remember, your plan will be more effective if it includes: (1) concrete, realizable objectives that you really want to achieve;

(2) practical strategies for moving toward these by overcoming obstacles and resistances; (3) a time line, especially when you'll begin; (4) rewards you'll give yourself as you take each step toward your objectives, or withhold if you backslide. (5) a record of your movement and new insights that emerge as you implement your plans. Try to keep what you do love centered and spiritually energized.

For starters, pick one or two especially attractive objectives and begin taking steps toward them in the next day or two.

If inner resistances threaten to stymie your progress, try creating a movie in your mind each day for a few minutes. Experience yourself doing what you plan successfully and enjoying it. Balance your serious intentions with a touch of playfulness so you'll enjoy giving yourself more self-care in this vital area of your life.

Using Laughter and Playfulness for Healing and Health

The best doctors in the world are Dr. Diet, Dr. Quiet and Dr. Merryman.

—Jonathan Swift

An important and joyful way to wellness is to let yourself experience the healing energy of playfulness and laughter—regularly! Laughing at yourself and the absurdities of life, and with others, is an inexpensive, easily available, drug-free form of stress reduction that certainly can add life to your years and probably some years to your life. It's one of the simplest, healthiest, and most liberating health gifts you can give your mind, body, and spirit. The goal of this chapter is to provide insights and methods for you to use to raise your AQ (Aliveness Quotient) by enhancing your PPQ (Play-Pleasure Quotient).

Laughter and Playfulness Well-Being Checkup

CHECKLIST

This checkup can be a useful tool in two important ways. (1) It's a way to evaluate quickly how well you're using laughter and playfulness to increase your wholeness. (2) The statements on the checkup are behaviors and attitudes that tend to enhance playful enjoyment of life.

Instructions: In front of each item put one of three initials: E = I'm doing great (excellently) in this; OK = I'm doing acceptably, but there's room for improvement; NS = I very much need strengthening in this.

_____ I enjoy laughing (or smiling) at myself and the crazy things in my life. When I get stuck in taking myself too seriously, I can usually deflate this by a chuckle at my self-inflation.

_____ I laugh and play with others regularly.

_____ I enjoy the playful child within me.

_____ My smile comes from my center and is seldom put on for appearances or to manipulate others.

_____ I frequently enjoy funny movies, comic plays, TV humorists, and written humor.

_____ In the midst of serious situations, I often can see something at least mildly funny.

_____ I enjoy sharing funny events and jokes with my friends and family.

_____ Laughing and playing with people I care about is a delightful way of enriching these relationships.

_____ When things get boring or tense, I often lighten the situation with humor.

_____ I can laugh inwardly (if not aloud) at stuffy bureaucrats and autocrats, thus staying empowered in their presence.

_____ I can laugh at the absurd expectations I put on myself or allow others to put on me, thus lightening my load of expectations.

_____ I practice the healing power of play, giving myself several laugh breaks and mini-vacations each day.

_____ I take one or two real days off each week, carefully protecting them for self-care and enjoyment.

_____ I take a substantial vacation each year, planning it carefully to make it genuinely fun and revitalizing.

_____ I'm able to play, take a vacation, or just loaf without feeling guilty and punishing myself before or afterward.

_____ I regularly enjoy a variety of playful activities that are relaxing and rejuvenating.

_____ I use light TV programs or light reading or other healthy escapes when things get too heavy.

_____ I enjoy playful activities alone as well as with friends and family.

_____ My work and play tend to overlap—I'm occasionally playful at work and productive when I'm playing.

_____ I have discovered that my laughter and tears can complement and enrich each other.

_____ I enliven my spiritual life by enjoying a playful relationship with God.

_____ I find a serious checkup on playfulness something of a joke.

Using Your Findings. First, scan your responses to get an overall impression of your PPQ.

Second, if it feels helpful, list in your *Self-Care Journal* the important items marked OK and NS that you might want to try so as to increase the fun and joy in your life. If you have any tentative ideas about how to do this, it may be helpful to jot these down for use at the end of this chapter.

The Healing and Stress-Reducing Power of Laughter

A cheerful heart is a good

medicine, but a downcast

spirit dries up the bones.

(Proverbs 17:22)

When man [sic] ultimately

faces his Maker he will have

to account for all those

God-given pleasures of life

of which he didn't take full

advantage.

—Sam Levinson

The belief that laughing promotes good health is an ancient one. Consider this gem from the wisdom literature of the Hebrew Bible: "A cheerful heart is a good medicine, but a downcast spirit dries up the bones" (Proverbs 17:22). The wise words of a fourteenth-century physician come to mind: "The arrival of a clown at a village does more good for the health of the inhabitants than a whole train of asses loaded with medicine."

In recent years scientific research has confirmed this ancient wisdom. Norman Cousins has pioneered in this. Reflecting on his recovery from collagen disease, he reported: "I made the joyous discovery that ten minutes of genuine belly laughter had an anesthetic effect that would give me at least two hours of pain-free sleep. When the pain-killing effect of the laughter wore off, we would switch on the motion-picture projector again, and, not infrequently, it would lead to another pain-free sleep interval."[1] Tests of his body chemistry taken just before and several hours after the laughter episodes revealed that there was a positive and cumulative improvement. Cousins's exploration has continued on a scientific basis with an imaginative, well-funded research program at the UCLA Medical School focusing on the influence of positive emotions on healing.

Dr. William Fry of Stanford has found that laughter not only increases muscular activity, heart rate, and oxygen exchange, it also stimulates the sympathetic nervous and cardiovascular system. It increases the production of hormones called catecholamines, which in turn stimulate the production of endorphins, the body's natural pain-reducing enzymes. Beta-endorphins probably are the cause of both the "runner's high" reported by some joggers and the "laughter high" some people experience during prolonged laughing.[2]

Because laughter tends to reduce stress, hypertension, and depression, it's possible that regular, vigorous laughing may increase life expectancy. Scientists involved in the "Laughter Project" at the

WINDOW OF WHOLENESS

NORMAN COUSINS

The healing power of laughter was given widespread credibility through a remarkable experience reported by Norman Cousins, then adjunct professor of medical humanities at the School of Medicine at UCLA and distinguished former editor of the *Saturday Review*. In 1976 he claimed that laughter had been a major factor in his recovery from collagen disease, a rare, painful, and nearly incurable degenerative disease of the body's connective tissues. While in the hospital he accidentally saw a disturbing letter from his physician to a mutual friend. When he saw the line "I'm afraid we're going to lose Norman," he decided it was high time to take some initiative.

Knowing that negative feelings can cause increased vulnerability to many illnesses, he speculated that laughter and positive emotions might contribute to recovery. So he checked out of the hospital and into a hotel room, having arranged to watch old Marx Brothers films and segments of the spoofing television program *Candid Camera*. At times a nurse also read to him from books of humor. He discovered that a session of laughter contributed appreciably to his body's capacity for self-healing. He reports, "It worked. I was greatly elated by the discovery that there is a physiological basis for the ancient theory that laughter is good medicine (*Anatomy of an Illness*, 39–40). Cousins labeled hearty laughter "inner jogging," noting its healthful effects on muscle relaxation, heart rate, and blood pressure.

Several years later Cousins suffered a heart attack. He again mobilized the healing powers of his body and mind in remarkable fashion. When he learned that his wife was planning a surprise party to celebrate his first year of recovery, he stopped at Universal Studios, where a makeup artist had agreed to transform him with a disguise. He showed up at his surprise party with an accomplice friend who introduced him as Professor Morton, who was visiting from London. His antics were hilarious. Even his wife and daughter were fooled by the disguise and by his speaking in a crackling voice with an English accent (Cousins, *The Healing Heart* [New York: Avon Books, 1983], 86–87).

Norman Cousins was one of the most remarkable journalists and authors of our time. He transformed the *Saturday Review* from a struggling literary journal into a highly respected weekly forum filled with ideas, world affairs, culture, and illumination of social issues. An indefatigable editor and writer with more than fifteen books to his credit, his interests and contributions were amazingly broad. With a blend of intellectual brilliance, creativity, enthusiasm, and optimism, he was a foreign correspondent, a presidential adviser, a university lecturer, a citizen diplomat, a crusader-activist on peace and ecology issues, and a researcher on whole-person health. At the dawn of the nuclear age he argued that humans must learn to live as "world citizens" or die as "world warriors." For ten years he was international president of the World Association of World Federalists. As an unofficial, behind-the-scenes ambassador,

wonderful book

he shuttled between President Kennedy, Pope John XXIII, and Nikita Khrushchev, carrying messages that eventually produced the Soviet-American nuclear test ban treaty.

Cousins obviously was committed to serious writing and to working to help heal some of the most deadly problems facing the human family. But his life was sprinkled with playfulness. In spite of his accomplishments, Cousins said that he "loves to goof off." His hobby was composing music as well as repairing and playing a century-old church organ. He continued to play baseball for years after he finished Columbia University's

Teachers College. He later enjoyed golf and tennis. In the *Saturday Review* he occasionally created elaborate, playful hoaxes. In one, a fictitious letter writer (K. Jason Sitewell) complained about a proposed congressional bill that would abolish golf. The journal *Golf World*, fooled by the prank, denounced the legislation in a heated editorial. Cousins commented on his literary hoaxes: "Spoofing has been a tradition here. We like to laugh and share our laughter with others, especially in times when there's not much to laugh about" (*Current Biography*, 1977, 120).

University of California at Santa Barbara found that a good old-fashioned thigh-slapping session of laughter reduced stress as much as a complex biofeedback training program. They point out that the laughter treatment required no special equipment or training, only a funny bone.

Psychological Rewards of Laughter and Playfulness

Beyond the physiological benefits, laughter may have these seven healthy psychological rewards:

1. Laughter can reduce stress and enhance wellness by letting you adopt a playful attitude toward the frustrating but unchangeable circumstances in your life. By changing your perspective in this way, you reduce appreciably the power of the situation to affect you with wholeness-diminishing stress. As you may have discovered, one way to avoid selling your soul to a bureaucratic institution (e.g., a job setting) is to decide to laugh (or at least smile inwardly) at the stupidity of some bureaucrats and bureaucratic policies. The same method can reduce the impact of boring meetings.

2. Laughter can reduce stress and enhance your wellness by providing a third option to flight or fight. Robert Eliot, a cardiologist on the medical faculty at the University of Nebraska, gives three rules for coping with stress: "Rule No. 1 is, don't sweat the small stuff. Rule No. 2 is, it's all small stuff. And No. 3, if you can't fight and you can't flee, flow."[3] All of your frustrations and stresses are

probably not from small things. But the next time you're in a situation where the fight-or-flight responses aren't possible or constructive—for example, with your boss, a pompous bureaucrat, or a traffic cop—try the third option, seeing if you can flow. It can save a lot of creative energy for better things than doing a slow burn.

Wholeness Exercise

> As an experiment, the next time you're stuck in a boring or frustrating meeting, from which it isn't feasible to escape, try the "inward smile" technique. See if you can find something ludicrous or silly in the situation. Or try looking at the situation through an extraterrestrial's eyes, as if you were from another planet. Then let yourself enjoy the absurdity of the situation inwardly at least.

3. Laughter can strengthen your self-esteem and sense of empowerment for handling challenging situations constructively. When you smile or laugh at the absurdity of a situation and those who perpetrate it, something transforming may occur. Whatever passive victim feelings you're experiencing will be shattered along with your anger as you allow yourself to thumb your nose (symbolically) at the situation. You thereby exercise and increase your sense of inner freedom and power. As you feel more empowered, you'll increase the chances that you'll be able to work with others to correct the injustices in the situation. In her illuminating discussion of women's strategic use of humor, Regina Barreca points to the value and empowerment of laughter in all human life: "A day during which we have laughed is a day that has not been wasted—to laugh is to affirm ourselves and our lives in a fundamental sense. . . . Humor is a way to . . . rise to meet a challenge, channel fear into pleasure, translate pain into courage."[4]

4. Laughter and playfulness can nurture wholeness by letting the little kid who's still inside you (whatever your age) act silly and clown around. Consider these familiar biblical lines from the First and Second Testaments: "A little child shall lead them" (Isaiah 11:6) and "Unless you become like a little child . . ." (Mark 10:15). A good laugh is one of the quickest and most reenergizing minivacations. There often is something freeing about being a little crazy and clowning around playfully.

   Transactional analysis (TA) sheds light on the dynamics of play as a resource for wellness. It makes it clear that the little boy or girl we once were is still within our personalities—very much alive, though not necessarily well. In TA's understanding, our inner child has two sides. Our natural child is playful, spontaneous, mischievous, fun loving, and creative. Our adapted child is under the thumb of the inner parents and therefore controlled by all manner of parent figures in the external world, seeking their approval by obeying them. Our adapted child often gets more of our attention and energy than our free-spirited natural child, who laughs spontaneously and plays with abandon. Learning to love your natural child by letting her or him play frequently can enrich your mind-body-spirit wholeness.

5. Laughing at yourself and your exaggerated self-expectations may help to lighten your stress load. As a Type A person, I sometimes allow my schedule to become absurdly packed by not practicing the art of saying no. Occasionally it's so jammed that I feel I have to wedge in time to "answer nature's call." Chuckling at myself and my crazy self-expectations is remarkably lightening, releasing the steam in the pressure cooker of self-stressing.

A friend once told of a dream in which he saw his workaholic pattern from a cosmic perspective—the way it must look to God. He saw himself as one of a frantically busy colony of ants, racing around in all directions. He reported hearing a kind of "cosmic laugh" at the sight.[5]

"Morton's on the cutting edge of pooped."

Wholeness Exercise

> Tell a friend or colleague a joke on yourself, or laugh with someone about something stupid you did. Risk being vulnerable and discover what happens in you and in that relationship.

6. Laughing at yourself and with others gives you and them a healthy "vulnerability break." If you're in a position where others tend to encourage you to wear a mask of some kind, it's important to break free of this load. Laughing at yourself can reduce your heaviness and open you to feel the renewing closeness to others that's impossible when you're "in role." There's truth in the statement attributed to Ethel Barrymore: "You grow up the first time you laugh at yourself." Psychologist Gordon Allport observed that relatively mature people have a sense of playfulness and lightness and can laugh at themselves. Lucille Ball won the hearts of a TV generation by helping us laugh at our own frailties and screwups, as we vicariously enjoyed hers.

7. Laughing and playing with others is a joy-full, healthy way to enrich those relationships. Letting your child sides frolic together is a delightful way of touching lives. In a recent survey, a sense of humor was identified as an attribute that both women and men find attractive in the other sex. When asked what they value most in a blind date, women rate a sense of humor first, followed by sensitivity and a great personality. Long-coupled people often lose the sparkle from their relationship by taking too many things with deadly seriousness. A shared laugh break in such relationships is like a breath of fresh air in a stuffy room.

   Regina Barreca highlights the communication facilitation function of humor: "Having a sense of humor about sex is like having a sense of humor about death—both allow you to have perspective on an otherwise potentially overwhelming prospect. . . . Humor breaks taboos by allowing us to talk about those issues closest to us. We should see humor as a way of making our feelings and responses available to others without terrifying our listeners."[6]

   Not all smiles are healthy, of course. Health-enhancing smiles and laughter must come from your center and be authentic. People often use smiling to manipulate others. Some folks keep smiling to manipulate themselves, hiding their despair from themselves. These are the so-called smiling depressives. There is a plastic quality about such smiles. Women and other one-down persons in our society often use smiles to hide their anger (and the pain behind it). Because of our society's taboo against anger in females, many women have learned to be sweet and smiling in

A laugh is the shortest

distance between two

people.

—Victor Borge

order to appear "feminine" and not threaten men. Unfortunately, humor often is used to put down or attack women as well as ethnic, religious, or national groups. All these forms of laughter are symptoms and causes of brokenness rather than aids to wholeness. (See Barreca's book for a discussion of the hostile, put-down nature of all sexist jokes about women.)

The Liberating Power of Laughter

I'm grateful for the healing ways laughter has helped my own life in recent years. In a period of being nearly stressed out, I enrolled in a ten-day seminar for therapists to increase my skills in using gestalt therapy methods. I went determined to appear highly competent as a therapist, learn some therapeutic techniques to use in my work, and solve a list of heavy personal issues. Because of these absurd self-expectations, the harder I tried, the more "uptight" and frustrated I became.

The night before the last day of the seminar, I went to bed in a mood of failure, convinced that I was hopelessly trapped in my defensive need to succeed. During the night I had what felt like a breakthrough dream—the key to getting free. I went to the last session with intense determination to work effectively on the dream with the gestalt therapist who was leading the seminar.

After a few minutes of talking about my dream in a labored, superserious tone, I was shocked when the therapist put a small, multicolored pillow on his head and began clowning around with his eyes and face. I instantly felt intense rejection and anger. Then from somewhere within me came a totally unexpected wave of laughter as I got a flash of the humorous absurdity of what I had been doing—making a federal case out of everything, including myself and my goals. For the first time in years I collapsed in spasms of uncontrollable laughter as my playful but long-neglected inner child was released to enjoy the freeing moment. The laughter was contagious. Soon everyone in the room was laughing uproariously.

When the outward laughter subsided, I was surprised that my inner laughter was continuing with light, bouncy, dancing feelings. A powerful image came to my mind—a wild mountain stream in the Sierras along which my sons and I had hiked years before. That stream was dancing with reckless abandon down the mountainside, its spray splashing wildly on the rocks, sparkling in the brilliant sunlight. I sensed that it was the rocks that made the stream so wild and so sparkling. (Later I realized that the rocks were the rocky problems in my life.)

Following the workshop, my inner smile continued. I was surprised and pleased to feel more in touch with my body, with nature, and with other people in a fresh, energizing way. A few days later I was walking alone on a deserted ocean beach in Santa Barbara early in the morning. As the dawning sun sparkled on the surf, a line from an old camp song from my teens began playing in my mind: "Like your dancing waves in sunlight, make me glad and free." Walking along the beach, I came upon a solitary egret fishing for breakfast in the surf. As I approached, the bird took off and soared in a gentle arc over the waves and then back to the beach. I felt my spirit soaring free as a bird with the egret.

The inner smile and lightness continued, with minor ups and downs, for several months, in spite of a series of difficult circumstances. Gradually, however, the old feelings of heaviness increased. Preoccupation with *doing* rather than *being*, with proving myself rather than enjoying being alive—all this diminished my awareness of the dancing waves and mountain stream. Then my mother became terminally ill in a nursing home two thousand miles away. The joy and freedom of the soaring bird and the laughing little boy inside me slipped away totally. Then my mother died. Her death under tragic circumstances hit me like two tons of bricks. Months of struggling to do my grief work resulted in only partial healing of my depressed heaviness.

After about a year, I attended an Ash Wednesday chapel service at the seminary where I was teaching. I went mainly out of a sense of duty, feeling no expectations of any healing of my pain. The students had planned a special ritual in which worshipers were invited to write on slips of paper what we would *give* up and what we would *take* up for Lent. Such rituals usually are not particularly meaningful for me. I thought to myself, "The last thing I gave up for Lent was giving up things for Lent." But I decided to go along with what they had planned. As I reflected on what to write, a surprising thought came to me: "Perhaps I should give up my heaviness for Lent." So I wrote this on my paper. Along with other slips it was burned ritually and the ashes used to make the sign of the cross on the foreheads of the worshipers.

To my complete astonishment, the effect was dramatic. I left the chapel feeling as though I were walking several inches above the floor. I had received a wonderful gift—my inner smile had returned with feelings of lightness and aliveness! I'm very grateful that the gift has continued for almost a decade since then, in spite of a variety of frustrations, stresses, and losses. Of course I have some heavy days, when I don't feel like laughing. But even on some of these days I'm able to experience my inner smile and thereby touch the playful little boy in me.

A variety of simple techniques may help you to awaken the inner smile with its aliveness. For example, breathing more completely, meditating for a few minutes, moving to music (actual music or music in your mind), recalling something funny you heard lately, or having a sensuous or outrageous fantasy trip may help. If you've been out of touch with the gift of healing playfulness for a long time, its recovery may come either gradually or quickly and dramatically. But befriending and enjoying your playful inner child is possible, even if you haven't been on friendly terms for years.

Your Laughter and Your Tears— Companions and Allies

If you're in an agonizing place on your life journey, you may wonder if you'll ever again feel like laughing. There is evidence that tears and laughter not only can coexist but can actually facilitate each other. Some people cannot laugh wholeheartedly because they are too afraid of drowning in the tears that may be released. When they are able to risk crying deeply, they often discover they can laugh more fully. Kahlil Gibran puts this truth lyrically:

> Your joy is your sorrow unmasked.
> And the selfsame well from which your laughter rises was
>   oftentimes filled with your tears.
> And how else can it be?
> The deeper that sorrow carves into your being, the more joy
>   you can contain.
> Is not the cup that holds your wine the very cup that was
>   burned in the potter's oven?
> And is not the lute that soothes your spirit, the very wood
>   that was hollowed with knives?[7]

Go back to the liberating mountain stream of laughter in my gestalt workshop. That probably could not have flowed in me without the preceding days of struggle to come alive. It took that painful self-confrontation to crack the protective shell of my defensive busyness. The laughter of my inner child had been sealed up too long in the cellar of my psyche. It took an experience of my own powerlessness to break the dam and let the rushing mountain stream flow with abandon.

For most of my adult years I had been unable to cry freely. My male programming had taught me a very unhealthy message: "Real men don't cry even when they're hurting like hell." Within an hour after the eruption of my laughter in the workshop, an emergency phone call informed me that a dear friend had just died. My tears flowed more freely and fully than ever before in my adult life. Surprisingly, the sense of inner joy was still there mingled with the tears. Opening the long-plugged inner channel had released the flow of both laughter and tears. What a gift!

The therapeutic uses of laughter in life-threatening illnesses is becoming increasingly prevalent. The Wellness Community is a southern California center whose purpose is to enable persons with cancer to overcome their "hopeless, helpless, passive, all-alone victim of the disease" feelings and participate in the fight for recovery, along with their physicians. The center offers a variety of resources, without charge, to help cancer patients enhance the quality of their lives and thereby increase their will to live. Along with personal counseling, nutrition classes, guided imagery, and relaxation groups, a vital part of the program is the First Sunday Brunch Joke Fest. For several hours patients take turns telling each other funny stories, including cancer jokes. As the gags get better and worse simultaneously, guffaws replace giggling and titters. A heartwarming mirth becomes contagious, and many are reduced to tears of unrestrained laughter. There are prizes for the best and worst jokes. The gales of laughter, shared enjoyment, and group support probably enhance the participants' cancer-fighting body chemistry, as their hope and their will to live are strengthened.[8]

Malcolm Boyd tells of this same close connection between joy and sorrow. Lucky, his warm, lovable dog, developed cancer. "Finally it became painful for her to set her feet on the ground. One morning I awoke to a luminous snowfall. I let the dog out into the yard and, to my astonishment, Lucky was able to run and pirouette over the soft snow, which yielded to her touch. She was buoyant. I laughed as I watched Lucky's last good run on earth. It was for her a moment of pure abandon—and for me a bitter-sweet memory."[9]

A counselor in Santa Barbara often uses laughter in her therapeutic work with cancer patients, people in deep grief, those with painful family problems as well as incest and rape survivors. In working with families she seeks to help them begin laughing and crying together again. This lets them experience the connections that were broken when they came for help.[10] In my experience of doing marriage counseling and enrichment, I find that couples often discover that playfulness is a low-cost but priceless resource for them to use in healing and nurturing their relationships.

The good news in all this is that it often is possible to choose a somewhat playful perspective on one's situation in the midst of the stresses and losses, crises and clutter. Moreover, the heavier and

Wholeness Exercise

> Pick a sore spot in your life—in your job, your relationships, or your health. / Let yourself reexperience the pain and express it in whatever ways you choose for a little while. / Now, see if you can discover anything about the situation that eventually could be seen, in retrospect, as so absurd that it might seem amusing. / If you discover such, look at your situation from that perspective for a few minutes and see if a smile begins to come. / Stay with whatever you are feeling.

more chaotic things are in your life, the more important it is to try to generate whatever playfulness you can in your attitude toward them. ✓

Laughing and Playing in a Shattered World?

With all the health values of laughter and playfulness, a troubling question remains. Is it appropriate to laugh and play in a world with so much tragedy, violence, and oppression, so much disease and death? Is it right to be playful when at least one-fourth of the children of the human family went to bed hungry last night, while we humans squander millions on ghastly weapons of planetwide suicide? If such questions have entered your mind, congratulate yourself for the ethical sensitivity it took to ask them.

Theologian Jürgen Moltmann wrestles with this dilemma: "Is it right to laugh, to play and to dance without at the same time crying out and working for those who perish on the shadowy side of life?" Moltmann answers by making it clear that he's writing about the values of play for "those who are mourning and suffering with others, who are protesting and feeling oppressed by the excess of evil in their society, who are weighted down by their own impotence so that they are either ready to despair or seek to forget it."[11] In fact, persons who care intensely about suffering people have a special need for the perspective of playfulness. Such a perspective can help prevent what aptly has been called compassion fatigue. It can help prevent the burnout that is epidemic among those committed to peace, justice, hunger, and ecology work. (and the helping professions)

Using Playfulness for Wholeness

A certain Brother Jeremiah shared these reflections about his life:

If I had my life to live over, I'd try to make more mistakes next time. I would relax. I would limber up. I would be sillier than I have been this trip. I know of a very few things I would take seriously. I would take more trips. I would climb more mountains, swim more rivers and watch more sunsets. I would eat more ice cream and fewer beans. I would have more actual troubles and fewer imaginary ones. You see, I am one of those people who lives prophylactically and sensibly and sanely hour after hour, day after day. Oh, I've had my moments; and if I had it to do over again, I'd have more of them. In fact, I'd try to have nothing else. Just moments, one after another, instead of living so many years ahead each day. . . . If I had my life to live over, I would ride more merry-go-rounds, . . . pick more daisies.[12]

These reflections brings to mind the lapel button a lively older friend sometimes wears: SOME MISTAKES ARE TOO MUCH FUN TO MAKE ONLY ONCE! A playful attitude toward living is a precious asset for stress reduction. For this reason, not taking yourself and life too seriously is one of the most serious contributions you can make to your mental, spiritual, and physical health.

It is significant that the self-healing methods developed by Carl

Wholeness Exercise

A few years ago my friend Erma Pixley gave me a delightful list by an unknown author entitled "Mini-Ways to Wellness." Perhaps you'd like to use it to stimulate your imagination as you decide on ways to give your inner child more fun breaks or mini-vacations. Here it is, with some additions of my own:

Keep a journal. Pull weeds. Don't pull weeds. Play a musical comb. Sign up for a yoga class. Look at the clouds. Take the stairs, not the elevator. Make herb tea. Drop a note to a friend. Listen to your favorite music. Dance around the living room (with or without your clothes). Listen to the rain. Have a good cry. Express appreciation. Watch a sunset. Go fishing. Plant a garden. Listen to children laugh. Run on the beach. Clean up a mess. Pet a dog. Get up early and listen to the quiet. Take a brisk walk. See a funny movie. Make a list of your good qualities. Find something good in everyone you meet. Watch the sunrise. Recycle your cans and newspapers. Laugh at yourself. Eat out. Hug a child. Eat with a friend by candlelight. Do something for peace. Sit by the fire. Cook a vegetarian meal. Chop wood. Take ten deep breaths. Take a fun trip in fantasy. Get and give a back rub. Sing your favorite song. Sit in a hot tub.

Meditate. Write a poem. Do something kind (without taking credit). Read something full of hope and love. Dance. Take a nap. Walk in the grass barefoot. Do stretching exercises. Phone someone who's lonely. Take a pottery class. Forgive yourself. Forgive someone else. Spend a weekend in a beautiful, quiet place. Row a boat. Sail a boat. Play with a new idea. Fly a kite. Comfort a child. Make love. Climb a tree. Go to the zoo. Walk around the block briskly. Hug a friend. Take a bike hike. Roller skate. Daydream. Donate blood. Clean out a closet. Go camping. Smell a flower. Plant a tree. Let yourself be silly. Reward yourself for reaching a goal. Visit a sick friend.

Let your mind play with this list. Jot down other ideas that come to you for mini-vacations. / From your list, pick three of these that you'll do today. / Plan how you'll have at least three mini-vacations every day from now on, as gifts to your wholeness.

Simonton and Stephanie Matthews-Simonton (see chapter 9) include techniques for enabling patients to give themselves permission to have fun. They recommend that participants in their retreats make a list of all the good things they do for themselves when they are sick—like resting more, not working without feeling guilty, more attention to body comforts, saying no without worrying about displeasing others. Then they suggest that participants do these things for themselves *before* they get sick, to help themselves stay well. (If you're feeling stressed out, I suggest that you pause while you try this exercise now.)

Playfulness can be a remarkably transforming, stress-reducing attitude toward your whole life. Play can also be a fertile and nurturing environment in which you activate your latent creativity. The so-called incubation period of the creative process discussed earlier (see chap. 3) is a time when relaxation and playfulness are blended. The phrase "toying with an idea" describes this phase of creativity. I invite you to let your creative inner child play now, using the exercise on p. 172 in your own way to enhance your self-care.

Using the New Leisure for Wholeness

If you're in a people-helping profession or you're a single parent or mother employed outside the home, you're probably feeling that the "new leisure" is very slow in coming to you. Unfortunately, most single parents and mothers have two full-time jobs. But the average American male has something over four months of leisure available per year—eight holidays, eight to ten vacation days, and fifty-two weekends. Typically, Americans spends only 13.5 percent of time at work, leaving more than forty hours each week for leisure activities.[13] How people spend their leisure obviously has a huge impact on their overall health levels.

What is the quality of most people's leisure? Even though we spend more than two hundred billion dollars a year on leisure, Americans on the average spend 75 percent of their leisure time in their homes, three-fourths of it watching TV. Considering the impoverished quality of much TV fare, this addiction to the plug-in-drug (and the junk food that accompanies it) diminishes the general wellness of many. With the four-day, thirty-two hour work week and earlier retirement coming before long, and as the computer revolution gathers speed, patterns of uncreative uses of leisure pose both unprecedented threats and challenging new opportunities for enhancing our wholeness.[14]

As you plan how to make your leisure more fun and more renewing, it's also well to keep a playful attitude toward your nonleisure. I like the way Richard Bolles puts this:

> When I think of the happiest and best people I know, one quality about them really sticks out. That is, while enjoying their leisure,

Wholeness Exercise

Is your life too full of oughts and shoulds? Is fun and self-care often crowded out of your schedule? If so, here are three simple steps you can take to spend more time doing things that will help lighten up your life.[15]

1. A week or two ahead, reserve blocks of time in your date book for yourself, to use in whatever self-caring, playful ways you choose.

2. Write out brief plans concerning what you'll do during these times to make them pay off with fun, renewal, and health. Richard Bolles, pioneer in life and career planning, wisely recommends: "In deciding what to do with your leisure, the principle of alternating rhythm suggests that your leisure complement your work. . . . Look for your oldest and most enjoyable skills. If your work does not employ them, choose leisure activities that will. If your work does satisfactorily employ them, . . . use your leisure to explore your newest and potentially most enjoyable skill."[16] One "leisure counselor" identifies eight directions in which many people find it helpful to plan satisfying leisure activities: culture, fitness, learning, art, religion, volunteerism, entertainment, and developing relationships skills.[17] Make such a list for yourself, asking, How are these activities balanced in my life?

3. Put the activities on your list in order of attractiveness, jotting down an approximate date for beginning each of them. Then move ahead with number one.

they never wait for their leisure to come, before enjoying themselves. They seem to be endlessly playing, no matter where they were, or what they were doing. They were determined that the monotonous round of their daily appointed tasks would be transformed by the alchemy of their humor, and their light touch.

Clowns, you may say. . . . Kids who have never grown up. Ah, yes, and what a delicious compliment that is. Remembering that Man who said—two thousand years ago—"Except you become like little children, you cannot enter the kingdom of heaven." So, let's drink a toast to all those who refuse to let their playfulness be fenced-in solely within the compound of their leisure time. But allowed it to spill outside of those bounds, into every compartment of their lives. Playful in the way they learn. Playful in the way they work. Playful in the way they make love. Playful in everything. Their whole life is their leisure.[18]

Using Laughter and Play to Enrich Your Spiritual Life

Unfortunately for our well being, many approaches to religion make it difficult for people to dance their spirituality. Anthropologists report sad behavioral changes in certain African tribes after "successful" missionary activity converted them to Christianity. "Before the missionaries came the natives were noted for their hearty, full-bodied laughter. But unrestrained laughter seemed 'pagan' to the missionaries. After their reeducation in 'Christian' ways, the natives developed a nervous, suppressed, embarrassed laughter known as the 'mission giggle.' "[19] What an impoverished caricature of the "good news" the missionaries were trying to communicate. It's reminiscent of the Puritan clergy who opposed bearbaiting not because it was cruel to the bears but because it gave the spectators pleasure.

For people who try to walk (but sometimes stumble) on the path of the Christian way, a more liberating as well as accurate picture of healthy spirituality is Jesus' life-style. Elton Trueblood in *The Humor of Christ* cites thirty examples from the Bible to show that Jesus was a person of wit and humor who laughed and expected others to laugh. In contrast to John the Baptist, who came "neither eating or drinking," Jesus first used his special powers at a marriage party to supply more wine when the refreshments ran low. His enjoyment of eating and drinking with friends undoubtedly threatened and angered the superpious of his day. It gave some who couldn't understand his life-celebrating, people-loving life-style an excuse to accuse him of being "a glutton and a drunkard." He was one who said a rousing yes! to life and to people. At the last meal with his closest friends he said: "These things I have spoken to you, that my joy may be in you, and that your joy may be full" (John 15:11). As I recall, it was the deeply spiritual scientist Pierre Teilhard de Chardin who once said that the most certain sign of the presence of God is joy.

Some other religious traditions put laughter in a central place. The creation story of a certain tribe of aborigines in southern Australia depicts us humans as being created from excrement. After being molded into human form, it was *tickled,* causing it to laugh and come alive. The Jicarilla Apache have a delightful story that pictures the creator standing back after he had made all the animals and laughing at their hilarious appearance and habits. When the creator had made a man, he said to him, "Speak!" and he began to talk, then "Laugh!" and he began to laugh. Then, when the creator made a woman, the man spoke to her and, to his amazement, she answered back. Then they began to laugh together. They laughed and laughed![20]

Taking a serious but playful attitude toward your faith helps liberate your spirituality from sterile legalisms and shallow moralisms, enriching it with joy. If your spirituality tends to be somber and joyless, you might want to get a second opinion.

C. S. Lewis in *The Screwtape Letters* (alleged to be from the senior devil Screwtape to his nephew Wormwood, who is in training to become a demon) writes:

My Dear Wormwood,

. . . I divide the causes of human laughter into Joy, Fun, the Joke Proper, and Flippancy. You will see the first among friends and lovers reunited on the eve of a holiday. Among adults some pretext in the way of Jokes is usually provided, but the facility with which the smallest witticisms produce laughter at such a time shows that they are not the real cause. What the real cause is we do not know. Something like it is expressed in much of the detestable art which the humans call Music, and something like it occurs in Heaven—a meaningless acceleration in the rhythm of celestial experience, quite opaque to us. Laughter of this kind does us no good and should always be discouraged. Besides, the phenomenon is of itself disgusting and a direct insult to the realism, dignity, and austerity of Hell.

. . . Fun is closely related to Joy—a sort of emotional froth arising from the play instinct. It is of very little use to us. It can sometimes be used, of course, to divert humans from something else which the Enemy [God] would like them to be feeling or doing; but in itself it has wholly undesirable tendencies; it promotes charity, courage, contentment, and many other evils.

Your affectionate uncle,
Screwtape.[21]

I'm glad that the psalmist pictures God as laughing at the arrogant kings of the earth (Psalm 2:4). Laughing at puffed-up authority figures seems both appropriate and healthy. I have some empathy for the philosopher Nietzsche's declaration that he "would only believe in a god who could dance." Socrates' statement in one of his dialogues that "the gods too are fond of a joke"[22] reflects a healthy dimension of the religion of ancient Greece. In my more playful moments I've considered calling my current understanding of spiritual things "The theology of the divine smile." Or, in my more irreverent moments (after encountering some of the heavies in the field of religion), I've toyed with "The theology of the cosmic chuckle." I hope the divine Spirit has a hearty sense of humor. Otherwise, we're all in big trouble.

One of the ways a playful perspective on life can enrich your spirituality is by helping you transform your fear of death (existential anxiety) into a stimulus to aliveness and creativity rather than causing stifling idolatry. Two familiar Woody Allen quips illustrate a humorous means of coping with existential anxiety: "I'm not afraid of death, I just don't want to be there when it happens" and "If I knew where I was going to die, I wouldn't go there."

I'm not afraid of death, I just don't want to be there when it happens.

—*Woody Allen*

If I knew where I was going to die, I wouldn't go there.

—*Woody Allen*

A monk at a Zen Buddhist center located halfway up 10,050-foot Mount Baldy, which I could see from my office window in southern California (at least twice a year—whenever the smog lifted), once quoted to me the wisdom of a Zen seer who centuries ago had written, "Angels can fly because they take themselves so lightly."[23] Good advice for any of us who tend to take ourselves too seriously!

Wholeness Exercise

> **Guided Imaging Exercise.** In the spirit of that ancient Zen seer, try this Zen laughing meditation. Get comfortable and close your eyes. Notice your breathing for a moment, relaxing as you exhale. / Now imagine that you're in a beautiful, serene place in nature. / It's just before sunrise. Watch as it slowly gets light. / Note the peaceful feeling in you and let yourself experience a quiet joy as you watch the light begin to bathe whatever is around you. Enjoy letting a gentle inner smile grow, as you appreciate the dawn. / Feel a twinkle in your eyes as you let yourself go and just enjoy being alive. / When you feel ready, stretch and open your eyes as you come back, refreshed and energized.[24]

Create Your Playfulness Self-Care Fitness Plan

Go back and review the things that aroused your playfulness as you read this chapter, including the important items from the checkup.

Pick at least six things you will do to let your inner child enjoy more play. Using your creativity, write out a realistic Self-Care Plan to do these things. Remember, your plan will be more effective if it includes: (1) things you'll really enjoy; (2) practical strategies for doing these things; (3) a time line, including how often you'll do them.

Pick one or two especially attractive things in your plan and start doing them today or, at the latest, tomorrow. Playful self-care is inherently rewarding, so you won't need to create special rewards. Also, I recommend that you create a movie in your mind each day experiencing yourself laughing at yourself and at the craziness of some things in your life.

You also may enjoy dipping into one of the books on humor in the Recommended Reading for this chapter at the end of the book.

Remember, as someone has said, she or he who laughs, lasts! Enjoy!

yes!

* *Edwin Keister, Jr., "The Case Against Growing Old," Longevity (9-90) re: Ashley Montagu's exploration of neotany: carrying childlike qualities into adulthood (curiosity and flexibility; openness and friendliness; spontaneity and joyfulness).*

Enhancing Your Well Being by Helping Heal a Wounded Planet

Every day Americans jog twenty-seven million miles, eat three million gallons of ice cream, and produce one and a half million tons of hazardous waste.

—CBS News, February 17, 1986

Mahatma Gandhi, on an important mission to England, was asked by a dozen reporters, "What do you think of Western civilization?" Gandhi responded: "I think it will be a good idea."[1]

 Once upon a time three foolish young California gray whales lingered too long feeding on the aquatic abundance of the Arctic Ocean off Point Barrow, Alaska. They became trapped by the early freeze of the Arctic winter, which left them only a few small holes for breathing once every four minutes. The environmental group Greenpeace heard of their plight. As ice began to close their air holes, a massive effort was launched to save them from certain death. A rear admiral coordinated the liberation effort. Skilled Native American Inuits were hired to work around the clock cutting air holes with chain saws. A huge array of heavy equipment was used in a frantic but failing effort to cut a channel through the towering packed ice to the open sea.

The passionate sympathies of millions of people in many countries were aroused. The story was front-page news day after day. It was reported via worldwide TV networks with heartrending video shots of the gasping whales bleeding from the sharp edges of the ice. The U.S. president phoned the rescue workers on behalf of our nation to wish them success.

After almost three weeks of nonstop efforts, hope was wearing thin. The smallest whale (affectionately named Bone by the Native Americans) died. Then the Soviet Union made an unprecedented move, sending two huge ice-breaking ships to clear a channel. Before long, people around the world cheered as the two surviving whales were freed. They followed more than twenty thousand uncles and aunts and cousins on their incredible six-thousand-mile annual migration to the warm lagoons of Baja, California, to mate and bear their babies. Perhaps you cheered with all the others and felt as I did, as though something in *me* had been freed!

Then an unsettling picture intruded into my mind. A news item reported the cost of the rescue—over three million U.S. dollars. I visualized millions of human children and women and men, around the planet, trapped in an icy sea of stifling poverty, lethal hunger, deadly disease. How many of them, I wondered, could be saved with such a passionate, all-out international expenditure? But then I remembered that the magnificent grays had been slaughtered almost to extinction three different times during the past one hundred years, killed ruthlessly to make things like cheap dog food. The all-out effort to save members of that species seemed wonderfully appropriate, like a symbolic gesture of repentance by the human family. But I still wish that we could do the same for trapped humans around the globe.

Is it possible that the whales' trappedness in a freezing sea captured our attention so powerfully because we resonated from some dim awareness of our own captivity? Perhaps we identify with the whales' plight because of the trappedness in our inner lives, in toxic relationships, frustrating jobs, and in dying dreams. Do the powerful images of this contemporary parable express how millions of us feel about life on our spaceship earth—trapped in a potentially terminal global environmental crisis? From our own inner depths do we not yearn for freedom to move ahead on our journeys to the warmth and loving joy of healthier lives in a healthier environment?

What is the ultimate health challenge confronting you and your loved ones today? The bottom-line health challenge we all face is to create effective ways to save the planet's wonderful web of life from environmental disaster by moving to ecologically sustainable lifestyles and a just global economy! This is the most critical health issue not only for our times but for all times. For if, as a global community, we don't solve this planet-cidal challenge in our times, a healthy future for our children, our children's children, and all the children of the human species and all other species will be impossible.

In a powerful appeal to the new leader of their country, astrophysicists Carl Sagan and Sann Druyan declared: "It is no longer enough to love, feed, shelter, clothe, and educate a child, not when the future itself is in danger. . . . We have been treating the environment *as if there were no tomorrow,* as if there will be no new generations to be sustained by the bounties of the earth. But they, and we, must drink the water and breathe the air. They and we are vulnerable to deadly waste, ultraviolet light, and climatic disasters."[2]

Every creature in earth's interdependent network of life is threatened by a common reality. For the first time in the five-billion-year story of life on this earth, one species—homo sapiens (us)—threatens all the species. One species continues to overpopulate irresponsibly. One species has used our superb intellectual endowment to create a technology capable of destroying a livable planet. We have created the awesome power to damage irreparably, with deadly radiation, the gene pool on which the future of all life depends. But we also have the power and the intelligence to save the earth, if we have the will.

Unless our species rises to this unprecedented challenge and devises innovative ways to heal and protect our planet, your personal health and mine and that of the human family, as well as of all the animals and plants, cannot have a viable future. Therefore, *nothing* is more important for health than our learning to live with more down-to-earth love for the planet. Only thus can we save it as a healthful place for all living things.

A short item appeared in the *Los Angeles Times* not long ago reporting that the last Palos Verdes blue butterfly in the world was dead. The butterfly, only discovered in 1977, was on the endangered species list. It was wiped out when the city of Rancho Palos Verdes destroyed a stand of locoweeds, its only food and habitat, for some type of city development. The city was being taken to court for destroying an endangered species—a mere misdemeanor.

As I read the item, I experienced an unexpected wave of sadness and anger. Surprised, as I stayed with the feelings they took me to the awareness that my children and grandchildren will never see a Palos Verdes blue butterfly! In the larger scheme of things, the death of a butterfly species may not seem all that important. "Stop being so sentimental!" I said to myself. Yet I felt then and feel now deep grief for what my children and grandchildren, and yours, have lost forever. And then I remembered that their losses continue each day, with over 1,070 species on the endangered and threatened list. I recalled that in the last seventeen years, some 300 species of animals and plants have been declared extinct while awaiting government approval to be included on that list.

As I was completing this book, I spent a few glorious but sobering days in the Amazon basin of Brazil. One day we crossed the majestic river which carries eleven times the water in the Mississippi. We took a canoe up a small stream into the rainforest. The beauty and aliveness of the forest was awesome. Our guide led us along a trail through the forest to a place where the trees had been slashed and burned to make a soccer field near a rural school. As we stood in the middle of that field, he suggested that we examine the soil under our feet. It appeared much like the sand on a beach.

The guide explained that, when the rainforest is destroyed, the nutrients in the shallow topsoil are soon leached away by the torrential rains. Within four years it can no longer grow food crops. In about seven years it cannot even provide pasture for cattle. The incredibly alive rainforest through which we had just walked becomes a barren desert. As we stood there stunned, I realized that if I buy a hamburger in California made from cheap imported beef raised on denuded rainforest land, I am, in effect, cutting down a magnificent tree in that forest!

If you live in North America, consider these wise words by Jose Lutzenberger, Secretary for the Environment in Brazil: "When the U.S. and Canada chop down their primitive forests on the Pacific coast, or Sweden and the USSR do the same to their taiga forests in the far north, the results are just as devastating for the global ecosystem as the destruction of rain forest in Africa or tropical forests in New Guinea—and should be condemned by international public opinion" (*WorldWatch*, September–October 1990, p. 8).

In this chapter we'll look at how the sickness of the biosphere and the pathology of our major social institutions affects our personal wholeness every minute of every day. Our individual wellness will be short-lived—a passing luxury of privileged persons in affluent circles and nations—unless we understand health globally while we work for it at home through healing outreach to our community's people-serving institutions.

Peace-Ecology Well-Being Checkup

This checkup can be useful in two important ways. (1) It will give you a quick evaluation of the health of your life-style and values in relation to the health of the wider social systems in your community and world. (2) The checkup suggests a variety of practical options you can use in developing your own plan to help heal the planet's life-threatening collective illnesses.

Instructions: In front of each item put one of three initials: E = I'm doing excellently in this area; OK = I'm doing all right, but there's definitely room for improvement; NS = My life-style definitely needs strengthening in this area.

_____ I know that my personal wholeness and that of my loved ones is inextricably interwoven with the wholeness of my society and the natural world.

_____ I love the Earth and feel deeply connected with the wonderful web of life of which I'm a tiny but significant part. I find joy and renewal in getting close to plants, animals, and places of natural beauty.

_____ I feel a deep bond with the incredibly diverse peoples of the human family.

_____ I enjoy sharing the beauty and wonder of nature with the people I care about most.

_____ I'm aware that the basic causes of growing damage to the Earth are the population explosion in many regions of the world, the violence of poverty caused by economic injustice, the life-styles of greedy consumption by (us) affluent individuals and nations, and the squandering of the planet's limited and precious resources in the global arms race.

_____ I recognize that violence against nature and violence against persons defined by society as lesser (women, children, minorities) are rooted in the same causes—the social evils of injustice, poverty, patriarchal valuing of violence, and socially inflicted powerlessness.

_____ I examine and correct my life-style and the values that guide it regularly, to make it more expressive of my love for both my health and the health of the planet.

_____ For my own health and the healing of the planet, I'm actively involved in supporting and working with others in environmental and peacemaking groups dedicated to healing and protecting the health of the Earth.

_____ I know and use methods of healing my numbing feelings of despair, denial, and powerlessness, so as to recover hope and energy for doing environmental and peace work.

_____ I experience the mystery and wonder of the eon-spanning process of continuing creation.

_____ I use methods that work for me to enrich my spiritual core, the empowering center of my loving-the-planet work.

_____ I'm growing beyond narrow or exclusivistic faith and value commitments to make these more inclusive and bridge building with other traditions and species.

_____ I'm practicing parenting and "friending" for peace, justice, and environmental wholeness.

_____ I have a clear, evolving image of a healthy future for the planet, a future toward which I'm working.

_____ I use my sense of humor and laugh with peace and ecology partners as a release valve and to empower action.

Using Your Findings: To gain the most from this checkup, I recommend that you scan your self-evaluation to get an overall impression of the health of your life-style in relation to the wider society and world. In your *Well Being Self-Care Journal* (or elsewhere) list the OK and NS items that seem important enough to cause you to consider making constructive changes in your life. Beside these jot down your tentative thoughts about what you might do to enhance your wholeness by helping heal the planet.

Privatized Wellness Seeking—A Dangerous Fallacy

If you try to maximize your wholeness while ignoring the brokenness of your community and the wider world, you'll be walking into a dead end. To be fully effective, well being for you and your family must include doing all that you can to help heal the planet, thus reducing the social causes of individual and family brokenness. These social malignancies include sexism, racism, ageism, militarism, classism, consumerism, species-ism (treating other animals as existing for our exploitation), tribal nationalism, pathological religious movements, political and economic oppression, and the tragic destruction of a livable environment. These institutionalized sicknesses hurt your wholeness and mine every minute of every day, whether or not we're aware of their impact. They damage the health of everyone on the planet and are particularly cruel to those suffering from economic, ethnic, racial, and political oppression.

A public health physician raises the crucial question we should all be asking about the M.A.S.H. approach to medical treatment: "The illness-care system for the most part tries to patch people up and return them to the battle from whence they came. No effort is made to change the rules of the battle, much less to make peace. . . . Why do we have to structure our society in such a way as to create ill health? Is there a way to structure our society so as to *create* health?"[3]

Let's bring this down to you and me. What is the impact of a deteriorating environment on our health? *Well Body, Well Earth*, a powerful book by a physician and an ecologist, helped to open my eyes to the reality of this health threat. The authors declare: "All living things are both *in* and *of* the environment. . . . It is an interdependency with no beginning, middle, or end. If any one part of the whole is unhealthy, we must assume that each other part of the whole is affected. . . . We are not separate from the earth; we are as much a part of the planet as each cell in our bodies is a part of us. . . . All disease must of necessity be environmental."[4]

The Dalai Lama, speaking in Claremont shortly before he received the Nobel Peace Prize, put it straight: "When the situation becomes desperate, there's no time to pretend." There's no time in our fractured world to pretend that privatized wholeness seeking can be sustained. In the long run, it's unhealthy for our individual and

> When the situation becomes
>
> desperate, there's no time
>
> to pretend.
>
> —*Dalai Lama*

"The picture's pretty bleak, gentlemen. . . . The world's climates are changing, the mammals are taking over, and we all have a brain about the size of a walnut."

family wellness to focus solely on our own health while ignoring what must be done to heal a deeply wounded planet.

But the problems of an ailing planet pose a threat not just to the physical side of our lives. The bleak predictions and enormous tasks of trying to solve such gigantic, complex problems can lead us to inner turmoil, frustration, anger, despair, and paralyzing feelings of helplessness. Is there any real hope in the planet's desperate situation? Yes! If we reorient our priorities and values, we can use the same incredible human intelligence and creativity that released the atom and landed men on the moon, to save the planet. That's the challenge that faces all of us in the human family.

A No-Lose Investment in the Future

Norman Cousins provided a dramatic illustration of how your feelings about the world situation can affect your personal health. Cousins did an ingenious experiment on himself. He had two blood samples taken and tested at the medical school where he was a faculty member. The first sample established a base line for the effectiveness of his immune system. Then for only five minutes he imagined that the superpowers each had truly rational foreign policies. A second blood sample was taken. Within those five minutes of experiencing in his mind the dramatic positive changes in the world, Cousins's immune cells increased an average of 53 percent in all categories![5] To replicate Cousins's experiment today, all you would have to do is let yourself image that a major breakthrough had occurred in environment healing or peacemaking in one of the many anxiety-arousing areas of global conflict.

The good news is that putting some of your energy, creativity, passion, and money into working for the healing of problems in your community, or for ecological-nuclear healing, is a no-lose investment. Simultaneously it's an investment in both your own and the planet's health. Active outreach with others to help heal your community or world will probably enhance your fitness, even if it doesn't produce rapid or radical changes in your community or world.

A high school junior named Bill was referred to our counseling and growth center by the school psychologist. Bill was failing in all his courses, in spite of being intellectually gifted with an IQ of around 145. The pastoral psychotherapist knew that when one member of a family is suffering such painful dysfunction, the whole family is hurting at some level. So she wisely invited Bill's parents and two teenage siblings to join him at the first session.

Here is a crucial interchange, after rapport had been established in that session:

Therapist: Bill, you must have some reasons why you're not cracking your books. I'd be interested to know what your thinking is on that.

Bill: (Shrugs his shoulders dejectedly, looking very depressed.)

Therapist: What do you mean by this (shrugging her shoulders)?

Bill: (blurts out with pained intensity) Why bother when the world's going to hell in a basket?

Therapist: Things look terribly hopeless to you.

Bill: (nods) Yeah, the world sucks!

Bill's despair came pouring out, totally surprising his family. (The nuclear-ecological issue was part of their "family secret"—things a family subconsciously agrees not to talk about.) A turning point toward health came for the family when Bill's father admitted, "The mess in the world worries me, too, Bill." The family did much more therapeutic work together over the next few months. Opening up about the ecology-nuclear issue proved to be the key that unlocked their paralyzed communication. Not surprisingly, as the family communication improved, Bill began to pull himself out of his self-defeating tailspin resulting from what Yale psychiatrist Robert Lifton has called "radical futurelessness."

It is noteworthy that one of the most helpful things that Bill and his family did as part of their therapy was to become involved in a loving-the-earth peacemaking study and action group at their church. In my professional experience, such involvement often proves to be the most healing therapy for hopelessness about the world's future, particularly among teens and young adults.[6] Again it becomes clear that helping to save the planet is simply enlightened self-interest.

Learning to Be a Lover of the Planet

How does all this relate to love, the heart and power of whole-person health? One of the most loving things we can do for ourselves and those we care about (including our unborn great-grandchildren) is to live more lovingly in and for the biosphere on which all our futures depend. To love ourselves and others effectively involves loving in widening circles of caring, like a pebble dropped into a pond. These widening circles of care for the whole human family and for the biosphere can link us with those in other lands and traditions who also care about the earth.

The wise words of an inspired Pacific Northwest Native American named Chief Seattle, spoken in 1854, are powerfully relevant today: "Teach your children what we have taught our children: The earth is our mother. . . . This we know. The earth does not belong to humans; humans belong to the earth. This we know. All things are connected like the blood which unites one family. . . . Whatever befalls the earth befalls the children of the earth. People did not weave the web of life, they are merely a strand of it. Whatever they do to the web, they do to themselves."[7]

This deep respect for and affinity with the earth is still reflected in the memories of Paula Gunn Allen, a contemporary Native American woman. She remembers: "When I was small, my mother told me that animals, insects, and plants are to be treated with the kind of respect one customarily accords to high-status adults. 'Life is a circle, and everything has its place in it,' she would say. That is how I met the sacred hoop."[8]

The ecological and nuclear crisis of the planet is both an unprecedented challenge and an unprecedented opportunity for humankind. More than any previous generation, we have the opportunity to learn to love the planet in new ways, to love it enough to do what must be done to save it as a beautiful place for all of God's creatures everywhere.

After visiting peace action groups across North America, Henri Nouwen concluded that most peacemakers are living in what he called the "house of fear." To be effective, he declared, we must move from the house of fear to the house of love. I agree. Only as we move from the house of fear and despair to the house of love and

WINDOW OF WHOLENESS

HELEN CALDICOTT

A brilliant pediatrician from Australia was doing research at Columbia University's Presbyterian Medical Center in New York City seeking a cure for a devastating but relatively rare disease of children. As she became aware of the increasing threat to the children of the whole planet posed by the nuclear arms race, she resigned from her tenured position and became one of the most dedicated, passionate, and untiring peacemakers in our times. She sparked the mobilizing of doctors in her leadership role in Physicians for Social Responsibility. Later, convinced that the vision and special experiences of women held the key to interrupting the lemminglike stampede of humankind toward the abyss, she helped form WAND, Women Against Nuclear Destruction. In July 1982 she spoke these powerful words to the annual meeting of the Association of Humanistic Psychology:

> Nothing we do makes any difference if God's creation is going to be destroyed this year, next year, within ten years or twenty years, does it? We are put here, I believe, by God to save the planet. No other generation has had such a responsibility placed on its shoulders. That's why you are here. . . . And it's up to people like you to take the responsibility to save the planet. And do you know it's the most joyous thing to work together to do this. It unites everybody: rich and poor, black and white, Russians and Americans, because we're all the sons and daughters of God, we're all brothers and sisters. And if we don't spiritually evolve now (we're at the crossroads of time), if we don't spiritually evolve, we're not going to make it.

After many exhausting years of intense, dedicated work as leader of Physicians for Social Responsibility, Helen Caldicott withdrew from peace activism in that organization. The burnout she suffered apparently came from her uphill struggle against the resistance to fundamental changes by the male-dominated medical profession. She continued her involvement in WAND.

Then in October 1990, Helen Caldicott keynoted a powerful conference of more than seven thousand college students sponsored by Student Environmental Action Coalition on the University of Illinois campus. She joined with such justice and peace luminaries as Robert Redford, Ralph Nader, Jesse Jackson, and Cesar Chavez in encouraging this networking bonanza of environmental activism among young people. In challenging the students she declared: "This is the day I've been waiting for. This is the beginning of the revolution to save the earth!" (Reported in *Nuclear Times*, Winter 1990, p. 5.)

Wholeness Exercise

Peacemaking Exercise. Pause and let yourself feel the joy and hope in the words of Helen Caldicott in this chapter's Window of Wholeness. Experience the challenge of ecology and peace activism transcending the many walls that divide us. / Jot down the images and ideas that came to you during this exercise, including your thoughts about what you can do.

hope can we sustain the energy to make the radical changes in ourselves, our life-styles, and our society that must occur if our world is to be healed. Social activist burnout is epidemic partly because many who work for community improvement and justice seem to be motivated mainly by fear and anger. Both these feelings can be appropriate and valuable. But a healthier motivation for social change work is love—of ourselves, other people, and our planet home.

How does this environmental and peacemaking talk relate to the spiritual heart of our well being? This challenge is our most spiritual task. It's the spiritual imperative that confronts us all. The joyful call of the divine Spirit is to work with other persons of goodwill, across all boundaries and differences that divide us, as active lovers of the planet. For what? To create a global community of eco-justice in which all persons will have an opportunity to develop their fullest possibilities. To work for this dream is to become co-creators with the loving Spirit who is the ultimate wellspring of all love, health, justice, and peace.

In the summer of 1991, my best friend and I enjoyed an exciting twelve-day oar rafting, whitewater trip through 188 miles of one of the Creator's most beautiful natural wonders—the Grand Canyon. As we flew in a small plane toward the departure point, we were saddened but also angered to see the brown haze that often shrouds this awesome canyon. Only sixteen miles from the canyon we saw the huge, coal-burning generating plant, the source of much of the sulfur dioxide that is thought to produce the beauty-obscuring air pollution. This will not change until the U.S. Environmental Protection Agency forces the plant to install scrubbers to reduce the emissions. Ironically, another governmental agency, the Bureau of Reclamation, is one of the operators of the offending plant.

Ways to Help Heal Our Planet

John Seed, pioneer in the struggle to protect the rainforests in his native Australia and around the globe, invites us "To Hear Within Ourselves the Sound of the Earth Crying."[9] The Earth is crying at the breakdown of its life support systems as indicated by

Wholeness Exercise

Hope-Empowerment Exercise. This picture of planet earth taken from near the moon provides a new, potentially saving perspective for our species. As you look at it, see it as a small, precious living spaceship in the vast, cold immensities of space. See it as home, to you and all the people and creatures of this marvelous network of life. Try looking at your life with all its problems and possibilities from this planetary perspective, the only really whole perspective for seeking health today. Pause now, close your eyes, and let your mind and heart feast on this healing image.

In your *Well Being Self-Care Journal* jot down the thoughts and images that came to you during this exercise.

- the poisons poured into the rivers, lakes, and oceans;

- oil spills in the pristine wilderness of Alaska and elsewhere;

- acid rain destroying the forests and the lakes;

- holes in the protective ozone layer;

- tragic disasters such as Bhopal and Chernobyl;

- global warming and the greenhouse effect;

- the vast erosion of precious topsoil and the creeping growth of deserts;

- deforestation and particularly the destruction of the tropical rain forests in which more than half of all plant species on earth live;

- toxic and nuclear waste dumps created by the arms race and uncontrolled industrial pollution;

- the expected extinction of an average of one hundred species per day in the next three decades;

- the threatened pollution resulting from economic exploitation of the antarctic continent;

- the pollution of our own bodies from toxic substances in our food and homes;

- making our planet home a garbage dump.

As someone has observed, the immune system by which the planet heals itself is being irreparably injured so that it is as if the body of our world has AIDS.

What is the key to getting ourselves moving so that we will do what we must to save the planet? The key is for us to hear and feel the sound of the earth crying within ourselves, to experience the environmental crisis in our own bodies and minds and spirits. This means awakening to wider awareness of the terrible personal price we're already paying, and will pay many times over in declining health, unless we change drastically our planet-desecrating ways. The authors of *Well Body, Well Earth* put this point powerfully:

> There is nothing that seems more immediate and important than personal health, our own and that of our loved ones. It is here that we feel the greatest urgency to solve problems of environmental pollution, and it is here that the consequences of our actions are the most dramatically demonstrated. . . . Like radio buoys guiding a ship at sea, disease and health can guide our lives. Steering our course by these signals not only leads to a life relatively free of disease. It can also guide us to the upper limits of personal fulfillment. Again, because of our interconnectedness, the fulfillment of any single individual or system ultimately benefits all systems around it. Guided by disease and health, Gaea, the living Earth, benefits from every person's human fulfillment.[10]

Another key to awakening hope for planetary survival is the vision and understanding of the "ecofeminists," a contemporary movement that focuses feminist insights on the ecology crisis. Judith

Plant, ecofeminist writer and activist, declares: "Making the connection between feminism and ecology enables us to step outside the dualistic, separated [male-dominated] world into which we were all born. From this new perspective, we begin to see how our relations with each other are reflected in our relations with the natural world. The rape of the earth, in all its forms, becomes a metaphor for the rape of women, in all its many guises. . . . By understanding that we are all part of the same organic flow of life, we are reminded, with a stirring that excites our deepest selves, of who we really are. We are part of this earth, and thus the world becomes a place of infinite mystery, of delight to the senses and the intellect."[11]

African-American novelist Alice Walker, in an essay written to celebrate the birth of Martin Luther King, Jr., declared: "Some of us have become used to thinking that woman is the nigger of the world, that a person of color is the nigger of the world, that a poor person is the nigger of the world. But, in truth, Earth itself has become the nigger of the world. It is perceived, ironically, as other, alien, evil, and threatening by those who are finding that they cannot draw a healthful breath without its cooperation. While the Earth is poisoned, everything it supports is poisoned. While the Earth is enslaved, none of us is free. . . . While it is 'treated like dirt,' so are we."[12]

Ecology and Peacemaking Action Checklist

CHECKLIST

What can you and I do to express our love for the earth and its network of living things? You already have a variety of suggestions from the checkup in this chapter. Let me add some other things that people like you are doing to help. Treat this as a checklist of options to which you can add your own ideas.

Instructions: In the blank before each option, put a number from 0 to 5, 0 meaning "not interested," and 5 meaning "an outstanding idea! I'll use it!"

_____ *Enjoy the healing pleasures and mind-body-spirit renewal of frequent communion with flowers and trees, birds and animals, and with wild and beautiful places in nature.* As suggested above, learning to enjoy our deep connection with the earth is a vital way to enhance our motivation to save her. Experiencing your organic relationship with nature, in and through your body, can provide the energy to engage in difficult, ongoing environmental and peace activism. It can also reduce stress overload and help heal your hurts. Surgeon Bernie Siegel observes that hospital patients heal faster when their room has a view of the sky.[13] In my experience even a mini-vacation (ten to fifteen minutes) spent soaking up the life energies and rhythms of nature can be surprisingly renewing. Enjoying the wonders of

nature with people you love can enrich those relationships. Nurturing your inner peace can lessen the danger of burnout in your peacemaking in the world.

Gary Doone, a Native American singer, healer, and writer, describes the Lakota sense of bondedness with the earth: "Every parent feels a bond with his or her children that goes beyond what words can explain. It doesn't have to do with logic or reason; it is a bond deeper and fuller and more mysterious than that. . . . This is the kind of connection that we will have with All-Our-Relations-on-Mother-Earth as we . . . awaken to the incredible bond which exists between ourselves and all things. . . . Our deep bonding will not only block destructive attitudes and actions, it will also give us the harmonious and truly ecological solutions to the issues we face today."[14]

Writing nearly twenty-six hundred years ago in China, Lao-tzu expressed beautifully this healing, childlike openness to nature:

> Can you hold the door of your tent
> Wide to the firmament?
> Can you, with the simple stature
> Of a child breathing nature
> Become, notwithstanding, a man?

With keen insight, he observed:

> Those who would take over the earth
> And shape it to their will
> Never, I notice, succeed.
> The earth is like a vessel so sacred
> That at the mere approach of the profane
> It is marred.[15]

———— *Equip yourself with the most accurate facts available about the changing ecological and nuclear crisis.* Although this may not be easy (as the cartoon above reminds us), getting the best information you can is essential homework for helping save the planet. It can help you avoid getting on your activism horse and riding off in all directions. Such consciousness raising can be done via study (see Recommended Reading for this chapter) or by organizing a loving-the-earth study and action group among your friends, in your community, or in your congregation. Your knowledge pool should include understanding of how violence against Mother Nature and violence against those defined as weaker, less important, or odd—e.g., women, children, minorities, the aged, gays, the disabled, the poor, developing nations, and animals—are rooted in the same causes. The causes are lack of love (for oneself, other people, and nature), and injustice, meaning the unfair distribution of power, status, money, and resources.

———— *Help children learn constructive ways to settle conflicts; to respect, love, and care for people and for the natural world; and to engage in ecology-peacemaking with you.* (Especially helpful is the book by Kathleen and Jim McGinnis *Parenting for Peace and Justice.*) Among the many rewards of such parenting, the one identified by conservation pioneer John Muir, the founder of the Sierra Club, is not often recognized. In discussing our society's warped attitudes toward death, he recommended, "Let children walk with nature, let them see the beautiful blendings and communions of death and life, their joyous inseparable unity, as taught in the woods and meadows, plains and mountains and streams of our blessed star, and they will learn that death is stingless indeed, and that the grave has no victory, for it never fights. All is divine harmony."[16]

_____ *Let yourself experience the constructive anger, guilt, and grief that is appropriate when you become aware of the continuing rape of the earth and the violence inherent in the tragic waste of the earth's precious resources in mega-armaments.* The energy generated by these fiery feelings can get you moving in wholistic ecological and peacemaking action.

_____ *Examine your life-style (and the values that guide it), and then adopt a more ecologically constructive, peacemaking way of living day by day, week by week.* If you're one of the overprivileged minority of the human family living in an affluent country, there is a disturbing fact about your life-style that may be difficult to accept. It is the socioeconomic reality that our greedy, nonecological life-styles (which depend on our consuming a disproportionate share of the world's limited resources) and our support of a massive military establishment are major contributors to the destruction of the planet. Our affluent life-styles are riding on the backs of the poor nations and contributing to pollution of the planet. The international economic system, on which our life-styles depend, fosters proliferating poverty and violence.

The greenhouse effect and global warming, caused in part by the destruction of the tropical rain forests, illustrate the problem. Brazil, like many developing countries, is caught in a debt trap. It owes huge debts it will never be able to repay to the rich countries of the northern hemisphere and the world bank. In a vain attempt to pay even the interest, thousands of acres of precious rain forests are being cut and burned to raise cattle to sell to fast food chains of North America for cheap hamburger meat. After this the land becomes desert, is abandoned, and more rain forests are devastated. Individuals can help some by boycotting the chains that import this meat. But until institutional changes occur, through the international banking and governmental communities in rich countries, Brazil probably will continue to be trapped in the vicious cycle of impossible debts and rain forest destruction.

_____ *Join hands with other lovers of nature and peace in the local chapters of one or more of the numerous national and international ecology and peace organizations.* The political clout of such broad-based groups is impressive, and it needs to be increased by your participation and support.[17] Grass-roots action must accompany networking in national and international organizations. Many of the effective local recycling programs came into being because small, dedicated groups became active in promoting them in their communities. The familiar motto "Think globally and act locally" makes sense. Organizations that seek to help developing countries cope with their huge environmental crises must do so in a spirit of genuine partnership. An Australian aboriginal woman put the issue well: "If you have come to help me you can go home again. But if you see my struggle as part of your own survival then perhaps we can work together." (Cited in "The Manila Declaration on People's Participation and Sustainable Development.")

It's important to continue to support nuclear peacemaking groups, in spite of the wonderful thawing of the cold war. Remember the doomsday clock the atomic scientists who developed the first A-bomb created in 1947 to symbolize the danger of nuclear war? The Union of Concerned Scientists recently moved the big hand back—by four minutes—as peace between the superpowers appeared to be breaking out. But it's now only at ten minutes before the doomsday hour of midnight! Columnist Ellen Goodman asks, "It is reasonable to ask whether Americans have to be terrified in order to go on thinking about the human capacity for self-destruction. After all, it's [still] 10 minutes to midnight. Do you know where your 50,000 nuclear warheads are? . . . The risk of accident is as great as ever. Four more countries have the technology to produce bombs. And at home we are still 'modernizing' our nuclear weapons [to make them more deadly]. . . . In short, at 10 minutes to midnight, it's not time yet to stop worrying."[18]

_____ *Update your patriotism to include the planet.* No wholeness is possible for any nation unless the planetary home of all nations is safe and whole. If something seems good for my country but is bad for the world, it's really bad for my country in the long run. In her book *Three Guineas,* author Virginia Woolf declared, "As a woman my country is the whole world."[19] From an ecological perspective, this is now true of all persons, male and female, on the planet, whether or not we know it. This makes all noninclusive definitions of patriotism potentially hazardous to everyone's health. Making the earth and the human family the bottom line of your caring and commitment does not diminish your love and loyalty for your own country. It's actually more loving, in our modern world, because it is the only way to give your country the best chance of having a healthy future.

The original Native Americans in my part of Southern California were called the Chumash people. This is a saying from the wisdom of their culture: "All the world is a canoe, and whether paddlers or passengers, we are all one people together in that vessel." Let's put this in contemporary terms: Whether we recognize it or not, we're all in the same boat, for better or for worse.

In this spirit, here is a "Pledge of Allegiance to the Family of the Earth" that we keep on the refrigerator in our home:

"I pledge allegiance to the Earth, and to the flora, fauna and human life it supports, one planet, indivisible, with safe air, water and soil, economic justice, equal rights and peace for all."[20]

_____ *Contribute time and money to elect political leaders on local, state, and national levels who have strong social consciences and commitments to sound ecology and peace principles and programs.* Such legislators are dedicated to turning back the runaway armaments race; increasing health, housing, and education programs; protecting wilderness areas from continuing degradation; and nurturing nature through constructive political and economic policies. Adopting a more ecologically sound, peacemaking life-style on a personal level, as vitally important as that is, will never change the laws and social practices that are threatening the planet on a wholesale basis. Only as personal health is understood as having crucial social and political dimensions will the political action be taken that will change these.

_____ *Do the simple things that have symbolic as well as literal value in helping save the planet.* Here are some down-to-earth things you can do today. Many of these ideas and the supporting facts cited are from a valuable little book, *Fifty Simple Things You Can Do to Save the Earth.*[21] It will provide you with the reasons and methods for these actions.

- Recycle and reuse everything you can, including aluminum, glass, newspapers, junk mail (and office paper), motor oil, tires, plastic bags, and cardboard cartons. Many of the 500,000 trees that are cut down to supply paper for Sunday newspapers each week in the U.S. could be saved.

- Buy food and other products produced by companies that are socially and ecologically responsible, thus putting your money where your conscience is. Hit socially irresponsible companies where it hurts, in their pocketbook. A valuable booklet to take when you go grocery shopping is *Shopping for a Better World: A Quick and Easy Guide to Socially Responsible Supermarket Shopping* by the Council for Economic Priorities.[22] It rates companies and products on these issues: concern for the environment, advancement of women and people of color, community outreach and giving to charity, military contracts and nuclear power, investment in South Africa, animal testing, and family benefits to employees.

• Buy foods in bulk and other products in biodegradable or recyclable packaging whenever possible.

• Plant a tree to reduce carbon dioxide (the main greenhouse gas), enjoy its shade on hot summer days, and reduce your need for energy by planting it where it will shade your house. A friend tells of a woman he knew who planted at least one tree in every place she lived. How's that for a living investment in the planet's future?

• Eat lower and healthier on the food chain by cutting down or eliminating meat and eating more vegetables and fruits grown organically without pesticides. (See Frances Moore Lappé's *Diet for a Small Planet* and John Robbins's *Diet for a New America*.)

• Car pool, take mass transit, and drive your automobile much less; walk or ride your bicycle much more. When you drive 10,000 miles in the average gasoline-driven vehicle (the yearly average mileage in the U.S.), your car emits some 650 pounds of carbon monoxide, 105 pounds of hydrocarbons, and 50 pounds of nitrogen oxides into the air we all breathe. (The co-head of the European Greens, Sarah Parkin, recently observed: "In London, traffic really doesn't move any faster now than it did in the Middle Ages.")[23]

• When you purchase a motor vehicle, select one that goes the farthest on the least amount of gasoline or, better still, one that burns a clear fuel such as propane or alcohol.

• When you walk, carry a trash bag and pick up litter, including recyclable cans and bottles.

• Stop junk mail by sending it back in the return envelopes with a note. If only 100,000 people did this, some 150,000 trees a year could be saved.

• Use only clean (phosphate-free) detergents. Over half the phosphates that are killing many lakes and streams come from detergents.

- Use latex instead of toxic, oil-based paints. Paint products account for over half the hazardous waste individuals dump.

- Boycott styrofoam packaging and cups—they're toxic and completely nonbiodegradable.

- Take a reusable cloth or web shopping bag to the store (as people in Europe do), thus saving both paper and plastic bags.

- Don't buy ivory or other products from endangered animals or plants.

- Use cloth and not disposable diapers, which take five hundred years to decompose and put three million tons of untreated feces in landfills rather than sewers each year.

- Use only nontoxic pesticides, and compost grass, garden clippings, and vegetable material from the kitchen to produce your own rich soil and planting mulch.

- Save energy and water by installing low-flow shower heads and faucet aerators and by putting a plastic displacement bottle in your toilet tank or, better still, installing a water-saving toilet.

- Help save the rain forests by not buying tropical hardwoods or fast foods with imported meat raised on deforested land in the Amazon basin.

- Support national and international groups working for family planning to stop the population explosion, a fundamental cause of world-wide poverty, hunger, and the destruction of the environment.[24]

- Encourage your office, club, or congregation to help save the planet by doing things like those listed above.

Becoming an environmental activist is your vote for the future. It's a much-needed investment in your children's and grandchildren's future. It's never too late to make such an investment. Melquiades Orttiz was still farming his land in the Himbres Valley of southwest New Mexico when he was 104 years old. He enjoyed his relationship with the earth as he grew alfalfa, apples, and grain, using a horse-drawn single walking plow. When he was 101, he expressed his commitment to water and soil conservation (and to the future of his community) by becoming involved in a five-year group plan to rehabilitate the local community irrigation system.[25]

Doing Your Despair and Empowerment Work

For your health it's important to work through and release whatever subconscious denial and fears may be stealing your creative energy. You could be using that energy to live more productively and help save the planet. I invite you to try these steps (developed by Joanna Rogers Macy) now with a friend.[26]

Step 1: Bring your denied and repressed fears and other feelings into consciousness by talking them through in a relationship of mutual trust. Do this by hearing each other's nuclear-ecological stories—how each of you became aware of the precarious state of the earth. Express your feelings about this fully. (The first time I experienced despair work, I couldn't believe how much emotional baggage I had been carrying around in subconscious feelings of anger, fear, and guilt about the pain of the planet.)

Step 2: Validate each other's pain for the world as based in reality and appropriate. Say to yourself and each other, "You're not crazy! It is appropriate to feel pain about the world's pain in this unprecedented global crisis!"

Step 3: As you talk, get in touch with the underlying source of your pain—your caring love for the wonderful network of life that is threatened with irreparable damage.

Step 4: Open the doorways of your heart to receive hope and empowerment. This comes from working through and releasing your despair, mobilizing your inner resources, deepening your sense of connectedness with the web of life and with the divine Creator of all life.

Step 5: Using this hope and power, identify your action goals and resources, and move into earthkeeping and peacemaking with others.

Discovering the Spiritual-Ethical Heart of Wholistic Ecology-Peacemaking

Let's take a deeper look at why we must evolve spiritually if we are to survive. The deep spiritual and ethical emptiness and dis-ease in us as individuals and in our society are root causes of the ecological and nuclear crises. Only to the extent that this spiritual-ethical pathology is healed can wholistic peace on a whole planet become a reality. Here's a diagnostic overview of the spiritual pathology.

A crucial dimension of our dangerous spiritual sickness is our unfulfilled need to befriend the dark, denied, potentially destructive side of our personalities that Carl Jung called our shadow. We try to avoid seeing this rejected side as a real part of us. Instead, we project it onto others, defining them as "other" and sooner or later demonizing them as dangerous, threatening enemies. It then feels appropriate, of course, to hate and attack them to protect ourselves. This pathological need for an enemy group or nation is a form of collective paranoia. In a nuclear age this enemy making is more dangerous than ever before in the long, sorry history of human violence.

Consider our tendency to see "wild" animals as enemies to be tamed or killed, and wilderness as enemy space to be "civilized" by building neat, boring subdivisions and huge shopping malls with endless parking lots. These are examples of the enemy-making process stemming in part from fearful rejection and then projection of those wild, wilderness dimensions of our own deeper lives. Healing requires that we become acquainted with our wild shadow side and discover how to make it our friend. If we do this, our inner wilderness can become a place of power and zest for living which enriches and enlivens our "civilized," socially "acceptable" side.

A second and closely related spiritual-ethical malady is being cut off from a wonderful sense of our organic oneness with the biosphere's web of life, the human family, and the divine Spirit, which is the source and energizing sustainer of all life and love. A whole range of destructive I-it behaviors flow from this deep alienation from our unity with all of life. Alienation from our bodies— the part of nature we are closest to—is one consequence. Our alienation from nature spawns grandiose feelings that we human beings somehow have a God-given right to exploit the earth and misuse the other species.

Healing involves the discovery of our profound oneness with the whole interdependent network of life, including all human beings. As the most aware co-members of the community of living things, we have a precious trust, a sacred responsibility to protect and nurture it. Getting in touch with our oneness brings the great gift of renewing aliveness and a sense of being partners, co-creators with the divine Spirit. We must learn to live in the truth of the ancient wisdom that "the earth is the Lord's" (Exodus 9:29). We have it only in trust to be loved responsibly for future generations. We will really love the earth when we claim the profound truth of the refrain in the first creation story in Genesis. The Creator's response after each stage of creation was a ringing "It is good!" "It is good!" "It is very good!"

Martin Buber describes how a sense of the sacredness of living things changes our relationship with the natural world. The great teacher-philosopher writes: "I contemplate a tree . . . and if will and grace are joined as I contemplate the tree, I am drawn into a relation, and the tree ceases to be an it."[27]

A third spiritual-ethical sickness is our tribal religious beliefs and ethnocentric consciences with narrow, constricting boundaries ending with our own in-group. These narrow faith and value systems express themselves as classism, religious exclusivism, and jingoistic nationalism, as well as racism and sexism. They enable us to maintain a false sense of defensive, pseudosuperiority over "foreign" or "heathen" religions and groups.

Nothing but inclusive religious beliefs and consciences can draw the human family together to save the planet, rather than splintering us divisively as tribal religions now do. Only inclusive beliefs and values can provide spiritual vision and healing for wholeness with one another and nature in this fractured time. Matthew Fox's expression of this spiritual challenge is on target:

> How can humans deal with cosmic energy and their responsibility for it, without a cosmic spirituality? . . . The human chauvinism that so narrows our vision that . . . we spend a million dollars a minute on weapons of cosmic destruction must cease. It is religion's task to reintroduce a cosmic vision, a less arrogant and less humanly chauvinistic way of seeing our world. . . . Today it is more and more evident that the time has come for humanity to let go of war, to admit that it has outgrown war, and to move beyond war as a way of settling differences. Just as humanity one hundred years ago outlawed slavery, so it is capable of outlawing war.[28]

A fourth deadly spiritual disease consists of magical beliefs that let us expect to be rescued from ecological or nuclear catastrophes by the divine intervention of a heavenly quick fix. These obscene religious beliefs are dangerous defenses against terror because they cut the nerve of responsibility for doing what we must to help save the planet. Rescue fantasies of being pulled back from the brink of eco-nuclear disaster by political leaders whom we foolishly endow with godlike wisdom and power is a secular variation of the same pathological spirituality.

Another dangerous pathology that must be healed if we are to survive in a livable world is our spiritual deadness that keeps us from cherishing and celebrating the incredible gift of just being alive on a living planet. People who are having a love affair with life and the Source of life would not tolerate the tragic destruction of the environment or the colossal wasteful violence of global armaments. Our inner deadness makes the deadness of our social systems feel less

ghoulish. This inner deadness flows from the fact that the divine within us is a stranger to us. This alienation from our transcending self narrows the inner channel of love. It constricts the free flow of the spiritual power from the divine Spirit within us. Love of yourself, of other people, of the earth, and of God flow from this one inner Source.

To remain effective, peacemaking and ecology groups must be spiritually empowered, love-of-life groups. Healing our spiritual deadness involves opening ourselves to receive the gift of the transforming presence of the divine, available in every moment. By so doing, you may discover the lift of living with something akin to the spirit of Saint Francis of Assisi. He had a lover's relation with nature and referred to the birds as his brothers and the wind as his sister. By opening yourself to the divine in the wonders of nature, you may find the joy of living Saint Francis's prayer "Lord, make me an instrument of your peace," and doing so by helping heal the world's brokenness.

Planetary Well-Being Exercise

As you picture the future, do you see the world alive and well and free? Does your vision of the future energize you to work to make it a reality? The purpose of this exercise is to experience the hopeful energy that can pull you forward toward that future.[29] I'm indebted to Joanna Rogers Macy for the heart of this right-brain exercise. I have modified her exercise to include the environmental dimension.

Instructions: Sit in a quiet, comfortable place where you will be undisturbed for fifteen minutes or so. Have your *Well Being Self-Care Journal* within easy reach. Begin by tightening all your muscles and relaxing by deeper breathing and allowing tension to flow out with each exhalation. Use other full-body relaxation methods that work for you, until your body-mind organism is deeply relaxed but keenly alert. /

Now, using one of your many creative abilities, form a picture in your mind of your favorite place in nature. See it vividly and in color. / Be there enjoying the awesome beauty and serenity of that place. Let yourself be nurtured by the healing rhythms of nature. Immerse yourself in the aliveness of that place, letting that energy flow throughout your body, touching every cell with new life and healing. /

Now, imagine that it's a day just like today but thirty years in the future. Imagine that the devastating environmental trends of the 1990s continued unabated through the past three decades. The pollution of the earth has increased and thousands of species have become extinct. The population has soared from six billion to between nine and ten billion, with a cruel impact on the natural world as well as widespread starvation and disease. You're still you (even though you may be a little ancient), and you're sitting in that same place in nature. Look around and experience what it's like, being aware of whatever you're feeling. /

Shift gears now, to a different scenario. Imagine that in the early 1990s people like you around the planet decided to love and protect the earth so that their children and grandchildren would inherit a more beautiful planet. They also decided to interrupt the insane arms race totally, destroying all the nuclear, chemical, and biological weapons that had held the whole planet hostage. Furthermore, the population explosion was halted and the problems of hunger and sickness were resolved by the nations of the planet working together. Be aware of how it feels to be in a world with an effective international environment-protecting, peacekeeping force—a sane, healthy world where all children have enough food, health care, housing, and education to develop their gifts fully. /

Be in your favorite place in nature again. Look around and enjoy experiencing it even cleaner and more beautiful than it was thirty years ago. / Watch now as a child approaches you. She looks about eight or nine. She seems shy but she's also very curious. She has heard something about the way the world was thirty years ago. Watch as she comes up to where you're sitting and begins to ask you questions. Listen to her eager questions about the old days and to your responses as she asks, "What was it like back then? Was pollution poisoning the air and the water so people and animals were getting sick? Were there really bombs so big that they could blow up the whole world? Were millions of children like me poor and hungry and sick because governments were spending so much on bombs? Wasn't it scary to be alive then? What did *you* do to keep strong so you could help make the good world we have today?" /

The little girl spontaneously flings her arms around your neck and gives you a big hug of gratitude, saying with deep feeling, "Thank you! Thank you! Thank you!" Then she leaves, and you close your eyes and reflect on the whole experience. What was it like when you realized you were in a peaceful, healthy world without environmental and nuclear threats? Did you find it terribly hard to believe? Or did your heart feel like a heavy weight had been lifted? If it did, you are now aware of the load of chronic anxiety about the world that you carry like a heavy pack on your psychological back, every hour of every day. / How did you feel when the little girl asked you what you did to help give her and other children such a wonderful world? / Continue to process your trip into a more whole future. Ask yourself perhaps, What do I need to do now to get more involved in helping heal the planet for all children of the future, including those as yet unborn? / When you are ready, make notes in your *Well Being Journal* of things you discovered and plan to do as a result of visiting a transformed world.

**Create Your
Eco-Peacemaking
Fitness Plan**

Take time now to jot down your plans for enhancing your own wellness by doing more to help heal our planet. Go back and review things that interested you as you read this chapter, including the items you marked for attention on the checkup and the subsequent shopping list. Pick at least six things you want to do.

Using your creativity, write out a realistic Self-Care Through Earth-Care Plan. Remember, your plan probably will be more effective if it includes: (1) concrete, realizable objectives that you really want to achieve; (2) practical strategies for moving toward these; (3) a time line; (4) rewards you'll get or give yourself as you take each step toward objectives, or withhold if you backslide; (5) a record of your progress in your *Journal.* You may want to include further reading (from the Recommended Reading at the end of the book) in your plan.

Pick one or two especially attractive and achievable objectives and begin moving toward them immediately. Also, to empower your efforts, I recommend that you create an empowering movie in your mind each day, experiencing the joy and struggles of successfully implementing your plan.

Also, keep a record of your progress as you implement your plan. It's important to keep what you do love centered and spiritually energized. Activate your inner child, balancing your serious intentions with a touch of humor. As Milton Berle once said, "The world's in terrible shape. Pessimists never had it so good!"[30]

The multiple crises on our planet might well remind us of the ancient Chinese proverb: "If we do not change our direction, we'll probably end up where we're headed!" Changing our direction, as individuals or as a society, is tough, to say the least. But it's the only way out of our global health crisis, the only way to ensure that our children inherit a beautiful, livable planet.

A healthy reminder to frazzled planet-savers from environmentalist Edward Abbey: "Do not burn yourself out. Be as I am—a reluctant enthusiast, a part-time crusader, a half-hearted fanatic. Save the other half of yourself for pleasure and adventure. It is not enough to fight for the environment; it is important to enjoy it. While you can. While it's still here."[31] I wish you heart-stretching, deeply satisfying self-care that includes earth-care.

PART TWO

Coping Constructively with Detours, Challenges, and Opportunities on the Journey of Well Being

Growing Through Crises and Losses, Disabilities and Addictions

 Not long ago our local paper's sports page quoted a classic comment by the basketball coach at the University of California at Irvine. Describing the abysmal loss by his team to the University of Nevada by a score of 125 to 59, he declared, "We got off to a terrible start and then things started to deteriorate." Ever have a day like that? Or a week? Or a year? If so, you can identify with Charlie Brown's complaint: "As soon as I get up in the morning, I feel like I'm in over my head." Crises and losses are a part of everyone's journey, sooner or later. As the author of the ancient Book of Job observed, we humans are born to trouble as the sparks fly upward from a fire (Job 5:7).

What can we do to sustain some measure of well being at our center when agonizing crises and losses strike? The light of the ancient wisdom of the Far East is reflected in two Chinese characters. The character on the left (pronounced *way*) means danger. The character on the right (pronounced *gee*) means opportunity. Together they mean crisis![1] In these characters we find the theme of this chapter. Most of us are painfully aware of the danger in our crises and losses. But we often miss the opportunities! Using the opportunities in your crises involves learning how to transform miserable minuses into at least partial plusses. This means learning how to grow through crises and losses. To do so is tough, but possible. And it's essential to our well being to learn how to do this.

Sooner or later all of us know the pain of shattered hopes and dreams. The more intensely you love, the deeper the pit of grief when your love is gone. The more passionately you care about a cause, the deeper your anger and pain if, in spite of all you do, it fails.

(danger) *(opportunity)*

Well being involves learning how to cope with this grief without being permanently embittered and crippled by the losses. It involves having the guts to accept your failures, finitude, and fracturedness; your addictions, disabilities, and diseases; your agonizing losses and painful transitions. It is learning to use these painful intruders in your life to leaven your wholeness with humility, new strengths, and some real down-to-earthness.

In my memory bank, I prize these wise words of the minister of my boyhood church (who was like a second father to me): "Walk softly, for everyone you meet is carrying some cross."[2] These words ring true today, much more so than when I heard them a half-century ago. It's often easy to miss this reality. Most of us are skilled in hiding our personal crises from others. We're experts in appearing on top of things when at our center we're having to look up to see bottom. The degree to which you love and accept yourself, with all your imperfections, is a barometer of your wholeness. This includes accepting what's most difficult for most of us—the hidden, unattractive areas of brokenness and captivity. Getting to know, accept, and befriend this shadow side (Carl Jung's term) is crucial to your overall well being.

The considerable time I spent on my grandparents' farm in southern Illinois each summer, during my childhood and youth, provides a vivid image. In the springtime, I remember the horse-drawn plow cutting deep furrows through the prairie soil. I can still experience and enjoy the smells of spring including the freshly turned earth. I can still see the robins and meadowlarks following the plow to harvest the exposed earthworms.

Crises and griefs are like that. The blades of their pain cut deep channels through our souls. The plow also cuts the roots of our comfortable beliefs and life-styles. But, by the very turbulence, it also prepares the soil to nurture new seeds. These can take root and eventually flower in ways that could not have been imagined before the soil was so rudely prepared for new life. The deeper the furrow cut by grief, the more can flow through it. Fortunately we can choose what runs in this channel to some degree. At first it usually carries the torrent of our tears. These can be followed by the acid flow of continuing bitterness and resentment. Or, gradually, we can let the living waters of compassion, empathy, and love—ours and God's—flow through this channel in our souls. When this happens new flowering can be nurtured in grief-parched lives—beginning with our own.

Professor Jack Matson of the University of Michigan Business School teaches a class he calls Failure 101. It is based on a series of "hurdle-jumping exercises" that confront students (who are used to succeeding) with repeated failures and humiliations. When things go wrong later in life, he explains, "they'll understand those are natural,

IN CASE OF A TIDAL WAVE

REMAIN CALM,

PAY YOUR BILL—

AND RUN LIKE HELL!

—*sign in a hotel lobby*

in Hawaii

WINDOW OF WHOLENESS

HELEN KELLER AND ANNE SULLIVAN

The lives of Helen Keller and her dedicated teacher and companion, Anne Sullivan, are stories of inspiring wholeness, despite personal crises, losses, and disabilities. Helen was born in 1880 without physical disabilities. Until just before her second birthday, she enjoyed hearing the mockingbirds and seeing the flowers and trees on the Alabama plantation where she was raised. Then she suffered a severe brain fever that destroyed both her sight and hearing.

Her parents' frustrating efforts to handle their doubly handicapped daughter produced only a deeply disturbed child. They sought the help of Alexander Graham Bell, a former teacher of the deaf. He helped them find a twenty-year-old woman, Anne Sullivan, who came to be a live-in teacher for Helen. Anne had had a miserable childhood with an illiterate, alcoholic immigrant father. At age ten she experienced the humiliation and rejection of being sent to a poorhouse, where she was listed as blind. Four years later she was transferred to an institution that had developed innovative methods for teaching the blind. Surgery restored her sight. Gradually the shame and hatred of her childhood trauma gave way to understanding and love. She was selected as valedictorian of her graduating class.

The day she came to be Helen's teacher she brought a doll, which she handed to Helen, spelling D-O-L-L on Helen's hand with her fingers. The marvelous moment of learning came when Anne poured water from a pump on one of Helen's hands while she spelled out the word on her other hand. Helen realized that everything has a name! This opened up the mystery of language to her. She became an avid, rapid learner. By age ten she had learned to read and write. Eventually she learned to talk, a difficult feat, in French and German as well as English. She entered Radcliffe College, accompanied by Anne, graduating cum laude with excellence in English literature, history, and foreign languages.

After graduation she found her lifelong passion and calling, working and writing on behalf of the blind. She published extensively and lectured widely in America and abroad. She broadened her interests and became involved in the women's suffrage movement and in other political activity on behalf of the poor and oppressed. With all of her work, she also enjoyed horseback riding, bicycling, sailing, playing with her dogs, and gardening. She enjoyed music, hearing through the vibrations she could feel. She had a sparkling sense of humor and a vitality and optimism that attracted a wide circle of friends, including a host of literary, political, educational, and entertainment leaders.

Recognized as one of the stellar women of her times, she received many honors. In 1936 she and Anne were awarded the Roosevelt Medal for Cooperative Achievement of Far-Reaching Significance. Mark Twain described her as "a wonderful creature—the most wonderful in the world." Of herself, she said, "My life has been happy because I have had wonderful friends and plenty of interesting work to do. I seldom think of my limitations and they never make me sad. Perhaps there is just a touch of yearning at times, but it is vague, like a breeze among the flowers. The wind passes and the flowers are content" (*Current Biography*, 1942, 444). Helen Keller's buoyant spirit was expressed beautifully in her autobiography when she wrote: "One can never consent to creep when one feels the impulse to soar."

EASY WHEN HAVE ALL THE ADVANTAGES ? (RETURN TO LEFT COLUMN PREVIOUS PAGE !)

Helen Keller died in 1968, having inspired millions by her writings and even more by her vital, courageous life. Her wholeness and that of Anne Sullivan are a continuing blessing to all of us in the human family who suffer losses and disabilities, large or small, and yet feel the impulse to soar.

normal sensations and by knowing that, they'll be more confident to forge ahead. If we really want to succeed, we have to take risks." And risks mean we often fail.[3]

Crises and Losses Well-Being Checkup

CHECKLIST

This checkup can increase your well being in two ways. (1) It's a self-discovery instrument. It can give you a quick evaluation of your present strengths and weaknesses in coping constructively with crises and losses. (2) The checkup offers options for use in developing a personal plan to increase your fitness in this vital area. The checkup is also a preview of many of the self-help ideas and methods explored in more depth in this chapter.

Instructions: In front of each item on the checkup, place one of three initials: E = I'm doing very well (excellently) in this; OK = I'm doing acceptably but there's room for improvement; NS = I definitely need strengthening in this.

_____ When trouble strikes, I take better care of myself physically and emotionally, and also turn to other caring people for help.

_____ When the future seems horribly dark, I take my life an hour at a time. I avoid the temptation to retreat for long into denial or despair. I know that hope eventually will be reborn, if I do what I can to improve things bit by bit.

_____ I'm able to express my full range of agonizing feelings and talk them through so that I can eventually release them.

_____ I don't waste creative energy feeling discriminated against by life, for long, when losses happen, because I know they're a normal part of everyone's life.

Wholeness Exercise

The purpose of this brief exercise is to remind you of what you already know about how to grow from your losses and crises.

Go back in your memory and recall a painful loss, crisis, failure, accident, or disabling problem in your life. Relive that experience in as much detail as you can, experiencing whatever pain was there. / If you feel unhealed pain, fear, or anger, remember that it's good to become aware of these energy-wasting feelings on which you need to do more healing work. /

Reflect on what you just relived. In your mind (and then in your *Self-Care Journal*) list the personal strengths, bits of wisdom, and spiritual growth you gained as a result of handling this tough experience as well as you did. Even if you only muddled through, remember that you *did* mobilize the strength to do this. Commend yourself for whatever fragments of wisdom about coping you acquired from your crisis. / Become aware of the things and the people who enabled you to survive and perhaps even to grow a bit through this crisis. Remember, you can use these tested-in-the-fire learnings in your future crises and losses.

_____ I have the courage to seek the guidance of a competent counselor if I feel wiped out by a crisis or loss.

_____ I've discovered how mutually helpful it can be to reach out to others going through crises and losses similar to mine.

_____ I do anticipatory grieving to help prepare myself for expected or ongoing losses, such as a terminally ill loved one or a major life transition.

_____ I've learned how to find some spiritual comfort and meaning even in tragic situations that seem unfair. If my old faith feels shattered, I'm able to hang in there until spiritual renewal slowly begins to occur.

_____ When I experience physical, mental, or interpersonal pain, I try to listen to what it is telling me about my need to change something in my life.

_____ After making corrective amends, I forgive myself and accept God's forgiveness for whatever I have contributed to my crises and losses.

_____ When I'm in a major crisis, I continue to eat and rest adequately, even when I don't feel like doing so. I also avoid the trap of seeking to deaden the pain by excessive alcohol or drugs, or fleeing from the pain in frenetic busyness.

_____ Whenever possible, I avoid making major decisions while I'm still in shock after a shattering crisis or loss.

_____ I'm usually able to sort out the pieces of my crises and take action on one part at a time, rather than being paralyzed by the whole intertwined mess of problems.

_____ If I experience a socially stigmatized loss—such as a loss by suicide or AIDS—I have resources for coping with the judgmentalism and lack of social support.

_____ Among the uninvited learnings that have come through crises is the discovery that I can survive things I couldn't have imagined surviving.

Using Your Findings: Scan your responses and get an overall feel for your strengths and weaknesses in handling crises and losses growthfully. Then in your *Well Being Self-Care Journal* write down key words to remind you of the items that feel most important among the ones you marked NS or OK. These are your "growing edge" areas, where you can increase your crisis fitness with the most benefits to yourself. Also jot down any tentative thoughts you have concerning actions you might take in these areas of need and opportunity.

Transforming Miserable Minuses into Partial Pluses

In the early 1940s there was a terrible loss of human life in a nightclub fire near Boston. This tragedy motivated Harvard psychiatrist Erich Lindemann to begin a scientific study of how people recover from crises and grief. His research and that of many others since then have produced a wealth of understanding. This understanding can help us cope more constructively with painful experiences. Here is a summary of these discoveries.

All significant crises and life transitions bring losses and therefore a measure of grief. Surprisingly this includes even the good changes, like a job promotion, graduation, or retirement. Experiences of crises and grief are intertwined. To have a crisis there must be some loss, actual or feared. Crisis experiences happen *within* you, rather than *to* you. The external pressures make you emotionally vulnerable to have the inner experience of a crisis. The fact that a crisis happens *in* you means that you have at least some power to choose your response to it.

There are these predictable stages in most crises:

1. You face a problem or loss that robs you or threatens to rob you of something very important to you. This produces feelings of fear, shock, anger, and anxiety.

2. You use the problem-solving skills you already know and have used before. If these are effective, crisis feelings subside.

3. If your old problem-solving skills don't work because the situation is somehow new, you may well try new coping strategies.

4. If these also are ineffective, severe crisis feelings flourish—for example, painful feelings of confusion, disorientation, helplessness, floundering, hopelessness, panic, rage, and guilt.

5. If the need-depriving problem is not resolved, either by your own efforts or the help of others, the crisis pressure gradually will rise to a breaking point. You come apart at the seams in one way or another, feeling overwhelmed by a tidal wave of what could be called copelessness.

It's important to know that the health-threatening stress of crises, changes, and losses are cumulative. A loss followed closely by another, before the first wound heals, produces much more total stress than the two would if separated by more healing time. So if you're going through one of those "when it rains it pours" times, be especially gentle, caring, and forgiving with yourself. Also, remember that if unexpected crises or losses strike out of the blue, it usually takes much longer for full healing to occur than when crises are expected. Unexpected crises and losses are more likely to produce infected grief wounds that may not heal on their own without therapeutic help. Expected losses give you time to learn how to cope, tie up loose ends in a relationship by saying good-bye and "I love you," and time to do some of your grieving work before the loss occurs (anticipatory grief).

Research has shown that to stay as fit as possible during severe, multiple, or unexpected crisis and grief, it's essential to increase your self-care and your receptivity to the care of others. In other words, be kind and gentle with yourself and also let your friends and loved ones know that you need extra support and care.

All this came closer to home than I would have liked while I was finishing this book. Within a few months I ended three decades of teaching at the same school; we sold and moved out of a home in which we had lived and reared our three children for almost thirty years; and I vacated an office I had occupied for nearly half of my life. (Just sorting and pitching what I had accumulated was a major trauma for this charter member of Packrats Anonymous.) Then we moved to a new community and into another home, which had to be remodeled while we lived in it. Being stressed out, I was an accident waiting to happen. And it did—totaling the car and almost totaling me.

I wish I could report that my self-care was increased, as I knew it should be during this pressure-cooker time. Unfortunately, I let my self-care be diminished by the barrage of pressures on my time and psyche. As I gradually learned (again) to laugh at the crazy rat race and load of expectations I was putting on myself during those frantic months, a degree of something closer to sanity returned.

The potential growth opportunities in crises and losses usually are well disguised. But they're actually forks in the road of your life journey. If you take the fork of facing and coping constructively, you'll discover in retrospect that you've grown a little bit stronger and wiser, and perhaps a tad more empathetic as a result. If, in contrast, you take the fork of avoiding facing the problem, your crisis-handling muscles will be weaker when you encounter the next crisis or loss down the road. You'll also be wasting creative energy carrying around the unresolved loss in your deeper mind.

To grow through crises and thus sustain your wholeness you need three things: *First, caring people* who can hold up a light for you by supporting and loving you in your darkness. Millions of persons who are caught in our society's epidemic of loneliness have a terribly difficult time surviving, not to mention growing, during severe crises. It's crucial that communities and congregations develop strategies for giving such persons caring support during their crises.

The second thing needed is *some sense of meaning in your crisis.* Studies of prisoners of war and death camp inmates revealed that those who had even a short-term sense of purpose could survive enormous deprivation and suffering that destroyed those with no sense of meaning.

The third thing needed is *some small hope for a better future.* Studies in the psychology of hope have produced clear evidence of a simple but profound fact: while there's hope there's life. Our human ability to cope with the present is intertwined with memories of the past and expectations for the future. When hopes for a good future are shattered, people lose a powerful magnet drawing them forward toward their future. Studies by Yale psychiatrist Robert Lifton show that "radical futurelessness" is widespread among North American youth. It flows from their awareness of the ecological-nuclear crisis on planet earth. Futurelessness is epidemic among poor youth. This deep hopelessness cuts the nerve of constructive living now and also action aimed at helping build a better future. (Remember the high school youth, Bill, in chapter 8?)

Rose Campbell-Gibson, a research scientist at the University of Michigan, came up with some remarkable findings regarding the human ability to cope with crises and losses. In her analysis of a national survey of Americans,[4] she discovered that elderly black women, the poorest group in America, live longer and cope better with aging than white women, or men of either race. They also have the lowest suicide rate of any group of elderly people. (White males, the most affluent group, have the highest suicide rates among the elderly.) Once black women reach seventy-five, they can expect to live longer than any other group.

Older black women suffer from five forms of social oppression, all of which tend to diminish well being in most people—racism, sexism, ageism, poverty, and working at boring, menial jobs. How do they manage to cope and survive? The researcher found that black people are far better than whites at getting caring support from a network of family, friends, neighbors, and (she should have added) their church. She observed that blacks are more likely than whites to use prayer as a method of coping and as a way of bonding with others. But in her explanatory comments, she misses the crucial fact that the religious life and church community of many black Americans is a primary source of their love, hope, and faith. From the days of slavery on, the black congregation has been a life-saving oasis from the searing, debilitating heat of institutional racism. Its family-like network provides mutual support in times of crisis and sorrow, as well as repair for black self-esteem damaged by their constant humiliation in our white racist society. It is also a place to develop leadership, express and release pent-up hurt, and drink deeply from the spiritual spring of moving, rhythmic singing, rituals, and worship.

Growing Through Grief: The Five Tasks of Healing

What do you need to do to use losses as opportunities for healing and growth? The same basic process—labeled "grief work" by Erich Lindemann—is involved in what could be called crisis recovery work. There usually are five overlapping tasks that make up the journey to healing. As I walk you through these tasks now, I recommend that you relate them to a painful crisis, loss, or transition—past or present—in your own life.

1. **The first task on the path of healing is gradually to let go of denial and accept the painful reality of the problem or loss.** When something traumatic hits us like a ton of bricks, our minds mercifully protect us from overload by the psychological defense of denial. "It seems like a horrible nightmare from which I expect to wake up. I go in and out of feeling that it's unreal." These are the words of a father whose teenage son was killed by a drug-intoxicated driver. Some denial is essential at first for our sanity in such a huge loss. But for healing to continue, this protective denial must gradually lift. The grim reality must be gradually accepted.

   What kind of help do most of us need right after a shattering loss? The warm, loving presence of trusted family and friends is most important. Practical help with the countless things that must be done is also important. And, depending on the person's religious background, the presence of their trusted pastor, priest, or rabbi bearing the comfort of their spiritual tradition may also be desired and helpful. During the early days of a severe crisis, taking life one hour, then one day at a time is the only way many of us make it through. Stop to recall what kind of support you found helpful in moving through the denial stage of your loss.

2. **The second task is to experience and express fully all your agonizing feelings, talking them through so that you can gradually release them.** This task begins and is intertwined with the first. Anything that prevents the full experiencing, expressing, and talking through of the pain will retard or block the healing. The wisdom of the Second Testament puts the same insight this way: "Blessed are those who mourn, for they shall be comforted" (Matthew 5:4).

The presence of loved ones who will really listen enables those in grief to gradually let go of their denial and express their agony. They do this by talking—again and again—about their loss as they experience the emotional release of active mourning, often including deep weeping. Full release of the swirling waves of feelings after a cruel loss usually takes a long time, often a year or more. As the excruciating feelings slowly diminish, the problem-solving abilities of the mind become more available for coping with the new situation brought by the loss.

What kind of help do people usually need as they struggle with the second task? Someone who can "hear us into speech," to use Nelle Morton's apt phrase.[5] This means someone who will listen without judging or giving advice, listen with warm, caring acceptance of the person's sorrow, whatever form it takes. This includes expressing those messy, conflicted feelings that aren't polite, easily accepted, or easily expressed. It also includes hearing the feelings between the lines, too painful to put in words. All this is what I call healing listening.

In practice what is required is to say (and really mean), "Tell me about what happened," and then practice the fine art of keeping your mouth shut. If you do this, you create an inviting silence into which the person can pour the bitter brew of rage, longing, remorse, resentment, confusion, self-pity, hopelessness, denial, emptiness, disorientation, and, in some cases, relief, release, and hope. Listening in this depth is a gift. It's also a skill that doesn't come easily, particularly if our anxiety and pain make us fall into the traps of trying to give quick-fix advice or making the pain go away. Pause and ask yourself, was I fortunate enough to have someone to do healing listening during my big crisis or loss? Do I still need to talk through some pain?

3. **The third essential task on the path to healing is to put your life back together gradually, in some workable shape, without whatever you have lost.** What makes this task very difficult is that it usually must begin almost immediately after a death or other major crisis, long before the second task of healing is very far along. The crisis situation forces you to make tough decisions and take difficult actions when you are struggling to keep your head above water in the whirlpool of overwhelming feelings.

Putting your shattered life back together involves unlearning all those old ways of satisfying your essential needs in relation to whomever or whatever you have lost. It also means learning new ways to satisfy these needs. This unlearning and relearning is a scary, painful process for most of us. If your loss was of a vitally important person in your life, you know that deep relationships are irreplaceable, in one sense. But I hope you will discover that it is possible to develop new friendships that can supply some of the lost satisfactions and help you get on with living.

A friend named Jean described her struggles after the death in midlife of her dear husband: "It has taken three years to finally come to some sense of peace and to find my way again as a single woman. I want to share with you some of this journey. First, I never knew how much I could hurt, how many tears there could be, how alone one can feel in the midst of many friends and a wonderful family. While support is so vital, I knew this was my journey and no one could 'fix it' for me."

She went on, "After about six months I was so distressed, I went for counseling. My therapist opened doors for me but, most of all, she affirmed me. She assured me that my grief was healthy. . . . She helped me sort out practical decisions and plans. After about nine months, she encouraged me to 'fly' and to call her when needed. As you might guess, I am now a true advocate of therapy. . . . The journey continues. The pain and loss are ever there but healing does come . . . [to me], as a person working hard at a new identity."[6]

4. **A fourth healing task is to stretch your faith so as to find some meaning in your new situation.** Traumatic crises confront us with opportunities for spiritual growth. They often shatter our illusions of invulnerability. Crises expose the inadequacies of our little gods, the values we have worshiped by our life-styles like achievements, success, security, power, prestige, and possessions. Crises invite us to see our idols as unworthy of being given so much of our precious passion and devotion. Crises may even shatter our

ultimate human idolatry—the protecting shell of pseudo-self-sufficiency, feeling that we don't *really* need other people or the divine Spirit.

As I was finishing this chapter, a cruel disease struck a dear member of my family. The central question of the biblical Book of Job—Why does a good person suffer so unfairly?—hit us where we live and love. We humans usually ask the big *why me* question out of anger and resentment, on the one hand, protesting the unfairness of it all, or out of irrational guilt on the other—"I must have done something to deserve this, though I haven't a clue what it is." However we ask it, there's really no adequate or fully satisfying answer. But there are, I remind myself, a few constructive things we can do to ease the pain.

• One is to face the fact that often life is anything but fair. Sorrows and joys rain on the just and the unjust, and on the rest of us in between.

• A second thing we can do is to avoid going on an unproductive guilt trip, at the same time that we take an honest look at anything we might have done to contribute to our crisis; and to take responsibility for correcting anything that we discover.

• A third thing we can do is to use the energy we save by not continuing for long to rage at life for being unfair, to cope with the loss as constructively as we can.

• A fourth thing is to reframe our situation by deciding to learn all we can from this agonizing part of our life journey.

As we mature in other areas, most of us retain residues of magically protective, though obsolete beliefs from childhood. These usually are a variation on one theme: "If I do or don't do certain things, God will protect me from all tragedy." Such beliefs sooner or later are shattered by a head-on collision with reality. Many people feel like Ron did when his wife, Cathy, contracted a fast-spreading cancer and died at thirty-two, just as their careers, family, and fortunes were beginning to flourish. Here's what he cried out in rage to his pastor, Mike: "It's so unfair! What I've always believed turned out to be a lie! I've lost my faith!"

What kind of help encourages spiritual growth after faith-shattering losses? What helped Ron most in his agonizing struggle was the caring presence of his trusted pastor, who, fortunately, had been trained in grief counseling. The minister listened to Ron with warm, nonjudgmental acceptance as he raged against God and fate. He heard and let Ron know he heard his cries of awful despair and the emptiness in the dark night of his soul. Ron gradually discovered, with Mike's help, that the shattering of his cherished childhood beliefs had forced him to let go of his innocence and to grow up in both his heart-level and head-level understanding of the ways spiritual reality works. He also found helpful understanding in a book the pastor loaned him, *When Bad Things Happen to Good People* by Harold S. Kushner. Gradually he accepted the fact that we live as very vulnerable creatures in a universe still in process, where destructive forces impact our lives every day, that we are in a universe where we may be broken by toxic forces in our social and natural environment, and where we hurt ourselves by not living in harmony with the working principles of an orderly world, many of which principles we do not yet fully understand.

Thus the minister helped Ron do his double grief work, about the loss of his wife and also his spiritual grief at the loss of his childhood faith. Over several months of counseling, Mike encouraged Ron to think and feel his way through to a stronger, more workable faith, which helped him to open himself to a healing relationship with God. The pastor also helped him make some tough decisions about his getting-ahead-at-whatever-price lifestyle, and about changing the "screwed up priorities" (as Ron eventually put it) implicit therein.

Did your personal faith and life-guiding values survive the storm of your crisis intact? Did they help you handle it? Is there still some growth to be done in this area of your life?

5. **The fifth task of growing through crises and losses is to join hands with others going through similar deep water, giving each other mutual understanding and help.** When you have a crisis and learn something useful from it, you have a new asset for helping others find healing. To reach out in this way is a no-lose strategy. It may help the other but it almost certainly will help your healing. To paraphrase the wisdom of a young carpenter, a spiritual genius who lived some twenty centuries ago: To find life in all its fullness in the midst of brokenness, you must reach out to others in pain. To keep life clutched to yourself is to lose it. To give it away is to find it, in mutual caring and healing. If your life crises have taught you some valuable things about handling times of agony and grief, don't waste these small fragments of wisdom. Your brokenness will be either a bridge or a barrier to others who are broken by crises and grief. If you try to hide your brokenness, other suffering persons will be aware that you are somehow not for real. But if you own your pain and learn from it, it becomes a bridge of empathy and a spring of healing for others' brokenness. You become a wounded healer and thereby help heal yourself.

In his powerful little book *Lament for a Son,* written after the death of his twenty-five-year-old son, Nicholas Wolterstorff reflects on the future of his own life: "Sorrow is no longer the island but the sea. . . . I shall look at the world through tears. Perhaps I shall see things that dry-eyed I could not see."[7] The valuable things you have seen through your tears can be used by reaching out to help others.

Here are some words that I wrote several years ago, soon after both of my parents died:

On Not Wasting Your Pain

For my pain, O God—which I did not choose, and do not like, and
    would let go of if I could—
Give me the wisdom to treat it as a bridge
A crossing to another's pain—to that person's private hell.
Grant me the courage not to live alone
Behind my shell of hiding,
My makebelieve side which tries to always seem "on top,"
    in control, adequate for any crunch, not really needing others.
Let me own my inner pain so that it will open me
To those I meet,
To their pain and caring—
That in our shared humanity,
We may know that we are one—in You.

A Tool for Coping Constructively with Crises

Putting your life back together following a huge crisis or loss (the third task of grief work) involves many difficult decisions and new, scary actions. Here's a do-it-yourself version of the ABCD approach to crisis counseling.[8] This has proved to be a simple but valuable tool for helping yourself or others cope constructively with crises and perhaps even grow a little in turbulent times. If you're in a crisis (major or minor) currently, I strongly recommend that you apply this strategy now. To cope effectively with a crisis, do four things:

A. **Achieve a relationship with a trusted person (or persons) who can be your caring guide and ally.** When your head is whirling from the shock and grief of a crisis, it's crucial to ask at least one caring person you trust to give you support. Such persons often can help you understand your situation more accurately and, on that basis, plan reality-based solutions to it. They can walk beside you as caring guides through the dark valley. They can give you encouragement and reality testing in the process of talking through and resolving your crisis. Such help can come from a trusted family member, friend, clergyperson, counselor, congregation, or a crisis support group.

WINDOW OF WHOLENESS

CLEM LUCILLE

When Clem's little daughter, Ruth, died on her first birthday, the whole family was shattered by the tragedy. With intuitive awareness, Clem knew that she must do something to bear the crushing load of her grief. Her response was an expression of her deep faith. For several years she watched her hometown paper carefully. When she read of the death of a child, she wrote a brief note to the parents saying very simply how sorry she was, that they were in her prayers, and that she knew something about the dark valley through which they were walking, because she, too, had lost a dear child. Clem never discussed how much the grieving parents to whom she wrote were helped. But it is clear that Clem herself found deep healing in sending those little notes. She felt that she was responding to God's intention for her life in those dark days. I'm profoundly grateful for what Clem taught me when I was very young, by reaching out with healing love to others, during our family's darkest hours. Clem Lucille Clinebell was my mother.

B. **Boil down your complicated crisis situation by dividing it into its major problems.** One thing that makes big crises so overwhelming is that they hit you with a tangled jumble of interrelated problems all at once. It helps to sort out the pieces of your crisis, separating the most urgent parts from those that can wait for solutions, and distinguishing problems you can solve from those that are beyond your control. Avoid wasting your precious energy on the latter. To do this is to use theologian Reinhold Niebuhr's familiar Serenity Prayer: "Grant me the serenity to accept the things I cannot change, the courage to change the things I can, and the wisdom to know the difference." A New York psychiatrist I once knew observed that if her patients could learn to live by this prayer, many of them would no longer need her help. If you're using the ABCD strategy with a current crisis, list all the pieces of your problem in your *Self-Care Journal*, and then sort them out with your trusted guide, as described above.

C. **Choose one or two parts of your crisis you can do something about, and challenge yourself to take action soon.** List all the solutions you can think of to each sub-problem, and then list the probable consequences of each approach. Discuss all this with your guide. Then decide on which solution(s) you'll try and work out a realistic plan, including the small steps you'll take to make the plan work for you. After doing this, commit yourself to moving ahead to implement this plan ASAP, deciding on a time line and asking for the help you need from others.

As crisis counselors have discovered repeatedly, the human personality is like a muscle. Exercise it by actively solving problems and it will grow stronger. Don't use it and it will gradually grow flabby and atrophy. As you implement your action plan, remember that your coping muscles are being strengthened by your strenuous, though sometimes frustrating, efforts. Equally important, as you take small steps toward solving one part of your crisis, you'll probably find that your shaky self-confidence is strengthened and your hope reawakened. Gradually you'll feel more self-empowered.

> The human soul is virtually
>
> indestructible, and its ability
>
> to rise from the ashes
>
> remains as long as the body
>
> draws breath.
>
> —Alice Miller

D. Develop and implement an ongoing action plan for coping with the other parts of your crisis, one by one, thus gradually rebuilding your life in each of the troubled areas. When some of your action plans don't work, go back to the drawing board. Consult with your guide and together devise a better plan for that issue, or shift to another part of your crisis. As you let go of old patterns that don't work and surrender (in a positive, active sense) to the reality that some things cannot be cured, changed, or recovered, your energy level will tend to rise slowly. The creative energy that you were wasting by batting your head against the wall of your crisis will become available for living, loving, and coping.

Psychologist Joan Borysenko, director of the Mind/Body Clinic at Harvard Medical School, describes a research study that sheds light on why some people cope and others collapse in crises. Suzanne Kobasa and her colleagues studied business executives and lawyers under severe stress. Three attitudes were found to be prominent in stress-hardy subjects, protecting them from physical illnesses in their crises: (1) *commitment*, meaning curiosity and involvement in whatever happened; (2) *challenge*, meaning they believed that the stressful changes could be used to grow; (3) *control*, meaning the willingness to act on their belief that they could influence what happened. Borysenko declares: "People who feel in control of life can withstand an enormous amount of change and thrive on it. People who feel helpless can hardly cope at all."[9] The ABCD strategy works for many people, as I understand it, because it enables them to strengthen their sense of courage, challenge, and control.

When the Wound in Your Heart Does Not Heal

It's important to know that grief and crises are not illnesses. They're normal human responses to the psychological amputation caused by a significant loss and trauma. Most people can mobilize resources within themselves and their caring community to cope with even severe losses. Like a cut on your hand, the crisis or grief wound will gradually heal over time, unless it is infected. But in our

"I can tell you one thing right off—you can't solve your problems by running away."

death-denying culture of massive loneliness, many people experience some degree of infection when they are so wounded. The infection may retard or totally block the healing process.

Here are some danger signs that can alert you to an infected grief wound, *if* they continue unabated.

- Ongoing denial of the reality of the loss, or continuing to overidealize whatever has been lost (pointing to repression of those negative feelings that are present in all close relationships);

- The absence of mourning or, at the other extreme, undiminished mourning;

- Severe depression, guilt, rage, phobias, or deadening of zest for living;

- Continuing withdrawal from people and everyday human activities;

- The onset of severe or multiple illnesses with a psychophysiological component—for example, heart disease, hypertension, arthritis, diabetes, neurodermatitis, thyroid malfunctions, and cancer of the gastrointestinal tract (the seven illnesses that proliferate, according to Erich Lindemann);

- Continuing escape into alcohol or drugs (prescribed or street) or into overwork (a favorite escape for men);

- The onset of addictions of any kind; or either overt or covert suicidal ideas or actions (like crazy driving);

- Ongoing sleep or eating disturbances;

- Craziness-making, toxic relationships, sexual deadness and severe hang-ups beginning in the months after the trauma;

- Radical personality changes (e.g., a neat person becomes super-messy);

- Loss of faith or fleeing into toxic, fanatical religious ideas or groups.

Most of these symptoms may be present, to some degree, in the awful agony of the first days and weeks after a huge crisis or loss. Only if they continue unabated for several months or longer are they warning signs of infected grief wounds.

What can you do if you know or suspect that someone you love (including yourself) is suffering from a grief wound that's not healing? Short-term crisis and bereavement counseling by a clergyperson with training in counseling will probably help. Powerful buried feelings—especially rage, guilt, shame, and fear—are usually the hidden causes of infected grief. If these denied feelings are deeply buried, it may require the skills of a pastoral counselor or psychotherapist to enable the person to bring them back into awareness where they can be worked through so that healing can occur. The longer grief work has been delayed, the more costly it becomes to the person's creativity and health, and the more important it is to get the help of a counselor skilled in treating infected grief.

Enormous losses and devastating crises usually wipe us out for a time, perhaps for a long time. Just to survive seems too much. Even to think about learning and growing from such a crushing experience is impossible when you're struggling to survive. But if your grief wound isn't infected, when you look back, after several years perhaps, you may make a surprising discovery. You realize that your grief no longer has its cutting-to-the-bone quality. It has changed to a quiet sadness. You may also discover that you've acquired new strengths that have deepened who you are as a person. The strengths have come as a result of having had the courage to keep on keeping on, even when the future seemed hopeless and utterly without meaning.

AIDS, Suicide, and Other Stigmatized Losses

Crises and losses caused by any illness or death that society views as stigmatized usually produce painfully infected grief wounds. Conspiracies of silence and hiding make recovery prolonged and complicated. Deaths from AIDS, for example, are surrounded by social rejection and abandonment, often complicated by homophobia. The AIDS epidemic is confronting the whole human family with massive medical, economic, ethical, educational, sexual, and theological problems which we are only beginning to face. This unprecedented health crisis highlights the urgent necessity of developing innovative, global solutions to the horrendous brokenness and grief it has already caused and promises to produce in the next decade. As I write this, I feel wrenching sadness for the death from AIDS of a gifted young graduate student I knew. Fearing rejection if his secret illness became known, he hid in his room alone for days, as he slipped into a coma. For me his death makes painfully personal the unprecedented challenges with which the AIDS epidemic confronts all of us.

Deaths by suicide still carry stigma in many circles. This often is true, unfortunately, even when they are self-chosen mercy deaths enabling persons to gain release from intractable pain, staggering costs, and meaningless dying prolonged by medical technology. Divorces, though much less stigmatized in most circles than in the past, still may produce infected grief wounds. If you or someone you love is suffering such grief, be especially alert to the need for extra measures of acceptance, listening, and loving. Healing help usually is needed for much, much longer than for persons suffering "respectable" losses during which they're surrounded with abundant social rituals of mourning and community support.

Well Being in the Crises of Having a Disability

The millions of children and adults with serious physical and developmental disabilities (more than thirty million in America) are a frequently ignored and alienated minority. This is in spite of the much-needed equal rights legislation passed in recent years. Gaining and maintaining inner wholeness is a difficult achievement when your body is disabled in obvious and profound ways. Our culture's glorification of a "perfect" body image in the Hollywood–Madison Avenue media circuit contributes to the self-esteem and body-acceptance problems of those whose bodies deviate radically from this stereotype. The popularity of cosmetic surgery reveals the multi-million-dollar social pressure to conform. The grief of not being able to come close to the body-beautiful image is one of a variety of self-esteem and grief problems that persons with disabilities must work through if their gifts are to be developed fully. Parents, siblings, and children of severely disabled persons often live with chronic grief, "a dark cloud that won't go away," as a friend named Heather put it.

What can persons with disabilities and their families do to maximize their well being? They can begin by becoming aware that equating any human being's value as a person with her or his body image is a cruel, irrelevant put-down. It's an esteem-damaging prejudice from which victims need to exorcise themselves. A vital part of this self-liberation is becoming aware that it is indeed possible to be a whole person without having a whole body.

Twenty-year-old Tom came to counseling to get help with crippling feelings of inferiority and shyness stemming from a short leg caused by a birth defect. His breakthrough came when he learned to think of himself "as a man with a short leg rather than a short leg with a man attached," as he put it. That fundamental change in self-definition (called reframing in counseling and therapy) is the key to affirming your wholeness, whatever limitations you have in any area of your life.

In my early midyears, a serious disability (diabetes) hit me out of the blue. My macho sense of physical invulnerability was shattered. As I wrestled with my shaken body image and grief, I had a flashback that helped me cope. I remembered an inspiring man named Glenn Cunningham who had spoken at my local YMCA some twenty-five years before. He told us a story about a boy whose legs had been terribly burned in a fire. The doctors informed his distraught parents he would never walk again. By holding on to the back of a horse-drawn ice wagon driven by his father, the boy made his scarred legs slowly learn to walk again, in spite of the pain. Eventually he learned not only to walk but to run. At the end of the story Glenn said, "That boy was me." We knew that he held the world's record at the time for the fastest mile ever run!

My disability has forced me to learn many lessons I did not want to learn. It made me listen to my body's long-ignored messages, especially its cry—"Stop treating me like an obedient machine! Take more loving care of me!" I learned (reluctantly, with abundant resistance) that losing weight, eating more healthfully, and exercising regularly were no longer elective options if I wanted to survive. As a result, I'm thankful that I feel more physical energy and well being today than when my disability was diagnosed three decades ago. As a therapist I've noticed that my relationships with clients who have disabilities have changed for the better since I've had to face my own grief, vulnerability, and finitude.

As is true of any grief experience, persons with disabilities and their families can move toward greater wholeness by accepting the reality of their situation and doing their grief work. This includes working through their anger and repairing their self-esteem, often with the assistance of a caring listener. It's also important for persons with disabilities to learn to live as fully, independently, and productively (including working for pay) as can become possible with rehabilitative therapies, courage, and perseverance. Joining a support group of those with similar limitations often is of tremendous help in rebuilding self-esteem on a new foundation. Participating in advocacy groups by and for persons with disabilities is also empowering and politically astute.

One of the marvelous human capacities that persons can develop is the ability to compensate for weaknesses by developing other skills, gifts, and competencies more fully. The term *otherwise-abled* points to the challenge of growth in other areas of their lives, which can be very important for anyone with a significant physical or mental limitation.

WINDOW OF WHOLENESS

HAROLD WILKE

A friend of mine named Harold Wilke has inspired countless persons by his remarkable life. Soon after he was born without arms, an acquaintance who encountered his mother at the grocery store said to her, "I heard the church bells this morning toll the death of an infant, and I was hoping it was your poor little crippled baby."

His parents, strengthened by a deep faith, struggled mightily with the shock and emotional trauma of having a child without arms. Fortunately, they resisted institutionalizing Harold and instead helped him develop a robust sense of responsibility and self-reliance. Harold gradually discovered that he could do almost everything (mainly with his feet) "except play the piano."

After completing college and seminary, he was ordained and went on to what he calls his "six careers"—local church pastor, army hospital chaplain, denominational leader, author and editor, professor, and founder of the Healing Community, a worldwide network to help congregations enable persons with disabilities to join the mainstream. He has spoken in thirty-seven countries as well as all fifty U.S. states, and has taught at the Menninger Foundation and Union Theological Seminary. Harold and his wife, Peg, have raised five sons. On July 26, 1990, when President George Bush signed into law the historic Americans with Disabilities Act of 1990, Harold Wilke was honored by being invited to ask God's blessing. After the ceremony on the South Lawn of the White House, he accepted (with his left foot) a pen from the president with thanks. But then Harold added that he wanted to give the pen to a woman who deserved it more. When he gave it to her, the president responded by giving Harold *his* pen!

The Crisis and Grief of Addictions

The epidemic of addictions in Western society is another expression of our planet's massive brokenness. Addictions produce profound suffering in the lives of millions of persons with illnesses such as alcoholism, drug addictions, compulsive gambling, sexual addictions, food and nicotine addictions, and addiction to fanatical religions. Many persons today are trapped in several addictions simultaneously. For example, many sex addicts are also addicted to alcohol and drugs. The driving force behind these compulsive-addictive behavior patterns is a desperate loneliness and a hunger for love, self-worth, and an intimate relationship with the divine Spirit.[10] An addiction becomes a fierce, consuming idolatry, as that substance or activity becomes their highest and eventually the only goal, value, and devotion in their lives. Other values are squeezed out as the person's life is strangled by the powerful tentacles of the addictive process.

In all the long, despairing history of addictions, the most effective treatment is the spiritually centered Twelve-Step recovery program, developed first by AA and now used by countless groups focused on other addictive-compulsive problems. I will always be grateful for what AA has taught me about life and recovery. I am also thankful for the way Bill W., cofounder of AA, encouraged and supported my plan to explore the spiritual dimension of the causes and recovery from alcoholism for my dissertation research. A statement he made the first time we met influenced my thinking deeply: "Before AA we alcoholics were trying to drink God out of a bottle."

Bill W. once wrote to Carl Jung to thank him for the guidance he had given Roland, Bill's friend who had gone to Zurich seeking Jung's help with his alcoholism. Jung had told him that only a spiritual awakening could help him. Roland told Bill what Jung had said. This helped point Bill toward the spiritual approach that eventually evolved into AA. In responding to Bill's letter of appreciation, Jung wrote that the craving for alcohol was "a spiritual thirst for wholeness" and that only by breaking out of their isolation from society and getting back in touch with a Higher Power could addicted persons find the power to stay sober.[11] The primacy of spiritual factors among the multiple causes of addictions means that a dynamic spiritual component is an indispensable part of any full and effective recovery program. (If you're interested in an in-depth exploration of this issue, see my book *Understanding and Counseling the Alcoholic, Through Psychology and Religion*.[12])

There are multiple griefs involved in most addictions. These must be healed in effective treatment. Elizabeth, a single parent in her late forties, had been a controlled social drinker until the tragic death of her son in the Vietnam War. Within a few months her bitter grief had driven her to compulsive-addictive drinking combined with increasing self-medication and addiction to tranquilizers. As her addictions escalated, she suffered one loss after another—her self-respect, faith, friends, and eventually her job. After about eighteen months of out-of-control drinking she hit bottom in the alcoholic ward of the city hospital with alcoholic hallucinations. At that point she suffered the grief of losing her "best friend"—the bottle, the god who had betrayed her. Elizabeth had a heavy load of multiple griefs to deal with as a central part of her recovery, including the infected grief wound around her son's tragic death. Only as she began to experience some healing of these griefs did she move ahead to a spiritual awakening in the fellowship of AA. Doing her grief work as a part of her therapy freed her to continue her healing, a process that enabled her to stay recovered.

Most family members of addicted persons also have a lot of grief healing work to do in their recovery from codependency—their obsessive dependence that traps them in the ineffective role of rescuer of the addicted person. Their multiple grief is tangled with their own shattered self-esteem and damaged family identity, as a part of the family illness of addiction. At the heart of grief healing and recovery for them is learning how to release the addicted loved one, by surrendering their futile efforts to cure (control) that person's addiction by overprotecting or punishing behavior. They must learn to practice tough love and to nurture their own well being, whatever the addicted person does.

Finding a Crisis and Grief Healing Group

With the walking wounded everywhere in our loneliness-wracked world a new societal strategy for their healing is desperately needed. The heart of such a strategy is to make sharing-caring groups more easily available to everyone who needs them. The flowering of self-help groups like AA is evidence of their incredible power to heal grief, shame, and addictions, awaken hope, and stimulate growth toward whole-person well being. (Each week in the U.S., fifteen million people attend some five hundred thousand self-help groups.) To have a healthier society, crisis-grief sharing and support groups must become even more widely available to all those living "lives of quiet desperation," Henry David Thoreau's poignant phrase for garden-variety silent suffering.

Congregations of all faiths have a wonderful opportunity to take a leading role in creating such a network of healing. Health facilities and counseling agencies also have an important role in this. My experience with grief-healing groups over more than two decades provides convincing evidence that many people find them immensely helpful in coping with all manner of losses, crises, disabilities, painful transitions, and addictions. Such groups are not difficult to set up and lead. Clergy who are trained in counseling, as well as carefully selected and supervised nonprofessionals who have grown from coping with their own crises and griefs, can provide effective leadership. I cannot imagine anything that clergy or their congregations could do that would contribute more to healing and wholeness than making crises and grief recovery groups readily available to anyone in their communities who needs such groups. (Two series of videotapes, "Growing Through Grief, Personal Healing" and "Healing Your Grief Wound," have proved to be surprisingly useful as resources to show in grief-recovery groups, as well as in grief and crisis education programs. See Recommended Reading for details.)

For your continuing well being, it's very important to do everything you can to prepare to handle anticipated developmental crises constructively—crises such as getting married, having a child, or retiring. One of the benefits of a crisis-grief education program in a congregation is to encourage and guide people in experiencing what have been called "emotional inoculations" to prepare for such normal, expected crises.

Relaxation Imaging for Healing Your Body-Mind

Here's an imaging exercise that can be a valuable gift you give yourself for healing and health. It may help you stay fit in the midst of crises and losses. By using this blend of deep relaxation and creative imaging, you probably can stimulate and maximize the remarkable self-healing resources of your mind, body, and spirit. There is evidence that approaches like this can help activate your immune system, which helps protect your body from the attack of viruses, germs, and malignancies. Such a method is not a cure-all, of course. But many folks who try it make a welcome discovery. Rachel, a client suffering from multiple psychophysiological problems, put it this way: "It's a neat way of being an active partner, not a passive recipient, in my therapy." This type of self-empowerment exercise also can be used preventively to nurture higher-level wellness in your body, mind, spirit, and relationships.

What follows is a modified version of an approach developed by physician O. Carl Simonton and psychologist Stephanie Matthews-Simonton in their pioneering work with cancer patients.[13]

Instructions: Do this exercise in a quiet room, sitting comfortably with your spine in a vertical position and your feet flat on the floor, to facilitate the flow of energy in your body. Until you learn the steps, you may find it helpful to record the instructions, leaving a few minutes between each step to do what has been suggested. (Don't record my comments in parentheses.)

Before beginning the steps, select a physical ailment, psychological problem (perhaps a crisis or loss), or painful relationship about which you have an intense desire for healing. Choose a problem that's heavy enough to motivate you to continue using the exercise for at least a week, while you learn how effective it may be for you.

Step 1:   Take a few minutes to become as deeply relaxed throughout your body as possible, accompanied by quiet alertness in your mind. Use whatever relaxation methods you've found to be effective. (Instructions for one such method are in chapter 4.) Being relaxed but alert allows your body-mind organism to be maximally receptive to the healing messages you'll send it via images.

Step 2:   When you are deeply relaxed, form a clear, moving picture on a movie screen in your imagination of the problem you have selected for healing. Experience the reality and pain of that problem. (If you chose a physical ailment, form a picture in your mind—realistic or symbolic—of how that part of your body looks. For a headache, picturing hammers pounding in the head does well.) If you picked an emotional or spiritual problem, picture it in some vivid, symbolic way. If you're focusing on a troubled relationship, see and experience those persons in painful alienation and conflict. / Let yourself experience each step intensely for several minutes.

Step 3:   Form a moving picture of any treatment or therapy you are receiving, visualizing and experiencing it as being wonderfully effective. (For example, if you're taking aspirin for a headache, picture thousands of aspirin grains going through your bloodstream bringing freedom from all pain. If you're having psychotherapy, spiritual direction, or relationship counseling, form a moving picture in your mind of that being highly effective.) Let yourself actually enjoy the warm feelings of increasing well being for a few minutes.

Step 4:   Now form a clear picture of your body's natural defenses and healing forces, seeing these functioning powerfully and assertively in overcoming the problem. For example, if you're dealing with an infection, see a picture of the millions of health-restoring white blood cells coursing through all your blood vessels. See them like millions of tiny vacuum sweepers, for example, cleansing your whole body and especially the afflicted parts of the infection or other causes of the problem. It's important to choose an image that is meaningful to you and fits your way of approaching problems. Some young people like the figure from the video game Pac-Man. A woman with breast cancer imagined small, delicate birds eating the crumbs (cancer cells) in her blood. Bernie Siegel suggests that, in selecting your image, it's important to make sure it appeals to the sense faculty on which you tend to rely most heavily—visual, auditory, tactile, or olfactory. For example, one woman whose tactile faculty is dominant, "felt" her immune system as a cleansing stream washing over her.[14] If you're seeking healing of a psychological, spiritual, or relationship problem, form a symbolic picture of your many resources of mind and heart that can be used for self-healing. Let yourself experience self-healing resources doing their work in remarkably effective ways.

Step 5:   Now picture a gentle but powerful light, a little above your head and just in front of you—the healing light of God's wonderful love and total acceptance. / Experience this light flowing in and throughout your whole body, bathing your mind and spirit and enveloping your important relationships with a mantle of healing energy. / Now, focus this light intensely on the body area, psychological problem, or relationship that is in special need of healing. (If you're doing healing of fears and guilt feelings, focus the light on those in some symbolic way, or see yourself and the other person in a troubled relationship surrounded and drawn together by the healing light.) Keep the light focused there for several minutes, enjoying the feelings of increased wellness. / Open yourself to experience warm thankfulness to the divine Spirit of Love—the source of all healing.

Step 6:   Picture the troubled area(s) of your life fully healed and your whole self in wonderfully robust health. Be *in* the experience. Let yourself enjoy the relief and good feelings in your whole body-mind, free of pain, full of energy, joyfully alive, close and loving in your relation- ships, moving zestfully toward your life goals, and making a con- structive difference in the world around you. Let yourself actually experience all this with inner joy for several minutes.

Step 7:   Using the glow of the experiences you've had, create a clear picture of someone you care about who needs healing or help. / See him or her surrounded by warm healing light—the light of your caring mingled with the healing energy of God's love. / Now see her or him in robust health, enjoying life and contributing to the needs of oth- ers. / Be aware of how reaching out in this caring-healing way makes you feel. /

Congratulate yourself for participating actively in self-healing and in helping heal others. Give yourself a loving pat on the back, even if the experience was only slightly meaningful at this early stage. (It often takes a week or two of practice to discover how effective it can be for you.) / Picture yourself doing this exercise two or three times each day, staying awake and alert, and completing each session feeling renewed hope and love. The exercise can be helpful, particu- larly as a preventative, if used only once a day for as little as five to ten minutes. But for healing it's wise to use it three times a day— before breakfast, before lunch, and before going to sleep—for ten to fifteen minutes each time.

Before using this exercise with any major illnesses, such as cancer, I recommend that you discuss its use with your physician. And it's important to read *Getting Well Again* by O. Carl Simonton and Ste- phanie Matthews-Simonton, to prepare you for using this self- healing technique. (See Recommended Reading.) After trying this tool a few times, you may decide to modify it to make it more effective for you.

Create Your Crises and Losses Self-Care Fitness Plan

Now take time to go back and review things that interested you as you read this chapter, including some of the items you marked NS or OK on the checkup. Select at least six things you'd like to do in this area. / Using your creativity, write out a realistic Self-Care-in-Crises Plan. Remember, your plan probably will be more workable if it includes: (1) concrete, realizable objectives concerning particular problems you want to handle better; (2) practical strategies for moving toward these objectives; (3) a time line; (4) and (very important) rewards you'll give yourself as you implement your plan step-by-step, or withhold if you backslide; (5) a record of your progress as you implement your Self-Care Plan. You may find it helpful to include in your plan some further reading from the Recommended Reading at the end of the book.

Pick one or two especially important objectives and begin moving toward them immediately. Be sure to keep what you do spiritually energized. If you backslide, don't waste energy castigating yourself. Just recommit yourself to action in that or another important area and move ahead.

I wish you hope-awakening self-care in your crises, losses, disabilities, and addictions.

CHAPTER 10

Sex and Well Being: 10 Ways to Enjoy Sensual Love

The joy of your wholeness can be enhanced through celebrating your sexuality, with yourself and also in a relationship of love, mutual respect, and responsibility. I invite you to enjoy these passionate words from two long-ago lovers. (Would you believe some twenty-five centuries ago?):

Sex is one of the few

pleasures in life that isn't

yet taxed!

—J., The Sensuous Woman

O that you would kiss me with the kisses of your mouth! For your love is better than wine.

My beloved speaks and says to me: "Arise, my love, my fair one, and come away; for lo, the winter is past, the rain is over and gone. The flowers appear on the earth, the time of singing has come, and the voice of the turtledove is heard in our land."

Upon my bed by night I sought him whom my soul loves.

How fair and pleasant you are, O loved one, delectable maiden! You are stately as a palm tree, and your breasts are like its clusters. I say I will climb the palm tree and lay hold of its branches.

Set me a seal upon your heart . . . ; for love is strong as death. . . . Many waters cannot quench love, neither can flood drown it.[1]

I hope this passionate poetry from the Song of Solomon puts you in touch with your own sensual lovingness, one of God's most delightful gifts. We can be glad that these ancient words survived as a part of the Bible, a minor miracle in light of the way Western religions have often said a resounding no! to the body and to sexuality. I also hope you enjoyed the intimation that these lovers had discovered the joy of making love outdoors in the blossoming springtime. A friend of mine was raised in a conservative religious denomination that required children to sit through long church services. She laughs now when she recalls how she discovered the Song of Solomon in the pew Bibles when she was nine or ten. Reading it helped her survive long, boring sermons.

As you know from this morning's paper, if not from personal experience, contemporary human sexuality often seems to produce more hurt than well being. In spite of many advances in this area, sexuality is still rife with human suffering, self-alienation, wrenching guilt, and bruising conflicts. Painful sexual problems are epidemic, including

> TODAY THEY'RE PRINTING
>
> ANSWERS ABOUT SEX
>
> I DIDN'T EVEN KNOW
>
> THERE WERE QUESTIONS FOR.
>
> —bumper sticker

- proliferating sexual addictions, producing widespread individual and family tragedies;

- sexually transmitted diseases of which there are at least twenty different ones. The most deadly of these is the tragic, planetwide AIDS epidemic, which raises the specter that "even the most loving acts may be the vehicle of a life-threatening virus."[2]

- crippling erotophobia (fear of the erotic);

Other symptoms of our society's sexual pain and pathology are

- unwanted pregnancies (including millions by teenagers);

- the compulsive sexuality of males driven by macho programming who try to prop up their shaky masculinity by sexual conquests;

- widespread homophobia and discrimination against gay men and lesbians;

- the awful plague of sexual violence against children and women present at all socioeconomic and educational levels of society.

Fortunately, in today's mixed-up world there are hopeful rays of sunlight concerning sex and wholeness. Celebrating your sexuality, it turns out, may actually increase the length as well as the quality of your life. It can give you more joy on your journey, and may even increase its duration. Summarizing the key factors identified by various research studies on extended life spans, Kenneth Pelletier gives this good news: "Sexual activity . . . comprises the fifth component noted by longevity researchers. . . . One study documented in both film and print, of the Vilcambaba people, reported that a man named Capio Mendieta 'was sexually active at 123 years of age.' "[3] Let's hear it for Capio and all those who add life to their years by valuing their sexuality!

The way you feel about and express your sexuality has an impact on all the other dimensions of your wholeness, for better or for worse. Wellness-nurturing sex flourishes best in loving relationships where there is mutual respect and responsibility, caring communication, continuity, and commitment to one's own and each other's growth and well being. It's in such relationships that sensual-sexual pleasuring can flower best on a continuing basis. In a recent study of the sex life of Americans, married couples who said they are the happiest also had the most sex—each of these probably being both an effect and a cause of the other.[4] Among today's multiple sexual options, celibacy can be a healthy choice for some (about 3 percent of Americans). But that decision doesn't eliminate the need to affirm one's sensual needs and rechannel one's sexual energies in other creative directions.

Fortunately, significant steps have been taken toward healthier sexuality in recent decades. Sex has been brought out of the closet for open discussion (sometimes ad infinitum if not ad nauseam). Many people report they're enjoying higher levels of sexual satisfaction. Many women have discovered and are enjoying their wonderful, previously suppressed pleasure potentials, including the capacity for multiple orgasms. Some men are gaining release from their defensive, power-oriented uses of sex that diminish sexual joy by making sex a flunkable test of their masculinity. There is wider social acceptance of a variety of sexual and gender preferences.

Further good news about sex is the clear evidence that sex-rejecting feelings, attitudes, and behaviors are learned in our early lives. And what has been learned can often be unlearned. Sex education and sex enrichment workshops have demonstrated repeatedly that new, body-loving feelings, attitudes, and pleasuring skills can be learned to replace the old joyless, guilt-laden patterns. More sophisticated sex and relationship therapies have proved helpful to many persons suffering dysfunctional sexuality, including inhibited sexual desire.

Chris, a superstressed high school teacher in his midforties, described his sex life to his therapist: "It's like a bottle of soda left open too long in the refrigerator." If your sexuality feels like that at times, this chapter may provide ways to recover some sparkle. It offers insights and methods you can use to enrich your sex life and thereby enhance your overall fitness. If you're married or in a committed relationship that includes sex, it may be mutually helpful to share this chapter with your partner.

Sexuality and Well-Being Checkup

CHECKLIST

This checkup can enhance your sex life in two ways. (1) It can give you a quick evaluation of your overall sexual fitness. (2) Checkup items offer a variety of things you can do to help make your sexuality more satisfying and healthful.

Instructions: In front of each item place one of three initials: E = I'm doing excellently in this; OK = I'm doing acceptably, but there's room for improvement; NS = This area really needs strengthening.

_____ The ways I express my sexuality increase my well being *and* that of my partner.

_____ I feel at home with my sexuality, including my gender identity.

_____ I've drastically diminished or let go of sexually inhibiting inner messages I learned in my childhood.

_____ I enjoy my sexuality as a good gift of life and/or the divine Spirit of Love.

_____ The most fulfilling forms of sexuality for me are in a trusting, mutually respecting relationship of love.

_____ I (we) enjoy healthy hedonism by doing everything possible to practice safe and responsible sex, including avoiding unwanted pregnancies.

_____ I enjoy giving as well as receiving leisurely, whole-body pleasuring.

_____ I know my body's pleasure preferences and communicate to my sexual partner what I find most satisfying.

_____ I can enjoy guilt-free solo sex.

_____ I (we) have learned imaginative ways to re-eroticize the settings where I (we) make love.

_____ I enjoy my erotic fantasies without guilt trips and can use them to increase my sexual enjoyment.

_____ I (we) often extend the pleasuring of each stage of sexual arousal, without needing to have quick climaxes.

_____ We deal with distancing hurts in our relationship and get reconnected emotionally before making love.

_____ I avoid the four traps of being rushed, being exhausted, drinking too much, or needing to prove something when making love.

_____ We're able to talk through differences in our sexual preferences and work out win-win compromises to satisfy some of each person's desires.

_____ After making love, we feel more warmth and closeness, rather than distance.

_____ My spirituality and sexuality are connected and mutually enriching areas of my life.

_____ If I (we) experience temporary sexual problems, we don't make a federal case out of it, but just relax and enjoy being close.

_____ I don't use sex as a way of proving I'm OK as a man or woman or as a power trip to manipulate my partner.

_____ My sexuality is spontaneous and playful, not compulsive and driven.

_____ I (we) ignore advice from all so-called experts (including this chapter) when it's irrelevant, freeing us to enjoy my (our) own style of sexual play.

Using Your Findings: To maximize the benefits, follow these steps:

1. Scan your responses to get a rough feel for your strengths and the places where improvement is needed.

2. If your sexual partner also took the checkup, discuss responses on which you agreed and disagreed until you each more fully understand the other's sexual needs, preferences, and attitudes.

3. Jot down in your *Self-Care Journal* important items you (and perhaps your partner) feel need improvement (rated OK and NS).

4. Then note for later use your tentative ideas about enhancing sex in those areas.

Sex and Singlehood

Developing health-enhancing sexuality is challenging enough for most people who are paired in committed relationships. It may be even more complicated for many who, by choice or by chance, are single. These include teens and young adults prior to marriage, postmarrieds (including divorced persons, widows, and widowers), and those who have never married (both straight and gay). These singles constitute one-third of all adults in America. Traditional morality in our society (including most voices in mainstream religions) still holds that sex is off limits for singles. Yet it is both unfair and unhealthy for a society simultaneously to glamorize and market sex and try to prevent one-third of its adults from enjoying its delectable satisfactions. Fortunately, some courageous religious leaders are calling for more humanizing and reality-based ethical guidelines. Episcopal bishop John Shelby Spong stands out as an articulate voice among these leaders. In his groundbreaking book *Living in Sin?* he asks rhetorically: "Is it a legitimate demand of a moral society to say to the brightest and best of a new generation that they are to suppress their sexual drives from puberty, at perhaps age twelve, to the time of finishing law school, for example at age twenty-five? Can an ethical standard completely out of touch with biological reality be expected to survive? The fact is that the standard has not survived."[5] He then observes that the old guilt that has been used to try to enforce traditional standards is rapidly weakening.

The majority of younger and divorced singles probably choose to ignore what they regard as society's obsolete constrictions on their sexuality. Sexually active teens often do so rebelliously and irresponsibly, without contraceptives. The result is an epidemic of unwanted pregnancies. Some widows and divorced persons struggle with feelings similar to those of Michelle, who was widowed in her early fifties. She came for counseling because, as she put it, "I feel torn apart by guilt feelings over the ways I've been trying to deal with my loneliness and sexual desires, and my longing for closeness with a man." Promiscuity and so-called recreational sex outside healthy relationships of mutual love, trust, and commitment still result in enormous pain for many singles as well as marrieds.

Guidelines for Sexual Well Being

For many single and unsingle folks, sex produces more pain than joy, more frustration and despair than pleasure, satisfaction, and happiness. Often sex is a battleground both within persons and in their intimate relationships. Sex is sometimes more of a bed of nails than a lovers' boudoir of shared ecstasy. There are many reasons for this, including the fact that our society's values and norms about sex are in a time of chaotic, confusing transition. They offer few new or dependable guidelines for constructive, joyful sexual behavior. This makes some people's sex lives something like a ship in a storm without a rudder. Consequently many are searching for person-respecting, life-affirming inner guidelines relevant to today's real world.

To contribute to your overall health, sex should

- be in the context of both genuine self-love and a relationship of mutual love characterized by commitment and continuity, mutual respect, honesty, and trust;

- be physically safe for those involved;

- use the most effective measures to prevent unwanted pregnancies;

- be strengthened by good communication about things that really matter to both partners, including their sexual feelings and preferences;

- enrich other facets of the relationship;

- produce increased respect, self-esteem, and responsible hedonism; and joyful mini-vacations from daily stresses.

To contribute to your overall health, sex should not

- be laden with guilt, shame, fear, rebellion, or irresponsibility;

- be coerced or rooted in feelings of powerlessness expressed in drives for conquest, power over others, and physical or psychological violence;

- be compulsive or driven, as in sexual addictions;

- produce unwanted pregnancies;

- spread sexually transmitted diseases;

- be joyless, boring, or mechanical.

Obviously sex for us humans is much more than a biological drive. Sex is also a way of seeking to meet a variety of emotional and interpersonal needs. Some of these are healthy and constructive, such as the need for love, closeness, pleasuring, touching, caring, and moments of transcending ecstasy. Other needs are hurtful, such as the need to control, dominate, conquer, or hurt, to prop up shaky self-esteem, or prove one's masculinity or femininity. If the needs people seek to satisfy via sex are mainly from damaged self-esteem and feelings of powerlessness, sex will tend to bring them pain and problems. If the needs are mainly healthy, sex will tend to enhance their wholeness and increase their love.

Sexual joy is much too valuable to be missing in the lives of countless persons who want it. Theologian Carter Heyward holds to the view that sexual pleasure is "a delightful relational happening that needs no higher justification."[6]

The remainder of this chapter describes ten practical tools for increasing the joy and well being of your sex life. These tools build on the communication skills in chapter 5. If you are doing this chapter with a partner, I recommend that you pause after each tool is described and discuss how you might use it. If you are doing the chapter solo, pause and jot down your thoughts about using a particular method to liven up your sex life.

Sexual Enhancement Method Number 1: *Nurture your total relationship by loving communication, so that your friendship will deepen and your mutual caring grow.* My years of doing couple enrichment and counseling has convinced me that couples who take care of their relationship lovingly tend to experience increased esteem and love, which usually enriches their sexual passions and joy together.

In ongoing committed and caring relationships (in contrast to superficial sex in one-night stands), sex is intertwined with and colors everything else in the relationship. Therefore, it's a barometer of the relationship's general emotional climate. Let's say a relationship is friendly, honest, loving, and growing via mutual caring, respect, and conflict-resolution skills. The chances are good that that couple's sex life will be playful and satisfying (though not without conflict, of course). If a relationship is filled with dishonesty, hurt, anger, and attempts to dominate each other, the vitality of the couple's sex life usually is greatly diminished.

In sex therapy it's often helpful to avoid focusing primarily on the sexual problems that brought couples to professional help. The sexual issues usually improve appreciably only as they learn love-nurturing communication and conflict resolutions skills. The same is true of couples for whom sex has become deadly dull—called inhibited sexual desire. Sex for most couples is important but it is far from being the only or even the major determinant of their happiness.

Sexual responsiveness begins in our heads, not in our genitals. Sex is a powerful means of communication intertwined with all the other verbal and nonverbal communicating our species has developed through the eons of bonding in families. It should come as no surprise that anything you do that increases caring communication in your relationship as a whole probably will nurture and enliven your sex life.

The various love-nurturing communication tools described in the relationship wholeness chapter (chapter 5) can be used to enhance sexual communication and responsiveness. Among these the most passion-awakening tool is expressing warm, honest appreciation to your partner—the first step of the Intentional Relationship Method. Appreciation from your lover is like ambrosia, the delicious food from and for the God or Goddess in each of us. It's also a powerful psychological aphrodisiac. Use of the conflict-reduction part of this exercise (steps 2 and 3) also can enhance sex by resolving distancing issues and feelings fairly via win-win compromises.

Sexual Enhancement Method Number 2: *Focus on enriching the other facets of intimacy in your relationship, and sexual intimacy will tend to flower.* This is a variation on the first method. What follows is a tool for discovering and developing the hidden treasure of your many-faceted intimacy.[7]

The Intimacy Inventory

Instructions: In front of each facet of intimacy, place a number from 1 to 5: 1 means "This is an intimacy vacuum that I'd like to fill with my partner"; 3 means "We're doing acceptably but I'd like for us to develop this facet; 5 means "We're doing wonderfully in this dimension of our intimacy." /

If you and your partner are sharing this chapter, each of you should take the inventory separately. If you're working solo, use the inventory to discover all that you can about your intimacy needs and how you can meet them more fully in your relationships. /

After completing the inventory, if you're using it solo, reflect on what you learned and make some notes in your *Self-Care Journal* about your plans for change. / If you're working with a partner, compare your responses, discussing the meaning of your agreements and disagreements. / In areas where one or both desire improvement, brainstorm some concrete steps you can take to increase intimacy, jotting down ideas and plans on which you agree. /

_____ *Communication intimacy* = Feeling more connected through verbal and nonverbal communicating, including touching.

_____ *Conflict intimacy* = Connecting via struggling with painful differences and negotiating fair compromises.

_____ *Crisis intimacy* = Closeness that comes by coping constructively with crises and losses.

_____ *Work intimacy* = The bonding that comes from sharing common tasks.

_____ *Play intimacy* = The delightful connecting via fun, play, and just being together enjoying doing nothing.

_____ *Emotional intimacy* = Shared emotional resonance from being tuned to each other's feeling wavelengths.

_____ *Intellectual intimacy* = Closeness by sharing the world of stimulating ideas, challenging issues, and books.

_____ *Spiritual intimacy* = Bonding through sharing peak experiences of your Higher Power.

_____ *Individuation intimacy* = Connectedness from respecting each other's autonomy, differentness, and need for apartness for individual growth.

_____ *Caring intimacy* = Closeness that comes from caring for and about each other, in sunshine and shadows.

_____ *Creative intimacy* = Feeling connected through creating something together—rearing children, establishing a home or a business, realizing shared dreams, and so forth.

_____ *Aesthetic intimacy* = Bonding through sharing experiences of beauty.

_____ *Commitment-outreach intimacy* = Closeness via sharing common values and struggling side by side for causes aimed at helping others and making the planet healthier.

_____ *Journeying intimacy* = Deepening connection over time as a result of sharing the ups and downs of successive stages on the life journey.

_____ *Sexual intimacy* = Body-mind-spirit unity via sexual pleasuring.

Sexual Enhancement Method Number 3: *Clean up the emotional debris within and between you regularly—unresolved hurts, anger, resentments, injustices, and feeling unappreciated.* Do so particularly before trying to be close sexually. Neglecting this is the most frequent cause of dwindling sexual passion between midyears couples. When couples in deep conflict come for marital and sexual counseling, I often feel as if there is an icy (if not a fiery) wall growing between them. If they don't resolve these painful feelings, the wall will gradually block the flow of communication and erotic energies between them. Or sex may become a battleground on which they act out their hurt in mutually frustrating ways. Conflicts that need to be resolved by fair compromises may include differences in sexual desires.

Marge and Jeff, in their late twenties, came for therapeutic help with Jeff's impotence. It turned out that his problem was a symptom of pain in their total relationship. It produced further pain for both of them, which in turn increased his impotence. During their therapy they discovered that whenever Jeff felt angry at Marge and did not admit this to himself or respond openly, he would be unable to, in his words, "get it up." Jeff gradually learned to own his anger and to express it verbally. And, equally important, the two of them learned the skills needed to negotiate fair solutions to the painful conflicts that produced their anger. Jeff's impotence gradually diminished and their whole relationship, including their sex life, became more zestful and loving.

Sexual Enhancement Method Number 4: *Do everything possible to make your relationship fair, equal, and growth producing for both of you.* If you do this your creative closeness, including your sexual intimacy, will tend to increase. The deepest, most fulfilling forms of intimacy are possible psychologically only between true equals. Equals do not play the manipulative, mutually distancing control and power games that occur in all one-up, one-down relationships.[8] By increasing fairness in your closest relationship, you reduce the mutually manipulating games so prevalent between the genders in our sexist society.

During this time of radical change in women's self-identity and therefore troubling transitions in a close woman-man relationship, many couples are searching for fairer, more egalitarian ways of relating. In such a time many woman-man relationships are carrying a heavy burden of anxiety. It's not surprising that sex problems seem to be proliferating in such a climate. Some men's sense of inner power and worth is dependent on having the women in their lives hide their real intelligence and power by behaving in a subordinate way. Such men are deeply threatened when women decide they will no longer overprotect vulnerable male egos in this way. The men's feelings of psychological impotence may be expressed in the sexual area. Here males (unlike females) cannot fake it if they can't make it.

I once invited students in a large undergraduate class on human sexuality to submit written questions so that they would raise touchy issues they might find embarrassing to ask orally. A worried male student wrote, "How does one cure male omnipotence?" His humorous slip of the pen actually points to a painful issue many males are encountering today. It happens as they feel pushed out of the automatic one-up position when the women in their lives insist that long-standing male-female inequalities be remedied.

If you're a man, helping your sexuality to be more whole for you and wholeness-sustaining for your partner may involve some reprogramming of yourself. What may be needed is to separate sex, power, and self-worth issues in your attitudes and feelings. To the degree that you do this, you'll be freer to enjoy sex without the old burden reflected in the feeling that your penis isn't big enough. This widespread distress is a symbol of having to prove your masculine power and adequacy in relations with both women and men. The compulsive drivenness from this old programming fuels sexual aggression against women. Compulsive male sexuality also makes "failure" both more likely and something of a disaster when it happens. Such male sexuality is a barrier to emotional intimacy between men and women. It robs sex of its greatest ecstasy and keeps many men from knowing the sweet mutuality of their sexuality and spirituality. As men, we have much to gain by liberating our masculine identity from its macho programming. This involves redefining on a deep feeling level what real male strength is.

Sexual Enhancement Method Number 5: *Let your inner child sides play together often.* Family physician, humorist (like his dad), and consultant on sexuality Steve Allen, Jr., has a playful therapy for couples feeling uptight in bed. His prescription is to laugh together uproariously in a spirit of whimsy, not taking themselves too seriously. He declares, "Sex at its best is great play."[9] Couples who laugh and play together frequently (as well as cry together when they're hurting) are usually more playful when they make love. A laugh-tinctured touch in your relationship helps avoid the trap of taking your problems—including your sexual problems—too seriously. In TA (transactional analysis) terms, it's easy to get stuck in either the being-responsible-for-others (parent) side or the coping-with-problematic-realities (adult) side of our personalities. Healthy, joyous sex is letting your child sides frolic together sensuously, taking pleasure breaks from both the inner adult and inner parent sides of your personalities. Woody Allen is said to have observed that sex reduces stress but love increases it. Fortunately, sex and love can enhance each other if you can get them together!

Sexual Enhancement Method Number 6: *Adapt the basic principles and methods of sex therapy to enrich your mutual pleasuring and arouse your sexual responsiveness.* Problems of diminished sexual responsiveness are sometimes rooted in deep psychological disturbances requiring long-term psychotherapy. But often they are not. They are caused by faulty learning in two areas. One is negative feelings toward sex, learned in childhood. The other is not learning the skills of both effective self-pleasuring and mutual pleasuring. Much of the treatment in sex therapy is not therapy in the usual sense but simply individualized reeducation. Couples gradually overcome performance anxieties (fear of failure) and develop more sex-affirmative attitudes and feelings via two interrelated experiences. They set aside time for leisurely practicing of prescribed "sensate focus" pleasuring skills in which they have been coached by the therapist and

"I must say that was a fine, clean, wholesome picture . . .
The popcorn was lousy, too."

Wholeness Exercise

> **Hedonism-for-Wholeness Exercise.** Here is a playful, left- and right-brain experience to use as a way of increasing the PQ (Pleasure Quotient) in your life and intimate relationships.
>
> Quickly complete this sentence as many times as possible in six minutes, writing down your answers: It would be fun to experience this playful, sensuous, or sexual activity, with myself and, if possible, with my spouse or lover . . .
>
> Let your fantasies frolic as you list everything you can think of that would be silly or sensuous, frivolous or fun, without worrying about feasibility. /
>
> Then use your list for planning to do two or three of these sensuous, fun things during the next week. If you're doing this exercise with your partner, discuss your two lists and discover at least ten shared pleasures that you both would find fun and feasible, and select two or three to do during the week. Enjoy! / Devise a plan to try at least two each week.

their reading. (See the books in Recommended Reading for this chapter.) Constructive changes in their behavior gradually produce positive changes in their feelings and attitudes. In addition, their negative attitudes about sex are changed as they identify with the therapist's knowledge-based, pleasure-affirming attitudes.

Sexual Enhancement Exercises

Try the following self-help approaches, adapted from sex therapy.

Self-exploration and discovery. People's pleasure preferences vary tremendously. If you haven't explored your entire body to discover its most pleasurable areas, do this research before trying the other exercises below. Take time to enjoy doing it leisurely and thoroughly.

Communicating about your sex life. If you're in a coupled sexual relationship, this exercise facilitates open discussion of ways you can enhance your sexual relationship. (It uses a modification of the Intentional Relationship Method.) When you're both feeling reasonably good about yourselves and your relationship, set aside an hour or so to talk about your sex life.

Step A: Focus your initial discussion on these questions: What do you appreciate about your partner's body and your sex life together? What things that your partner does really turn you on, giving you the most sensual pleasure? (Don't slip into criticism here. Just stick with expressing what you appreciate.)

Step B: What would you like more or less of in your sex life? Which areas of your body would enjoy more caressing, kissing, sucking, or otherwise being loved by your partner's lips, tongue, hands, or genitals? Tell each other in detail what would make sex more satisfying. / Jot down some insights you've gained from this sexual dialogue session. / Discuss how talking about these things made you feel.

Step C: What can you do together to make your sex life more exciting (or awaken it if it's dozing)? Work out together a plan to enliven your love life. Avoid trying to resolve conflicted needs and desires at the start. If one of you wants something that the other finds unacceptable, table that conflict and begin by enhancing mutual satisfactions in agreeable areas of your sex life.

Keeping adventure and variety in long-term sexual relationships involves using creative playfulness. If you are bored with the "missionary position" or with always making love at a certain time in your bedroom, why not use your creativity to spice things up? Try a variety of different positions. Or set aside a couple of hours on a rainy (or sunny) afternoon when your energy levels are high and you feel up for leisurely loving. Re-eroticize the setting (adding music or candles or flowers, or a mirror on the ceiling perhaps). Or figure out a way to make love outdoors (avoiding such hazards as poison ivy, insects, and police persons). For keeping sexual boredom away and the fires of passion alive, Dagmar O'Connor's *How to Make Love to the Same Person the Rest of Your Life, and Still Love It* and Joseph Nowinski's *A Lifelong Love Affair* are sexual smorgasbords of neat ideas.

Extending the length of your enjoyment of the successive stages of the sexual arousal cycle is another valuable learning from sex research and therapy. As identified by William Masters and Virginia Johnson, the stages are (1) gradual arousal of sexual excitement; (2) sustaining a prolonged state of high arousal without a climax (a high plateau); (3) orgasm; and (4) resolution, when couples enjoy the mellow afterglow of warm closeness. Of course, a spontaneous roll in the hay can be great at times. But to have leisurely, extended pleasuring can add a delicious dimension to your shared sensual enjoyment.

Here are two other learnings from sex therapy. One is not to give power to the inner "judge" (or judging inner parent), who is often involved when people have sexual response problems. Many people have occasions when latent inhibitions and hang-ups get reactivated temporarily. Instead of making a federal case out of such times (which gives the judge-parent voice within more power), simply relax into a nondemand, no-lose pleasuring mode. This is also the best way to avoid making the problem self-perpetuating. By treating it as a passing episode, you avoid getting caught in a vicious cycle of escalating performance anxiety and fear of failure, which increase the

Wholeness Exercise

A Mutual Pleasuring Exercise. Loving takes time and time is in short supply in our overstuffed schedules. The "one minute orgasm"[10] is inherently frustrating—like gulping down a delicious meal so that you hardly taste it. Sex becomes mechanical and boring because it gets shoved to the end of long, exhausting days, when both persons are also often burdened by anticipating tomorrow's pressures and problems.

One way to correct this is to set aside regular times to experiment playfully with new pleasuring techniques, positions, and approaches, including nondemand mutual pleasuring ("nondemand" simply means mutual pleasuring for its own enjoyment, without any other goals, expectations, or demands).[11] Such pleasuring may be *the* key to restoring sexual zest to your life. (The full-body massage described at the end of this chapter is a delightful way to do this.)

Instructions: Set aside an hour or so of uninterrupted time for a mutual-pleasuring session. Unplug the phone, childproof the door to your bedroom (or other setting), and decide not to answer the doorbell if it rings. Then take turns giving pleasure to the other for at least a half hour each, with no agendas and no other goals. Be sure to coach each other so that you'll know what is most sensuously pleasurable for the other. (This is why your sexual self-exploration and playful experimentation together is so important. It lets you discover what positions, music, scents, pictures, body lotion, flowers, jokes, drinks, or loving caresses really turn you on.)

During your time to receive, just relax and enjoy. Go with your flow of sensual pleasure. When it's your turn to give, be playful and also lovingly sensitive to your partner's pleasure preferences. Your skills will grow with practice. Wherever the pleasure takes you probably will be good—perhaps very good. To stimulate your pleasure-giving creativity and broaden your repertoire of skills and positions, have a look at the illustrations of playful, nondemand pleasuring in Alex Comfort's *Joy of Sex* or *More Joy of Sex*. If you prefer something that seems more "scientific," try the drawings of sensate focus pleasuring in Helen Singer Kaplan's *Illustrated Manual of Sex Therapy* (see Recommended Reading for this chapter).

likelihood of response problems and increased performance anxiety the next time.

Another valuable learning from sex therapy is to avoid the triple traps of excessive fatigue, hurry-up-itis, and too much alcohol before having sex. Many men, particularly those past fifty, have occasional erection problems. These usually result from falling into one or more of these traps.[12] Remember that, though a glass of wine helps some folks turn off the inner parent and turn on the playful child, drinking too much depresses the sexual responsiveness of one's body.

Sexual Enhancement Method Number 7: *Liberate your body's pleasure potentials.* When you were a young child, the most meaningful language of love was the language of touch. The love messages your whole body-mind understood were being hugged and held and caressed, warmly and tenderly. This longing of the inner child is one we humans never outgrow. Yet, in uptight, low-touch families and cultures, hugging children after a certain early age and adult-to-adult touching (particularly among males) is blocked by punitive attitudes and erotophobia. This produces high levels of body-pleasure anxiety, making it difficult to enjoy sensual satisfactions without guilt or shame. Sexual impulses and responsiveness may be muted, or sexuality may become addictive, causing the person to think obsessively about sex much of the time.

Unfortunately, in our culture pleasure anxiety is often attached to solo sex (masturbation). Solo sex can be a healthy dimension of anyone's sex life. It's a godsend for some single persons and for those who are paired but whose partners are away, sick, or not interested in as-frequent sex. Learning self-pleasuring, including masturbation, has been demonstrated repeatedly in sex therapy to help women awaken their suppressed sexual responsiveness. Once awakened, it can then be enjoyed with a partner if they choose. Self-pleasuring can include many things—self-massage, long sensuous baths, satin sheets, stimulating your erogenous zones. A couple I know relax and talk (to get reconnected) while they enjoy body-to-body closeness in their hot tub after work. Body-awareness exercises and self-pleasuring help many people awaken their senses and learn to love their body and its pleasures more lustily and joyfully. A more alive body will tend to enhance your responsiveness as a lover.

Sexual Enhancement Method Number 8: *Develop and enjoy your capacity for "sensual spirituality."* Think about religion and sex in your life. Are these two friends or enemies, or perhaps strangers who exist in isolated compartments of your life? Getting your sex life and your spiritual life together can enrich both.

Ginny and Doug are a couple in their midforties with three kids. Their sixteen-year marriage had been going reasonably well, with the usual ups and downs of intimate relationships. Their major area of chronic conflict had been sex. Doug wanted it more often and Ginny,

Wholeness Exercise

> **Self-Caring Exercise.** To enjoy the self-nurture of satisfying your skin hungers, take a few minutes now to give yourself a firm, gentle but vigorous face and scalp massage. If you prefer, give yourself a loving foot massage. Energize your whole body by intentionally breathing more deeply as you give yourself the gift of a mini-massage. /
>
> If you liked this brief self-caring, I recommend that you do it regularly for different parts of your body.

who got little satisfaction from sex, seldom was interested. After years of frustrating attempts to change each other, they both felt defeated. Intercourse, when it happened, was tense, rushed, and generally unsatisfying for both of them.

The couple finally talked to their minister about the problem. Sensing that they needed deeper therapy than he had the time or training to provide, he referred them to our counseling center. There they worked with a specialist in pastoral therapy, trained to help couples deal with the spiritual as well as the psychological and interpersonal dimensions of such problems.[13] Both Doug and Ginny discovered that some of their conflict stemmed from their different levels of sexual drive. But they also became aware of some very old feelings behind their ongoing conflict. Many of these feelings came from the "sex-is-dangerous-and-bad" messages each had internalized as children in superconservative churches. Both now rejected this indoctrination, but the old feelings were still spooking around in them. Bob had responded rebelliously. This gave his sexual drives a compulsive, driven quality. Ginny had responded by blocking conscious awareness of her sexual impulses.

Using both joint and individual sessions, the therapist helped them to replace crippling religious attitudes with attitudes celebrating sex as God's good gift. One homework assignment proved especially helpful to them. It was to read together several chapters of James Nelson's *Embodiment*. They were particularly helped by several of Nelson's statements, including: "We need to speak of the erotic and sexual dimensions of our love for God. . . . Love for God devoid of passion and power does little to gladden either the human or the divine heart" (pp. 112–13). Later the therapist loaned them a copy of Helen Singer Kaplan's *The Illustrated Manual of Sex Therapy*. These assignments gave them a sense of having permission as well as some visual coaching in how to make love with more playfulness and imagination.[14] In these ways Ginny and Doug gradually interrupted the religiously rooted sabotage of joy in their sex life.

Wholeness Exercise

Sexual-Spiritual Wholeness Exercise. If you suspect that your sex-diminishing attitudes and feelings are rooted in up-tight childhood religious training, try this exercise used by Ginny and Doug during their therapy. For the next ten minutes, ask yourself these two questions, one at a time, closing your eyes and reflecting on your responses and your feelings: Would God have made sex so much fun if God hadn't intended for us to enjoy it? / How would my sexual feelings and behavior change if I really believed that sex is a glorious gift from God to be used joyfully as well as responsibly? /

Take a few minutes to jot down in your *Self-Care Journal* the thoughts, images, and feelings that came to you. / Then share what you experienced with your partner.

Sexual Enhancement Method Number 9: *Discover and enjoy the special romance of your present life and relationship stage.* The good news from sexologists is that sensual enjoyment can be continued almost indefinitely in successive life stages. "Use it and you won't lose it" is valid advice for your sexuality as well as your mind. A common ageist fallacy holds that sexual passion and satisfaction are mainly for the young. This ignores two facts—that sexual skills can improve with practice and that intimate relationships may become deeper and richer through the joy and pain of the shared years. Many midyears and beyond couples have made a delightful discovery: There's a special romance and closeness that becomes possible only as couples weather the ups and downs of their journey together, providing they have kept their love nurtured and growing. More about this exciting possibility in the final chapter.

Sexual Enhancement Method Number 10: *Take better care of your body and your sex life probably will improve.* Keeping your body fit by exercising and eating right can enhance your sexual enjoyment, particularly when you're over forty. Researchers at Bentley College studied 160 people ages forty to eighty, all active in swimming competition. Their sex lives were found to be more like people in their early thirties or even late twenties. Some medical experts on impotence speculate that clogged blood vessels from eating saturated fats and other cholesterol-rich foods may contribute to erection problems in men by reducing circulation around the penis.[15]

What if all the do-it-yourself methods don't bring the satisfactions you desire? Or what if you suffer from chronic sexual dysfunction? (For males this includes premature ejaculation, chronic impotence, or retarded ejaculation; for females, sexual unresponsiveness, orgas-

W I N D O W   O F   W H O L E N E S S

ALEX COMFORT

London-born Alex Comfort is most widely known for the two books on sex he edited. But he is a multi-faceted Renaissance person with wide-ranging creative contributions in a remarkable variety of fields. His central life work has been human biology, with a special focus on the aging process. He's also a physician and surgeon with a diploma in child health and a Ph.D. in biochemistry. For nearly twenty years, he did research on the aging of animals and how to slow it down. He has served as director of research on gerontology at London's University College and lecturer on physiology at London Hospital Medical College. He was the founder-editor of the journal, *Experimental Gerontology.* Although he has authored textbooks and other scholarly works on physiology, biology, and gerontology, he is also a well-published poet, playwright, and novelist with some eighteen books of fiction to his credit.

Alex Comfort has helped many people to learn to affirm and enjoy the good gift of their sexuality in more spontaneous, playful ways. His delightful bestseller, *The Joy of Sex: A Gourmet Guide to Lovemaking,* features sensuous line drawings and beautiful full-color paintings by Charles Raymond and Christopher Foss. These show a couple enjoying the freedom of adventuresome love making. This book has helped countless people discover and celebrate their bodies' pleasure potentials more fully. The sequel, *More Joy: A Lovemaking Companion to the Joy of Sex,* takes the next steps by helping couples explore and enhance the all-important

relational aspects of sex. It shows how mature adults can use joyful sex to grow as people. Comfort declares: "As a result of our basic cultural miseducation we have three hangups to lose: we have to learn that people aren't dangerous, that the body isn't shameful, and that no rewarding sexual sensation is abnormal or bad unless it's antisocial in some way. It sometimes takes a physical demonstration to change the mind of the child inside us, even if we know these things to be true." The book aims at diminishing the massive blocks that most people have against physical spontaneity, against touching, and against showing affection" (p. 10). The author observes, "Half the joy which a couple get from good sex is their mutual regard and acceptance" (p. 8).

A person with the courage of his convictions, Comfort has never been afraid to express controversial views on sex or other issues which he regards as important for human well being. He has worked for innovative approaches and international cooperation on global problems of overpopulation, hunger, and environmental destruction. He was an early exponent of zero population growth as the only long-term option that can provide a good life for the human family on a healthy planet. A long-term political activist, he was a conscientious objector during the Second World War and was temporarily blacklisted from broadcasting because of his attacks on the indiscriminate bombing of nonmilitary targets by the Allies. He was jailed in 1962 for helping to organize a massive "ban the bomb" demonstration in London's

Trafalgar Square. For several years Comfort was associated with the Center for the Study of Democratic Institutions in Santa Barbara, California—an international think tank of scholars devoted to the solution of basic problems of the contemporary world.

In addition to his significant contributions to the science of gerontology and to sexual joy, Alex Comfort has worked to help ordinary people retain or discover vitality, vigor, and a sense of fun (including sexual fun) in their older years. In his guidebook *A Good Age,* illustrated by Michael Leonard (New York: Crown Publishers, Inc., 1976), he gives numerous examples of the wide range of rewarding options and new opportunities now open to people beyond the midyears. With his challenging activism, he declares that the urgent need is for "old" people to learn to fight back against the hogwash, put-downs, and rip-offs which, because of only the passage of time, society attaches to the roles of people who could still be young in essential ways. With his characteristic spark of humor, he observes: "Two weeks is about the ideal length of time to retire." I agree! (Much of this information is taken from *Current Biography,* 1974, pp. 80–83.)

tic dysfunction, and vaginismus.) If you suffer from severe pleasure anxiety, body alienation, touch phobia, or sexual dysfunctions, you may require the help of a competent therapist who is trained in sex and body therapy and also in individual psychotherapy and couple therapy.[16] The remedial reeducation and coaching of sex therapy may be enough to resolve your problem. But if the roots of your problem are deep in childhood pain and unconscious conflicts, individual psychotherapy as well as body therapy may also be needed. If sex problems stem from communication and relationship problems, as is often true, couple counseling is essential. In a healthier society, such therapies would be readily available on an ability-to-pay basis. This would enable countless persons now plagued by sexual hang-ups and hangovers to know the gift of more joyful sex.

Enjoy a Sensual, Full-Body Massage

A massage can be profoundly relaxing and healing, or it can produce full-body sensual arousal, depending on how it's done.[17]

Instructions: Do the massage on a narrow table or the floor so that you can easily approach the recipient from all sides. Use a foam rubber mat to make it comfortable. Or, best of all, use a folding massage table, which you can make or buy. Get a supply of fragrant body oil to enable your hands to apply pressure and also to move smoothly over the skin. You can make your own using vegetable oil (olive or safflower) and adding a scent you both like. Warm the oil to near body temperature. The room temperature should be at least seventy-five degrees F. If it's winter, a blaze in the fireplace is great for the ambience. Put on your favorite music to provide an auditory environment of soothing or sensuous sound. A relaxing soak in a hot bath before the massage may add to the pleasure.

With warm hands, oil one side of the massagee's entire body before beginning the rubbing and stroking. If you touch with caring love, whatever you do will be welcome and good for the other, in all likelihood. But the recipient may want to give signals (verbal or hand) indicating how much pressure is most enjoyable and what needs more or less attention. Start by giving the face, neck, and scalp a leisurely massage. Then move gradually down the body, giving each part at least a few minutes of caressing. Slow, firm strokes usually are best, though rapid, vigorous strokes in some areas may be preferred by your partner.

The areas where stress accumulates, such as the neck and shoulders and the jaw, invite special attention. Go with the flow, enjoying both giving and receiving love in the wonderfully expressive language of your hands.

Create Your Sexual Enhancement Plan

Take time to go back and review the insights and methods that you liked as you read this chapter, including the important items from the checkup.

Pick at least six things that you'd like to do, and develop a tentative plan for including more love-enhancing sex in your life. Do this in a playful spirit, linking it with your Relationship Fitness Plan from chapter 5. If you're doing this chapter with a partner, work out a joint plan, making sure that it satisfies each person's desires as fully as possible, in equitable ways.

Bear in mind that your plan's effectiveness will probably increase if it includes (1) concrete, realizable objectives—such as the things you have chosen; (2) practical strategies for moving toward these objectives; (3) a time line; (4) a record of your progress in your *Journal*.

Pick one or two especially inviting things and begin doing them soon.

Some find it helpful in overcoming sexual hangups and hangovers to enjoy a sensuous movie, in their minds or on home video. Fantasies, images, and pictures can enable people to experience the luscious pleasures of joyful sexuality without guilt, which gradually changes old programming.

If you experience resistances from old habits and anxieties as you try to implement particular parts of your plan, table those and shift to other parts.

Keep your sexual enhancement loving and sprinkled with sensual spirituality. Stay playful and enjoy!

Challenges to Your Well Being as a Woman or Man—Creative Coping

Being raised in a sexist society can be dangerous to your health. If you're a male, consider the fact that boy babies in most if not all cultures have a considerably shorter life expectancy than girl babies from the same background. In America the longevity gap is over eight years. Think about the statistics on stress diseases among males in hi-tech societies. Women live longer in part because they practice healthier life-styles. In a recent study, American men were found to be 15 percent less likely to limit cholesterol than women, 12 percent more likely to drink too much, and 19 percent more likely to drive after drinking.[1] (See the books by Herb Goldberg, Warren Farrell, James Dittes, and Anne Steinman and David Fox in the Recommended Reading for this chapter for elaboration of the health costs to men of male programming. The books by Rosalind Barrett et al. and Georgia Watkin-Lanoil document the illnesses suffered by both sexes because of nonliberated programming.)

The high costs of female programming in a sexist society are painfully illustrated by the soaring incidences among women of depression and addiction to alcohol and prescribed, psychoactive drugs.[2] Poet Adrienne Rich states powerfully the price women have paid for having been trained to distrust and reject their bodies. She declares, "The fear and hatred of our bodies has often crippled our brains."[3] Sexist programming has damaged women's self-esteem, making them much more vulnerable than men to emotional illnesses. A review of psychological studies of self-esteem levels associated with sex roles confirmed that "successful socialization into the feminine role is accompanied by low levels of self-regard."[4] The primary harm to women's esteem comes from being systematically excluded from decision-making positions in all our institutions except the family. (For further documentation of the damage of sexism to women's health, see the books by Phyllis Chesler, Jean Baker Miller, Maggie Scarf, Mary Daly, and Herbert Freudenberger and Gail North in the Recommended Reading.)

The good news is that our society is in a time of transition when many women and men are becoming aware of the wholeness-constricting impact of traditional sex role programming and are struggling to liberate themselves from it. This makes it a time of hope as well as struggle and conflict in women-men relationships. Many women are deeply frustrated by the slow pace of change toward a more just and egalitarian society. But some significant changes are occurring.

The checkups that follow can be useful to you in two ways. First, they'll give you as a woman or as a man a rough indication of

"We're trying to figure out how to tell our father that his son flunked auto mechanics and his daughter made an A."

the degree to which you have freed yourself from wholeness-diminishing sex-role images and behaviors. Second, the checkups offer you a smorgasbord of concrete attitude and action options for use in liberating yourself further. There are separate checkups for each gender because women and men come from such different places in moving toward liberation. I suggest that you read the other checkup to get a sense of some issues confronting that gender.

Well-Being Checkup for Women

Instructions: In front of each of the items on the checkup designed for your gender, place one of three responses: E = I'm doing excellently in this aspect of my liberation; OK = I'm doing acceptably, but there is room for improvement; NS = I definitely need strengthening in this area.

CHECKLIST

_____ I like myself as a woman and feel a sense of inner power.

_____ I take loving care of the little girl inside me.

_____ I have good friends of both genders.

_____ I relate to women friends as sisters for mutual support and enjoyment.

_____ I have forgiven my parents for whatever inadequacies they had as models of women and men.

_____ I have made peace with my mother (both my actual mother and the mother I carry inside me), so we are now mutually respecting adult friends.

_____ I have made peace with my father (my actual father and the one inside me), so that we are mutually respecting adult friends.

_____ I don't give my power away to men by automatically deferring to them, being submissive, or being defiant. I express my intelligence and power openly when I am with men, rather than hiding these strengths and expressing them in covert, manipulative ways.

_____ I'm aware of the frequent put-downs women receive every day, but I refuse to internalize these attitudes in my image of myself.

_____ I feel equally comfortable with female and male professionals and leaders (e.g., doctors, therapists, clergy, airline pilots), evaluating them on the basis of their competence, not their gender.

_____ I like individual men who are relatively liberated from sexism, even though I reject and challenge the male establishment as destructive to both women's and men's well being.

_____ I am active in groups committed to the full liberation of women and men.

_____ I find spiritual healing power in the symbols, images, and stories that affirm the spiritual discoveries of women and the "feminine" dimension of the divine Spirit.

_____ I enjoy but avoid overidentifying with my role as caretaker of others.

_____ I feel equally joyful when I hear of the birth of a girl or a boy.

_____ I like my body with its wonderful capacity to give birth to a new person, and I care for it lovingly.

_____ I enjoy and celebrate my female sexual responsiveness.

_____ I feel and enjoy my sense of deep connectedness with Mother Earth.

_____ I feel equally female when I am assertive, analytical, independent, and managerial and when I'm expressing more traditional female attitudes and behaviors. I have redefined being feminine to include both kinds of behavior.

_____ I do not use my sexuality to manipulate men.

_____ I encourage the boys and men I care about to liberate themselves from destructive male programming, although I know that only they can free themselves.

_____ If I had my life to live over, I would enjoy being either a man or a woman.

Well-Being Checkup for Men

_____ I like myself as a man and feel a sense of inner power that prevents me from using external power to oppress women and others.

_____ I take care of the little boy inside me lovingly.

_____ I have close friends of both genders.

_____ I enjoy close relationships with some men as brothers and can be open and noncompetitive with them.

_____ I have forgiven my parents for whatever inadequacies they had as role models of liberated manhood and womanhood.

_____ I have made peace with my father (my actual father and the one I carry inside me), so that we are mutually respecting adult friends.

_____ I have made peace with my mother (my actual mother and the one inside me), so that we are mutually respecting adult friends.

_____ I feel equally comfortable with female and male professionals and leaders (e.g., doctors, therapists, clergy, airline pilots), evaluating them on the basis of competence, not gender.

_____ I have cleaned up my language and jokes by eliminating all sexism and put-downs of women.

_____ I'm aware of the wholeness-diminishing programming I received as a boy and am working strenuously to liberate myself from the health hazards of the male "success" treadmill.

_____ I enjoy relating to women as persons as well as sexual beings.

_____ I'm making determined efforts to practice equality and justice in my personal relationships with individual women.

_____ I don't use my male power to hurt, control, or limit the women in my family, work, and community.

_____ I'm aware of my passive if not active role in perpetuating the sexist status quo in the important institutions in my life (including my family and work); I'm using the influence I have there to make them more just and equal for women (and other disempowered people).

_____ I feel as strong when I'm being gentle, receptive, vulnerable, nurturing, dependent, or expressing "soft" emotions such as tenderness and grief, as I do when I'm expressing more traditional male behaviors and feelings.

_____ I feel no shame in enjoying non-macho pleasures, such as the arts and doing non-macho work such as cooking and nurturing children.

_____ I care for my body lovingly rather than treating it like a male machine.

_____ I don't use my sexuality to express power or prove my masculinity.

_____ I'm active in groups committed to the full liberation of men and women.

_____ I find spiritual healing power in the symbols, images, and stories that express the spiritual discoveries of women, as well as men, and in the so-called female as well as male dimensions of the divine Spirit.

_____ I feel equally joyful when I hear of the birth of a girl or a boy.

_____ I support the girls and women I care about in liberating themselves, in their own way, from wholeness-diminishing female programming.

_____ I have redefined "male strength" to affirm mutually empowering ways of relating and to exclude dominance over others.

_____ If I had my life to live over, I'd enjoy being either a woman or a man.

Using Your Findings: I recommend that you do a rough tally of the initials you put in front of the items. This will give you an overall view of your degree of liberation on these vital issues.

In your *Self-Care Journal* jot down for future reference the issues on which you feel it's important to make some changes (from among the OK and NS items). Also note your tentative ideas about what you might do to enhance your wellness in some of these areas.

The Goal of Liberation for Health

As you think of liberating yourself, your intimate relationships, and the social institutions in your life from health-damaging sexism, you probably know what you're against. It can also help to have an image of what you're for. The psychological goal of health-enhancing liberation for both women and men is androgynous wholeness. As used here, this simply means *the balanced development of the feelingful, nurturing, vulnerable, intuitive, receptive right-brain gifts of your personality and your rational, assertive, analytical, lineal-thinking left-brain capacities.* Traditional social pressures push men to develop their left-brain abilities to such a degree that they neglect their right-brain capacities. Comparable pressures also push women to neglect developing their left-brain abilities fully. These two complementary sets of potential strengths and abilities seem to be distributed equally among men and women. They are basic human capacities of the mind. To become more whole, our society must value equally the human capacities it has pressured women to overdevelop in lopsided ways—caring for relationships, nurturing behaviors, sensitivity to feelings—and those human capacities men have been pressured to overdevelop in lopsided ways—rationality and technical, verbal, scientific, and lineal-thinking skills.

There is empirical evidence that developing both sides of your personality fully is good for your mental health. Psychologist Sandra Lipsitz Bem studied the way women and men define themselves and behave with respect to stereotypical versus androgynous styles. She found that the most androgynous men and women were the most able to respond appropriately to the demands of radically differing situations; for example, to take charge when there is an emergency requiring strong leadership or, in contrast, to reach out and pet a kitten when it comes near. Macho males were more inflexible and less able to respond appropriately than androgynous males when the situation called for nonaggressive behavior. Women who fit the traditional feminine stereotype were more inflexible than even the macho men. They were unable to respond appropriately to the needs of a crisis situation.[5]

How does this picture of wholeness look in terms of live human beings? Karen, a woman in her midthirties, has a graduate degree in environmental engineering, a specialty that brings together her passion for science and her love of the earth. She's a respected leader among her colleagues in her workplace. She's comfortable with the assertiveness required in this position. When two (threatened) male colleagues tried to give her a problematic compliment about "thinking like a man," she simply pointed out to them that thinking like a woman today includes thinking in a rigorous, disciplined way.

Karen enjoys being wife to Jonathan and mother to their delightful four-year-old daughter, Nancy. There are the inevitable time crunches and conflicts of juggling home and job responsibilities. But fortunately she and Jonathan worked out an understanding before they decided to marry, that homemaking and child rearing would be shared by the two of them as fairly and equally as possible. It isn't easy for them to implement the agreement, even though Jonathan is a self-employed architect. It often takes schedule juggling and negotiations. They had trouble not reverting to traditional programming about parenting when Nancy had an ear infection and a decision had to be made about who would stay home with her. (Jonathan stayed home that day.)

Jonathan, who is about to turn forty, also has a considerable degree of androgyny in his personality and life-style. He likes the blend of the technical and the artistic sides of his work. He also enjoys fathering Nancy, and, although it's not his favorite occupation, he finds some satisfaction when he takes his turn preparing supper. Jonathan and Karen are tennis buffs and both enjoy a drama-reading group. Jonathan shares Karen's love of nature, and he's proud of her vocational passion to develop new ways to protect the environment. The two of them were avid backpackers during their courting and pre-Nancy years, and plan to begin that again, soon.

The ancient wisdom of the East about wholeness, expressed by Taoism's founder, Lao-tzu, included the awareness that creativity flows from developing both sides of our mind's potentialities:

> One who has a man's wings
> And a woman's also
> Is in himself a womb of the world,
> Continuously, endlessly,
> Gives birth.[6]

One who has a man's wings

And a woman's also

Is in himself a womb of the

world,

Continuously, endlessly,

Gives birth.

—Lao-tzu

Wholeness Hazards Confronting Women and Men

WOMEN	MEN
Sexist programming by society	Sexist programming by society
Caretaker treadmill	"Success" treadmill
Diminished self-esteem from social put-downs	Self-esteem dependent on proving oneself via achievements
Self-body alienation—as sex object	Self-body alienation—as success object
Alienation from full sexual responsiveness and enjoyment	Sexual alienation by compulsive, defensive sexuality
Repression of anger and assertiveness	Repression of tenderness and the playful child side
Derivative identity from being dependent on a man	Identity dependent on having a woman as satellite and support
Economic dependency and exclusion from power and opportunities	Stressed by constant competitiveness
Learned helplessness (giving power away to men)	Misusing power and/or feeling impotent in male competition
Alienation from in-depth relations with both men and women	Alienation from in-depth relations with both women and men
Ageism particularly oppressive	Retirement often an infected grief wound
Impoverished, male-dominated spirituality	Impoverished, male-dominated spirituality

The hazards to wholeness listed above overlap and are mutually reinforcing. Those after the first item on each of the two lists above are all variations of that theme—the sexist programming we receive as women and men. As we take a closer look at how our gender programming hurts well being, you may find it useful to reflect on the particular sex-role patterns you learned in your own childhood family.

In traditional families girls learn to derive much of their identity and sense of worth from being caretakers, particularly of males and children. When they become women, this orientation causes them to neglect needed self-care and to suffer from irrational guilt feelings about being "selfish" when they do healthful self-nurture. In a parallel way boys are taught in traditional families to derive their sense of identity and worth primarily from achievements and being "successful," success being defined as getting ahead of others. This sets up adult males to feel "unsuccessful" (lacking in power) or to misuse the power they do have to dominate and control those defined by society as less important or weaker—women, children, minority persons. Our society's hierarchical understanding of success means that only a few men can feel really successful, that is, on top of their job's pecking order. Consequently most men live with some feelings of diminished esteem, a nagging sense of not having made it. The male success treadmill makes it easy to become workaholics, in a frantic but vain effort to prove our worth and feel empowered.

To the extent that you feel valued and value yourself only as an object (either a sex or success object), alienation from your genuine self and your body, including your sexuality, follows. Many women and men have an I-it relationship with their bodies, rather than an affirming, loving I-thou relationship. They see their bodies as flawed machines, which they frantically try to fix or force to shape up. Many women try obsessively and at great expense to make their bodies fit the superficial media image of youthful beauty and attractiveness to men. Many men have a comparable obsession: to make their bodies meet a jock standard of male attractiveness or to make them serve obediently in the punishing, workaholic world of the super-competitive male success rat race.

For both genders alienation from full enjoyment of the pleasures of one's body results from the body rejection and diminished self- and body-esteem produced by the scenarios just described. For men the process is intensified by the compulsive-addictive need to prove one's masculinity. All this tends to depersonalize sexual relationships and to focus male sexuality in the penis rather than encouraging men also to enjoy full-body sensuality.

Traditional sexist programming also spawns dishonest, manipulative power games between the sexes. The female taboo on anger and the male taboo on tenderness and vulnerability alienate women and men from their full range of feelings and behaviors. This further impoverishes their relationships as well as limits their inner lives. Ageism and the shrinking self-esteem that result from it are particularly cruel to women who have internalized our culture's youth-worshiping, sex-object misunderstanding of their worth. Many men whose identity and esteem are grossly dependent on job achievements are devastated by retirement, or by prolonged unemployment. Severe health and sexual problems often result.

Liberating Your Wholeness as a Woman or Man

How can you protect yourself from the negative impact of gender-specific health hazards in your society? One thing you can do is to open yourself to consciousness-raising (CR) experiences. By reading and by joining a support CR group of other women or men, you can increase your awareness and resistance when stereotypes are being reinforced. This occurs constantly by the impact of TV, advertising, the press, sports, and the sexist practices of the institutions in your life. Consciousness raising often makes life more painful, but defending yourself against sexism is impossible if you are not aware.

Taking part in a women's support CR group helps many women become aware and resist the innumerable ways they are put down each day. A CR group for men can identify the macho influences that pressure us to define male strength according to Rambo and Superbowl images. Such experiences can awaken slumbering anger about sexism, constructive anger that provides energy for remedial action. Such a group can also give mutual support, hope, and empowerment via the rich experience of bonding with sisters or brothers who are also struggling for self-liberation for wholeness.

As we were growing up we all learned powerful messages from our society about the "right" way to be a woman or man. These old tapes are deeply imprinted, emotionally charged, and very seductive. All this makes them devilishly difficult to change even when rational evidence of their fallacious, hurtful nature is very strong. The key to protecting yourself is deprogramming the old tapes, a process that includes interacting with and learning from encounters with liberated books and with persons of your gender who are further along on the road of gender wholeness. When something starts an obsolete sexist tape playing in your mind, try turning the volume down by saying to yourself the healthier things you now believe about men or women. It also may help to laugh at the old messages' ridiculousness. Ridiculing old tapes can defuse whatever harmful power they may still have in your mind. In fact humor can play a vital and empowering role in the self-liberation of any oppressed group.

David Richardson's cartoon (whose caption you may have seen on a T-shirt worn by a woman) uses satirical humor to debunk our

SHE WHO WAITS FOR HER

KNIGHT IN SHINING ARMOR

USUALLY FINDS HERSELF

CLEANING UP AFTER HIS HORSE!

—bumper sticker

A woman without a man is like a fish without a bicycle.

culture's traditional indoctrination of women to believe that they're really OK and whole only if they're attached to a man.

There are other things that men can do to deprogram their sexist social programming. They can redefine their inner pictures of success and male strength. This means rejecting the illusions that the workaholic treadmill produces healthy success and that macho strength is normal or healthy strength. It means redefining male success to include more attention to self-care flowing from self-love and loving care of those nearest to us. It means owning and valuing the soft, so-called (erroneously) unmasculine feelings. It also means freeing sexuality from the shackles of being used to overcome feelings of powerlessness.

Many women have internalized the negative messages of their sexist society in their own sense of self. This is an inner saboteur of their empowerment. Jean Baker Miller, a psychiatrist, points out that women can enhance their well being by recognizing that their traditional "womanly strengths" are valuable and need to be developed by both women and men in today's world. She identifies five such strengths: vulnerability, emotionality, cooperation, creativity, and valuing participation in the development of others, as in raising children, teaching, and caring for the elderly.[7]

Women friends have reported that these things are helpful in changing their sexist programming: learning to balance receiving with giving care; learning to enjoy the pleasures of their bodies more fully; learning to avoid giving their power away to men by acting dumb; discovering sources of self-esteem and empowerment within themselves by learning new skills and competencies; doing more good things for themselves; taking self-defense, assertiveness training, and body-building classes.

Societal Benefits of Personal and Relational Liberation

An important thing you can do for your own wholeness, as a woman or a man, is to become active in social liberation, in both individual ways (such as writing letters to editors and congress people), and in groups committed to eliminating sexist-caused brokenness in our society. Whatever your efforts accomplish on a societal level, putting some appropriate anger and energy into this crucial cause can be healing and empowering for you. It's good for your personal wholeness to use whatever influence you have to help eliminate the social and institutional practices that diminish wellness for all women and men. In other words, personal liberation includes using whatever personal, political, and economic clout you have (or can develop), to erase the social roots of gender health hazards.

Many exciting gains in well being for our world probably will result from self-liberation by more and more women and men, together with the liberation of our social institutions. Riane Eisler in her breakthrough book *The Chalice and the Blade: Our History, Our Future* paints a well-documented picture of what will happen as we move from a male-dominated to a partnership world: "The changes in woman-man relations from the present high degree of suspicion and recrimination to more openness and trust will be reflected in our families and communities. There will also be positive repercussions in our national and international policies. Gradually we will see a decrease in the seemingly endless array of day-to-day problems that now plague us, ranging from mental illness, suicide, and divorce, to wife and child battering, vandalism, murder, and international terrorism."

She continues, "Along with the celebration of life will come the celebration of love, including the sexual love between women and men. Sexual bonding through some form of what we now call marriage will most certainly continue. But the primary purpose . . . will be mutual companionship, sexual pleasure, and love. Having children will no longer be connected with the transmission of male names and property. And other caring relationships, not just heterosexual couples, will be fully recognized. All institutions, not only those specifically designed for the socialization of children, will have as their goal the actualization of our great human potential."[8]

The stakes in all this are very high. The healing and even the survival of a livable planet may depend on both men and women learning to prize and practice in the public sphere the so-called feminine values and priorities—caring, compassion, and concern for

WINDOW OF WHOLENESS

TAI-YOUNG LEE

In 1981 I met a remarkable woman in Seoul, Korea. Tai-Young Lee is South Korea's first woman lawyer. She is a tireless and courageous worker for women's rights and human rights in a country where male-dominated laws and customs have traditionally treated women as second-class citizens. We met at her office in the Women's Legal Aid for Family Relations Center, in a building constructed from contributions made entirely by women. The center has a twofold objective: to give legal assistance to women suffering from discriminatory divorce and inheritance laws and to work to change these unjust laws. In the first twenty-five years of its existence, the center served over one hundred thousand women clients with legal assistance and, when appropriate, called in husbands to discuss constructive changes that could save marriages.

Born in a poor family in a small mountain village in what is now North Korea, Tai-Young Lee and her family fled as refugees to South Korea. Her mother inspired her to a life of service to the oppressed and the powerless. Her husband, who later became South Korea's foreign minister, was imprisoned by the Japanese for five years during their occupation of Korea. When he was released in 1945, he broke with ancient tradition by staying home to care for their four young children while she studied law to prepare for a career of advocacy for women. After passing the bar exam she started the center in the rented corner of a small office. She was the only staff. In the first year she helped 149 desperate

women with legal assistance and family guidance. In 1977 she and her husband were given a suspended sentence and stripped of their civil rights for reading a declaration at an ecumenical church service accusing the country's dictatorial president of trampling on human rights. When a few friends tried to persuade her to give up her struggle for human rights, to protect the center's development, she refused, declaring: "Human rights are indivisible. There is no point fighting for women's rights if we are not equally zealous in defending the human rights of others!" (The source of this statement and much of the present profile is David Finkelstein, "Korea's 'Quiet' Revolutionary: A Profile of Tai-Young Lee," *The Christian Century*, April 29, 1981.)

Tai-Young Lee has spent over four decades battling against heavy odds for women's rights. When I visited her again in June 1990, she spoke with excitement of the new Korean Family Law for which she had led the struggle for thirty-seven years—legislation that eliminates 90 percent of the legal discrimination against women. She told of the network of legal aid centers for women and families her program had established all over South Korea, as well as in the U.S., to serve Korean war brides and other immigrants.

As a grandmother of ten, Tai-Young Lee holds passionately to the view that peace and harmony in the home, based on justice and equality, is the path to justice and peace in the world. This revolutionary grandmother calls herself "a very ordinary woman." She blends human warmth, compassion, and idealism with a tough, pragmatic sense of political realities, and a "fierceness for freedom." Her biographer describes her as "demure as dynamite," a phrase originally used to describe American poet Emily Dickinson. All this power is rooted in her deep religious commitment and her profound respect and love for persons. She reminds the center's staff that when a woman comes with a painful family problem, they should ask themselves, "What love can I give to this person?" (from a biography of Tai-Young Lee by Sonia Reid Strawn, *Where There Is No Path* [Seoul: *Klacer*, 1988], 189).

nurturing people and relationships. For their well being and the well being of the planet, men must listen to and learn from the wisdom of women about increasing loving strength and strengthening love.

A Whole Spirituality For Wholeness

The Adam and Eve story

"shows, among other

things, that if you make a

woman out of a man,

you are bound to get

into trouble."

—*Carol Gilligan*

In Alice Walker's novel *The Color Purple*, Corrine (Celie) is asked by her dear friend Shug why she pours out her burdens in letters to her sister Nettie rather than to God, as she formerly did. Corrine responds: "What God do for me? . . . He gave me a lynched daddy, a crazy mama, a lowdown dog of a step pa and a sister I probably won't ever see again. Anyhow, . . . the God I been praying and writing to is a man. And act just like all the other men I know. Trifling, forgitful and lowdown." Shug responds worriedly, "Miss Celie, you better hush. God might hear you." Corrine says with passion, "Let 'im hear me. . . . If he listened to poor colored women the world would be a different place, I can tell you."[9]

The triple oppression of racism, poverty, and sexism by which Celie's self-esteem had been mangled was reinforced by religious beliefs with oppressive male images. Learning to challenge and reject these beliefs was for her a step toward wholeness. Most theologies, in the religious systems of both the West and the East, have been derived primarily from the religious experiences of males and are dominated by male authority figures. Nelle Morton, a pioneer in helping recover the neglected and often suppressed spiritual wisdom of women, puts the problem in these confronting words: "Any theology developed by one sex, out of the experience of one sex, and taught predominantly by one sex cannot possibly be lived out of as if it were whole theology. For whole theology is possible only when the whole people become part of its process, and that includes women." Then she adds a word of hope for the future, "And in time, whole theology may be approximated when men can hear women . . . and when men and women together can participate fully and equally in bringing faith to expression."[10] The parallel process of men not listening to the spiritual insights of women and Celie's God not listening to her is noteworthy.

Many women find that female images, stories, and religious leaders help them develop their full spiritual potentialities. Women who have been trained to base their identity and worth on satellite relationships with males have this dependency strengthened by male images, stories, and symbols of deity. The often-voiced protest "My God is not a male or a female!" does not alter the spiritually limiting impact on women of constantly repeated male images by male religious leaders. The spiritual hunger of both women and men in our society is increased by the deep sexism of our theologies and religious institutions.

Carol Christ makes a convincing case for the ways in which the symbol of the Goddess enhances women's wholeness by affirming the beauty and legitimacy of female power, the female body, and the life cycle expressed in it. The Goddess imagery also helps them value women's heritage of healing and spirituality, and strengthens bonding among women in sisterhood.[11] Nelle Morton gives a moving account of how her experience of the Goddess healed her fear of flying.[12] (For a full documentation of women's powerful spiritual need for a whole theology see the books by Nelle Morton, Mary Daly, Charlene Spretnak, Carol Christ, Riane Eisler, and Joan Engelsman in the Recommended Reading.)

I'm convinced that men also need to experience and value the Goddess, the female aspects of divinity. We need a whole theology to help us experience a more whole and empowering spirituality. "Whole" in this context means the joining of two complementary, mutually enriching spiritual streams—those dimensions of traditional religious wisdom that are liberating and androgynous and the stream of wisdom from women's spiritual discoveries through the ages. There is much in the Jewish and Christian heritages that can provide pathways to experiencing God's loving, healing Spirit. Fortunately valuable fragments of the ancient heritage of women's spirituality survived in the wisdom literature of the First Testament and in beautiful passages such as this one from Isaiah: "As one whom his mother comforts, so I will comfort you. . . . You shall see and your heart shall rejoice" (66:13–14). Furthermore, Jesus' attitudes toward women, in sharp contrast to the prevailing sexism of his day (and ours), were strikingly liberated.[13]

A part of the richness of Native American spirituality *is* its deep awareness of the feminine dimension of divinity, an awareness that was central in its respect for the natural world. Paula Gunn Allen remembers her Native American tradition of the Sacred Hoop of Be-ing: "In the beginning was thought, and her name was Woman. . . . She is the Old Woman who tends the fires of life. She is the Old Woman Spider who weaves us together in a fabric of interconnection."[14]

As I have gradually become more open to experiencing the God-

Wholeness Exercise

A Healing Exercise from Women's Wisdom. Psychotherapist Diane Mariechild draws healing images and methods from the centuries-spanning heritage of women healers. She has given us a valuable exercise for connecting with the wisdom within each of us.[15] Experience it now, after you have taken a few minutes to breathe more deeply, release tension, and get your body-mind in a relaxed but alert state.

"Let yourself sink deeply into the realm of intuitions, images and archetypes. Deep within this sea of images is the image of the wise old woman. She lives very deeply within you. You may uncover her and enjoy the benefits of her great wisdom . . . the wisdom of the ages that is unfolding within you." / "And now you are at the foot of a mountain. And you begin to climb this mountain, making your way along the stony mountain path. Climbing higher and higher now and the ascent is becoming steeper but you are drawing on inner strength and the climb is almost effortless. The air is getting thinner now, yet it is clean and clear. And you eagerly make your way upward, almost running the last few steps as you reach the door to the cabin. Here in this cabin lives the wise old woman. She is here to greet you now and you will spend some very important time with her. . . . *Pause about ten minutes.* / And now you thank the old woman for her advice and support, . . . leave the cabin and descend the mountain, moving down the mountain path and back to your usual waking reality. Return now, relaxed, refreshed and filled with energy. Open your eyes and stretch your body."/ Note in your *Journal* what you learned from the wise old woman within you. /

On another occasion, I suggest you experience the same exercise substituting an encounter with a wise old man. / Compare the two experiences after you complete this second encounter.

dess, I have learned to enjoy the soft, receptive, mystical side of my religious life. I feel gratitude to the feminist vision of whole spirituality for the way it has helped open me to experience my oneness with the wonderful web of life. This continuing discovery has helped to heal my male illusion of separateness. My anxiety about death has diminished as I have become aware of death not as enemy but as an essential transition in the continuing cycle of birth, growth, death, and rebirth. I suspect that many men are searching for the Goddess experience, often without being aware of the nature of their spiritual hungers.

**Create Your
Gender Liberation
Fitness Plan**

Go back and review key insights and methods that seemed relevant in this chapter, picking a half dozen or so that you want to use. Include important items you marked OK or NS on the checkup.

Using your creativity and playfulness, write out a realistic Self-Care Plan for your double liberation—liberation from gender-related health hazards and liberation to enjoy your life as a woman or man more fully. If you're working with a partner, create a joint plan aimed at encouraging each other's self-care and self-transformation.

Again, your plan probably will work better if it includes these things: (1) concrete, realizable objectives that you really want to achieve; (2) practical strategies for moving toward these; (3) a time line; (4) rewards you'll get or give yourself or each other as you implement your self-liberation plan, or withhold if you backslide; (5) a record of your progress in your *Journal*.

Pick one or two attractive parts of your plan and begin doing them immediately. Keep what you do love centered and spiritually energized. Also activate your inner child so your serious intentions will be spiced with playfulness.

If it's helpful, create a movie in your mind each day for a few minutes, experiencing the satisfactions of more liberated relating to both genders. You may find it helpful to include some reading (from the Recommended Reading) in your plan.

I wish you the joy of self-liberation from the male box if you're a man or the female programming prison if you're a woman!

Maximizing Love-Centered Well Being in Your Present Life Stage and Throughout Your Life

 Love-centered well being involves staying alive all your life! Or, in the wise words of a friend, it's the way to "die young as late as possible."[1] It's a pity that so many people hit the midyears doldrums and stop savoring life with gusto and zest. Their loss of life loving is indeed a great loss. Nicholas Murry Butler, when he was president of Columbia University, described a colleague on whose tombstone he said should be inscribed the words DIED AT FORTY, BURIED AT SEVENTY.

In contrast, remember Rosa Beyer, whom you encountered in the first chapter? Her life embodies the good news that it is possible for you to sustain playful, love-empowered wholeness through all the stages of your life journey, in spite of painful losses. Actress Katharine Hepburn was interviewed when she turned eighty. She said she wasn't going to make much of her birthday, adding, "There are 20 million books I haven't read, 20 million walks I haven't taken and 20 million parts I haven't played." She still digs in her garden and cleans refuse in front of her brownstone in Manhattan. She complains (with a refreshing touch of humor) about gradually getting shorter with aging: "I used to be 5 foot 7½ inches, now I'm 5 foot 6. Pretty soon I'm going to disappear."[2] Katharine Hepburn and Rosa Beyer are vivid demonstrations that wholeness in the older years is possible and is the achievement of a lifetime.

Well being through life's stages is something like a rainbow, with each life stage reflecting an important but different color in the spectrum of aging. Each complements the others. Whether you're young or old, in your present stage you know valuable things you could not have known without the struggles and learnings of earlier stages. You can understand and do things now that were impossible before life taught you these hard lessons. Many older people have jewels of insight about living that younger folks have not had the experience yet to know. (In age-affirming societies these insights are respected for what they are—precious fragments of wisdom.) On the other hand, young people, having grown up in a very different world, understand things from their experiences that we who are older cannot understand, unless we're open to learning from them.

The rainbow image reflects the real world of human experience more accurately if seen in the context of the storm that produced it, a storm with its fury, its dark, swirling clouds, its thunder and lightning, its lashing wind and pouring rain. During the storms of life the light that eventually produces a brilliant rainbow is often obscured by the clouds of pain and loss. Then, as the storms clear, the sunlight breaks through and a rainbow is born as sunlight is refracted through billions of tiny prisms—nature's tears still in the air from the storm.

Here's a moving description of the life journey by Henri Nouwen and Walter Gaffney, using the rainbow image: "Aging is the most common human experience which overarches the human community as a rainbow of promises. It is an experience so profoundly human that it breaks through the artificial boundaries between childhood and adulthood, and between adulthood and old age. It is so filled with promises that it can lead us to discover more and more of life's treasures."[3]

If you prefer another image, see your life as a hike of wholeness. This metaphor highlights healing and health as a way of walking in which you provide the muscle and choose the direction. As you've undoubtedly noticed, each major transition on your journey has brought a new set of losses, liabilities, and challenges. But what is often overlooked is that each life stage also brings new strengths, assets, and possibilities not available before. Your life journey, like mine, probably has taken you through some very deep, shadowed valleys. But very likely it also has taken you to some high points, lookouts where breathtaking vistas awakened your lost awareness of the incredible beauty and wonder that life sometimes brings.

Gail Sheehy describes the challenge of the growth journey that is

"The best thing you can do is to get very good at being you."

well being: "The willingness to move through each passage is equivalent to the willingness to live abundantly. If we don't grow, we are not really living. Growth demands giving up familiar but limiting patterns. . . . The courage to take new steps allows us to let go of each stage with its satisfactions and to find the fresh responses that will release the richness of the next. The power to animate all of life's seasons is a power that resides within us."[4]

What is the key to maximizing well being in your present age and stage? It's to transform the new problems and pains this stage holds by developing the new possibilities and gains it offers you. This is a down-to-earth strategy for staying alive all your life. It's the secret of maturing wholistically. By developing more of the new possibilities of mind, body, spirit, and relationships in your present life stage, you prepare yourself to continue developing the fresh possibilities of the future. This chapter describes ways to do this, whatever your age. It includes a robust emphasis on life's second half because that's when, in our ageist culture, it's easiest to miss the rich possibilities for enhanced well being.

**Life Stage
Well-Being
Checkup**

Instructions: This inventory can be useful in two interrelated ways: as an evaluation of your wholeness in your present stage and as a rich variety of options to use in enhancing wholeness in areas where you discover it is needed. In front of each statement put one of three symbols: E = I'm doing excellently in this area; OK = Things are acceptable but there's room for improvement; NS = Things definitely need strengthening in this area.

CHECKLIST

_____ I enjoy keeping my body tuned up and trim by age-appropriate exercising, a healthful diet, adequate rest, and loving cultivation of my circle of family and friends.

_____ In my present life stage I've learned to cope with the problems by developing some of the new possibilities.

_____ I have realistic goals for this stage and am taking steps toward them.

_____ I've made peace with my past so that I don't waste creative energy on unproductive regrets or futile self-criticism.

_____ I've learned to prize the things I've learned the hard way in the past and use these as preparation for what I can do today and in the future.

_____ I've made peace with my tomorrows by planning carefully, not wasting valuable energy on unproductive worry, and maintaining reality-based hope.

_____ I enjoy living in this here-and-now moment, aware of both its pleasures and pain, thankful for the good gift of just being alive.

_____ My experience today is enriched by enjoying cherished memories from my past and hopeful expectations about my future.

_____ I enjoy friendships with persons of all ages and am open to learning from and sharing my understandings with friends, whatever their chronological ages.

_____ I've accepted my own mortality, so awareness that my time on this planet is limited motivates me to live today more fully.

_____ I enjoy doing everything I can to make the world a little better and more whole when I leave it than when I arrived.

Using Your Findings: Do a rough tally of the three types of initials you placed in front of checkup items to get a quick sense of your life-stage wholeness. Congratulate yourself on all the E items that you know are for real. Then in your *Self-Care Journal* or the book's margins, jot down your ideas about constructive changes you want to make in areas initialed OK and NS that seem important to you.

Some Guidelines for Your Well-Being Journey

Here are some ways to enjoy more wholeness in your present life stage. (You'll find tools for implementing these guidelines in the pages that follow as well as elsewhere in this book.)

1. Become aware that life itself, including your life, is a precious gift to be used well in each new chapter.

2. Make better friends with time, in all three of its dimensions. Do this by moving from the house of regrets about the past and fears about the future to the house of gentle self-forgiveness for past stumblings, action-empowered hope for the future, and thankfulness for just being alive in the present moment.

3. In the midst of the daily-ness of life, measured by your wristwatch and calendar, become aware of any special spiritual meanings and opportunities of this particular stage of your journey. In the time-tested wisdom of the Bible, the Greek word *kairos* was used to distinguish the spiritual significance of time. This quality is present in the midst of the humdrum, everyday *chronos* (clock and calendar time) of your daily life. *Kairos* is when time stands still for a moment of transcendence, you forget about your schedule, and you sense that you indeed stand in a precious little sliver of eternity.

4. Discover the fresh strengths and possibilities of your present situation. By developing these gifts you help to generate the self-esteem, hope, and love you need to cope with whatever painful problems you're having at this time in your life. Be sure to prize those fragments of wisdom that life has taught you. Use these understandings and skills. They are precious resources for living and loving today.

5. Awaken a dream in your heart of a transformed future with greater well being for yourself and those you love, but also for the human family and the network of living creatures called the biosphere. Open yourself to be lured by your dream, energized for doing what you can to make it a reality. As I look up from writing, I see the poet Langston Hughes's powerful words on a poster near my desk: "Hold fast to dreams, for if dreams die, life is a broken-winged bird that cannot fly." It's true, you know. Giving your dream hands and legs and a voice can generate the actions needed to help create a better future.

Empirical studies of adult development have confirmed what most adults already knew from experience: that the years of adulthood are times of continuing changes. These changes are in one's self-identity, career, meanings, sense of time, significant relationships, and lots more. The next three sections highlight the wholeness problems and possibilities that many people experience in the three major stages of adulthood. People's life journeys vary tremendously, of course. Your developmental pains and gains may be similar at points to what follows, but they may also be radically different. These generalizations are designed to inspire reflections on your own life journey.

Well-Being Challenges of the Young Adult Years	**Problems and Pains**	**Strengths and Gains**
	Intense life-styles and pressure-cooker demands of leaving one's childhood home, completing formal education, beginning one's career, developing intimate relations, having children, and so on.	High levels of energy to invest in the multiple demands. Growing autonomy and competence. Enjoying new, challenging work and, in some cases, beginning a new family.
	Unfinished identity may result in fear of intimacy and responsibility.	Untarnished dreams and motivation to be all that one can.
	Problems of balancing time for job, close relationships, and for oneself.	Lots of zest for living life fully and in the fast lane.
	Heavy financial pressures.	
	Coping with either marriage or singlehood without adequate preparation for either.	Opportunities to learn by "on the job training" in intimate communication and conflict resolving.
	Frequent uprooting by moving away from supportive relations.	Opportunities to grow and build new relationship networks in new places.
	Being able to neglect one's body and seem to get away with it.	The challenge of including a healthy diet, exercise, and rest in a busy life.

A central task of maturing in the high-pressure young adult years, according to Erik Erikson, is to develop one's capacity for intimacy. This brings a new strength—self-giving love. But young adults who suffer from leftover fears of getting hurt in close relationships and unfinished identity issues from adolescence may avoid intimacy. This leads to painful isolation. To risk giving yourself to another with intimate, joyful abandon requires a firm sense of your own identity and self-worth.

Wholeness issues encountered frequently by struggling young adults include

- conflicts and resistances to transferring primary emotional bonding from their family of origin to their new family or peer support group;

- learning to balance the need for emotional intimacy with your need for autonomy. Women tend to shortchange autonomy and men intimacy;

- struggling to integrate sex with mutual respect, equality, and love in an ongoing relationship;

- learning the know-how required to make their work both effective and fulfilling;

- developing all the new interpersonal skills needed for either creative singlehood or for marriage and parenting.

Well-Being Challenges of the New Midyears	**Problems and Pains**	**Strengths and Gains**
	A quiet, often unrecognized crisis.	A challenge to keep growing.
	Work pressures very high.	Work satisfactions also potentially high.
	Problems with teenagers.	Satisfactions with teenagers.
	Aging, increasingly dependent parents.	An opportunity to deepen adult-to-adult relations with parents.
	Signs of bodily aging increase.	A challenge to care for one's body to keep it trim and healthy.

Heavy financial pressures.	Increased income potential.
Marital boredom and distancing.	A challenge to deepen marital intimacy.
Spiritual-value issues become more pressing.	An opportunity for major spiritual-value maturing.
The emptying or empty nest necessitates significant adjustments.	The emptying or empty nest creates potential for other fulfilling activities.

Middle adulthood is a two-phase stage for those who have children. Phase one, with teenagers in the home, is often hectic. Phase two has radically different pressures and possibilities. It's the emptying and then empty nest. Stressful family issues often arise today as young adult children postpone leaving the nest or move out and then back in. This pushes both generations into a revolving-door adjustment—now empty, now unempty nests. The central task of maturing in these years is developing *generativity*, from which the strength of caring emerges or is enhanced. Generativity is a beautiful idea. It involves caring about and for the future by investing something of yourself in that future by caring for and about children and young people, institutions, work, and causes that may live after you. If generativity flowers, it enhances wholeness at any life stage, not just the midyears. If this capacity is not developed at least by the midyears, self-absorption constricts wholeness.

For many people the midyears are good times of savoring life and contributing in satisfying (though sometimes exhausting) ways to their families, jobs, and communities. Wholeness challenges often encountered in midyears include marital and/or job burnout, teen-parent crises, painful spiritual-value crises, chemical dependencies and addictions (including alcoholism, prescription drugs, sex, and work), and being the sandwich generation pressed between adolescing teens and increasingly dependent aging parents. People often experience a reorientation of their awareness of time. They move from time-since-birth to time-left-to-live. This may trigger a spiritual crisis, causing them to question their meanings, priorities, and lifestyles.

I once saw a book in an airport paperback stand entitled *How to be 30 for 40 Years*. (I'm sorry now I didn't get a copy.) Although this title smacks of ageism, it also points to the extended midyears, which have provided us with a whole new set of problems and opportunities for wholeness. The midyears now last for three or four decades for many people in developed countries. This life extension is a welcome but very recent gift to humankind derived from dramatic increased life expectancy in this century. Many people are staying healthy enough to enjoy active, productive living through the fifth, sixth, seventh decades and beyond. Living more wholistically is the secret of wellness in the midyears. It's also the best preparation for the so-called mature years.

Well-Being Challenges of the New Mature Years	Problems and Pains	Strengths and Gains
	Health problems tend to increase, though the majority of seniors are healthy.	Challenge to enhance self-care for physical well being.
	Diminishing energy for *doing*.	More time and incentive for *being*.
	Vocational losses and grief at retirement.	Active retirement as a challenging new chapter in life.
	Diminished income (poverty for some).	Need for "things" may decline.
	Ageism may diminish self-esteem.	Challenge to find inner sources of self-esteem.
	Regrets about opportunities not taken in the past.	Satisfaction with the achievements of one's life.
	The pressure and grief of a rapidly contracting future.	Challenge to enjoy the present and use the available time well.
	The anxiety of unstructured time after retirement.	Freedom for choices about uses of time, plus more time for satisfying activities, including outreach to help others.
	Increasing griefs from deaths of close friends and/or spouse.	The challenge to do one's grief work and strengthen one's friend network.

Confrontation with one's own mortality.	The challenge to come alive by facing death with vital faith and love.
Temptations to neglect health-sustaining exercise and diet.	The challenge of preventing premature aging by exercise and diet.

The mature years actually include two or three distinct phases for most of us: the vigorous, active early retirement years; the years of widowhood or widowerhood (for those who are coupled); and years of diminishing vigor leading eventually to death. Each of these phases has potentialities for sustaining well being at your center. Each is a time when the hope-wholeness perspective is an invaluable resource for staying alive all your life. For those whose intimate relationships have been nurtured like good wine (which improves with age), these years can be rich and cherished times of intimate sharing. As the couple in Eugene O'Neill's play *Ah, Wilderness* declares: "Spring isn't everything. There's a lot to be said for fall and winter, too, if you're together."[5] Those who live alone have a special challenge sustaining their friend-family support circle in these years.

The central wholeness task of the mature years is *ego integrity* according to Erikson, the opposite of which is despair. Wisdom is the strength that matures if this task is accomplished well. Ego integrity means accepting your finitude and making some peace with the swiftly passing years. It means forgiving life for its imperfections and accepting the reality that being alive is basically good, in spite of the limitations and losses of living. This acceptance frees you to enjoy living now rather than cutting off your aliveness by remorse, depression, resentment, despair, and retreat into the past.

Inventory of Your Present Life Stage

This simple inventory can help you get a clearer picture of the gains as well as the pains of your present stage. Based on this awareness you can make workable plans for using the gains more fully to cope with the pains.

Instructions: Close your eyes and become aware of the losses, liabilities, and limitations of this life stage. / Look at the columns in this inventory. In the far left column, jot down words to remind you of these negative factors in your life now. / Close your eyes again and reflect on the assets, strengths, and new possibilities of your present life stage. / In the center column list these positive factors in your current life experience. / Now decide on ways to use your assets in this life stage to handle the liabilities and enhance your wholeness.

Losses and Pains	Assets and Gains	Using Gains to Handle Pains

As action strategies come to you, jot down notes to yourself in the right hand column, for later use.

This simple inventory has proved to be surprisingly useful to people of various ages, particularly during transitions when they're struggling to reorient their lives or careers. During a life-career planning workshop in the Pacific Northwest, Carl, age thirty-nine, declared after using this inventory: "It blows my mind to discover that I've been focusing so hard on the problems that I've been ignoring some new possibilities right at my fingertips." Later he asked the group for feedback about a vocational redirection plan that was developing in his mind after he used this inventory.

How to Make Better Friends with Time

The folk art of bumper stickers occasionally communicates surprisingly sound advice. There's some down-to-earth wisdom in this one: DON'T LET YOUR YESTERDAYS AND TOMORROWS GOBBLE UP YOUR TODAYS! One way to enjoy more wholeness in the present is to spend more time there. This probably will require two things: healing leftover wounds from your past and recovering energy wasted on unproductive worry about the future. During my early life I spent too much time five miles ahead on the road (with unproductive fantasies

MAGGIE KUHN

Margaret E. Kuhn—better known as Maggie—is a human dynamo of ebullience, steely determination, tough-mindedness, and moral fortitude. At age sixty-five she was put out to pasture by mandatory retirement from a church-and-society job with the United Presbyterian denomination. With a welcome sense of liberation from the bureaucracy, she banded together with four friends, all of whom had opposed the war in Vietnam. Together they launched a national network of older, middle-years, and young activists to work for human liberation from the widespread oppression of ageism, sexism, and other forms of social injustice. This rapidly growing group eventually came to be called the Gray Panthers. As Maggie reminds us, gray is the color you get when you mix all the colors of the rainbow. In her words, "We are on a pilgrimage but also a lark"(*Current Biography*, 1978, 239). College student volunteers were among those who helped the Gray Panthers get set in their first office, in a Philadelphia church basement. In Kuhn's words: "We realized that the young and the old in this society are equally discriminated against. Both groups have identity crises. Both groups can't get credit from banks. Both groups are in the drug scene, although there are different drugs and different pushers" (*Current Biography*, 1978, 241).

Maggie Kuhn quotes Simone de Beauvoir's powerful insight: "The meaning or lack of meaning that old age takes on in a given society puts that whole society to the test" (Dieter Hessel, ed., *Maggie Kuhn on Aging: A Dialogue* [Philadelphia: Westminster Press, 1977], 65). Her panthers help "recycle" (train) older people to monitor insurance companies, banks, courts, zoning boards, municipal agencies, and the media to change negative stereotyping and discriminatory policies affecting older people. They eventually joined forces with Ralph Nader's Retired Professional Action Group to mobilize citizen action for constructive legislation. They have worked and lobbied for nursing home industry reforms and tax-supported health insurance for all ages. Maggie is convinced that elderly folks are natural coalition builders and empathizers with others. When they become social activists, they not only improve their own lot but also become agents of change for people of all ages.

Here is her exciting vision of the challenges she sees in the present: "This is a new age—an age of liberation, self-determination, and freedom. Winds of change are blowing from every quarter, disturbing . . . every human group. . . . Many groups are struggling for freedom. Their struggles are all of a piece: The nonwhites struggling against racism; The women struggling against the domination of men and sexism; The young and the old struggling against ageism; The developing nations in the Third World struggling against U.S. Imperialism and Pax Americana" (Hessel, ed., *Maggie Kuhn on Aging*, 13).

Maggie Kuhn quotes one of her favorite epitaphs: "HERE LIES MARY, MY BELOVED WIFE, UNDER THE ONLY STONE SHE EVER LEFT UNTURNED." Obviously she likes it because it describes her caring-for-people-and-the-planet life-style. As she says, "All of this sure beats Geritol!"

about future problems) or five miles back on the road (doing postmortems on things I had or hadn't done). This didn't leave much energy for enjoying the daisies along the road. The exercises that follow are ways of making friends with the three dimensions of time that are crucial for maximizing your wholeness—past, future, and present. Have your *Self-Care Journal* or other paper and a box of crayons available as you do the exercises.

A Guided Meditation on Reparenting

This exercise is useful at any stage from adolescence on. It's designed to help you make peace with the past by healing emotional wounds and griefs from your childhood. I recommend that you do this one when you're with a trusted friend or support group, so that you'll have support if you encounter very heavy feelings.

Begin by tensing all the muscles of your body very tightly, holding for the count of three, then releasing the tension. Repeat this several times, resting for a count of three between each tensing. Do this until your body and your mind are very relaxed but also very alert. / Breathe deeply and fully for a few minutes, as described in chapter 3, to energize your relaxed body-mind. /

Now, using one of your many creative abilities, form a moving picture of the house or apartment you call home, in as vivid detail as possible. Become aware of all the sounds, colors, sights, people, pets, plants, and smells you associate with that place. / Be inside your home now. / Become aware of the emotional and relationship climate in that place, including how you feel about yourself when you're there. How safe and loved do you feel? /

Now, go back in your memory and form a similar moving picture of the home you lived in as a small child, seeing it as vividly as you can. (If your childhood was relatively happy but your teens were painful, picture the home where you lived as a teenager.) / See yourself as a little child (from here on, substitute "teenager" if this applies) entering that home and going to your favorite place there. / *Be* that girl or boy now, in your early home now. How do you feel about yourself? About your body and your sexuality? About life? About God? / Now, bring one of your parents into the room; experience what happens between you. / How does your parent really feel about herself or himself as a woman or man? About you as a little girl or boy? Talk with that parent for a while. / Bring your other parent into the room and experience what happens. / How does this parent feel about you? How do your parents feel about each other—really? (If you lived with only one parent, stay in touch with your feelings about that.) /

Be with your whole family having dinner together now. Be aware of the emotional climate of your family. How healthy are relationships? Are people's self-esteem (especially yours) enhanced or diminished by being there? What's the spirit of this family? Is there much joy or grief there? How safe and loved and connected do you feel? /

Drawing on your memory bank, recall a particular time when as a child you felt affirmed, respected, appreciated and loved uncondi-tionally for who you were. Relive that experience as fully as you can, luxuriating in that warm, delicious experience. (If you cannot re-member such an experience, learn all you can from the pain that brings.) /

Now, recall and relive an incident when you were punished, rejected, unfairly criticized, terrified, abused, or degraded as a child. (If you're doing this alone and sense that you may unleash over-whelming feelings, postpone the remainder of the exercise until you can do it with the loving support of a person you trust.) If the pain feels manageable, relive that incident now in as much depth as possible, experiencing the wounded feelings that still cling to the memory and need healing. / Let one or both of the parents you carry within you comfort and love you and bring some healing of those painful memories, if they can. /

Now, try a second healing approach. Picture your present loving, capable adult self entering your childhood home. Be there alone with your inner child. / Give all the love and strength you can to your child, doing whatever you sense is needed to help heal that old wound. You may want to pick up the little one and hold her or him on your lap tenderly. Rock and sing to this little person, letting him or her know that your protection, love, respect, and wise guidance are available whenever they're wanted. / Be aware of how your little child responds. If she or he begins to feel safer, less afraid, and more loved, you'll know that healing is occurring. (Junior, the little boy inside me, usually relaxes and smiles as I rock, hug and tell him he's OK.) / This second method is called reparenting. (For a full discus-sion of this, see Muriel James and Louis Savary, *A New Self.*)

Now, if your inner child is feeling better, why not have some fun together for a little while? Play a game, for example. This child part of you can teach your adult self how to be playful again, if you've been neglecting that joyful art. / Before telling each other good-bye, make a date to meet again soon so you can continue getting to know, care for, learn from, and enjoy each other. If these two valuable sides of you have been largely out of touch, spend some quality time together so that you can become good, mutually enriching friends. / Give each other a warm hug before you say good-bye.

Here's a third approach to inner-child healing. Try it if your child still feels wounded, and this method seems likely to be meaningful. Form a picture of a wise, strong, caring person who represents the loving parent of the universe (God) for you. / Let this spiritually empowered person be with your hurting child now in your childhood home, relating in a loving, healing way. Be open to receive comfort and healing of your memory wounds, perhaps remembering these ancient words: "As one whom his mother comforts, so I will comfort you" (Isaiah 66:13). Some Christians find the familiar picture of Jesus with the children meaningful in this kind of healing work. Their inner child hears his loving, affirming words, "Let the children come to me . . . for to such belongs the kingdom of God" (Mark 10:14). /

Complete the guided meditation in your own way to give it a sense of completion for you. / Come back to the present time and place, and sit quietly, eyes closed, reflecting on what you discovered on this memory trip. What feels unfinished about this experience? What will you do to continue the healing process? Perhaps you haven't forgiven your parents for their inadequacies? Until you do, you're still hooked on the past. This wastes energy that could better be used for enjoying life more in the present. Think about any connections you see between your feelings in your present home and what you experienced when you revisited your childhood home.

It may be helpful to jot down notes to yourself about what you experienced and discovered concerning self-healing of your inner child. I recommend that you draw some sketches with crayons of your childhood (or teen) home especially with the people in it. / It's very important to debrief this exercise with a trusted friend or family member. If you got in touch with raw, painful feelings that were not healed fully by the three approaches, I urge you to debrief your experience with a trusted clergyperson or other counselor. Becoming aware of residual pain from the past, even if it's not fully healed yet, is an important step you've taken on the healing path. Decide what the next steps will be for you on this vital inner journey. /

I hope very much that you experienced some self-healing of memory wounds by doing this exercise. I hope that something you did in this exercise gave your inner child that all-important esteem-enhancing affirmation and love without strings attached that your parents couldn't give. They probably couldn't because they had experienced a shortage of such unconditional love from their parents, and so on back through the generations. I've used this blend of TA reparenting and healing of memories in workshops, counseling, and teaching for over a decade. It can be a powerful path to healing for some people. Its three options lets users choose what works best for them.

The point of this healing exercise is that you don't need to continue wasting valuable creative energy by having your life controlled so much by painful events long passed and people long gone. Using an exercise such as this one may enable you to experience something of the truth in the slogan Bernie Siegel reports seeing: IT'S NEVER TOO LATE TO HAVE A HAPPY CHILDHOOD![6]

In all this you may find Milton Berle's quip a helpful light touch: "You didn't choose your ancestors but the chances are they wouldn't have chosen you either."[7]

You can apply these healing methods to the painful memories and grief wounds from any period of your life. Here's how. First, do a memory search, starting with the present. Go back year by year to your earliest memories, becoming aware of unhealed griefs and painful memories at each stage. Note these in your *Self-Care Journal* for future healing work. Take the memories and griefs one at a time, on different occasions, reliving each by being in the home where you lived at that time. Simply adapt the exercise to fit each situation.

If you're having trouble with your kids (or someone else's kids, if you're a teacher), try reliving being a child or teenager about their ages. I remember taking a sack lunch to our high school–age daughter who'd forgotten it one day, years ago. As I walked across the campus, I noticed a skinny, pimply-faced boy sitting alone on the ground, leaning against a building, munching a sandwich. A sudden wave of sad, frightened feelings came over me. Long-forgotten and unhealed memories from my own lonely high school years came flooding back. This surprising experience pushed me to use exercises like the above to help heal those memories. As I did this I began to like the adolescent within me much better. And, not surprisingly, my relationships with my own teenagers improved.

A chaplain I know was called to the bedside of Lydia, a woman about forty, hospitalized for multiple addictions. With deep grief she told him that she had had a meaningful prayer life, but now "God is gone. I have no sense of his presence or reality at all, and it is such a lonely, desolate feeling." She was terribly agitated. The chaplain asked her if she would like for him to see if he could help her to relax. She agreed. He led her in a guided imaging meditation using images of still waters and green pastures from the Twenty-third Psalm. She relaxed readily.

On an impulse the chaplain suggested that Lydia look off to the horizon in her imagination, and see a person approaching her. As the two moved toward each other, the woman saw that the person was a child, someone she knew. Gradually she saw that the child was herself about five or six. When they reached each other, they joined hands. The child began to play, inviting her to join in. They played and played—tag, leapfrog—eventually collapsing in a heap on the grass, where the woman took the child in her lap. The child told her what it was like to be a child—the fears and frustrations and unfair situations. The woman comforted her saying that she was there and would help her. Finally they parted, agreeing to come together often so that the child could continue to teach her to play and she could continue to comfort and help the child grow. When the woman finished the imagery, there were quiet tears. She said softly, "God is back." From that point her recovery, which had been blocked, was fairly rapid.[8]

Creative Futuring

We humans have the remarkable ability to create futures in our minds. The kinds of futures we picture there have a powerful impact on our feelings and our behavior in the present. Envisioning and experiencing an attractive future of increased well being in your mind can help you move toward such a future. The goal of this exercise is to gain increased control in shaping such a future for yourself.[9]

Step 1: Pick a time in the future (e.g., a year or more hence) and create a winsome picture of yourself transformed in whatever ways you'd like to be. If it's meaningful to you, see if you can blend your dreams with your understanding of God's dream for your life. In this way you may gain a sense of partnership with the divine Spirit in co-creating your future well being.

Step 2: For the next few minutes *be* your transformed self. Let yourself *experience* the satisfactions of increased well being in areas where your sense of need is strong. For example, you may want to let yourself feel how it is to be more creative and serene in your consciousness; more sensuously loving in your intimate relationships; more effective in your work or in helping to heal society's brokenness; more childlike and celebrative in your play; more aware of your oneness with the nurturing web of life; or more empowered by a growing, loving friendship with the divine Spirit. Whatever goals you choose, enjoy experiencing yourself wonderfully transformed.

Step 3: Keeping the images from this experience in your mind, form a moving picture of yourself outwitting any resistance that might sabotage your dream's fulfillment. Experience how good it feels to overcome both inner and outer blocks to making your dreams become positive reality.

Step 4: Write down your step-by-step Self-Change Plan for moving from where you are now to become the person you enjoyed being in Step 2. Make sure your concrete objectives are clear. It will help you achieve them if you prioritize your objectives in order of importance. / Make a wholeness covenant with yourself in which you spell out precisely what you'll do to move toward your more whole, joyous self. If it helps, sign your covenant to strengthen your commitment to implementing it, and share your covenant with a trusted

The best thing about the
future is that it comes only
one day at a time.

—Abraham Lincoln

friend to get feedback for improving it. Agree to check in with that person periodically, sharing your experiences in creating your more whole future.

A quick way to enhance the Creative Futuring experience for yourself is to add visual stimuli in this simple way. Before you do Step 1, take your crayons and a blank sheet of paper and quickly sketch a picture of yourself. Don't plan it or worry about how it looks. (This isn't an exercise in art, and no one but you will see it unless you choose.) Just sketch yourself quickly and roughly with lines and colors to express the way you feel about yourself. / Draw a bubble by your head, as in a cartoon, and quickly write what the person you have drawn is thinking and feeling. / When you have completed Step 2, quickly do a second self-sketch expressing your feelings about your hoped-for self. / Then insert a bubble with words expressing your new thoughts and feelings about yourself. / Keep in mind what you taught yourself by these two pictures as you do Steps 3 and 4.

Learning to Live in the Now

There is only one time any of us can experience more love and wholeness—this here-and-now moment! There is wisdom in the saying "Today is the tomorrow I worried about yesterday, and the yesterday I'll feel guilty about tomorrow." A key to living with more aliveness in the present is sustained awareness of your stream of consciousness. This brief wholeness exercise is designed to increase your awareness of when you're living in this moment and when you're not, and to give you practice in moving in and out of the present moment intentionally.

Through stretching and breathing let your body-mind move into a state of relaxed alertness. Close your eyes and focus on what you are experiencing in the moment-by-moment stream of your awareness— bodily sensations, sounds, temperatures, images, smells, thoughts, fantasies, feelings—whatever enters your consciousness. Experience the here-and-now flow of your awareness for a little while. Notice how easy it is to distract yourself from what you are experiencing right now by having your attention pulled away into the past or the future. / Now, practice moving intentionally among the past, present, and future. / Relive something enriching that happened in your past. / Shift, becoming aware of something in the future. / Now enjoy a few moments of staying in the present. / You'll find that the ability to focus your mind as you choose grows stronger with practice, putting you more in charge of yourself.

Enhancing the Present

The purpose of this awareness exercise is to discover how your present can be more fulfilling, by viewing it from a longer perspective.

Imagine that you are standing at a point in your life journey, just a few months before your death, looking back at the way your life is in the present. How do you feel about its quality when you view it from this perspective? / Now decide what you need to do to enhance your present life in one or more of its seven dimensions, or in its overall quality. / Draw a rough picture with your crayons of how you'd like to be now and jot down precisely what you'll do to move in these directions.

One way to make peace with time is to maintain a sense of humor about it. You may enjoy this statement by an Australian humorist, "I had a terrible night. Today was going to be the first day of the rest of my life. Now it will have to be tomorrow."

Coming Alive (at Any Adult Age) by Facing Death

More than two decades ago, Joanne, a friend in her midforties, helped me begin to grasp a profound truth about wholeness. She did this by the way she chose to live as she was dying. Joanne had won a mighty struggle with the disease of alcoholism, thanks to her involvement in AA. During more than a decade of sobriety, her life flowered as she discovered her superb gifts for helping other addicted women. Then, out of the blue, she learned one dismal day that she had terminal, inoperable cancer. Joanne struggled in counseling to find nonchemical ways to cope with her devastated dreams for a long, fulfilling life.

Her breakthrough came when she made a simple but profound decision. "I've decided to die living rather than live dying." Joanne became even more alive and loving in her last precious months than she had been before. Her spirituality had been reborn for her in the Twelve-Step recovery program. It flowered in an empowering way as she coped with the shattering impact of cancer on her life. She enjoyed her friends and family and reached out in love. When she died after less than a year, countless friends in AA, her church, and the wider community poured out their grief. Many of us voiced our gratitude for all that she had meant to us, particularly for the inspiration she had been in her last year on earth. In spite of all the frustrations and pain of Joanne's tragic illness, it was crystal clear that she *had* died living!

I was a young adult then. I thought I understood how Joanne's way of dying had been such a dynamic part of her spiritual healing and well being. But the years since have taught me many things I didn't want to learn. Life and losses have increased understanding and appreciation of what this remarkable person was saying by her living while dying. She validates the ancient, audacious claim of the Song of Solomon that "love is as strong as death" (8:6).

Years ago I was hospitalized for a few days. The medical crisis was serious but not life threatening. But it turned high the volume on the background music of my awareness of my mortality. I was clobbered by several episodes of painful panic. This was embarrassing for one who thought he had it together in this area. When I left the hospital, I was amazed to see how incredibly blue the sky looked. The grass was unbelievably green. My head-on collision with my mortality had given me a gift. It had removed temporarily a veil from my eyes. Many people, after near-death experiences, report even more vivid awakenings, of coming alive to the wonder, the beauty, the miracle of just being alive.

A major stumbling block to growing older gracefully—from childhood through maturity—is our way of denying that we ourselves and those we love most are mortal. This awareness rises to the surface of consciousness during major transitions on our life journey (such as adolescence and retirement) and during shattering crises. In the second half of life, how we handle the underground awareness that we're all living-and-dying creatures influences how creatively we grow older and how alive we stay.

A crucial question thus becomes how we can use our feelings about the brevity and vulnerability of our lives as a stimulus to aliveness, serenity, and creativity. How can we transform these anxieties from a deadening force into a school where we learn how to enjoy staying alive all our lives?

We can begin, at whatever age, by confronting our feelings about death in the context of life rather than running from these troubling feelings. It's by risking looking into the abyss that we find a path that leads through it to the celebration of life in the present moment. Furthermore, many of us may find resources for facing our finitude constructively in a lively faith flowing from a growing friendship with the divine Spirit of Love. It may be more important than you think to keep your faith alive and growing as you mature in other areas. Many folks also need a caring community of shared faith to help them nurture death-transcending spiritual power.

The bottom line answer to our fear of dying (and the many mini-deaths that are a part of most people's lives) is to come alive as fully as possible in this moment. To do this is to discover moments of transcending the mundane, space-time world. This reminds me of a wise client who observed insightfully, after completing her journey to enhanced wholeness in therapy: "I came for help because I thought I was afraid of dying, but I discovered that I was really afraid of living!"

Coming alive in this sense involves opening ourselves to the awareness that our brief lives are a precious part of the wonderful, flowing, ongoing, interconnected web of life. In this awareness one experiences something of the eternal in the midst of the daily-ness of life. Death is accepted not as an enemy but as one essential phase of the continuing creation by which everything is reborn and transformed. In *Zorba the Greek*, Nikos Kazantzakis declares: "There is some Eternity even in our ephemeral lives, only it is very difficult for us to discover it alone. Our daily cares lead us astray. A few people only, the flower of humanity, manage to live an eternity even in their transitory life on this earth. Since all the others would therefore be lost, God had mercy on them and sent them religion—thus the crowd is able to live in eternity, too."[10]

From a vital relationship with the divine Spirit flows this experience of eternity in the now. With this comes a kind of existential trust that is the ultimate answer to existential anxiety. The Quaker poet John Greenleaf Whittier expresses this trust beautifully:

> I know not what the future hath of marvel or surprise,
> Assured alone that life and death God's mercy underlies.
> I know not where God's islands lift their fronded palms in air;
> I only know I cannot drift, beyond God's love and care.

The knowledge of our eventual death is what gives meaning, urgency, and beauty to every day of our lives.

—*Bernie Siegel*

From the perspective of his patients who have transformed the quality of their lives in response to a cancer diagnosis, surgeon Bernie Siegel declares: "The knowledge of our eventual death is what gives meaning, urgency, and beauty to every day of our lives."[11] In a similar vein, Saul Alinsky, who spent his life working to make our society healthier and more just, observed: "Once you accept your own death all of a sudden you are free to live. You no longer care about your reputation except so far as your life can be used tactically—to promote a cause you believe in."[12]

Adding Life to Your Years

A Harvard med school professor who heads a research program on successful aging declares: "I can describe to you a 75-year-old man with a history of heart disease and diabetes, and you can't tell me with any confidence whether he will be sitting on the Supreme Court or in a nursing home."[13] It's obvious that many factors, including how carefully you picked your grandparents, influence how long and how healthily you'll live. Many of these factors have been discussed earlier in this book. Let me summarize a few other strategies for adding life to your years (and perhaps years to your life), strategies for dying young as late as possible.

1. **Take extra good care of your body.** A friend who is a fitness buff observed that "health is a gift to the young. After that you have to earn it."[14] You earn it, of course, by consistent, aerobic exercise, good nutrition, and adequate rest and play. I recall hearing this right-on comment somewhere: "There's no such thing as a fountain of youth, but regular fast walking and a low fat diet is about as close as you'll come." In the pressure-cooker young adult years, and in the often nearly as pressured midyears, it's easy to get superbusy so that you neglect doing what you know is good for

your health. When you're younger, you seem to get away with this for a while, until you notice your spare tire, or the puffing as you climb the stairs, or worse. What is the best way to avoid premature aging in the midyears and help prevent the early onset of those degenerative diseases that flourish in our flabby society? It's to keep your body trim, flexible, and healthy and your mind alive and well by regular self-care. A lapel button worn by a midyears student elicited chuckles of recognition from several of us workaholics: DEATH IS NATURE'S WAY OF REMINDING YOU TO SLOW DOWN! Fortunately, lots of people are listening to their body-mind's cry for care before that happens.

DEATH IS NATURE'S WAY

OF REMINDING YOU TO

SLOW DOWN!

Regular moderate exercise (such as brisk walking) can be a genuine fountain of youth. An expert on lifelong fitness puts the case well: "Exercise can help you—no matter your condition or disease—by allowing you to do more and get more out of life. Then you will learn that aging is not so much a function of years as it is a function of fitness—or lack of it. The better your functional fitness, the younger you will be, the younger you will act, and the younger you will appear."[15] (Just a reminder: If you're in the midyears or beyond it's absolutely crucial to get your level of fitness assessed by a health professional before launching any vigorous exercise program.)

The eating patterns of many folks in the second half of their lives are nutritional disasters. But for postretirement people it's often because they're chronically depressed, living alone after the death of a partner and "don't feel like fixing meals for just me," or because they're poor. It's a social obscenity that in an affluent country, sales of dog food skyrocket in inner cities when food stamp programs for the poor are cut back by a short-sighted government. The majority of the poor folks who buy dog food (because it's cheap protein), are the elderly poor. Of these, over 70 percent are women, victims of the double economic whammy of ageism and sexism! A recent survey revealed that more than 50 percent of America's elderly don't have enough money to buy food at least part of the time.[16] We should all get politically involved and help correct this social atrocity.

2. **Keep learning and growing and excited about something.** In her early eighties, my friend Erma Pixley was still taking tough graduate seminars *for credit*. One day I asked why she didn't just audit the course on contemporary psychotherapies, thus avoiding the required reading, papers, and exams. She smiled mischievously as she replied, "Well, Howard, I never know when I might want to start another degree." Erma was excited by wrestling with challenging ideas, and she loved relating to other students— bright-eyed young adults a half century her junior. W. Somerset

Maugham described his amazement, as a youth, when he read Plutarch's statement that the elder Cato began to learn Greek at eighty. Much later Maugham commented with this gem: "I am amazed no more. Old age is ready to undertake tasks that youth shirk because it would take too long."[17]

Most older minds, with their treasure of experience, can continue to expand, given a certain minimal level of physical health. The human personality can continue to grow and become mellower and enriched with aging. So if you're in the middle or mature years (or getting ready for these), why not become a second-half bloomer? If you're a lifelong bloomer, you'll probably keep it up. Or you may need to plant a few more seeds or fertilize those already planted before you blossom in the second half.

If you're older perhaps you can remember assuming, as I did as a young adult, that when you reached your present age or a little older, you'd be winding down your activities and beginning to fold your tent. (I still feel that way about people who are ninety. I will probably continue to feel this way until I'm eighty-nine.) Ageist feelings, like other prejudices, are tough to exorcise, even when you know better. I feel very lucky that, although I've slowed down in some physical ways, I feel more zest about living and loving and get more enjoyment out of day-by-day life than when I was harboring those illusions about people my age.

3. **Keep using your talents to contribute something to others and to causes you care about.** A study of persons one hundred years of age and older reached this interesting conclusion: "[these] old people continue to be contributing, productive members of their society. . . . People who no longer have necessary roles to play in the social and economic life of their society generally deteriorate rapidly."[18] I'm sure you know at least one work-centered man who died soon after retirement. Such people "lose heart" because they have lost the heart of their existence from which they had derived their self-esteem and meaning.

It's crucial in the midyears and beyond to learn additional ways, beyond your work, to gain the satisfactions of productive, meaningful uses of your talents. Let's say you have launched or will launch soon on the potentially exciting life stage misnamed "retirement." There are many ways to use the wonderful freedom to do things you've always wanted to do. This includes volunteer work for causes you find really exciting.

Bertha and Harold Sodenquist are among those unretired "retired" people who explode the negative stereotypes of this life stage. They're also great examples of zestful contributors to a more whole world. They were the oldest persons who had volunteered for the Peace Corps when they enrolled and were assigned to teach in a secondary school in Western Samoa. She was seventy-six and he was eighty. The Peace Corps doesn't expect those over fifty to do well in learning new languages, but the Sodenquists refused to be let off the hook. Bertha reported, "We went home and crammed."[19] They both passed with flying colors!

There are so many things that need doing and are satisfying to lend your skill to. For example, whatever your age, why not participate in a group working to end economic discrimination against seniors—groups such as the Gray Panthers and the American Association of Retired Persons? The latter organization now has some 350,000 volunteers active in hundreds of communities using their skills and experience in a thousand and one public service causes.

Hamilton Fish, Sr., at ninety-nine the oldest living former congressman, recently married his live-in housekeeper, Lydia Ambrogia. Fish said of his bride, "She's done more for me in the last three years to keep me alive and I hope she can keep me alive for three or four more so I can spread my message about the disarmament of nuclear arms." She responded, "He wants to talk of nuclear arms—I say he ought to talk about my arms."[20]

A sense of purpose in your life is important to your health at any stage. Norman Cousins captures the power of this challenge eloquently: "I can imagine no greater satisfaction for a person, in looking back on his life and work, than to have been able to give some people, however few, a feeling of genuine pride in belonging to the human species and, beyond that, a zestful yen to justify that pride."[21]

4. **Stay (or get) playful.** Milton Berle comments that "one way to live longer is to cut out the things you want to live longer for."[22] This is humorous but misleading. Actually, keeping your playful inner child activated is an essential strategy for your well being in the midyears and beyond. Socrates, the great philosopher in ancient Greece, found time in his old age to learn to play an instrument and to dance.[23]

Being able to joke about even the darker side of aging can be therapeutic. Walter Cronkite is said to have commented, "When I go, I'd like to go like Errol Flynn—on the deck of my seventy-foot yacht with a sixteen-year-old mistress." Betty Cronkite, his spouse, responded: "You're going to go on a sixteen-foot boat with your seventy-year-old mistress." A Scottish humorist tells of a woman being interviewed on her hundredth birthday. Reporter: "At your age, do you have any worries?" She replied: "Not any more. Not since I got my youngest child into a good nursing home."

5. **Keep on loving.** The truth of the biblical wisdom "the greatest of

Life is full of misery,

suffering, loneliness and

pain—and it ends too soon.

—Woody Allen

these is love" becomes ever more important as the years pass. Keeping your network of friends and family strong isn't easy for many in the older years. Because friends and family members are dying it takes more intentional reaching out to keep your mutual support circle strong. There are multiple generation gaps cutting through our society like intertwining grand canyons. Making friends across these is good for the wholeness of all generations— older and younger. Relationships with children and youth help older persons stay young in heart. They also help the young learn from the hard-won wisdom of those who are older.

One of the cruelest myths about aging is that older women don't want sex and older men can't do it. Actually, those who have enjoyed sex in their midyears usually continue to be sexually active throughout most of their lives. Of course persons for whom sexual activity had low priority earlier in their lives tend to continue this pattern as they grow older. But some women become more interested in sex after menopause removes the fear of unwanted pregnancies. In any case, the need for sensual pleasure does not evaporate with age in anyone's life.

One of the humanizing changes in some nursing homes is to provide times of privacy for residents and their partners to be alone together if they choose. Not surprisingly the residents in such facilities are less depressed, consume fewer tranquilizers, and are generally happier than those in facilities where much younger staff members assume that of course aged residents are asexual. A delightful story about the great jurist Oliver Wendell Holmes tells of an incident alleged to have occurred when he was ninety. While strolling with a male friend along the streets of Cambridge, a beautiful woman passed them. Holmes commented wistfully (and I suspect with a smile), "Oh to be seventy again!"

A recent medical study reports a significant correlation between "coffee drinking and a higher rate of sexual activity in elderly women and a decreased prevalence of impotency among elderly men." One of the researchers suggested that the reason may be that coffee is a relaxant of the smooth muscles and a powerful stimulant of the central nervous system. A newspaper report of this research carried the headline, "Like Another Cup?" The reporter added another possible reason for the findings, "Then again, maybe they just can't fall asleep right away."[24]

Psychiatrist-gerontologist Robert N. Butler, former head of the National Institute of Aging, states the challenge of lifelong wholeness: "None of us knows whether we have already had the best years of our lives or whether the best are yet to come. But the greatest of human possibilities remain to the very end of life—the possibilities for love and feeling, reconciliation and resolution."[25]

Hear this affirmation of growing older on a spiritually and love empowered journey, words spanning some thirty centuries: "They shall bring forth fruit in old age, they are ever full of sap and green" (Psalm 92:14). Your life is a journey on which you can experience new dimensions of well being all through your years. For as an anonymous sage once said: "The heart that loves is always young!"

Create Your Life Stage Self-Care Fitness Plan

Take a few minutes now to finish a realistic plan to develop more of the possibilities of your present life stage (and thus also to cope constructively with the problems). Choose at least six insights and methods that raised your energy level in this chapter. Include items you marked OK or NS on the checkup. Using your creativity, write out (in your *Self-Care Journal*) a realistic plan for developing the special potentialities of this stage. Remember, your plan probably will work better if it includes five things: (1) concrete, realizable objectives that you really want to achieve; (2) practical strategies for moving toward these; (3) a time line; (4) rewards you'll give yourself as you implement your Self-Care Plan, or withhold if you backslide; (5) a record of your progress kept in your *Journal*.

You may find it useful to include some reading (from the Recommended Reading at the end of the book) in your plan.

Pick one or two especially attractive parts of your plan and begin doing them immediately. Keep what you do love centered, spiritually enlivened, and playful.

I wish you the joy of discovering and developing the treasure of new possibilities in your present time on your journey, whether you're young or old. Go for it!

Completing and Using Your Personal Well-Being Program

As a person of infinite worth and rich possibilities for enjoying more whole-person fitness, you deserve effective self-healing, loving self-care, and an alive body-mind-spirit. I trust you have found some useful tools for moving toward goals such as these in this book. I now recommend that you use what you have learned to move ahead to greater well being. If, as suggested, you already have developed plans for increasing your wholeness in the areas as suggested, chapter by chapter, congratulations! You now have a series of plans focused on wholeness in your *Well Being Self-Care Journal*. I hope you have begun to use parts of your plans and have already begun to experience the benefits! You can now combine these plans into an overall fitness program. Simply follow this process:

First, look over your *Journal* entries and also scan this book to see what you underlined or noted in the margins. This will refresh your memory concerning the insights and exercises you found most relevant and the self-care practices to which you were attracted. Pay particular attention to what you discovered and tentatively planned as you took the various checkups. /

Second, as you do this note how your change plans in each chapter relate to each other. Do they overlap or conflict? As you review them together, you may discover that they require too much time when taken together. Since you probably won't be able to do all the things, at least not all at once, take time now to prioritize and streamline the cumulative list of self-care objectives, using the topics of chapters 2 to 12 to organize your list. By doing this you can guide yourself to invest whatever time you can make available in those objectives you *now* see

"The hell of it is I've forgotten what they're reaching for."

as most important to your overall fitness. Write out your prioritized list of fitness objectives with notes to yourself about how you plan to move toward them. Prevent your overall program from becoming overwhelming by keeping your playful inner child active in whatever you plan and do. Also build in rewards you will give yourself step by step as you implement your program. This will sweeten your experience.

Third, from your overall program, select for immediate implementation several items related to those dimensions of your wholeness in which improved self-care now seems most important and appealing. As you begin implementing the parts of your program you've selected, keep notes in your *Journal* about your experience.

Fourth, team up with someone you like (a family member or close friend) as fitness partners. In this way form a mutual-support relationship to increase your enjoyment as you implement the changes you each want to make. Look over each other's personal wholeness programs and give feedback—both affirmation and suggestions for strengthening them. If possible, do some of your self-caring together or meet regularly to report on progress and problems and to encourage each other. You'll find it easier to avoid being seduced by resistances if you have a sense of support and mutual accountability with at least one other person who is also working and playing to increase wholeness. If you keep your relationship playful, you and your partner(s) will be more likely to achieve your objectives, since this will reward and reinforce the discipline it takes.

Fifth, once you have begun to practice your list of high priority choices, go back and add other important objectives from your plans list. Gradually implement more and more of your well-being program.

A Plan for Overcoming Resistances

The envelope of an ad for a New Age publication carried this warning: "Recipient: Please open only if prepared for quantum challenge and evolutionary growth!" The editor of the periodical commenting on the ad gave this choice response: "We're not even prepared for Monday mornings!" In the same vein, during the heyday of the human potential movement, a therapist friend commented, only half facetiously, that he was thinking of specializing in "post-self-actualization depression." Those of us with enthusiasm for well being run the risk of unwittingly encouraging exaggerated expectations that set people up for eventual disillusionment and self-blame.

Let me be clear. Unlearning old health-damaging patterns and implementing a self-care program as outlined above involves hard work. The rewards of healthier patterns of living usually don't come immediately. If you shape up, you'll eventually experience the self-reinforcing rewards of feeling more alive, trim, and attractive, with more zest for living. But before that happens, it may test your frustration tolerance and perseverance.

Your journey to enhanced well being involves learning effective ways to overcome those frustrating resistances to doing what you know is good for your health. The following outwitting-resistances plan uses a combination of imaging (right-brain) and contracting with yourself (left brain).

Step 1:   Select a self-care objective around which you're encountering resistances. See a picture in your mind of yourself the way you really want to be in that area. / Then allow yourself to enjoy experiencing (in your imagination) the rewards of this healthier way to be. (If you want to shed that spare tire around your middle, for example, see yourself as the slim, trim, energized, attractive, and sexier person you wish you were. Then experience how good it feels to be that way.)

Step 2:   Make a list of the behaviors that are keeping you from moving toward your goal. / Alongside these behaviors, list all the rewards of *not* changing them. For example, the self-comforting oral satisfactions of guzzling candy or potato chips when you're bored, sexually frustrated, lonely, or are simply in the well-practiced habit of doing this while watching TV.

Step 3:   Decide whether or not you *really* prefer the rewards of changing your behavior and whether these offset the rewards you'll lose if you do change. / If you decide not to change that particular behavior, choose another health-diminishing pattern that's not so rewarding and therefore not so hard to change. / When you decide in favor of the potential rewards of changing, say good-bye to the rewards of the old unhealthy behavior and do your grief work so you can really let go of that behavior.

Step 4:   Write out a self-care fitness agreement with yourself (a self-change contract) detailing the objective you have chosen and the healthier behaviors you will do to move toward the objective. Include a time line during which you agree to stick to your agreement, and, very important, include the rewards you will give yourself for each step you take toward your goal, or withhold if you backslide. / Sign your contract with yourself as a concrete indication of the seriousness of your commitment.

Step 5:   Discuss your resistances and your self-change contract with your fitness partner. Make yourself accountable to report to that person(s) regularly about how you are doing. Working out a shared fitness contract with someone who wants to improve in some of the same general areas can strengthen your motivation, lessen your resistances, and be mutually supportive as well as more fun.

Step 6:   Reward yourself in some tangible way (noncaloric, if you're trying to shed pounds) each day you fulfill your commitment, as well as each time you take a step toward your objective. Self-rewards for small steps may help you maintain the momentum of change until you eventually begin to experience the rewards inherent in healthier living. When that happens, your changes become self-rewarding and more likely to continue.

Step 7:   At the end of your planned time line, decide if you will renew it for another time period. Add one or other change objectives to your self-care agreement in areas where change is important and you're frustrated by your resistances. Do this as soon as you feel ready to take an additional step toward enhanced fitness. /

Don't waste creative energy giving yourself a bad time if you backslide occasionally. Resistances and backsliding are parts of being human. If you have a slip, withhold the rewards, as you agreed, but don't waste your energy on self-criticism. Just go back to revise your self-care agreement or choose another more feasible objective, and commit yourself to it. Recontract with yourself to practice the self-care you have decided is important to you. Backsliding will tend to diminish as you enjoy more of the satisfactions of good self-care over time—increased fitness, self-esteem, love, and aliveness. It takes time and persistence for these rewards to be experienced fully. Well being is a lifetime journey. To keep on keeping on should become easier as you experience the inherent satisfactions of living in a healthier, more loving relationship with your body and mind, other people, the natural world, and the divine Spirit.

Your Potential Rewards

Think of wholeness as a diamond with many facets. Each facet reflects different rays of light, potential rewards for the discipline and sweat required to grow in well being. Have a look at some of these facets now.

- Wholeness can bring the joy of having a love affair with life, your sometimes crummy, sometimes joyful life, with its crazy mixture of despair and hope, turmoil and serenity, agony and ecstasy.

- Wholeness can bring the zest of aliveness that comes from choosing to take the risks of being as alive and aware as you can in this moment, in spite of all the seductive temptations to deaden your awareness in order to hold off the pain.

- Wholeness can release the joy of singing your own special song, perhaps a little off key at times, by yourself or together with those you love.

- Wholeness can give the satisfactions of celebrating your finger-prints, those amazing symbols of your unique gifts among all your five billion sisters and brothers on planet earth. It can lead to the incredible discovery that (as someone has put it), you're both one of a kind and one with all kinds.

- Wholeness can bring the uplift of having a love affair with the Source of all life, the divine Spirit of Love and liberation.

- Wholeness can bring the spiritually empowered self-esteem that comes from claiming your irreducible worth as a person made in the likeness of God.

- Wholeness can bring the uplift of learning to cherish and love your spiritual Self, and making this transcending part of you the inte-grating core of your life.

- Wholeness can give the joy of saying Yes! to your body, in spite of its sometimes frustrating limitations.

- Wholeness can bring the wonderful gift of being more accepting and forgiving, more caring and compassionate with yourself and therefore with others.

- Wholeness can bring the serenity of making at least some peace with your continuing brokenness, after you've done as much as you can to heal it.

- Wholeness can give the continuing satisfaction of working for an "impossible" but empowering dream—the dream of a healthier world for yourself and your children, and all the children of the planet.

- Wholeness can bring the gift of listening
  to your body and its healing wisdom
  to those fragments of wisdom about living (that usually don't feel like "wisdom"), things life has taught you the hard way
  to persons who long for the transforming gift of really being heard
  to the healing music of the wind and stars, the gentle dawn and the swirling storm, of the blossoms and the birds.

- Wholeness can bring, to some degree, the gift of liberation
  from those inner blocks that retard your continuing growth
  to your full God-intended personhood
  with the people whose lives are intertwined with yours
  for helping to create a world that, when you depart, will be at least a little more whole because you walked on this earth.

I like the way *Megatrends* author John Naisbitt describes living in these times: "Although the time between eras is uncertain, it is a great and yeasty time, filled with opportunity. If we can learn to make uncertainty our friend, we can achieve much more than in stable eras. In stable eras, everything has a name and everything knows its place, and we can leverage very little. But in the time of the parenthesis we have extraordinary leverage and influence—individually, professionally, and institutionally—if we can only get a . . . clear vision of the road ahead. My God, what a fantastic time to be alive!"[1]

As Naisbitt suggests, if we are to live with creativity and courage today we must make friends with uncertainty, insecurity, and anxiety. Speaking from the perspective of women struggling for justice and equality, novelist Doris Lessing declares: "One certainty we all accept is the condition of being uncertain and insecure."[2] Her point is on target for all of us in today's world-in-radical-transition. Nurturing the wholeness of healthy love and spirituality at the center of our being is the secret of making friends not only with the profound uncertainties but also with the unprecedented opportunities we all face in our broken, birthing world.

A group of brilliant computer scientists at MIT are investing their technical creativity in perfecting computers for the future, computers with which people can interact as easily as with each other. Their goal is to stay two or three years ahead of industry. Among their impressive achievements is a computer program that will enable architects to see buildings in three dimensions before they're actually built. When these scientists were asked to predict the future, they responded: "The best way to predict the future is to invent it."[3]

That is true of your future levels of well being in all seven dimensions of your life. The most effective way to predict what your health will be a year (or two or ten) from now is to invent it as you go along, beginning by what you do today. The same is true of the health of the planet. You and I can help predict, in small but important ways, the future of the global village. We can do this by joining hands with other caring people to invent new ways to help the whole human family grow in well being. As you do this, may you experience more of *the joy of wholeness and the wholeness of joy. Let's go for it!*

Helping Your Organization, Congregation, or Workplace Support Whole-Person Well Being

 I hope you will share whatever you found helpful in this book with your friends and family, as well as with people in the important organizations in your life—your school, church, synagogue, club, or workplace. For several reasons it's crucial for people-serving and people-shaping institutions to develop more effective wellness programs. One reason is that your community (along with many communities throughout Western society) is in an unprecedented health-care crisis. This crisis has many expressions including

- the skyrocketing of medical costs (at nearly twice the rate of general inflation in America);

- the increase of chronic, degenerative diseases in our longer-living population;

- the lack of much attention by most health care professionals and institutions to positive prevention, to using alternative healing approaches, and to more whole-person approaches;

- the gross inadequacies of health care for the poor in the inner cities and in some rural areas of industrialized countries where health professionals and facilities are in short supply;

- the tragic shortage of adequate health care in many developing countries;

- the increasing depersonalization of much medical practice in this age of growing specialized, hi-tech, biochemically oriented medicine;

- widespread unnecessary surgery; addictions to prescribed drugs, particularly by women; overprescribing of drugs, particularly to the elderly; and clinical iatrogenesis—illnesses caused by hospitalization and physicians;[1]

- the staggering probable human and financial costs of the worldwide AIDS pandemic.

To resolve this crisis some fundamental changes need to occur. There must be drastic improvements in the medical delivery system so that the marvels of modern medicine become available to all who need them. Adequate health care should be respected as a basic human right, a right that is protected by comprehensive insurance plans in all countries. Medical education needs to become more wholistic and prevention oriented. And medical research on both conventional and alternative treatments needs to be increased dramatically.

Also needed is widespread education to help people everywhere discover the healing wisdom within each of us, and increase our awareness that we as individuals are ultimately responsible for our own self-care. Furthermore, our people-serving institutions and workplaces need to respond to the crisis with imaginative programs of whole-person, positive care and prevention. Such organizations should provide communities with a network of professionally staffed wellness programs, trained lay carers (as in the hospice movement), and support groups for those going through family crises, grief, health crises, chronic illnesses, disabilities, and addictions.

As never before in human history it is crucial that schools of all types and at all age levels, together with religious organizations, become lifelong wellness centers. The crisis in health care makes it essential that religious organizations develop innovative programs of whole-person-oriented prevention. Churches, through their monasteries and convents, were pioneering institutions in the early phases of modern medicine in the West. But with the rise of hi-tech medicine, most religious institutions have pulled back. For Christians (who try to walk in the footsteps of one called the Great Physician throughout much of church history), wholistic healing and health is a much-needed expression of this heritage in the modern world. Fortunately, numerous congregations are developing spiritually centered wholeness programs. These often include pastoral counseling centers, spiritual healing services, crisis support groups, wellness weeks (launched by religious services on the theme), and interfaith, communitywide health fairs.

Even if your organization has had some involvement in the area of healing and wholeness, the chances are that it has only scratched the surface of its exciting opportunities. Most schools, congregations, health facilities, and other people-serving organizations are like sleeping giants in this area. No other outreach program of your organizations has the potential to awaken more widespread response in your community than a dynamic wellness program. Such a program can bring concrete help to the persons who are yearning for both healing and higher levels of well being.

Quite apart from the current health-care crisis there is a deeper reason why concentrating on individual and family wellness, though vitally important, is not enough. As discussed earlier, wholistic prevention of personal problems must include working with others to enable our institutions to become better gardens where everyone's health can be sustained and, when needed, healed. To be involved in helping the institutions in your life do this more effectively may contribute to your own wellness and that of the people you care about most.

Guidelines for an Effective Program for Well Being in Your Organization

1. Work with the leaders of your group to encourage them to make wellness a high priority in the life and programs of the group. Since health is a widespread concern today, your leaders may be quite open to considering this. This book, and others in the Recommended Reading, can be useful resources for informing your leaders about the values of such a program.

2. Once a decision has been made to make a wellness program a regular service of your organization, the next step is to make sure that a particular committee or group within the organization takes responsibility for planning and implementing the program. If the present structure has no committee that would be the logical one on which to put this responsibility (such as an education, health, worker benefits, or personnel committee), a new ad hoc well being task group should be recruited, trained, and encouraged to take the lead. The committee should include members of the healing and therapy professions, teachers who can guide the health education events, and persons who know the health resources in your community well. Members of some of the self-help and Twelve-Step recovery programs can also be valuable members of a health task group.

3. This group can equip itself to plan and lead the program effectively by reading and discussing a book such as this, from the

perspective of how to shape a well being program designed to meet the special needs of people in your organization and community.

4. The well being task group will want to survey and evaluate the wellness needs of persons within the organization. It should find out what other comparable organizations are doing. And, very important, they should also evaluate the overall health impact of your organization. The inventory at the end of this section is designed to help you check this out. An analysis of the findings of this study will identify concrete ways to increase the overall healing, caring, and wellness impact of your organization.

5. By using whatever this inventory reveals, and perhaps also using the chapter topics of this book as an outline, the task group should decide on the major objectives that need to be achieved to make your organization a more wellness-nurturing environment for all those whose lives it touches. Be sure to prioritize these objectives in terms of their importance, feasibility, and urgency.

6. Next, devise a comprehensive plan for your wellness program. Include plans aimed at moving toward each of the high-priority objectives identified. Be sure to include who will take responsibility, how you will draw people into a particular program, funding, time lines for implementing each part of the program, and ways of measuring movement toward the objectives. One way to measure the effectiveness of any program is to ask all participants to fill out an evaluation form at the end of an event. By concentrating only on the higher-priority objectives, you avoid the trap of spreading your efforts too thin. Decide on objectives for the next year, two years, five years, and so on.

7. Celebrate an annual well being or wellness week in your organization, perhaps featuring a wholistic health fair. This is a way to highlight the importance of well being, giving your program visibility and making a wide spectrum of practical resources available to your group's members and to its larger community.

8. As a central part of the wellness program, develop ways of making lifelong wellness training easily available, attractive, and enjoyable to participants. In religious congregations it's good strategy to encourage ongoing classes and youth, couples, men's, women's, singles, and family groups to include wholeness study issues in their programs regularly.[2] Some Christian congregations have found it effective to offer such wellness series to their entire church family during special seasons of the church year—for example, a series of five to seven sessions during the weeks of Lent or after Easter. Comparable approaches

are usable in Jewish congregations and other faith groups. It's important to relate any program to an organization's purposes and traditions.

9. Make sure your organization encourages eating for wellness and practices environmental caring. It can do the former by serving healthy snacks rather than the usual junk food high in refined sugar, fat, and caffeine. It also can serve more nutritious meals at its gatherings. Environmental caring can be expressed by recycling all paper, cardboard, plastics, and metal waste, and reducing the use of throwaway materials to a minimum. Individual members can be encouraged to do their shopping from companies with socially and environmentally responsible policies and practices (see chapter 8).

10. As a part of the wellness program, mobilize the public and political influence of individuals within your organization and also the organization as a whole to support constructive health-care, peacemaking, and environmental legislation on all levels—local, state, regional, national, and international. The familiar line "Think globally and act locally" certainly applies here. Regional, national, and international branches of your organization can encourage well being programming in wider circles and enable you to join forces to initiate intergroup wellness action and legislation.

11. Make sure that your organization's funds are invested in socially responsible and wholeness-engendering ways. This means avoiding investments that support industries that damage personal or environmental health, such as the tobacco establishment, the junk food organizations, the arms industries. It means not supporting national or transnational corporations that wittingly or unwittingly encourage racial discrimination, economic exploitation, or political oppression in developing countries. Instead invest your organization's money in one of the funds that chooses investments on the basis of social responsibility as well as economic opportunity.

12. Make sure that the wellness needs of both genders, and of persons at all life stages and ethnic backgrounds are provided for in your well being program. In adult education organizations and in multigenerational institutions such as congregations, programs to enable parents to teach (explicitly and by modeling) wellness practices in their own families can be strategically important.

13. Develop an active strategy to provide care and support for persons in crises and losses, thus reducing their vulnerability to illness during those high stress times.

14. Encourage the "people" professionals in your organization, particularly those in health care and teaching, to develop ways to update their understanding of and commitment to whole-person-oriented prevention, education, and healing. Use these professionals to plan and staff your program. Such overstressed professionals often also need help in enhancing their own wholeness. In ways such as these your organization will help enhance the wellness of countless individuals whose well being will be impacted, often profoundly, by these professionals.

15. Encourage your organization's leaders to examine both the positive and negative impact on everyone's well being of its organizational structure—its rules, traditions, admissions criteria, and procedures. Then initiate structural changes to make its impact more wholeness-nurturing for everyone in it and its community.

16. Sprinkle the programs and life of your organization with caring love along with laughter and a playful spirit. The more serious your organization's purposes, the more salutary a light touch can be for increasing its overall impact on people's wholeness. The more conflict there is in your group, the more important it is for its leaders to have conflict-resolving and health-nurturing communication skills, but also a sense of humor.

Evaluating the Wholeness of Your Organization

How to Use This Inventory: There are a variety of ways to use this instrument. It can be helpful for each of the leaders to complete it prior to a group evaluation and planning session. If there is low morale within the organization, ask a cross-section of members to take the inventory, also. This can provide valuable information for diagnosing and developing a plan to correct the group's collective wellness problems. The use of such an approach also expresses the leaders' respect for the needs and views of individual members.

The items in Section A apply to all types of organizations. Those in Section B apply mainly to voluntary groups and organizations. Simply ignore items that do not apply to your organization. Or, if you prefer, create an evaluation form to fit your particular organization by selecting items from these two inventories and adding your own.

CHECKLIST

Instructions: In front of each statement, place one of three initials: E = This group is excellent in this area; OK = Things are acceptable, but there's room for improvement; NS = The group definitely needs strengthening in this.

Section A: All Organizations

_____ The group has a clear sense of its purposes, goals, and identity.

_____ Those associated with the organization understand and generally affirm its purposes and goals.

_____ The organization's goals and objectives are measurable, making it possible to know when progress toward them has been made.

_____ The group has a high level of productivity or accomplishment; its tasks usually get done on time and without major overload on those doing the work.

_____ The *esprit de corps* or emotional climate of the group is generally accepting and warm. There's a strong sense of belonging.

_____ People feel affirmed, respected, and cared about in this group.

_____ Those leading the organization are strong, firm, effective, and democratic in their leadership style. Leaders also are sensitive to the needs of people, including the need to receive warm appreciation whenever it is appropriate.

_____ Social malignancies such as sexism, racism, classism, and ageism are not present in the customs, structures, rules, or practices of the organization.

_____ People going through crises and grief receive caring support from their associates within the group.

_____ Conflicts are handled quickly, fairly, and constructively rather than being ignored or being handled unconstructively.

_____ Problem people are handled firmly and compassionately, and in ways that do not seriously lessen the organization's effectiveness in achieving its purposes.

_____ Newcomers are welcomed and given support in becoming a real part of the group, bringing their gifts to its life and work.

_____ The organization has an effective strategy for discovering and using the latent talents of its members.

_____ Those taking part in the work of the group usually feel more whole and more self-esteem as a result of the quality of relationships and the way the work is done.

_____ Group programs, objectives, plans, and meetings are evaluated regularly, by all group members as well as by leaders, so that learning from both mistakes and accomplishments occurs. The feedback from members guides leaders in their planning and functioning.

_____ Criticism from the organization's members is heard and considered seriously by its leaders.

_____ The group has an effective long-range planning group that generates plans for the future in light of a critical evaluation of past experiences. Input to this planning process is invited from all organization members.

_____ Communication within the organization is generally clear, open, and honest.

_____ The leaders and group standards reflect a strong sense of fair play and ethical integrity.

_____ People generally use their ideas, skills, and creativity freely within the group.

_____ As a result of participating in the organization, people generally feel trust, esteem, hope, empowerment, and zest for living, rather than depression, rejection, fear, or boredom.

_____ Women and men feel equally valued and at home within the organization.

_____ If the organization should disappear, those associated with it would feel a sense of loss.

_____ There's a spirit of lightheartedness at times in the group, with a sprinkling of laughter and nonhostile humor.

_____ I'm glad to be a part of this organization, in spite of its limitations.

_____ The organization increases rather than decreases my well being.

Section B:
Voluntary
Organizations

_____ The organization has a clear "contract" (goals, objectives, purposes, what members get and give, etc.), a contract that has general support among the members.

_____ Those who have belonged for a while know and often call each other by name, as they enjoy being together.

_____ Attendance, financial support, and shared responsibility is generally good, without heavy pressure from the leaders.

_____ People not present at meetings are missed and they know it.

_____ Members going through severe crises and losses feel free to turn to group members for help; the group has a functioning committee that reaches out to those experiencing personal crises.

_____ People feel safe enough in the group to be vulnerable when they choose, risking being honest about their real feelings, including critical feelings about the group.

—— The program planning and leadership functions are shared widely within the organization, rather than monopolized by a few persons.

—— The leaders are selected by a democratic process and rotated regularly, with leadership responsibilities being distributed widely among the members.

—— Decision making on major issues, including deciding on and revising the group's contract, is done democratically, with everyone's viewpoint being heard and respected. Decision making on superficial matters is done by key officers, without burdening the wider membership.

—— There is a wide consensus among group members concerning the importance of the group and its purposes to themselves and to the wider community.

—— Members have frequent opportunities to strengthen their mental muscles and broaden their intellectual horizons by encountering stimulating people, programs, or books and tapes from which they can learn.

—— Those who disagree with the majority point of view feel free to express their disagreement, knowing they'll be heard and their views considered.

—— When a member feels alienated from the group, others take the initiative in seeking reconciliation.

—— The programs of the organization are designed to meet the basic interests and needs of the members (not the hidden agendas of its leaders).

—— The group uses some of its energy to reach out to the needs of others and to increase the well being of its community.

—— Belonging to the organization tends to build bridges rather than barriers between its members and persons and groups with differing philosophies and purposes.

—— There is openness to interact and cooperate with other organizations, rather than being an exclusive or closed group.

—— Commitment to the group does not depend on feelings of superiority over nonmembers or members of other groups.

—— There is regular attention to the health of group process as well as the content of the program, to the well being of *means* as well as *goals*.

—— There is explicit concern within the organization's objectives and program for one or more of the major dimensions of wholeness—physical, intellectual-emotional, relational, work/play, environmental, institutional, and spiritual.

_____ There is a healthy balance within the group's life between intellectual, rational, and analytic matters (left brain), and intuitive, emotional, artistic, and playful matters (right brain).

_____ The organization's members seek and welcome new members who bring fresh resources to its life and work.

_____ Most persons feel more whole after participating in the organization.

_____ Many members of our group would feel that a questionnaire like this is not needed by the group because things are basically healthy and OK.

Recommended Reading to Enhance Your Health and Well Being

In the early years of my career as a professor, I was full of fantasies that many students would find the motivation and time to read avidly and voraciously for my graduate-level counseling courses. I began to come down to the actual world of the students' reality when the delightfully confronting cartoon below appeared in the weekly campus newspaper. It was drawn by David Richardson, one of my students. I thought it might provide you with a chuckle as you encounter the lengthy list of recommended books that follows. My hope is that the annotations will provide you with clues to guide you as you zero in on those books that interest you most because they promise to be useful as you implement your Well Being Self-Care Program.

"Only eighty-four more library books to steal, then Clinebell will have to reduce his reading requirements."

319

Instructions: Put an X in the blanks in front of the books you find interesting enough to read when you have time. Put an XX in front of those books that really interest you so that you want to read them as soon as possible. Put an XXX in front of those books that you want to read immediately.

General Books on Healing and Well Being

X Donald B. Ardell. *High Level Wellness: An Alternative to Doctors, Drugs and Disease.* Berkeley, CA: Ten Speed Press, 1977. Explores self-responsibility, nutritional awareness, stress management, physical fitness, and environmental sensitivity. In-depth descriptions and evaluations of many wellness books.

HAVE IT Boston Women's Health Book Collective. *The New Our Bodies, Ourselves.* New York: Simon & Schuster, 1984. An encyclopedia of useful health and self-care information on a wide variety of issues. Focuses on the special needs of women, but much of it is also useful to men.

HAVE IT Howard Clinebell. *Basic Types of Pastoral Care and Counseling.* Nashville: Abingdon Press, 1984. Focuses on whole-person, spiritually centered counseling. Includes approaches that are useful for self-care in a variety of areas, including marriage and family enrichment, crisis and bereavement, and spiritual and ethical well being. Annotated bibliographies at the end of each chapter.

HAVE IT Norman Cousins. *Anatomy of an Illness, as Perceived by the Patient: Reflections on Healing and Regeneration.* New York: W. W. Norton, 1979. A personal account of his recovery from a debilitating illness using humor, self-responsibility, and vitamin C.

XX Norman Cousins. *Head First: The Biology of Hope and the Healing Power of the Human Spirit.* New York: Penguin Books, 1989. A fascinating account of his ten years on the faculty of the UCLA School of Medicine and his discovery that positive emotions—faith, love, hope, determination, humor—can facilitate healing.

 XX René Dubos. *Celebration of Life.* New York: McGraw-Hill, 1981. Challenges human beings to use their creativity and intelligence to live whole lives in relation to the whole earth.

X Tom Ferguson, ed. *Medical Self-Care: Access to Health Tools.* New York: Simon & Schuster, 1980. A guide by health professionals to self-care in a wide variety of areas.

_____ Daniel Girdano and George Everly. *Controlling Stress and Tension, a Holistic Approach.* Englewood Cliffs, NJ: Prentice-Hall, 1979. Explores the psychosocial, biological, and personality causes of stress; and shows how to use meditation, diet, exercise, biofeedback, and relaxation techniques in your stress-management program.

X Carl Lowe, James W. Nechas, and the editors of *Prevention. Whole Body Healing.* Emmaus, PA: Rodale Press, 1983. Self-care approaches to exercise, massage, and other drug-free methods, as adjuncts to medical treatment.

X Kenneth Pelletier. *Holistic Medicine: from Stress to Optimum Health.* New York: Delta/Seymour Lawrence, 1979. Presents a holistic medical model, which includes a guide to nutrition and health.

XX Kenneth Pelletier. *Longevity: Fulfilling Our Biological Potential.* New York: Delacorte Press/Seymour Lawrence, 1981. Explores the relation between lifestyles, nutrition, and exercise in the length and quality of life.

X John W. Travis and Meryn G. Callander. *Wellness for Helping Professionals: Creating Compassionate Cultures.* Mill Valley, CA: Wellness Associates Publications, 1990. The authors share their growthful personal-professional journeys in ways that can be useful (in their words) "to anyone wanting to contribute to their own healing and to that of the planet." Contains a wealth of insights, models, and methods.

X John W. Travis and Regina Sara Ryan. *Wellness Workbook.* 2d ed. Berkeley, CA: Ten Speed Press, 1988. Explores wellness approaches to self-responsibility, feeling, breathing, sensing, eating, exercise, thinking, working, playing, communicating, sex, and finding meaning.

XX Donald A. Tubesing and Nancy Loving Tubesing. *The Caring Question.* Minneapolis: Augsburg Publishing House, 1983. A spiritually oriented guidebook balancing the major dimensions of self-care with reaching out to others. Useful in congregations.

Chapter 2: Reading to Enhance Your Spiritual Health and Well Being

——— Anne McGrew Bennett. *From Woman-Pain to Woman-Vision*. Minneapolis: Fortress Press, 1989. The lectures of a courageous, pioneer feminist theologian who inspired many of the women doing theology from a feminist perspective today. Begins with an account of Bennett's significant life and work by editor Mary E. Hunt. Concludes with two "Experiments in Mutuality," public dialogues Anne Bennett did with her husband John.

——— Carolyn Stahl Bohler. *Prayer On Wings: A Search for Authentic Prayer*. San Diego, CA: Lura Media, 1990. Explores ways of revitalizing your prayer life by selecting fresh metaphors for God and using your creative imagination.

——— Robert Brizee. *Where in the World Is God? God's Presence in Every Moment of Our Lives*. (Foreword by John B. Cobb, Jr.) Nashville, TN: The Upper Room, 1987. A minister-psychologist, using process theology, presents a freeing understanding of our relationship with God and how God is involved in all our crises and ordinary moments.

——— Martin Buber. *At the Turning*. New York: Strauss & Young, 1952.

——— Annie Cheatham and Mary Clare Powell. *This Way Day Break Comes: Women's Values and the Future*. Philadelphia: New Society, 1986. Two futurists journey thirty thousand miles to document the lives and visions of one thousand North American women.

——— Carol P. Christ. *Laughter of Aphrodite: Reflections on a Journey to the Goddess*. San Francisco: Harper & Row, 1987. An alternative spiritual focus for women and its connection to peace and justice.

——— Carol P. Christ and Judith Plaskow, eds. *Womanspirit Rising: A Feminist Reader in Religion*. New York: Harper & Row, 1979. A collection of insightful papers on feminist spirituality, including a section on "Creating New Traditions."

——— Gary Doore, compiler and editor. *Shaman's Path: Healing, Personal Growth, and Empowerment*. Boston and London: Shambhala, 1988. A variety of thinkers explore the ancient healing traditions and methods of native healers, and their relevance to Western medicine and psychotherapy.

——— Tilden Edwards. *Spiritual Friend*. New York: Paulist Press, 1980. Shows how to recover the gift of spiritual direction both individually and in groups.

HAVE IT Matthew Fox. *On Becoming a Musical, Mystical Bear: Spirituality American Style*. New York: Paulist Press, 1972. A playful approach to prayer and spiritual enrichment.

——— Matthew Fox. *Original Blessing: A Primer in Creation Spirituality*. Sante Fe: Bear & Co., 1983. A powerful introduction to Fox's thinking in four sections—Befriending Creation; Befriending Darkness; Befriending Creativity and Our Divinity; and Befriending the New Creation (including interdependence and erotic justice).

——— Carter Heyward. *Touching Our Strength: The Erotic as Power and the Love of God*. San Francisco: Harper & Row, 1989. A feminist theologian describes the intertwining of healthy religion and sex, infused with passionate involvement in the struggle for justice. Holds that sexual and gender injustice are linked to racial and economic injustices.

——— William Johnson. *The Still Point: Reflections on Zen and Christian Mysticism*. New York: Fordham Univ. Press, 1970. A Jesuit priest with expertise in and appreciation for Zen Buddhism explores the rich possibilities of relating Zen to Christian contemplation.

——— Merle R. Jordan. *Taking on the Gods: The Task of the Pastoral Counselor*. Nashville, TN: Abingdon Press, 1986. Explores the origins of neuroses in idolatry, and how to help individuals and families gain liberation from their false psychological gods.

HAVE IT Morton Kelsey. *The Other Side of Silence*. New York: Paulist Press, 1976. An in-depth guide to Christian meditation.

——— Lao-tzu. *Tao Te Ching, A New Translation*, by Gia-Fu Feng and Jane English. New York: Vintage Books, 1972. This edition of a classic of ancient wisdom about spiritual well being (written in the sixth century B.C.) is illuminated by beautiful photographs of nature and by the eighty-one brief chapters in Chinese characters as well as in English.

——— C. S. Lewis. *The Screwtape Letters*. New York: Macmillan, 1943. Letters from the senior devil Screwtape to his nephew Wormwood, who is in training to be a demon. A wise and playful critique of pompous, humorless religion.

——— Sallie McFague. *Models of God: Theology for an Ecological, Nuclear Age*. Philadelphia: Fortress Press, 1987. A metaphorical theology that explores new images for deity relevant to issues of justice, peace, and ecology—such as God as Mother, Lover, Friend.

_____ Robert Muller. *New Genesis: Shaping a Global Spirituality.* Garden City, NY: Doubleday & Co., 1982. A global UN statesman writes in the hopeful tradition of Dag Hammarskjold and Teilhard de Chardin, affirming the need to recognize the global transcendence of human values, religions, and humanity.

_____ John Shelby Spong. *Rescuing the Bible from Fundamentalism: A Bishop Rethinks the Meaning of Scripture.* San Francisco: Harper San Francisco, 1991. Writing from his knowledge of current biblical scholarship and his love of the Bible, the author shows how we can bring alive the biblical message by rethinking it in light of modern science and today's life-styles.

_____ Charlene Spretnak, ed. *The Politics of Women's Spirituality.* Garden City, NY: Anchor Press/Doubleday, 1982. Essays exploring spirituality and the rise of spiritual power within the modern feminist movement.

_____ Merlin Stone. *When God Was a Woman.* New York: Dial Press, 1976. Drawing on evidence from archaeology, mythology, and history, describes the prepatriarchal role of women during the era of the religions of the Goddess.

_X___ Gabriel Uhlein. *Meditations with Hildegard of Bingen.* Sante Fe: Bear & Co., 1983. A collection of Hildegard's beautiful poems on creation theology.

_____ Frances Vaughan. *The Inward Arc.* Boston: New Science Library, Shambhala, 1986. A wider vision of healing and wholeness in psychotherapy and spirituality, from the perspective of transpersonal psychotherapy.

_____ John Welwood, ed. *Awakening the Heart: East/West Approaches to Psychotherapy and the Healing Relationship.* Boulder, CO, and London: New Science Library, Shambhala, 1983. Papers exploring the spiritual dimension of healing and well being from Eastern and Western perspectives.

_____ Ken Wilbur. *No Boundary: Eastern and Western Approaches to Personal Growth.* Los Angeles: Center Publications, 1979. Develops a "spectrum of consciousness" integrating Western persona and ego levels with total organism and transpersonal (unity consciousness) levels of consciousness. The latter is found in Vedanta Hinduism, Taoism, Mahayana Buddhism, and mystical Islam, Judaism, and Christianity.

Chapter 3: Reading for Healing, Empowering, and Enjoying Your Mind

_____ Jeanne Achterberg. *Imagery in Healing.* Boston: Shambhala, 1985. Surveys the many uses of imagery by shamans, in medicine and in psychotherapy.

_____ Silvano Arieti. *Creativity: The Magic Synthesis.* New York: Basic Books, 1976. Describes what happens in the mind during the creative process, identifying nine factors in cultures where creativity is nurtured and valued, applying this understanding to education.

_____ Philip Baker. *Using Metaphors in Psychotherapy.* New York: Brunner/Mazel, 1985. Shows how metaphors and stories can be used to increase motivation to change and mobilize healing resources. Some of the approaches can be adapted to self-help.

_____ Mary Field Belenky, Blythe McVicker Clinehy, Nancy Rule Goldberger, Jill Mattuck Tarule. *Women's Ways of Knowing, The Development of Self, Voice, and Mind.* NY: Basic Books, 1986. Based on 135 in-depth interviews, reveals why many women feel silenced in their families, schools, and society. Valuable for women's intellectual self-empowerment.

_____ Herbert Benson. *The Relaxation Response.* New York: William Morrow, 1975. Describes the physiological benefits of a variety of meditative techniques and offers a simple way of achieving these.

_____ Milton Berle. *Milton Berle's Private Joke File.* New York: Crown Publishing, 1989.

_____ Thomas R. Blakeslee. *The Right Brain: A New Understanding of the Unconscious and Its Creative Powers.* Garden City, NY: Doubleday, 1980. Presents the scientific findings of the split-brain research and suggests how the intuitive half of our mind can be developed and used.

_____ Harold H. Bloomfield, with Leonard Felder. *Making Peace with Yourself: Transforming Weaknesses into Strengths.* New York: Ballantine Books, 1985. Offers techniques and exercises for self-forgiveness and self-acceptance and overcoming oversensitivity to criticism.

_____ Joan Borysenko. *Minding the Body, Mending the Mind.* Reading, MA: Addison-Wesley, 1987. The former director of Harvard Medical School's Mind/Body Clinic describes the methods used there for whole-person healing.

———— Barbara B. Brown. *Between Health and Illness: New Notions on Stress and the Nature of Well Being.* Boston: Houghton Mifflin, 1984. A practical book on stress reduction and the widespread malaise that is neither wellness nor illness.

———— Barbara B. Brown. *Supermind: The Ultimate Energy.* New York: Harper & Row, 1980. Explores evidence of prodigious resources for reason, judgment, self-healing, and altruism within the deeper levels of the mind in ordinary human beings.

———— George Isaac Brown. *Human Teaching for Human Learning: An Introduction to Confluent Education.* New York: Viking Press, 1971. Describes ways of making education more alive and whole-person oriented, as well as producing more learning that's relevant to real-life issues.

———— David D. Burns. *Feeling Good: The New Mood Therapy.* New York: William Morrow, 1980. A clinically based self-help program for interrupting depression and hopelessness by changing one's patterns of perception and thinking.

———— Gary Emery and James Campbell. *Rapid Relief from Emotional Distress.* New York: Rawson Associates, 1986. A psychologist and a psychiatrist present self-help methods from cognitive therapy for overcoming self-defeating thoughts.

———— Paulo Freire. *Pedagogy of the Oppressed.* (Translated by Myra Bergman Ramos.) New York: Herder and Herder, 1971. A powerful book by a courageous Brazilian philosopher-educator. Describes the way traditional ''banking'' education prepares people for submission to authority, in contrast to ''dialogic'' education, which equips people to practice freedom.

———— Shakti Gawain. *Creative Visualization.* Mill Valley, CA: Whatever Publishing, 1978. A workbook on using mental imagery and affirmations to enhance health, loving relationships, and prosperity.

———— William Glasser. *Take Control of Your Life.* New York: Harper & Row, 1984. Relates mental and physical health and relationship problems to the pictures in our heads, describing how to take charge of your life and your health.

———— Daniel Goleman. *The Varieties of the Meditative Experience.* New York: Irvington Publishers, Inc., 1977. Compares twelve systems of meditation including those of Zen, Sufism, Christianity, and Judaism, showing some basic unity in their goals.

———— Willis Harman. *Global Mind Change: The Promise of the Last Years of the Twentieth Century.* Sausalito, CA: Institute of Noetic Sciences, 1988. Explores the radical change in the belief structure of Western industrial society, which opens incredible potentials for human consciousness.

———— Jean Houston. *The Possible Human.* Los Angeles: J. P. Tarcher, 1982. A course in enhancing and awakening your body, senses, mind, perceptions, and hidden creativity.

———— Dennis T. Jaffe. *Healing from Within.* New York: Simon & Schuster, 1980. Techniques for using your mind to help heal your body.

———— Susan Jeffers. *Feel the Fear and Do It Anyway.* New York: Fawcett Columbine, 1988. Practical methods for self-empowerment by transcending fears.

———— Spencer Johnson and Constance Johnson. *The One Minute Teacher: How to Teach Others to Teach Themselves.* New York: William Morrow, 1986. A guide for teachers, students, and parents, to make the teaching-learning process more effective and esteem-enhancing by means of goal setting and praising.

———— Lawrence Le Shan. *How to Meditate: A Guide to Self-Discovery.* New York: Bantam Books, 1975. Describes the why and how of meditation in its various types.

———— *Managing Stress from Morning to Night.* Alexandria, VA: Time-Life Books, 1987. An illustrated guide for reducing stress on the job and at home.

———— Robert Ornstein and Paul Ehrlich. *New World, New Mind: Moving Toward Conscious Evolution.* New York: Doubleday, 1989. Shows how the obsolete ''old mind'' (fitting the world of the eighteenth century) misguides contemporary education, religions, politics, and popular thinking. Suggests directions for conscious evolution to develop a ''new mind'' that will meet the survival needs of humanity and the planet in the world of today and tomorrow.

———— Robert Ornstein and David Sobel. *The Healing Brain.* New York: Simon & Schuster, 1987. A neurobiologist and a physician describe ''Breakthrough Discoveries about How the Brain Keeps Us Healthy.''

———— Martin H. Padovani. *Healing Wounded Emotions, Overcoming Life's Hurts.* Mystic, CT: Twenty-Third Publications, 1987. A spiritually oriented approach to moving through depression, guilt, anger, and self-condemnation to self-love, compassion, affirmation, and giving.

_____ Kenneth R. Pelletier. *Mind as Healer, Mind as Slayer.* New York: Delta Books, 1976. A wholistic approach to preventing and healing stress disorders.

_____ Ira Progoff. *The Dynamics of Hope.* New York: Dialogue House, 1985. Uses wholistic depth psychology to explore anxiety, creativity, imagery, and dreams.

_____ Keith W. Sehnert. *Stress/Unstress: How to Control Stress at Home and on the Job.* Minneapolis: Augsburg Publishing House, 1981. A guide to five ways of managing stress.

_____ Bernie S. Siegel. *Love, Medicine and Miracles.* New York: Harper & Row, 1986. A surgeon shares lessons he has learned about self-healing from "exceptional patients" who participate in and influence their own recovery.

_____ Bernie S. Siegel. *Peace, Love and Healing: Bodymind Communication and the Path to Self-Healing, an Exploration.* New York: Harper & Row, 1989. Explores the self-healing system (a gift from the Creator), and shows how to send ourselves healing messages via meditation, relaxation, visualization, and loving.

_____ Charles T. Tart. *Waking Up: Overcoming Obstacles to Human Potential.* Boston: New Science Library, Shambhala, 1986. Offers insights and methods for self-liberation from being joyless automatons controlled by mechanical habits of thought, perception, and behavior.

_____ Donald A. Tubesing. *Kicking Your Stress Habits.* Duluth, MN: Whole Person Associates, 1981. A do-it-yourself guide for coping with stress.

Chapter 4: Reading to Enhance Your Body's Fitness

_____ Bob Anderson. *Stretching.* Bolinas, CA: Shelter Publications, 1980. An illustrated guide to stretching for fitness and sports.

_____ Covert Bailey. *The Fit-or-Fat Diet.* Boston: Houghton Mifflin, 1984. Enables you to evaluate any diet plan and tailor a diet to your tastes.

_____ Theodore Berland. *Fitness for Life.* Washington, D.C.: AARP, 1986. Designing your lifelong exercise plan to build endurance, flexibility, and strength.

_____ Boston Women's Health Book Collective. *The New Our Bodies, Ourselves.* New York: Simon & Schuster, 1984. An excellent guide to self-care for women, written by women. Also helpful for men.

_____ Alice Christensen and David Rankin. *Easy Does It Yoga.* San Francisco: Harper & Row, 1979. A daily program of yoga, exercise, breathing, meditation, and nutrition for older people.

_____ Kenneth H. Cooper. *The Aerobic Program for Total Well-Being.* New York: Bantam Books, 1982. A physician discusses integrating exercise, diet, and emotional balance to increase wellness.

_____ Martha Davis, Elizabeth R. Eshelman, and Matthew McKay. *The Relaxation and Stress Reduction Workbook.* Richmond, CA: New Harbinger Publications, 1980. A manual of many relaxation and stress-reduction techniques, including progressive relaxation, breathing, and meditation.

_____ *The Fit Body: Building Endurance.* Alexandria, VA: Time-Life Books, 1987. Aerobic fitness through walking, running, cycling, swimming, skiing, and so on. A guide to quick, twenty-minute workouts, eating on the go, fitness in the office and when traveling.

_____ Richard L. Hittleman. *Yoga for Physical Fitness.* New York: Warner Books, 1964. An illustrated guide to hatha yoga exercises.

_____ Frances Moore Lappé. *Diet for a Small Planet.* Rev. ed. New York: Ballantine Books, 1975. A plan for eating in healthier and more ecologically responsible ways, combining vegetarian foods for a diet rich in proteins.

_____ Alexander Lowen and Leslie Lowen. *The Way to Vibrant Health.* New York: Harper & Row, 1977. An illustrated manual of basic bioenergetic exercises.

_____ Robert Masters and Jean Houston. *Listening to the Body: The Psychophysiological Way to Health and Awareness.* New York: Dell Publishing, 1978. A program using mind-body awareness to reduce stress, increase pleasure, and enhance the body's functioning.

_____ Joyce D. Nash. *Maximize Your Body.* Palo Alto, CA: Bull Publishing, 1986. A sixteen-week program of weight management, using behavioral methods to control eating habits and become as healthy and fit as possible.

_____ Keith W. Sehnert. *Selfcare, Wellcare: What You Can Do to Live a Healthy, Happy, Longer Life.* Minneapolis: Augsburg Publishing House, 1985. A selfcare guide by a spiritually oriented physician.

_____ *University of California, Berkeley, Wellness Newsletter.* P.O. Box 10922, Des Moines, IA 50340. A monthly newsletter filled with current information about health, nutrition, fitness, and stress management.

—— Gary Yanker and Kathy Burton. *Walking Medicine.* New York: McGraw-Hill, 1990. A guide to walking in the most health-enhancing ways.

Chapter 5: Reading to Enhance Love and Well Being in Your Intimate Relationships

—— Ronald B. Adler, Lawrence B. Rosenfeld, and Neil Towne. *Interplay: The Process of Interpersonal Communication.* 4th ed. New York: Holt, Rinehart & Winston, 1989. A basic text for enhancing communication competence, beginning with understanding one's self-concept and developing more effective skills in expressing and hearing interpersonal meanings with understanding.

XX Susan M. Campbell. *The Couple's Journey: Intimacy as a Path to Wholeness.* San Luis Obispo, CA: Impact Publishers, 1980. A five-stage path to relationship wholeness—romance, power struggle, stability, commitment, co-creation.

—— Howard Clinebell. *Growth Counseling for Marriage Enrichment.* Philadelphia: Fortress Press, 1975. Describes a variety of ways of enriching intimate relationships and leading marriage enrichment events.

—— Howard Clinebell. *Growth Counseling for Mid-Years Couples.* Philadelphia: Fortress Press, 1977. Includes a variety of methods for enriching relationships in life's second half, including spiritual and value enrichment for use at any stage.

—— Howard J. Clinebell, Jr., and Charlotte H. Clinebell. *The Intimate Marriage.* New York: Harper & Row, 1970. A guide to cultivating the many facets of loving relationships. Useful for couples themselves and in leading couple enrichment groups.

—— Riane Eisler. *The Chalice and the Blade: Our History, Our Future.* San Francisco: Harper & Row, 1987. The feminist codirector of the Center for Partnership Studies traces the history of the disempowerment of women and the alienation of the sexes and charts the pathway toward a partnership future.

—— Riane Eisler and David Loye. *The Partnership Way: New Tools for Living and Learning, Healing Our Families, Our Communities, and Our World.* San Francisco: Harper San Francisco, 1990. A practical guide to moving from domination to partnership in relationships. A companion to *The Chalice and the Blade,* written by Eisler and her partner.

—— Herb Goldberg. *The New Male-Female Relationship.* New York: New American Library, Signet, 1983. A guide to liberating traditional male-female relations so as to enjoy relating as friends, lovers, parents, playmates, and equals.

HAVE IT Harville Hendrix. *Getting the Love You Want: A Guide for Couples.* San Francisco: Harper & Row, 1990. Describes insightfully and provides helpful exercises for moving from the "unconscious marriage," in which couples are controlled by childhood images and wounds, to the "conscious marriage" in which there is lasting love and companionship.

—— Margaret Frings Keys. *Staying Married.* Millbrae, CA: Les Femmes Publishing, 1975. TA approaches to handling problems and crises in marriages as growth opportunities.

X John R. Landgraf. *Singling: A New Way to Live the Single Life.* Louisville: Westminster/John Knox Press, 1990. Discusses four types of singles—because of death, divorce, delay, or design—and suggests positive methods for using the growth opportunities and coping with the problems.

—— Jim Larson. *A Guide for Strengthening Families.* Minneapolis: Augsburg Publishing House, 1984. Provides strategies, models, programs, and resources for generating family wholeness in congregations.

—— Harriet Goldhor Lerner. *The Dance of Anger: A Woman's Guide to Changing the Patterns of Intimate Relationships.* New York: Harper & Row, 1985. Explores how women can use their anger to gain a more autonomous, stronger sense of themselves, and thus facilitate constructive changes in their close relationships.

—— Harriet Goldhor Lerner. *The Dance of Intimacy: A Woman's Guide to Courageous Acts of Change in Key Relationships.* New York: Harper & Row, 1989. Provides steps to strengthen good relationships and heal relationships diminished by too much distance, intensity, or pain.

—— Ann Tremaine Linthorst. *A Gift of Love: Marriage as a Spiritual Journey.* Orange, CA: Pagl Press, 1979. Describes opportunities for spiritual growth and wholeness in marriages.

—— James L. McCary. *Freedom and Growth in Marriage.* Santa Barbara, CA: Hamilton, 1975. Explores creative marriage and sexuality.

—— Alan Loy McGinnis. *The Friendship Factor.* Minneapolis: Augsburg Publishing House, 1979. Ways of deepening relationships, cultivating intimacy, and handling crises in friendships.

James McGinnis and Kathleen McGinnis. *Parenting for Peace and Justice, Ten Years Later.* (See readings for chapter 8.)

Jordan Paul and Margaret Paul. *Do I Have to Give up Me to Be Loved by You?* Minneapolis: CompCare Publications, 1983. Describes ways of overcoming hidden obstacles to achieving creative intimacy.

Carol Pierce and Bill Page. *A Male/Female Continuum: Paths to Colleagueship.* Laconia, NY: A New Dynamics Publication, 1986. Describes women's and men's journey away from dominance-subordinance relationships and toward colleagueship, in which each person's wholeness is enhanced by mutual empowerment.

Virginia Satir. *Peoplemaking.* Palo Alto, CA: Science and Behavior Books, 1972. A classic, designed to help parents develop wholeness-nurturing families.

Anne Wilson Schaef. *Escape from Intimacy: The Pseudo-Relationship Addiction.* San Francisco: Harper & Row, 1989. Describes the underlying addictive process in relationships and the role of guilt, shame, and low self-esteem. Provides methods for untangling "love" addictions and moving toward genuine intimacy.

Tina B. Tessina and Riley K. Smith. *How to Be a Couple and Still Be Free.* North Hollywood, CA: Newcastle Publishing, 1980. Describes ways of balancing freedom and intimacy in loving relationships.

Barrie Thorne with Marilyn Yalom. *Rethinking the Family: Some Feminist Questions.* New York: Longman, 1982. Thinkers from a variety of disciplines discuss current feminist critiques of traditional views of the family and recent defenses of these views.

Charlotte Whitney. *Win-Win Negotiations for Couples.* Gloucester, MA: Para Research, 1986. Shows how to apply the win-win principle from business management to couple and family relationships.

Chapter 6: Reading to Enhance Well Being in Your Work

Richard Nelson Bolles. *The Three Boxes of Life and How to Get Out of Them.* Berkeley, CA: Ten Speed Press, 1978. A rich compendium of life-work planning information and resources, focusing on balancing three ingredients—learning, work, and leisure—during all the adult life stages.

Richard Nelson Bolles. *What Color Is Your Parachute?* Berkeley, CA: Ten Speed Press, revised each year. A leader in life-career planning presents an invaluable do-it-yourself manual for job hunters and career changers, filled with practical tools and guidelines.

Richard W. Gillett. *The Human Enterprise: A Christian Perspective on Work.* Kansas City, MO: Leaven Press, 1985. Explores critical ethical issues related to work—for example, the public policy and theology of economic dislocation and unemployment, militarization of the economy, racism and sexism in work.

John L. Holland. *Making Vocational Choices: A Theory of Careers.* Englewood Cliffs, NJ: Prentice-Hall, 1973. Presents useful theoretical understandings and a practical "Self-Directed Search" instrument.

Dorothy Jongeward and P. Seyer. *Choosing Success: Transactional Analysis on the Job.* New York: John Wiley, 1978. An illuminating application of TA theory to wholeness in the workplace.

Alan Lakein. *How to Get Control of Your Time and Your Life.* New York: Peter H. Wyden, 1973. A classic guide to doing what the title suggests.

Roy Lewis. *Choosing Your Career, Finding Your Vocation.* New York: Paulist Press, Integration Books, 1989. A step-by-step guide to career counseling with a spiritual orientation and an exploration of the developmental stages adults pass through during a career.

George Morrisey. *Getting Your Act Together.* New York: John Wiley, 1980. A guide to establishing a plan for discovering and achieving your important goals in terms of health, vocation, and recreation.

Thomas J. Peters and Robert H. Waterman, Jr. *In Search of Excellence: Lessons from America's Best-Run Companies.* New York: Warner Books, 1982. Shows the importance of human factors in business excellence and success.

Marsha Sinetar. *Do What You Love, the Money Will Follow.* New York: Paulist Press, 1987. Using the Buddhist concept of discovering your "right livelihood," an organizational psychologist provides guidance in overcoming internal self-doubts and external obstacles to becoming successful in doing work that one really loves.

Denis Waitley and Reni L. Witt. *The Joy of Working.* New York: Dodd, Mead and Co., 1985. An easy-to-follow guide to job effectiveness and satisfaction.

Chapter 7: Reading to Enhance Your Well Being by Laughter and Playfulness

———— Regina Barreca. *They Used to Call Me Snow White . . . But I Drifted: Women's Strategic Use of Humor.* New York: Viking, 1991. Shows how humor is different for women and men, and how women can use it effectively in the home, in the sexual battlefield, and in the workplace.

———— Adam Blatner and Allee Blatner. *The Art of Play.* New York: Human Sciences Press, 1988. "An Adult's Guide to Reclaiming Imagination and Spontaneity."

———— Harvey Cox. *The Feast of Fools.* Cambridge, MA: Harvard Univ. Press, 1969. Sees humans as creatures who by their very nature sing, dance, fantasize, dream, pray, tell stories, and celebrate (as well as work and think). Religion withers and the survival of humankind is in jeopardy if these festive capacities are repressed.

———— Matthew Fox. *Whee! We, Wee, All the Way Home.* Wilminton, NC: Consortium Books, 1976. A playful guide to sensual spirituality.

———— Conrad Hyers. *The Comic Vision and the Christian Faith: A Celebration of Life and Laughter.* New York: Paulist Press, 1981. Shows how comedy enriches and informs our religious lives.

———— Sam Keen. *To a Dancing God.* New York: Harper & Row, 1970. Explores his own experience playfully and seriously around such themes as "Education for Serendipity" and "The Importance of Being Carnal."

———— C. S. Lewis. *Surprised by Joy.* New York: Harcourt Brace Jovanovich, 1955. A "suffocatingly subjective" (his words, not mine) account of the author's movement from atheism to faith via the path he calls joy.

———— Werner M. Mendel, ed. *A Celebration of Laughter.* Los Angeles: Mara Books, 1970. A collection of psychoanalytically oriented papers on humor, including "A God Who Laughs" by Carlo Weber and "Laughter and Sex" by Martin Grotjahn.

———— Jürgen Moltmann. *The Theology of Play.* New York: Harper & Row, 1972. Explores the bold claim that God created the universe for his enjoyment; examines the nature of liberated enjoyment and the function of games and play in authentic human freedom and spirituality.

———— Raymond A. Moody, Jr. *Laugh after Laugh: The Healing Power of Humor.* Jacksonville, FL: Headwa-

ters Press, 1978. A physician writes on the role of laughter and humor in health and sickness.

———— Robert E. Neale. *In Praise of Play.* New York: Harper & Row, 1969. Holds that the essence of religion is the celebration of every aspect of our lives.

———— Laurence J. Peter and Bill Dana. *The Laughter Prescription: The Tools of Humor and How to Use Them.* New York: Ballantine Books, 1982. Explores the use of humor in reducing anxiety, depression, and ill health; coping with stress; and communicating effectively, all with hilarious examples. (The first coauthor is the Peter of the Peter Principle.)

———— Vera M. Robinson. *Humor and the Health Professions.* Thorofare, NJ: Slack, 1977. Discusses the nature of humor and its place in health and illness.

———— Elton Trueblood. *The Humor of Christ.* New York: Harper & Row, 1964. Discusses Christ's use of irony and humor, depicting him as a person of wit and wisdom.

———— Matt Weinstein and Joel Goodman. *Playfair: Everybody's Guide to Noncompetitive Play.* San Luis Obispo, CA: Impact, n.d. A compendium of games in which the fun of playing rather than winning is the main benefit.

Chapter 8: Reading to Help Heal Your Planet

———— Charles Birth and John B. Cobb, Jr. *The Liberation of Life: From Cell to Community.* Cambridge: Cambridge Univ. Press, 1981. A biologist and a theologian collaborate in producing an ecological model for understanding the interrelation of humankind and the natural world, as a basis for social and economic policy.

———— Lester R. Brown et al. *State of the World.* New York: W. W. Norton, 1991. The annual Worldwatch Institute report on the "earth's vital signs" and progress (or lack of it) toward a sustainable society.

———— Robert McAfee Brown. *Making Peace in the Global Village.* Philadelphia: Westminster Press, 1981. A Christian perspective on the crying need for peacemakers in our world.

———— Walter Brueggeman. *Living Toward a Vision: Biblical Reflections on Shalom.* New York: United Church Press, 1976. A leading scholar of the First Testament examines the concept of shalom (peace and wholeness) and its applications to today's world.

———— Fritjof Capra and Charlene Spretnak. *Green Politics: the Global Promise.* New York: E. P. Dutton, 1984.

Highlights the hope in the wholistic, ecological, and feminist Green movement in Germany and calls for an extension of this vision and movement to help transform the course of America and the world.

_____ Howard Clinebell, ed. *Global Peacemaking and Wholeness: Developing Justice-based Theological, Psychological, and Spiritual Resources*. Limited ed. Claremont, CA: Institute for Religion and Wholeness, 1985. Insightful papers from a theory-generating conference on the topic.

_____ Joseph Cornell. *Listening to Nature: How to Deepen Your Awareness of Nature*. Nevada City, CA: Dawn Publications, 1987. An inspired nature educator describes the principles and techniques of nature awareness, with beautiful color photographs by John Hendrickson.

_____ Joseph Cornell. *Sharing the Joy of Nature*. Nevada City, CA: Dawn Publications, 1989. Imaginative nature activities for persons of all ages.

_____ Joseph Cornell. *Sharing Nature with Children*. Nevada City, CA: Dawn Publications, 1979. A parents' and teachers' guidebook filled with activities and games.

_____ Ben Corson et al. *Shopping for a Better World*. New York: Council on Economic Priorities, 1991. "A Quick and Easy Guide to Socially Responsible Supermarket Shopping."

_____ Norman Cousins. *The Pathology of Power*. New York: W. W. Norton, 1987. An impassioned, illuminating exploration of the threat to freedom in the proliferation and misuse of government power and the arms race.

_____ Bill Devall and George Sessions. *Deep Ecology: Living as If Nature Mattered*. Salt Lake City: Gibbs M. Smith, 1985. Explores the environmental crisis in terms of both personal and social responses, emphasizing awakening to the wisdom of nature and the oneness of humans, animals, plants, and the earth.

_____ The Earth Works Group. *50 Simple Things Kids Can Do to Save the Earth*. Kansas City: Andrews & McMeel, 1990. A guide for children (as well as parents and teachers), explaining how they can release "kid power" to help keep the earth green, recycle, protect animals, and spend energy wisely.

_____ The Earth Works Group. *50 Simple Things You Can Do to Save the Earth*. Berkeley, CA: Earth Works Press, 1989. A practical guide giving both the why and the how of simple as well as more demanding

actions to help protect the threatened environment.

_____ Duane Elgin. *Voluntary Simplicity: Toward a Way of Life That Is Outwardly Simple, Inwardly Rich*. New York: William Morrow, 1981. Explores the basic changes in life-style that will be necessary to save the planet.

_____ Ruth Fletcher. *Teaching Peace: Skills for Living in a Global Society*. San Francisco: Harper & Row, 1983. Teacher's plans for sixty-four lessons in conflict management, nonviolence, cooperation, peace, and whole-earth thinking and living.

_____ Masanobu Fukuoka. *The Natural Way of Farming*. New York: Japan Publications, 1985. Describes the theory and practice of the Green philosophy as related to ecologically sound agriculture.

_____ Medard Gabel. *Energy, Earth, and Everyone: A Global Energy Strategy for Spaceship Earth*. New York: Doubleday, 1980. A creative plan for a crucial dimension of saving a viable planet.

_____ Susan Griffin. *Woman and Nature: The Roaring Inside Her*. New York: Harper & Row, 1978. A feminist critique of the voice of Western patriarchy in contrast to the voices of women and nature as they speak of the body, vision, and interrelatedness.

_____ Eugene C. Hargrove, ed. *Religion and Environmental Crisis*. Athens, GA: Univ. of Georgia Press, 1986. Essays exploring the sources of sacred power in various religious traditions needed to generate wholistic environmental consciences.

_____ J. Donald Hughes. *American Indian Ecology*. El Paso, TX: Texas Univ. Press, 1983. Describes the reverence for the earth of Native Americans.

_____ Sam Keen. *Faces of the Enemy: Reflections of the Hostile Imagination*. San Francisco: Harper & Row, 1986. A compelling study of the psychology of the "bad guys," with shaking illustrations of the twisted masks of hatred and a passionate appeal to discover more sane ways of resolving conflicts.

_____ Donald Keys. *Earth at Omega: The Passage to Planetization*. Boston: Branden Publishing, 1982. Offers a vision of the grand opportunities confronting humankind to solve the interrelated problems of the nuclear threat, overpopulation, pollution, hunger, and resource depletion by affirming planetary citizenship.

_____ J. B. Libanio. *Spiritual Discernment and Politics*. Maryknoll, NY: Orbis Books, 1982. A leading liberation theologian relates a theology of justice to concrete sociopolitical options.

—— Doris Janzen Longacre. *Living More with Less.* Scottdale, PA: Herald Press, 1980. A valuable guide to how to contribute more to world community, justice, and a healthy environment by the way we eat, travel, dress, and spend our money.

—— Joanna Rogers Macy. *Despair and Personal Power in the Nuclear Age.* Philadelphia: New Society Publishers, 1983. A teacher of world religions has written this valuable how-to book on helping people move through their denial and despair to hope and empowerment for action as peacemakers. Rollo May: "The bravest book I have read since Jonathan Schell's *Fate of the Earth.*"

—— Paul McCleary and J. Philip Wogaman. *Quality of Life in a Global Society.* New York: Friendship Press, 1978. Examines the issues of hunger, environment, energy, economics, and population from a biblical perspective and highlights the quality of life as a crucial issue for churches.

—— James McGinnis and Kathleen McGinnis. *Building Shalom Families.* St. Louis: Parenting for Peace & Justice Network, 1986. Two excellent videocassettes with a guidebook for use in workshops for parents.

—— James McGinnis and Kathleen McGinnis. *Parenting for Peace and Justice, Ten Years Later.* Maryknoll, NY: Orbis Books, 1990. An update of a valuable guide for parents and teachers who wish to help children learn peace and justice sensitivities and skills.

—— Carolyn Merchant. *The Death of Nature: Women, Ecology, and the Scientific Revolution.* San Francisco: Harper & Row, 1980. A feminist scholar explores how the scientific revolution produced a mechanistic worldview that led to unchecked industrial expansion, the exploitation of nature, and the subordination of women.

—— Eugene P. Odum. *Ecology and Our Endangered Life-Support Systems.* Sunderland, MA: Sinauer Associates, 1989. A citizen's guide and introductory textbook on the principles of ecology as related to the earth's life-support systems.

—— M. Scott Peck. *The Different Drum: Community Making and Peace.* New York: Simon & Schuster, 1987. A guide to moving beyond individual wholeness by creating the experience of genuine community, in small groups and ultimately in global community. A hopeful call for sanity in our personal lives and relationships, in the church and other institutions, in our nation, and in the world.

—— Judith Plant, ed. *Healing the Wounds: The Promise of Ecofeminism.* Philadelphia: New Society Publishers, 1989. A powerful anthology exploring the ecology of feminism, ecofeminist politics, spirituality, and community.

—— Rosemary Radford Ruether. *New Woman, New Earth.* New York: Seabury Press, 1975. A feminist theologian's vision of a more whole, ecologically nurturing society.

—— John Robbins. *Diet for a New America.* Walpole, NH: Stillpoint Publishing, 1987. An exposé of the high price we pay and the earth pays for our exaggerated nutritional dependence on animal protein.

—— Mike Samuels and Hal Zina Bennett. *Well Body, Well Earth.* San Francisco: Sierra Club Books, 1983. A physician and an environmentalist show how the health of our bodies and the earth are inseparable.

—— John Seed, Joanna Macy, Pat Fleming, and Arne Ness. *Thinking Like a Mountain: Toward a Council of All Beings.* Santa Cruz, CA: New Society Publishers, 1988. A powerful, moving book of essays, beautifully illustrated by line drawings of the rain forests, exploring the transformations of deep ecology.

—— Paul Shepherd. *Nature and Madness.* San Francisco: Sierra Club Books, 1982. Points to our collective mental and emotional immaturity as the cause of both environmental and human destruction.

—— Dorothee Soelle. *The Arms Race Kills, Even Without War.* Philadelphia: Fortress Press, 1983. Shows how the arms race stifles peaceful scientific research and cripples the hopes of the poor and the hopes for peace of people around the globe.

—— Bruce Stokes. *Helping Ourselves: Local Solutions to Global Problems.* New York: Worldwatch Institute, 1981. Provides encouraging examples of how groups around the world are empowering themselves by attacking health and quality-of-life problems.

—— William Irwin Thompson, ed. *Gaia: A Way of Knowing.* New York: Lindisfarne Press, 1987. Sets forth a vision of Gaia (originally the earth goddess) to examine the cultural implications of the new biology.

—— Jim Wallis, ed. *Waging Peace: A Handbook for the Struggle to Abolish Nuclear Weapons.* San Francisco: Harper & Row, 1982. The founder of the Sojourners community has compiled this grass-roots handbook of strategies against nuclear weapons.

World Commission on Environment and Development. *Our Common Future.* New York: Oxford Univ. Press, 1987. A powerful, action-oriented document on the interrelations of peace, security, development, and the health of the environment.

Chapter 9: Reading to Help You Grow in Crises and Losses

Sandra Albertson. *Endings and Beginnings.* New York: Ballantine Books, 1984. A moving account of her learnings around the death of her husband from cancer.

Howard Clinebell. *Growing Through Grief: Personal Healing.* Nashville: EcuFilm, 1984. Six thirty-minute video programs (with a *User's Guide*) showing a grief healing group led by Howard Clinebell. Designed for persons who want to help themselves or others find healing in the losses of death and divorce.

Howard Clinebell. *Healing Your Grief Wound.* Spiritquest Production and Distribution, P.O. Box 144, Claremont, CA, 91711, 1989. A two-part video resource designed to help grieving persons handle the grim early weeks and the first year after a painful loss.

Howard Clinebell. *Understanding and Counseling the Alcoholic Through Psychology and Religion.* Nashville: Abingdon Press, 1968. A guide for helping persons addicted to alcohol and for their families.

Glen W. Davidson. *Understanding Mourning: A Guide for Those Who Grieve.* Minneapolis: Augsburg Publishing House, 1984. A guide based on his study of twelve hundred adult mourners; clarifies misunderstandings, outlines healthy mourning and the use of religious resources.

Bob Deits. *Life After Loss: A Personal Guide for Dealing with Death, Divorce, Job Change and Relocation.* Tucson, AZ: Fisher Books, 1988. A valuable book for persons going through painful losses and transitions.

Ralph Earle and Gregory Crow. *Lonely All the Time: Recognizing, Understanding and Overcoming Sex Addictions.* New York: Pocket Books, 1989. A case-enriched approach to understanding and helping persons with sexual addictions.

Esther O. Fisher. *Divorce, the New Freedom.* New York: Harper & Row, 1974. A guide to constructive divorce and divorce counseling.

Charles V. Gerkin. *Crisis Experience in Modern Life:*

Theory and Theology for Pastoral Care. Nashville: Abingdon Press, 1979. Explores the nature and meaning of crises from theological and psychological perspectives.

Earl A. Grollman, ed. *Concerning Death: A Practical Guide for the Living.* Boston: Beacon Press, 1974. Chapters on Catholic, Protestant, and Jewish theology and rituals, suicide, children and death.

John W. James and Frank Cherry. *The Grief Recovery Handbook.* New York: Harper & Row, 1988. A five-step program for moving beyond losses.

Morton T. Kelsey. *Healing and Christianity.* New York: Harper & Row, 1973. A study of healing in the Jewish and Christian traditions.

Harold S. Kushner. *When Bad Things Happen to Good People.* New York: Avon Books, 1983. A guide to handling the most painful question raised by those experiencing tragic, unfair losses—Why me?

C. S. Lewis. *A Grief Observed.* San Francisco: Harper & Row, 1989. A moving account of his self-observations following his wife's death.

Gerald May. *Addiction and Grace.* San Francisco: Harper & Row, 1988. A spiritually aware psychiatrist who holds that everyone suffers from addictions tells of his awakening to the centrality of grace in recovery from addictions.

Alice Miller. *For Your Own Good: Hidden Cruelty in Child-Rearing and the Roots of Violence.* New York: Farrar, Straus, Giroux, 1983.

Ernest Morgan. *Dealing Creatively with Death.* Burnsville, NC: Celo Press, 1984. A valuable manual of death education and simple burials, with a list of grief support organizations.

Nancy O'Connor. *Letting Go with Love: The Grieving Process.* Tucson, AZ: La Mariposa Press, 1984. An insightful guide to facing painful losses, including the death of children.

Ronald W. Ramsey and Rene Noorberger. *Living with Loss.* New York: William Morrow, 1981. Guided confrontation therapy using the full reliving of painful feelings related to death, divorce, unemployment, and so forth.

Nan Robertson. *Getting Inside Alcoholics Anonymous.* New York: William Morrow, 1988. A veteran *New York Times* reporter explores AA and the recovery process, including her own moving story.

John A. Sanford. *Healing and Wholeness.* New York: Paulist Press, 1977. Integrates Jungian and biblical approaches.

———— Anne Wilson Schaef. *When Society Becomes an Addict.* San Francisco: Harper & Row, 1987. A psychotherapist shows how the "white male system" makes the addictive process proliferate in our society—both substance and process addictions.

HAVE IT Jim Smoke. *Growing Through Divorce.* Irvine, CA: Harvest House, 1976. Using divorce as a growth opportunity.

———— Ann Kaiser Stearns. *Living Through Personal Crisis.* New York: Ballantine Books, 1984. A self-help guide to dealing with the self-blame, anger, and bitterness related to large and small losses, and the process of self-care that is essential to healing.

———— Howard Stone. *Crisis Counseling.* Philadelphia: Fortress Press, 1976. A useful, succinct introduction to crisis theory and help.

HAVE IT R. Scott Sullender. *Grief and Growth: Pastoral Resources for Emotional and Spiritual Growth.* New York: Paulist Press, 1985. Valuable for both clergy and laypeople in understanding how to integrate psychological and spiritual resources in helping the grieving.

———— David K. Switzer. *The Minister as Crisis Counselor.* Rev. ed. Nashville: Abingdon Press, 1986. A thorough discussion of crisis counseling methods.

HAVE IT Judith Viorst. *Necessary Losses.* New York: Simon & Schuster, 1986. A depth psychology discussion of using developmental crises as growth opportunities by giving up our dependencies, illusions, and impossible expectations.

———— Emily B. Visher and John S. Visher. *Stepfamilies.* Syracuse, NJ: Lyle Stuart, 1980. A guide to helping stepparents and stepchildren.

HAVE IT Granger Westberg. *Good Grief, A Constructive Approach to the Problem of Loss.* Rock Island, IL: Augustana Press, 1962. A little book that summarizes the stages of grief healing; useful in grief groups.

———— *Women in Transition: A Feminist Handbook on Separation and Divorce.* New York: Charles Scribner's Sons, 1975. An illuminating and helpful feminist perspective.

———— Betty Jane Wylie. *The Survival Guide for Widows.* Rev. ed. New York: Ballantine Books, 1983. Based on her own experience, the author offers practical, compassionate guidance to widows.

———— Jack M. Zimmerman. *Hospice: Complete Care for the Terminally Ill.* Baltimore: Urban & Schwarzenberg, 1981. Describes the most hopeful development of this century in care for the dying.

Chapter 10: Reading to Enhance Sexual Joy and Well Being

———— The Boston Women's Health Book Collective. "Relationships and Sexuality"; "Controlling Our Fertility," parts 2 and 3 in *The New Our Bodies, Ourselves.* Helpful discussions of relationships, sex, birth control, and sexually transmitted diseases.

———— Alex Comfort, ed. *The Joy of Sex: A Gourmet Guide to Lovemaking; More Joy of Sex: A Lovemaking Companion to the Joy of Sex.* New York: Crown, 1972 and 1974. Two guides to developing more playful, joyful sex, each beautifully illustrated.

———— Barbara Ehrenreich, Elizabeth Hess, and Gloria Jacobs. *Re-making Love: The Feminization of Sex.* Garden City, NY: Anchor Press/Doubleday, 1986. Explores the dramatic changes and interrelations of contemporary feminist and sexual transformations.

———— Carter Heyward. *Touching Our Strength: The Erotic as Power and the Love of God.* San Francisco: Harper & Row, 1989. Affirms the spirituality of sexual pleasure as a delightful relational happening that needs no higher justification. Relates sexuality and justice issues.

———— Gordon Inkeles and Murray Todris. *The Art of Sensual Massage.* San Francisco: Straight Arrow Books, 1972. Beautifully illustrated with photos of a couple giving each other massages.

———— William H. Johnson, Virginia E. Johnson, and Robert C. Kolodny. *Masters and Johnson on Sex and Human Loving.* Boston: Little, Brown and Co., 1986. A discussion of the biological, psychological, and social complexities of sexuality, and how to avoid sexual burnout.

———— Helen Singer Kaplan. *The Illustrated Manual of Sex Therapy.* 2d ed. New York: Quadrangle, 1987. A well-illustrated guide to sex therapy, including sensate focus techniques.

———— Helen Singer Kaplan. *The New Sex Therapy.* New York: Brunner/Mazel, 1974. A whole-person approach combining psychotherapy, relational therapy with the reeducation of sex therapy.

———— Sam Keen. *The Passionate Life: Stages of Loving.* San Francisco: Harper & Row, 1983. An exploration of the erotic crisis of love, sex, and the human spirit.

———— *Massage: Total Relaxation.* Alexandria, VA: Time-Life Books, 1987. An illustrated guide to a variety of types of massage, including full body, quick, and self-massage.

_____ James B. Nelson. *Between Two Gardens: Reflections on Sexuality and Religious Experience.* New York: Pilgrim Press, 1983. A theologian-ethicist explores a wide range of sexual issues from the perspective of what sexuality has to say to the Christian faith.

_____ James B. Nelson. *Embodiment: An Approach to Sexuality and Christian Theology.* Minneapolis: Augsburg Publishing House, 1978. Discusses the theological implications of human sexuality, with a sensitivity to feminist insights.

_____ Joseph Nowinski. *A Lifelong Love Affair: Keeping Sexual Desire Alive in Your Relationship.* New York: Dodd, Mead, 1988. Self-help methods of keeping passion alive in intimate, committed, equal relationships, emphasizing the key roles of trust, power, self-esteem, and fantasy in this process.

_____ Dagmar O'Connor. *How to Make Love to the Same Person for the Rest of Your Life, and Still Love It.* New York: Doubleday, 1985. The director of a sex therapy program describes ways to "take the monotony out of monogamy."

_____ Ron Pion with Jerry Hopkins. *The Last Sex Manual.* New York: Wyden Books, 1977. A playful but serious guide to the "ten top sexual complaints," using behavior modification principles; includes a game called Up Your Orgasm.

_____ Jerry Rubin and Mimi Leonard. *The War Between the Sheets.* New York: Richard Marek Publishers, 1980. Explores with humor and candor the new sexuality emerging from changing female-male roles and the female orgasm. Includes "The Rubin-Leonard Non-Method for Feeling Good Sexually."

_____ John Shelby Spong. *Living in Sin? A Bishop Rethinks Human Sexuality.* San Francisco: Harper & Row, 1988. A courageous, well-researched book that describes a biblical foundation for an enlightened and contemporary understanding of sexuality for the Christian church.

_____ Maurice Yaffe and Elizabeth Fenwick. *Sexual Happiness: A Practical Approach.* New York: Henry Holt, 1986. A guide to improving your sex life for those with steady partners and for singles, with separate sections for women and men.

Chapter 11: Reading to Enhance Your Well Being as a Woman or Man

_____ Rosalind Barnett, Lois Biener, and Grace Baruch. *Gender and Stress.* New York: Free Press, 1987. Disentangles the sources of stress and the ways it is felt and expressed differently in women's and men's lives.

_____ Claudia Bepko and Jo-Ann Krestan. *Too Good for Her Own Good: Breaking Free from the Burden of Female Responsibility.* New York: Harper & Row, 1990. Provides step-by-step guidance out of the female "responsibility trap" and into increased self-nurture, self-esteem, and more constructive relationships.

_____ Charlotte Holt Clinebell (now Charlotte Ellen). *Counseling for Liberation.* Philadelphia: Fortress Press, 1976. Describes the pain women and men are experiencing because of being in sexist boxes, with methods for enabling them to move out into their full personhood.

_____ Mary Daly. *Gyn/ecology: The Metaethics of Radical Feminism.* Boston: Beacon Press, 1979. A powerful exposé of male destructiveness to women in many cultures. Documents the blindness of male scholarship to the meaning of massive cruelties against women, past and present, in male-dominated societies.

_____ James E. Dittes. *The Male Predicament: On Being a Man Today.* San Francisco: Harper & Row, 1985. A guide to moving beyond traditional, rigid "manly" roles to new, more fulfilling models.

_____ Joan Chamberlain Engelsman. *The Feminine Dimension of the Divine.* Philadelphia: Fortress Press, 1979. Taking exception to male images of God, the author offers feminine alternatives from psychological, biblical, and historical perspectives.

_____ Warren Farrell. *Why Men Are the Way They Are.* New York: McGraw-Hill, 1986. Explores the male-female dynamic today in light of the women's movement and the sexual revolution.

_____ Herbert J. Freudenberger and Gail North. *Women's Burnout.* Garden City, NY: Doubleday, 1985. Explores the causes of women's burnout and recommends ways to prevent and reverse it.

_____ Perry Garfinkel. *In a Man's World: Father, Son, Brother, Friend, and Other Roles Men Play.* New York: New American Library, 1985. Throws helpful light on male programming of stoic strength, emotional constipation, and isolation from ourselves and other men, all of which hurts our wholeness.

_____ Carol Gilligan. *In a Different Voice: Psychological Theory and Women's Development.* Cambridge, MA: Harvard Univ. Press, 1982. Describes highly significant differences in the moral and psychological development of females and males in our culture.

Herb Goldberg. *The Hazards of Being Male: Surviving the Myth of Masculine Privilege.* New York: New American Library, Signet Book, 1976. Discusses the suicidal pressures of the multiple traditional male roles—lover, husband, parent, breadwinner, strong-and-silent man—and suggests ways to escape.

Herb Goldberg. *The New Male: From Self-Destruction to Self-Care.* New York: New American Library, Signet Book, 1979. Explores men's trappedness further, including the double binds they experience in relating to women. Describes ways of liberation.

Dorothy Jongeward and Dru Scott. *Women as Winners.* Reading, MA: Addison-Wesley, 1976. Illustrates our culture's constrictions on women and how to liberate oneself physically, psychologically, and sexually, using resources from TA and gestalt therapy.

Catherine Keller. *From a Broken Web: Separation, Sexism, and Self.* Boston: Beacon Press, 1986. A scholarly critique of the patriarchal philosophies, myths, theologies, and psychologies, with a fresh vision of wholeness for women and men grounded in relatedness.

Diane Mariechild. *Mother Wit: A Feminist Guide to Psychic Development.* Trumansburg, NY: The Crossing Press, 1981. Exercises for self-healing, growth, and spiritual awareness drawn from the ancient healing wisdom of women.

Jean Baker Miller. *Toward a New Psychology of Women.* Boston: Beacon Press, 1976. A classic, groundbreaking book with a new understanding of women.

Nelle Morton. *The Journey Is Home.* Boston: Beacon Press, 1985. A pioneer feminist theologian describes the development of her personal and theoretical vision, including a moving account of her own experience of the goddess.

National Women's Health Network, 1325 G St., NW, Washington, DC 20005. Provides updated lists of books and other health resources.

James B. Nelson. *The Intimate Connection, Male Sexuality, Male Spirituality.* Philadelphia: Westminster Press, 1988. Describes how men can develop more reciprocal wholeness in the relationship between their sexuality and their spiritual lives.

Anne Kent Rush. *Getting Clear: Body Work for Women.* New York: Random House, 1973. Offers body work for women but also for men.

Anne Wilson Schaef. *Women's Reality: An Emerging Female System in a White Male Society.* San Francisco: Harper & Row, 1981. Explores the experience of women who have learned to adapt to the dominant white male system in our society and the emergence of a new female system that will be liberating to both women and men.

Anne Steinman and David J. Fox. *The Male Dilemma.* New York: Aronson, 1974. Describes the damage to men of traditional role stereotyping and the gains for them in a new relationship between the sexes.

Darlene Deer Truchses. *From Fear to Freedom: A Woman's Handbook for High Self-Esteem.* Denver: New Options Publishing, 1987. Methods for changing the self-destructive feelings and behaviors of being programmed as a woman in a sexist society.

Alice Walker. *The Color Purple.* New York: Pocket Books, 1982. A powerful novel on the devastating impact of racism, sexism, poverty, and oppressive religion.

Barbel von Wartenberg-Potter. *We Will Not Hang Our Harps on the Willows: Global Sisterhood and God's Song.* Oak Park, IL: Meyer-Stone Books, 1988. A former director of the Women's Department of the World Council of Churches reflects on viewpoints of sisters of the third world yearning for justice in sexist and economically oppressed societies.

Chapter 12: Reading to Enhance Well Being in Your Present Life Stage and Throughout Your Life

Theodore Berland. *Fitness for Life: Exercises for People over Fifty.* Washington, DC: AARP, 1986. Illustrated guide to exercises designed to enhance cardiovascular fitness, flexibility, muscle strength, endurance, leanness, and relaxation in older persons.

XX Eugene C. Bianchi. *Aging as a Spiritual Journey.* New York: Crossroad, 1985. Examines the challenges and potentials of midlife and elderhood from a spiritual perspective.

Edward M. Brecher. *Love, Sex, and Aging.* New York: Little, Brown & Co., 1984. A Consumers Union guide to sex in the older years.

William Bridges. *Transitions: Making Sense of Life's Changes.* Reading, MA: Addison-Wesley, 1983. Creative strategies for moving from endings through a time-out period to new beginnings in all types of perilous passages.

———— William M. Clements, ed. *Ministry with the Aging: Designs, Challenges, Foundations.* San Francisco: Harper & Row, 1981. A rich collection of essays on both theory and practice, by gerontologists, historians, psychologists, theologians, and clergy, edited by an eminent authority on religion and aging.

———— William M. Clements, ed. *Religion, Aging and Health: A Global Perspective.* Compiled by the World Health Organization. New York: Haworth Press, 1989. Multicultural understandings of the role of religion in healthy aging from the perspectives of Protestant and Catholic Christianity, Islam, Buddhism, Judaism, Confucianism, Taoism, and Shinto.

———— Howard J. Clinebell, Jr. *Growth Counseling for Marriage Enrichment: Pre-Marriage and the Early Years.* Philadelphia: Fortress Press, 1975. A guide for couples in the young adult years and those who work with them.

———— Howard J. Clinebell, Jr. *Growth Counseling for Mid-Years Couples.* Philadelphia: Fortress Press, 1977. Written for a dual readership—midyears couples wishing to enhance their own relationships and clergy as well as other professionals working with such couples.

XX Alex Comfort. *A Good Age.* Illustrated by Michael Leonard. New York: Crown Publishers, 1976. Provides inspiring guidance for living with dignity, vitality, and fulfillment in the advanced years of life.

———— Erik H. Erikson. *The Life Cycle Completed.* New York: W. W. Norton, 1982. A review of his basic theory, from a historical and autobiographical perspective.

———— Erik H. Erikson, Joan M. Erikson, and Helen Q. Kivnick. *Vital Involvement in Old Age.* New York: W. W. Norton, 1986. A portrait of enlivened old age today, based on interviews with octogenarians. (The Eriksons are superb role models of the book's theme.)

———— Marie Feltin. *A Woman's Guide to Good Health After Fifty.* Washington, DC: AARP, 1987. A physician's guidance on the major health challenges facing older women today.

———— James W. Fowler. *Stages of Faith: The Psychology of Human Development and the Quest for Meaning.* San Francisco: Harper & Row, 1981. A basic theory of faith development through five stages.

———— Naomi Golan. *Passing Through Transitions: A Guide for Practitioners.* New York: The Free Press, 1981. Examines in detail fourteen developmental stages from early young adulthood to the final years, and gives guidelines for helping.

———— Naomi Golan. *The Perilous Bridge: Helping Clients Through Mid-Life Transitions.* New York: The Free Press, 1986. A helpful book for midyears individuals and families as well as for professionals.

———— Dieter Hessel, ed. *Maggie Kuhn on Aging: A Dialogue.* Philadelphia: Westminster Press, 1977. The spirited founder of the Gray Panthers shares her insights about the possibilities and problems of the new old age.

———— William E. Hulme. *Vintage Years.* Philadelphia: Westminster Press, 1986. How to grow older with meaning and hope.

———— Muriel James and Louis Savary. *A New Self: Self Therapy with Transactional Analysis.* Reading, MA: Addison-Wesley, 1977. TA exercises for reparenting, rechilding, re-adulting, and developing the spiritual core of the self.

XX William F. Kraft. *Achieving Promises.* Philadelphia: Westminster Press, 1981. A spiritual guide to the stages of adulthood.

———— Pamela Levin. *Cycles of Power: A User's Guide to the Seven Seasons of Life.* Deerfield Beach, FL: Health Communications, 1988. From TA and human development perspectives, offers exercises to develop the potentialities of life stages.

HAVE IT Matthew Linn, Sheila Fabricant, and Dennis Linn. *Healing the Eight Stages of Life.* New York: Paulist Press, 1988. Spiritually centered, caring ways to develop the gifts and heal the hurts of each of Erikson's eight stages.

———— Michael E. McGill. *The Forty to Sixty Year Old Male.* New York: Simon & Schuster, 1980. A guide for men and the women in their lives to the crises of the male midyears.

———— Eugene Nelson, Ellen Roberts, Jeanette Simmons, and William A. Tinsdale. *Medical and Health Guide for People over Fifty.* Washington, DC: AARP, 1968. A program for maintaining good health.

———— Henri J. M. Nouwen and Walter J. Gaffney. *Aging: The Fulfillment of Life.* Garden City, NY: Image Books, 1976. Poetic, spiritually sensitive reflections on aging, with photographs by Ron P. Van Den Bosch.

———— James Peterson and Barbara Payne. *Love in the Later Years.* New York: Association Press, 1975. A specialist in marriage issues and a gerontologist explore love and sex among mature adults.

———— Natalie Rogers. *Emerging Women: A Decade of Midlife Transitions*. Point Reyes, CA: Personal Press, 1980. Describes her own journey as a woman in the uprooting and rerooting midyears. (Natalie is Carl Rogers's daughter.)

———— Isadore Rubin. *Sexual Life After Sixty*. New York: Basic Books, 1965. Discusses the importance, problems, and creative approaches to sex in the later years.

———— Maggie Scarf. *Unfinished Business: Pressure Points in the Lives of Women*. Garden City, NY: Doubleday, 1980. Discusses the need for and blocks to continuing growth in the six decades of women's lives, from teens through the sixties.

———— Gail Sheehy. *Passages: Predictable Crises of Adult Life*. New York: E. P. Dutton, 1974. A popular discussion of the developmental crises of the eighteen-to-fifty age span, drawing on in-depth interviews.

—X— Gail Sheehy. *Pathfinders: Overcoming the Crises of Adult Life and Finding Your Own Path to Well-Being*. New York: William Morrow, 1981. Builds on her understanding of adult crises, focusing on how some people cope constructively.

———— B. F. Skinner and M. E. Vaughan. *Enjoying Old Age: A Program of Self-Management*. New York: Warner Books, 1983. A positive guide to shaping your life and environment so as to develop the exquisiteness of the older years.

—X— Charles L. Whitfield. *Healing the Child Within*. Dearfield Beach, FL: Health Communications, 1987. A helpful book for adult children of dysfunctional families to heal the wounds of their childhood.

Notes

Chapter 1: Walking the Sevenfold Path of Well Being

1. Quoted by Aaron Antonovsky in his insightful book *Health, Stress and Coping* (San Francisco: Jossey-Bass, 1982), 54. (I have altered his definition to eliminate the sexist language.)

2. Tillich, *Love, Power and Justice* (New York: Oxford Univ. Press, 1954), 25.

3. From a filmed biography of Thomas Merton shown on Los Angeles public television, January 18, 1985.

4. *The Phenomenon of Man* (New York: Harper & Row, 1959), 265.

5. Alphonse Kerr, in *Say It Again*, ed. Dorothy Uris (New York: E. P. Dutton, 1979), 77.

6. See John 10:10 in the New Testament, NEB translation.

7. Personal communication, December 1981.

8. In healing, as in religion, yesterday's heresies often become tomorrow's valued orthodoxies. It makes sense, therefore, to stay open to the emergence of insights and methods from a variety of sources including chiropractic methods, the wholistic health movement, the spiritual healing movement, dietary approaches, indigenous Eastern and Native American healing, and women's ancient healing practices. Some "alternative" methods from these and other sources (e.g., acupuncture and hypnosis), already have proved very useful resources for healing work today.

Chapter 2: Enriching and Enjoying Your Spiritual Life

1. It was Erma Pixley and this idea that inspired the formation of the Institute for Religion and Wholeness in Claremont, California.

2. Eli S. Chesen, M.D. (New York: Collier Books, 1972). The book includes a section on "How to Teach Your Children a Healthy Attitude About Religion: A Parents' Guide" (chap. 8).

3. See William James, *The Varieties of Religious Experience. A Study in Human Nature* (New York: The Modern Library, 1902), 77–162.

4. For an overview of the key ideas of many of these thinkers see my book *Contemporary Growth Therapies* (Nashville: Abingdon Press, 1981). For a discussion of ways of healing pathogenic faith and facilitating salugenic faith and value systems, see my *Basic Types of Pastoral Care and Counseling* (Nashville: Abingdon Press, 1984), chaps. 5 and 6.

5. *Psychoanalysis and Religion* (New Haven: Yale Univ. Press, 1950), 24–25.

6. John B. Cobb, Jr., *Theology and Pastoral Care* (Philadelphia: Fortress Press, 1977), 17.

7. *The Road Less Traveled* (New York: Simon and Schuster, 1978), 286.

8. Cited by Matthew Fox, *Original Blessing: A Primer in Creation Spirituality* (Santa Fe: Bear & Co., 1983), 278.

9. *On Becoming a Musical, Mystical Bear: Spirituality American Style* (New York: Paulist Press, 1972).

10. *Prayer On Wings: A Search for Authentic Prayer* (San Diego, CA: Lura Media, 1990).

11. Quoted by James Fadiman and Robert Frager in *Personality and Personal Growth* (New York: Harper & Row, 1976), 347–48. Years ago I recall being inspired by the life of a medieval monastic, a Brother Lawrence, who worked in the monastery kitchen. He wrote of "practicing the presence of God" as a continuing experience. He was so attuned to divine love that he found he could pick up a straw from the monastery kitchen floor for the love of God. (Not exactly an easy way to get your spiritual highs!)

12. See Maslow, *The Further Reaches of Human Nature* (New York: Viking Press, 1971), 325.

13. Robert Hutchins, when he was president of the University of Chicago, coined this apt way of describing a value conflict that many people (including me) struggle to avoid.

14. *The Caring Question* (Minneapolis: Augsburg Publishing House, 1983), 96.

15. Cited by Matthew Fox, *Original Blessing*, 36.

16. *The Divine Milieu* (New York: Harper & Row, 1965), 60.

17. Quoted by Douglas J. Harris in *Shalom, The Biblical Concept of Peace* (Grand Rapids, MI: Baker Book House, 1970), 13.

18. *Beyond God the Father* (Boston: Beacon Press, 1973), 23.

19. *The Way of Life According to Lao-tzu*, translated by Witter Bynner (New York: Capricorn Books, 1944), 71.

20. *The Way of Life According to Lao-tzu*, 37, 40.

21. It's noteworthy that wholeness-oriented psychotherapists Erich Fromm, Carl Jung, and Roberto Assagioli were all deeply influenced in their understanding of wholeness by Eastern thought. Fromm drew heavily on Zen Buddhism in his understanding of healthy, non-authoritarian spirituality.

22. These three quotes are from Reshad Feild, *The Last Barrier, A Journey Through the World of Sufi Teachings* (New York: Harper & Row, 1976), 53, 172, 155.

23. Gabriele Uhlein, *Meditations with Hildegard of Bingen* (Santa Fe: Bear & Co., 1983), 70 and 63.

24. An earlier version of this healing waters meditation appeared in the *Newsletter of the Institute for Religion and Wholeness* 3, no. 4 (June 1984).

Chapter 3: Empowering Your Mind for Healing and Creativity

1. The researchers classified the doctors at graduation by use of a personality inventory that asked them if they agreed or disagreed with statements such as "Most people are honest chiefly through fear of being caught" and "I have often had to take orders from someone who did not know as much as I did." The study did not shed light on the reasons for the lethal effects of a negative life orientation—such as whether there are biochemical effects or less satisfying relationships resulting from chronic hostility and cynicism. "Cynical Attitude Harms Health," *USA Today*, October 18, 1984, D-1.

2. D. T. Suzuki, Erich Fromm, Richard DeMartino, *Psychoanalysis and Zen Buddhism* (New York: Harper & Row, 1960), 87–88.

3. *Medical World*, June 11, 1984, 101–2.

4. The most powerful predictor was the length of "disease-free intervals." "Body and Soul," *Newsweek*, November 7, 1988, 8–9.

5. See Barbara Brown, *Stress and the Art of Biofeedback* (New York: Harper & Row, 1977).

6. *Imagery in Healing* (Boston: New Science Library, 1985), 161.

7. A physician has called the mind-body movement the "third revolution in Western medicine," alongside modern surgery and the discovery of penicillin. "Body and Soul," *Newsweek*, November 7, 1988, 88–97.

8. Rollo May introduced the model of power over, power against, and power with. See his book *Power and Innocence: A Search for the Sources of Violence* (New York: W. W. Norton, 1972).

9. It's noteworthy that self-responsibility is a central theme in the approaches of many contemporary psychotherapies, including transactional analysis, gestalt therapy, psychosynthesis, reality therapy, and the wholeness approach I call growth counseling. For a discussion of these therapies, see my *Contemporary Growth Therapies* (Nashville: Abingdon Press, 1981).

10. Such professional guides may include wholistic physicians and nurses; nutritional, exercise, and stress-reduction specialists; those with chiropractic and osteopathic training; marriage and family counselors; and pastoral counselors and spiritual healers with expertise in enabling healing of spiritual pathology and in using spiritual resources in other types of healing.

11. A statement by Ralph Tyler in John Naisbitt's *Megatrends* (New York: Warner Books, 1982), 247.

12. George Isaac Brown, *Human Teaching for Human Learning: An Introduction to Confluent Education* (New York: Viking Press, 1971).

13. *Los Angeles Times,* 17 April 1988.

14. *The Way of Life According to Lao-tzu,* trans. Witter Bynner (New York: Capricorn Books, 1944), 30.

15. See Thomas R. Blakeslee, *The Right Brain* (Garden City, NY: Anchor Press/Doubleday, 1980), 45–46.

16. These stages were described in 1945 in a book by G. Wallas entitled *The Art of Thought.* Quoted by Blakeslee, *The Right Brain,* 49–50.

17. Perry W. Buffington, "Understanding Creativity," *Sky,* June 1984, 25.

18. *Minding the Body, Mending the Mind* (Reading, MA: Addison-Wesley, 1987), 3.

19. *Minding the Body, Mending the Mind,* 16.

20. *Between Health and Illness: New Notions on Stress and the Nature of Well Being* (Boston: Houghton Mifflin, 1984), 191.

21. *The Way of Life According to Lao-tzu,* 48.

22. Reported in *USA Today,* August 29, 1989, 1.

23. Quoted in Peter McWilliams and John-Roger, *You Can't Afford the Luxury of a Negative Thought* (Los Angeles: Prelude Press, 1989), 450.

24. *Peace, Love, and Healing* (New York: Harper & Row, 1989), 249.

25. "Dreams Before Waking," in *Your Native Land, Your Life* (New York: W. W. Norton, 1986), 46.

26. See Herbert Benson's *Relaxation Response* (New York: William Morrow, 1975), 70 and 71, for a summary of these fascinating findings.

27. "Study Finds Meditation Promotes Longevity," Santa Barbara *News-Press,* February 4, 1990, A8.

28. Borysenko, *Minding the Body, Mending the Mind,* 34.

29. Eileen Caddy, *Footprints On the Path* (Forres, Scotland: Findhorn Foundation, 1976), 26.

30. Quoted in McWilliams and John-Roger, *You Can't Afford the Luxury of a Negative Thought,* 44.

31. *New World, New Mind* (New York: Doubleday, 1989).

32. William M. Bueler, compiler and translator with the assistance of Chang Hon-Pan, *Chinese Sayings* (Rutland, VT and Tokyo: Chas. E. Tuttle, 1972), 118.

33. See Norman Cousins, *The Celebration of Life* (New York: Harper & Row, 1974), 34.

Chapter 4: Loving and Empowering Your Body for Fitness

1. CBS News, March 31, 1984.

2. *High Level Wellness* (Berkeley, CA: Ten Speed Press, 1986), 150.

3. *The New Our Bodies, Ourselves* (New York: Simon & Schuster, 1984).

4. 1 Corinthians 6:19–20, NRSV.

5. *Betrayal of the Body* (New York: Collier Books, 1969), 231.

6. *Love, Medicine and Miracles* (New York: Harper & Row, 1986), 4. Emphasis added.

7. See *The New Our Bodies, Ourselves,* 3. I'm indebted to Ruth Krall for raising my consciousness about this addiction (personal communication, November 24, 1989).

8. *Women's Reality: An Emerging Female System in a White Male Society* (San Francisco: Harper & Row, 1981).

9. The story is on file with the President's Council on Fitness and Sports, cited in Ardell, *High Level Wellness,* 159–60.

10. *University of California, Berkeley, Wellness Letter,* December 1989, 3.

11. Pelletier, *Holistic Medicine: From Stress to Optimum Health* (New York: Dell, 1980), 194–96.

12. Steven N. Blair, et al., "Physical Fitness and All-Cause Mortality: A Prospective Study of Healthy Men and Women," *JAMA* 262, 17 (November 3, 1989): 2395–2401.

13. *New York Times,* November 3, 1989, 1.

14. Lionel Tiger, "My Turn: A Very Old Animal Called Man," *Newsweek,* September 4, 1978, 13. Emphasis added.

15. Reported in *American Health,* March 17, 1987.

16. See Kenneth H. Cooper, *The New Aerobics* (New York: Bantam Books, 1970), 16–17.

17. Ellen Kunes, "The New Fitness Myths," *Working Woman,* August 1990, 87.

18. *The Wellness Workbook* (Berkeley, CA: Ten Speed Press, 1988), 100. Consider any of the following as red lights when you're exercising vigorously: dizziness or nausea, chronic fatigue, or if your heart rate doesn't decrease below 120 after five minutes and below 100 in ten minutes.

19. *University of California, Berkeley, Wellness Letter,* February 1987, 6.

20. *University of California, Berkeley, Wellness Letter*, June 1985, 7.

21. *Yoga Twenty-eight Day Exercise Plan* (New York: Workman Publishing, 1969).

22. The study was conducted by the federal Agriculture Department's Human Nutrition Research Center at Tufts University. Reported in the Santa Barbara *News-Press*, June 13, 1990, A3.

23. Several of these are adapted from Grete Waitz and Gloria Averbuch, "Staying Fit for Life," *MS* magazine, August 1985, 30–31.

24. The results of the study were published in the *Journal of the American Medical Association* in April 1990.

25. *University of California, Berkeley, Wellness Letter*, June 1990, 1.

26. The study was made by Lester Breslow and N. B. Belloc of UCLA. Reported by Kenneth R. Pelletier, *Holistic Medicine* (NY: Delta/Seymour Lawrence, 1979), 9.

27. *Los Angeles Times*, March 29, 1990, A1.

28. See Covert Bailey, *Fit or Fat* (Boston: Houghton Mifflin, 1984), 3–5.

29. See Travis and Ryan, *Wellness Workbook*, 70–71, for RDA and sources.

30. *Quotable Women: A Collection of Shared Thoughts* (Philadelphia: Running Press, 1989).

31. *Time Flies* (New York: Doubleday, 1987), 92–95.

32. *AARP News Bulletin* 30, 3 (March 1989): 7.

33. James Grant, executive director of the U.N. Children's Fund, estimates that 150 million children (40,000 a day) will die needlessly from hunger and treatable diseases in the 1990s, if present trends continue. To cut these tragic deaths in half would cost about as much each year as the tobacco company spends annually on advertising (about $2.5 billion). This is less than the nations of the world spend on armaments in one day. Nearly 7,000 children die each day from pneumonia because they don't have a dollar's worth of antibiotics. (*USA Today*, International Edition, July 13, 1990, A8.)

34. Organizations working to end world hunger include Oxfam America, 115 Broadway, Boston, MA 02116; Bread for the World, 802 Rhode Island Ave., NE, Washington, D.C. 20018; Results, 236 Massachusetts Ave., NE, Suite 110, Washington, D.C. 20002; The American Friends Service Committee, 160 N. 15th St., Philadelphia, PA 19102; Grassroots International, P.O. Box 312, Cambridge, MA 02139. See note 17, chapter 8 for a list of organizations working for peace, justice, and the environment.

35. "Smokers Ills Found to Cost $65 Billion a Year," *Los Angeles Times*, September 17, 1985, sec. 1, p. 8. Nonsmoking wives of smoking husbands have been found to have twice the probability of developing lung cancer as wives in nonsmoking couples do. The tobacco industry is an example of huge corporations profiting from people's illness and death.

36. Adapted from *The New Our Bodies, Ourselves*, 36.

37. The study was done at Stanford University and Brown University. Reported in the Tacoma, WA, *Morning New Tribune*, May 15, 1980, A6.

38. The researcher is Wilse Webb. See Daniel Grollman, "Staying Up: The Rebellion Against Sleep's Gentle Tyranny," *Psychology Today*, March 1982, 30–31.

39. Donald A. Tubesing and Nancy Loving Tubesing, *The Caring Question* (Minneapolis: Augsburg Publishing House, 1983), 53.

40. Morton Hunt, "What a Difference a Nap Makes," *Parade*, January 29, 1989, 16.

41. These instructions are paraphrased from Richard Hittleman's *Yoga for Physical Fitness* (New York: Warner Books, 1964), 47–48.

42. I am indebted to Dr. Bill Bray of Claremont, California, for this information.

Chapter 5: Nurturing Well Being Through Love

1. *The Seattle Times/Seattle Post-Intelligencer*, May 1, 1988, A15.

2. If you're in a lonely place on your life journey, this chapter may be painful to you. But it's also true that living in a close, toxic relationship can be very bad for your wholeness. Such a relationship can be agonizingly lonely, even though two people occupy the same space. If you have liberated yourself from such a "unholy deadlock" relationship, you know that living in a hot or cold war can be much more destructive to your health than the loneliness that may or may not accompany living alone.

3. This need is more basic than Sigmund Freud's will-to-pleasure, Alfred Adler's will-to-power, or even Viktor Frankl's will-to-meaning. For it's only in healthy, caring relationships that we human beings can satisfy our hunger for pleasure, power, or meaning in constructive ways.

4. David Gelman with Mary Hager, "Body and Soul," *Newsweek*, November 7, 1988, 88.

5. "You Live Longer If You're Sociable," *Modern Maturity*, March 1990, 18.

6. "Passionate Survivors, the Human Race," KPFK, Channel 28, Los Angeles, October 5, 1985.

7. *The Art of Loving* (New York: Harper & Bros., 1956), 4–5.

8. *The Way of Life According to Lao-tzu*, translated by Witter Bynner (New York: Capricorn Books, 1944), 47.

9. *Milton Berle's Private Joke File*, 400.

10. If your most intimate relationship has no negative feelings or pain, I suggest that you inform the folks who assemble Ripley 's "Believe It or Not" stories.

11. *Inside the First District*, Hall of Administration, Los Angeles, CA, Fall 1985, 3. It is estimated that more than 40 percent of American women will be the victims of physical abuse from male partners during their lifetimes.

12. Jeanette Lauer and Robert Lauer, "Marriages Made to Last," *Psychology Today*, June 1985, 22ff.

13. *Getting the Love You Want* (New York: Henry Holt, 1988), 127.

14. *The Intimate Marriage* (New York: Harper & Row, 1970), 179.

15. I'm indebted to Ruth Krall for this apt phrase.

16. If you do marriage counseling, family life enrichment, or creative singlehood work as part of your job, I think you'll find these communication tools to be useful there.

17. The RSJI was developed by Charlotte Ellen and me several years ago as an instrument to help couples revise their own relationship covenants.

18. Thomas Merton, *Love and Living*, ed. Naomi Burton Stone and Patrick Hart (New York: Farrar, Straus & Giroux, 1979), 33.

19. Elliot Beier, ed., *Wit and Wisdom of Israel* (Mount Vernon, NY: Peter Pauper Press, 1968), 32.

20. *Motivation and Personality* (New York: Harper & Row, 1954), 248–49.

21. *Love and Living*, 34.

22. *Singling* (Louisville, KY: Westminster/John Knox Press, 1990), 16–17.

23. John Shelby Spong's *Living in Sin? A Bishop Rethinks Human Sexuality* (San Francisco: Harper & Row, 1988), has three helpful chapters on homosexuality, including one on the Bible and homosexuality.

24. See Dolores Curran, *Traits of a Healthy Family* (New York: Ballantine Books, 1983).

25. For the names of well-trained relationship counselor-therapists, write the American Association of Pastoral Counselors (9504A Lee Highway, Fairfax, VA 22031, phone: 703-385-6967) or the American Association of Marriage and Family Therapists (1100 17th St., NW, 10th fl., Washington, D.C. 20036, phone: 202-452-0109).

26. *Living in Sin?* 61.

27. *The Chalice and the Blade: Our History, Our Future* (San Francisco: Harper & Row, 1987), 202.

28. See Sandra Hayward Albertson, *Endings & Beginnings* (New York: Ballantine Books, 1984), 91.

Chapter 6: Enhancing Well Being and Avoiding Burnout in Your Work

1. A national survey of working Americans revealed that an astounding 95 percent do not enjoy their work. See Marsha Sinetar, *Do What You Love, The Money Will Follow* (New York: Paulist Press, 1987), 8.

2. Nine million Americans are so severely injured in occupational accidents each year that they are at least temporarily unable to work. Some 100,000 die from occupational illnesses and another 400,000 new cases of occupational disease are recognized each year. See Trevor Hancock, "Beyond Health Care: Creating a Healthy Future," in *Global Solutions*, ed. Edward Cornish (Bethesda, MD: World Future Society, 1984), 42.

3. *Newsletter about Life/Work Planning*, 1981, nos. 3 and 4, p. 1 (The National Career Development Project of United Ministries in Higher Education, Walnut Creek, CA 94596).

4. I am indebted to John R. Landgraf, who devised this instrument. Used with his permission.

5. *How to Control Your Time and Your Life* (New York: Peter H. Wyden, 1973), 1 and 22.

6. Adapted from chapters 5 and 6 of Lakein's book. The second question is changed to one I prefer.

7. *How to Control Your Time and Your Life*, 61.

8. *The Joy of Working* (New York: Dodd, Mead, 1985), 3.

9. See John Naisbitt, *Megatrends* (New York: Warner Books, 1982), chap. 2.

10. Jim Farris, used with his permission.

11. *The Common Place*, limited ed. (1984), 45.

12. For a discussion of this understanding of work, see Waitley and Witt, *The Joy of Working* (New York: Dodd, Mead, 1985).

13. Personal communication from Susan Clinebell, used with her permission.

14. Write Workaholics Anonymous, c/o Westchester Self-Help Clearing House, Westchester College, 75 Grasslands Road, Valhalla, NY 10595.

15. *In Search of Excellence* (New York: Warner Books, 1982), 238–39.

16. Report on CBS television program *Two on the Town*, June 18, 1985.

17. See appendix of Bolles, *What Color Is Your Parachute?* (Berkeley, CA: Ten Speed Press, revised annually), for guidelines in starting such a group. A church in Edina, Minnesota, has had a thriving job transitions support group for over a decade. It has helped hundreds of people from the community as well as the congregation deal constructively with numerous types of job transitions, including unemployment. The program includes a seminar on "Faith in the Marketplace" for helping people integrate their spiritual life with their work. (For information, write Dr. David L. Williamson, Colonial Church of Edina, 6200 Colonial Way, Edina, MN 55436.)

18. "Work Spirit: Channeling Energy for High Performance," reprinted from *Training and Development Journal,* May 1985.

19. See Sinetar, *Do What You Love.*

Chapter 7: Using Laughter and Playfulness for Healing and Health

1. Cousins, *The Anatomy of an Illness, as Perceived by the Patient: Reflections on Healing and Regeneration* (New York: W. W. Norton, 1979), 39–40.

2. *University of California, Berkeley, Wellness Newsletter,* June 1985, 1.

3. "Stress: Can We Cope?" *Time,* June 6, 1983, 48.

4. Regina Barreca, *They Used to Call Me Snow White . . . But I Drifted: Women's Strategic Use of Humor* (New York: Viking Press, 1991), 201.

5. Merle Jordan shared this story as told by our mutual friend Cal Turley.

6. Barreca, *They Used to Call Me Snow White,* 200–201.

7. *The Prophet* (New York: Alfred A. Knopf, 1969), 29.

8. Dick Roraback, "Cancer Is a Laughing Matter at this Clinic," *Los Angeles Times,* March 12, 1986, part 5, p. 1.

9. "I'd Rather Be Laughing," *Parade,* August 13, 1989, 10.

10. Anne Goodheart is the counselor. Santa Barbara *News-Press,* April 24, 1986, D1–6.

11. *The Theology of Play* (New York: Harper & Row, 1972), 2.

12. *The Benezet Gazette,* vol. 7, no. 4 (Spring 1982).

13. Madison Kane, "Making the Most of Leisure Time," *Extra,* October 1982, 15.

14. Kane, "Making the Most of Leisure Time," 15.

15. Adapted from Richard Bolles's insightful suggestions in *The Three Boxes of Life and How to Get Out of Them* (Berkeley, CA: Ten Speed Press, 1978), 376–95.

16. Bolles, *The Three Boxes of Life,* 382.

17. Madison Kane, "Making the Most of Leisure Time," 16.

18. *The Three Boxes of Life,* 396–97.

19. See Conrad Hyers, *The Comic Vision and the Christian Faith: A Celebration of Life and Laughter* (New York: Paulist Press, 1981), 17.

20. Hyers, *The Comic Vision and the Christian Faith,* 14–15.

21. *The Screwtape Letters* (New York: Macmillan, 1943), 57–58.

22. Quoted by Hyers, *The Comic Vision and the Christian Faith,* 32 and 2, respectively.

23. I had a good chuckle when I later heard that this "ancient wisdom" has been attributed to the English author-journalist, G. K. Chesterton, who died in 1936. Was the Zen monk pulling my leg, or were he or Chesterton illustrating the cynical definition which says that "originality is the art of concealing your sources"?

24. Adapted from Deane H. Shapiro, Jr., *Precision Nirvana* (Englewood Cliffs, NJ: Prentice-Hall, 1976), 278.

Chapter 8: Enhancing Your Well Being By Helping Heal a Wounded Planet

1. *Milton Berle's Private Joke File* (New York: Crown Publishing, 1989), 37.

2. "An Open Letter to the New President—For the Sake of Our Children's Future . . . Give Us Hope," *Parade,* November 27, 1988, 4. Emphasis added.

3. Trevor Hadcock, M.D., in *Global Solutions*, ed. Edward Cornish (Bethesda, MD: World Future Society, 1984), 40.

4. Mike Samuels, M.D., and Hal Zina Bennett, *Well Body, Well Earth* (San Francisco: Sierra Club Books, 1983), 75 and 82.

5. From "New Winners in Healing," a lecture at the Cambridge Forum, March 19, 1986.

6. A survey was conducted by me and a colleague, of members of the Pastoral Care Network for Social Responsibility, a peacemaking group of clergy trained in pastoral psychology and counseling. A number of respondents told of adolescent and young adult clients who had come for help with nuclear depression and despair, often suicidal in intensity. The most effective help in awakening hope, they reported, was for the person to be encouraged to join with others in peace-with-justice action groups.

7. For the full text of his oration, see "Chief Seattle's Message," in John Seed, et al., *Thinking Like a Mountain: Toward a Council of All Beings* (Philadelphia: New Society Publishers, 1988), 67–73.

8. Paula Gunn Allen, *The Sacred Hoop: Recovering the Feminine in American Indian Tradition* (Boston: Beacon Press, 1986), 1.

9. John Seed, et al., *Thinking Like a Mountain*, 5.

10. *Well Body, Well Earth*, 92, 94.

11. Judith Plant, ed., *Healing the Wounds: The Promise of Ecofeminism* (Philadelphia: New Society Publishers, 1989), 5.

12. "Everything Is a Human Being," in Alice Walker, *Living by theWord* (San Diego: Harcourt Brace Jovanovich, 1988), 147.

13. *Peace, Love and Healing: Bodymind Communication and the Path to Self-Healing* (New York: Harper & Row, 1989), 11.

14. Gary Doone, comp., *Shaman's Path: Healing, Personal Growth and Empowerment* (Boston and London: Shambhala, 1988), 212–13.

15. *The Way of Life According to Lao-tzu*, trans. Witter Bynner (New York: Capricorn Books, 1944), 30, 43.

16. Quoted by Peter McWilliams and John-Roger, *You Can't Afford the Luxury of a Negative Thought* (Los Angeles: Prelude Press, 1988), 118.

17. Environmental action groups include: Greenpeace, 1436 U St, NW, Washington, DC 20007; Friends of the Earth, 530 7th St., SE, Washington, DC 20003; Sierra Club, 730 Polk St., San Francisco, CA 94120; Rainforest Action Network, 300 Broadway, San Francisco, CA 94133; Environmental Defense Fund, 275 Park Ave S., New York, NY 10010; National Wildlife Federation, 1400 16th St., NW, Washington, DC 20036; The Nature Conservancy, 1815 N. Lynn St., Arlington, VA 22209; The Wilderness Society, 1400 Eye St., NW, Washington, DC 20005; World Wildlife Fund, 1250 24th St., NW, Washington, DC 20037; The Cousteau Society, 930 W. 21st St., Norfolk, VA 23517; Conservation International, 1015 18th St., NW, #1000, Washington, DC 20077; Natural Resources Defense Council, P.O. Box 96048, Washington, DC 20077.
Peacemaking groups include: Union of Concerned Scientists, 1384 Mass. Ave., Cambridge, MA 02138; International Physicians for the Prevention of Nuclear War, 635 Huntington Ave., Boston, MA 02115; American Friends Service Committee, 1501 Cherry St., Philadelphia, PA 19102; Educators for Social Responsibility, Box 1041, Brookline Village, MA 02147; Council for a Livable World, 11 Beacon St., Boston, MA 02108; Center for Defense Information, 1500 Massachusetts Ave., NW, Washington, DC 20005; United Nations Association, 300 E. 42nd St., New York, NY 10017; Sane-Freeze, 1819 H St., NW, Suite 1000, Washington, DC 20006; Council on Economic Priorities, 30 Irving Place, New York, NY 10011; Fellowship of Reconciliation, Box 271, Nyack, NY 10960; Interfaith Center to Reverse the Arms Race, 132 N. Euclid Ave., Pasadena, CA 91101; Pax Christi, 3000 N. Mango, Chicago, IL 61634; Worldwatch Institute, 1776 Massachusetts Ave., NW, Washington, DC 20036; Beyond War, 222 High St., Palo Alto, CA 94301.

18. "Buying Time on the 'Doomsday Clock,'" Santa Barbara *New-Press*, March 9, 1990, A11.

19. *Three Guineas* (London: Penguin, Harmondsworth, 1977), 24. Her statement came from her sense of deep alienation because of the societal sexism she experienced.

20. Women's Foreign Policy Council, 1133 Broadway, New York, NY 10010.

21. Earth Works Press, Box 25, Berkeley, CA 94709.

22. Thirty Irving Place, New York, NY 10003.

23. *Worldwatch*, Sept.–Oct. 1990, 8.

24. One such group is Zero Population Growth, 1400 Sixteenth St., NW, Suite 320, Washington, DC 20036. It required hundreds of thousands of years for the world's population to reach two and one-half billion in the 1950s. But it doubled to over five billion by 1990 and is expected to exceed six billion by the year 2000. If this

continues, the consequences will be enormous increases in world poverty, hunger, environmental pollution, global warming, and depletion of non-renewable resources. (See Jean Cousteau, "How Many People Can Earth Support?" Santa Barbara *News-Press*, August 25, 1990, A11.)

25. Alex Comfort, *A Good Age* (New York: Crown Publishers, 1976), 52–53.

26. The five-step process is adapted from Joanna Rogers Macy's book *Despair and Personal Power in the Nuclear Age* (Philadelphia: New Society Publishers, 1983).

27. *I and Thou*, trans. Walter Kaufmann (New York: Charles Scribners Sons, 1970), 58.

28. Matthew Fox, *Original Blessing: A Primer in Creation Spirituality* (Santa Fe: Bear & Co., 1983), 13.

29. See "Thirty Years Hence" and "Imagining a World Without Weapons," in Joanna Rogers Macy, *Despair and Personal Power in the Nuclear Age*, 140–42.

30. *Milton Berle's Private Joke File*, 297.

31. A notice posted in the Environmental Defense Center in Santa Barbara.

Chapter 9: Growing Through Crises and Losses, Disabilities and Addictions

1. My thanks to Hwai-En and Kaofang Yeh of Taiwan for their help in clarifying these characters.

2. This remarkable pastor was A. Ray Grummon.

3. Santa Barbara *News-Press*, September 11, 1988, A2.

4. Janice Mall, "Black Women Live Longer, Cope Better, Survey Reveals," *Los Angeles Times*, April 8, 1984, sec. 2.

5. See Nelle Morton, *The Journey Is Home* (Boston: Beacon Press, 1985), 202–10.

6. I'm grateful that Jean Dickinson said, "Yes, of course," when I asked if I could share these insights from her moving letter.

7. Nicholas Wolsterstorff, *Lament for a Son* (Grand Rapids, MI: Wm. B. Eerdmans, 1987), 47 and 26.

8. I'm indebted to psychiatrist Warren A. Jones, who developed the original version of this tool to train lay volunteers staffing a community crisis center. (See Jones, "The A-B-C Method of Crisis Management," *Mental Hygiene*, January 1968, 87.) This is my adaptation, which adds the "D," of his model.

9. See Borysenko, *Minding the Body, Mending the Mind* (Reading, MA: Addison-Wesley, 1987), 22–23.

10. See the books by Ralph Earle and Gregory Crow, and by Gerald May in the Recommended Reading for this chapter.

11. From a report by Bill in *The AA Grapevine*, January 1963.

12. *Understanding and Counseling the Alcoholic, Through Psychology and Religion* (Nashville: Abingdon Press, rev. and enlarged ed., 1968).

13. See O. Carl Simonton, Stephanie Matthews-Simonton, James Creighton, *Getting Well Again* (Los Angeles: J. P. Tarcher, Inc., 1978).

14. See Bernie Siegel, *Peace, Love and Healing* (New York: Harper & Row, 1989), 112–14.

Chapter 10: Sex and Well Being

1. The Song of Solomon 1:2; 2:10–12; 3:1; 7:6–8; 8:6–7.

2. Carter Heyward, *Touching Our Strength: The Erotic as Power and the Love of God* (San Francisco: Harper & Row, 1989), 121.

3. See Pelletier's *Holistic Medicine, from Stress to Optimum Health* (New York: Dell, 1980), 197–98.

4. Santa Barbara *News-Press*, February 19, 1990, A5.

5. Spong, *Living in Sin? A Bishop Rethinks Human Sexuality* (San Francisco: Harper & Row, 1988), 180.

6. *Touching Our Strength*, p. 5.

7. Adapted from Charlotte's and my book, *The Intimate Marriage* (New York: Harper & Row, 1970), chap. 2, "The Many Facets of Intimacy."

8. John Shelby Spong observes, "For centuries sexual attitudes, sexual taboos, and sexual practices have been used by the dominant group [males in our society] to keep others subordinate" (*Living in Sin?* 23). Fortunately, this misuse of sex is changing in female-male relationships in our society.

9. Quoted in Cathy Permutter, "Thirty-One Facts and Tips on Sex after Thirty," *Prevention*, July 1989, 57.

10. Sex therapist Dagmar O'Connor's apt term.

11. Nondemand pleasuring requires letting go of the pressure to succeed, which creates performance anxiety in many men and some women (striving for multiple orgasms). This anxiety sets people up for failure, since self-pressure works against sexual arousal, erections, and orgasms (except premature ejaculations). By reducing performance anxiety, nondemand pleasuring frees people to flow spontaneously with their own body-mind arousal.

12. A midyears male client told of coming home exhausted form a high stress, esteem-depleting job. He had three

double martinis before he tried to make love with his wife. When he couldn't get an erection, he experienced panic and fear of "losing his manhood." The next night he had heightened anxiety about "failing" again, so he had extra drinks to "quiet his nerves," which made failure almost certain. This anxiety-drinking-failure cycle was interrupted through therapy by explaining what was occurring and encouraging him to have sex when he was rested and had not been drinking.

13. To find a competent pastoral counselor, contact the American Association of Pastoral Counselors, 9504A Lee Highway, Fairfax, VA 22031, (703) 385-6967.

14. James B. Nelson, *Embodiment: An Approach to Sexuality and Christian Theology* (Minneapolis: Augsburg Publishing House, 1978), 8–151; and Helen Singer Kaplan, *The Illustrated Manual of Sex Therapy* (New York: Quadrangle, 1975), 29–59.

15. Permutter, "Thirty-One Facts and Tips on Sex after Thirty," 58–59.

16. In addition to AAPC, consult The American Association of Marriage and Family Therapists (1100 17th St., NW, Washington, D.C. 20036, 202-452-0109) for a competent therapist.

17. For more detailed instruction on massaging different parts of the body and giving various types of massage, including a quickie (ten-minute) massage, a massage for lovers, and a self-massage, see *The Massage Book* by George Downing, illustrated by Anne Kent Rush; or see *The Art of Sensual Massage* by Gordon Inkele and Murray Todris.

18. e. e. cummings, *Poems: 1923–1954* (New York: Harcourt, Brace and Co., 1954), 129.

Chapter 11: Challenges to Your Well Being As a Woman or Man

1. The full results of this Harris survey were carried in a periodical, *Men's Health*. Reported in *USA Today*, February 10, 1989, D1.

2. See "The Feminine Face of Depression," in Roy Fairchild, *Finding Hope Again* (San Francisco: Harper & Row, 1980), pp. 10ff.

3. *Of Woman Born* (New York: Bantam Books, 1977), 62.

4. Reesa M. Vaughter, "Review Essay, Psychology," *Signs: Journal of Women in Culture and Society* 2, 1 (Autumn 1976): 127.

5. See Bem, "Gender Schema Theory: A Cognitive Account of Sex Typing," *Psychological Review* 88, 4 (1981): 354–64.

6. *The Way of Life According to Lao-tzu*, trans. Witter Bynner (New York: Capricorn Books, 1944), 42.

7. *Toward a New Psychology of Women* (Boston: Beacon Press, 1976), 29ff.

8. *The Chalice and the Blade: Our History, Our Future* (San Francisco: Harper & Row, 1988), 199, 202.

9. *The Color Purple* (New York: Pocket Books, 1982), 175.

10. "Toward a Whole Theology," *Lutheran World*, January 1975, 14.

11. See "Why Women Need the Goddess: Phenomenological, Psychological, and Political Reflections," in *The Politics of Women's Spirituality*, Charlene Spretnak, ed. (Garden City, NY: Anchor Books, 1982), 71–86.

12. See Nelle Morton, *The Journey Is Home* (Boston: Beacon Press, 1985), 157–58.

13. See Leonard Swindler, "Jesus Was a Feminist," *Catholic World*, January 1971, 177–83.

14. Paula Gunn Allen, *The Sacred Hoop* (Boston: Beacon Press, 1986), 11.

15. Diane Mariechild, *Mother Wit, A Feminist Guide to Psychic Development* (Trumansburg, NY: The Crossing Press, 1981), 78.

Chapter 12: Maximizing Love-Centered Well Being

1. I am grateful to Chuck Benison for this apt phrase, which he used in a sermon to describe the aim of the Christian life. It's also the aim of those from other spiritual traditions for whom life is a precious gift. The fact that zest for life is associated in the statement, as in life, with being young (in spirit) could be described as a sad commentary on society's glum stereotype of aging.

2. Santa Barbara *News-Press*, November 7, 1989, A2.

3. *Aging: The Fulfillment of Life* (Garden City, NY: Image Books, 1976), 19–20.

4. *Passages: Predictable Crises of Adult Life* (New York: E. P. Dutton, 1974), 253–54.

5. O'Neill, *Ah, Wilderness and Two Other Plays* (New York: Modern Library, 1964), 141.

6. Siegel, *Peace, Love and Healing* (New York: Harper & Row, 1989), 153.

7. *Milton Berle's Private Joke File* (New York: Crown Publishers, 1989), 34.

8. I am indebted to J. Kent Borgaard for sharing this moving experience from his ministry.

9. This futuring exercise is an elaboration on an approach to which I was introduced by Patricia Zulkosky.

10. Quoted by Frederick J. Streng in *Understanding Religious Man* (Belmont, CA: Dickenson, 1969), opposite p. 1.

11. *Peace, Love and Healing* (New York: Harper & Row, 1989), 234.

12. Quoted in Peter McWilliams and John-Roger, *You Can't Afford the Luxury of a Negative Thought* (Los Angeles: Prelude Press, 1989), 100.

13. Dr. John Rowe, quoted in "Why We Age Differently," *Newsweek*, October 20, 1986, 60.

14. Pierce Johnson shared this insight.

15. Theodore Bertland, *Fitness for Life: Exercise for People over Fifty* (Washington, DC: AARP, 1986), 5.

16. Santa Barbara *News-Press*, January 8, 1990, D4.

17. Cited in Alex Comfort's *A Good Age* (New York: Crown Publishers, 1976), 95.

18. Cited in Kenneth J. Pelletier, *Holistic Medicine, from Stress to Optimum Health* (New York: Dell, 1980), 199.

19. See Comfort, *A Good Age*, 212.

20. Santa Barbara *News-Press*, September 11, 1988, A2.

21. Norman Cousins, *Human Options* (New York: W. W. Norton, 1982), 224.

22. *Milton Berle's Private Joke File*, 389.

23. Comfort, *A Good Age*, 152.

24. The study was described in the *Archives of Internal Medicine*. Reported in the Santa Barbara *News-Press*, January 20, 1990, A2.

25. Robert N. Butler, *Why Survive? Being Old in America* (New York: Harper & Row, 1987), 421.

Completing and Using Your Personal Well-Being Program

1. *Megatrends: Ten New Directions Transforming Our Lives* (New York: Warner Books, 1982), 252.

2. Doris Lessing, *A Small Personal Voice*, cited in J. D. Zahniser, compiler, *And Then She Said . . .* (St. Paul, MN: Caillech Press, 1989), 48.

3. Reported on CBS News, February 20, 1988.

Helping Your Organization, Congregation, or Workplace Support Whole-Person Well Being

1. See Ivan Illich, *Medical Nemesis: The Expropriation of Health* (New York: Pantheon Books, 1976).

2. See Karen Granberg-Michaelson, *In the Land of the Living: Health Care and the Church* (Grand Rapids, MI: Zondervan, 1984), is a useful guide to whole-person health care in the church.

Grateful acknowledgment is given for permission to reprint the following:

Midtown Athletic Club cartoon from *The New Yorker;* Man's Best Friend Cartoon from *The New Yorker;* Santa cartoon from *The New Yorker 25th Anniversary Album* copyright © 1986 by Harper & Row, Publishers, Inc.; James Thurber, from *The New Yorker* 25th Anniversary Album, copyright © 1986 by Harper & Row, Publishers, Inc.; Wellness Unto Death cartoon from *The New Yorker;* Hagar reprinted with special permission of King Features Syndicate, Inc.; The Keeping Up cartoon by William Hamilton is reprinted by permission of Chronicle Features, San Francisco, CA; Glasbergen cartoons reprinted by permission by Randy Glasbergen; The Keeping Up cartoon by William Hamilton is reprinted by permission of Chronicle Features; One Amazing Slam Dunk cartoon from *The New Yorker;* The Better Half reprinted by special permission of King Features Syndicate, Inc.; Truck cartoon from *The New Yorker;* Pontius Puddle reprinted by special permission of Joel Kauffmann; Charles Adair, from *The New Yorker 25th Anniversary Album,* copyright © 1986 by Harper & Row, Publishers, Inc.; Runner cartoon from *The New Yorker 25th Anniversary Album,* copyright © 1986 by Harper & Row, Publishers, Inc.; Martha Campbell cartoon reprinted by permission of Martha Campbell; Dennis the Menace used by permission of Hank Ketchum and © by North America Syndicate; Richard Decker, from *The New Yorker 25th Anniversary Album,* copyright © 1986 by Harper & Row, Publishers, Inc. Reprinted by permission.